The

MIRACLE

of

AMERICA

Other Books by
André Maurois

The
MIRACLE
OF AMERICA

By ANDRÉ MAUROIS

Translated from the French by
DENVER and JANE LINDLEY

ILLUSTRATED

HARPER & BROTHERS *Publishers*
New York and London
MCMXLIV

THE MIRACLE OF AMERICA

Copyright, 1944, by André Maurois
Printed in the United States of America

6-4

FIRST EDITION

D-T

This book is complete and unabridged
in contents, and is manufactured in strict
conformity with Government regulations
for saving paper.

PREFACE

A number of years ago the author of this book published *The Miracle of England.* English and American critics at that time gave a not unfavorable reception to a work that had been submitted to them with misgivings, for it is always rash to talk about a foreign people, and especially so to speak on that subject to the people themselves.

The author experiences those misgivings anew as he offers the American public *The Miracle of America,* an attempt to trace the amazingly rapid development of a great nation and to describe how a people translated a splendid ideal into a working democracy. There are many books on the growth of the United States and several of them are excellent. What can a Frenchman add? Certainly not new facts, but perhaps a different way of presenting well-known facts, and an impartial observer's impression of old controversies.

I should like the American reader to understand that this work is presented to him with sincere modesty. That my knowledge of American history is less complete than that of native historians I am well aware. I have done my best to acquaint myself with it. I have read numerous works, a list of which will be found at the end of this book; I have journeyed through the whole country so that I might know the various scenes of the epic I was planning to recount. But I have not been able to do, nor do I claim to have done, any original research.

I hope this work will be useful, first to the French reader, who is more eager than ever to know about the United States now that he is its ally and who will find here the facts arranged in a fashion conformable with his habits of mind, and then perhaps to the American reader, who will see what a foreign friend thinks of his great men, his institutions, his past, and his future as well. I believe it is of advantage to the French at the moment of rebuilding their country and founding the Fourth Republic to study the histories of other societies of free men. This book will help them, I hope, to understand why one of those societies has succeeded so well.

I owe a debt of gratitude to the following authors whose works proved exceptionally illuminating and helpful: A. M. Schlesinger, A. F. Pollard,

D. W. Brogan, Morison and Commager, Vernon Parrington, Charles and Mary Beard.

I also wish to comment upon the usefulness to me of CHRONICLE OF AMERICA Series, edited by Allen Johnson and published by the Yale University Press.

A. M.

CONTENTS

Book Four: GROWING PAINS

Book Five: THE GILDED AGE

Contents

ix

Book Six: WORLD POWER

ILLUSTRATIONS

MAPS

The

MIRACLE

of

AMERICA

SIR WALTER RALEIGH

From the 1677 edition of Sir Walter's *Historie of the World*. Courtesy
of the William L. Clements Library, University of Michigan

Book One

EUROPE DISCOVERS AMERICA

CHAPTER I

The Country and the People

LESS than five centuries ago the peoples of Europe, Asia, and Africa were not aware of so much as the existence of those lands that today are called *America*. Between them and the European and Asiatic centers of civilization lay oceans of such size that navigators had neither the idea nor the daring nor the means of crossing them. The only territories relatively close to the Old World were situated to the north in Arctic regions difficult to reach. Over immense distances was scattered a population which today could be gathered together in a few New York City blocks. These virgin lands became a proving ground for experiments. For the first time Europeans were able to free themselves, by a few months' voyage, from the age-old quarrels that had made division among them; for the first time the problems of property ownership and the horde of hatreds connected therewith fell into second place; for the first time since prehistory man's most dangerous enemy was not man but nature. Because of this meeting of an unexploited continent and an advanced civilization, social history suddenly took a new turn.

The results of this meeting would have been less startling if the climate of America had not been so favorable to Europeans. In that case American settlements might have remained isolated colonies inhabited by a few scattered planters. As it turned out, the European adapted himself easily to the climate of North America. The changes of season were more sudden, the weather more capricious than in Europe, but many of the colonists felt healthier than in their native lands, although some of them maintained that this sense of well-being was short-lived. Since the difficulties of the voyage and the wildness of the country had eliminated at the start all those who were timid of soul or weak of body, the new people were vigorous by nature. There was not much danger of their lacking food. European grains were not to be found in America, but there were excellent native plants which were cultivated by the Indians. The forests provided fruits and game; the sea, fish. If the first settlers almost died of hunger it was because of ignorance and because through greed they went in search of gold and silver instead of corn and cod. When cattle and barnyard animals were imported from Europe they multiplied with surprising rapidity in a climate that was no less favorable to them than to the white man. For the construction of houses and ships, the wooded coast of the Atlantic assured the colonists of inexhaustible materials. Later their descendants were to discover that metals, coal, petroleum, and almost all the natural products necessary to man were to be found in these miraculous lands. The unexploited continent proved a continent worth exploiting.

And, finally, it was a continent easy to penetrate. America was turned toward Europe as Europe toward America. The deeply indented east coast of the New World, rich in natural harbors and navigable rivers, was hospitable to mariners. The hilly barriers were by no means insurmountable and did not present a serious obstacle to the advance of the white man. If the coast opposite Europe had been like California, a narrow strip, separated from the central plains by high mountains, the development of this country would have been delayed. On the east coast were the mouths of a number of navigable rivers which furnished natural means of access. Farther west the Mississippi and its tributaries unified an immense territory. Thanks to these waterways, the coast would be able to exchange its products with the interior as soon as the latter was cleared. In the north toward the region which today is Canada lay another giant system of lakes and rivers which issued into the valley of the St. Lawrence and, as a finishing touch in this natural design, between the Mississippi system and that of the St. Lawrence the distance was very small. The sources of the rivers in one system were so close to those of the other that a canoe could be carried on a man's back from the basin of the Ohio to the region of the Lakes. Whoever controlled the waterways, if he proved capable of defending them, would become the master of America.

Although the continent was colonized principally by Europeans, they acquired there new characteristics. It was the peculiarity of America to have, for a period of three hundred years, a moving frontier which retreated toward the west. On this extreme fringe of civilization the harshness of life, the struggle against the forest and the Indian, the abundance of land, and the necessity of mutual aid created a new type of man: the pioneer, generous, independent and rugged, who recognized no inequalities save those of physical strength and enthusiasm for work. In this setting men of very different countries came to resemble one another. All showed a spirit of co-operation that could hardly be found in Europe. On the frontier envy was curtailed by equality in the face of danger. Because government could not reach them, the pioneers fell into the habit of governing themselves. One's neighbor was not a rival but a partner. From this there resulted a gaiety and good will which astonished, and still astonish, the Europeans accustomed to parochial feuds. From this also came an easy acceptance of liberty which is a rare phenomenon. In the old countries liberties were conquests wrung by individuals from established governments; but here in the New World a new political theory was developed: That men were superior to governments.

CHAPTER II

The Indians

WHEN the first Europeans landed in America they encountered tribes which were at different levels of civilization but all of which seemed to belong to the same race. The explorers called these natives *Indians* because the geographers of that day placed the Indies on the western shore of the Atlantic Ocean. In point of fact, the first Americans were not of the Indian type; they resembled the Mongols with whom they had in common brown skin, prominent cheekbones, and coarse black hair. Where had they come from? Had their race originated on the American continent? This seems unlikely, for there has been no discovery on this continent, as there has been in Europe and Asia, of very ancient human remains. It is certain, however that during the glacial epoch there were men in America. In order to believe that their race originated here one must maintain: (a) that the skeletons of all intermediate forms analogous to Cro-Magnon man or to the Neanderthal have been lost or have not yet been found, which would be very surprising in view of the explorations that have been made in the caverns and caves where these pre-Americans might have lived; (b) that an independent but parallel evolution has miraculously produced men of a Mongoloid type in America as well as in Asia, which is incredible and even absurd. It is simpler to believe that the Indians were of Asiatic type because they came from Asia.

How? And at what period? The most generally accepted theory is that they migrated from Siberia to Alaska by crossing the Bering Strait. This strait is only fifty miles wide; the Diomede Islands provide a stopping place in the middle; the sea is frozen over for part of the year. Such a migration is, therefore, not improbable. And why did these tribes cross from Asia to America? Perhaps as a result of a change in climate, perhaps from the necessity of finding new pastures, perhaps by chance. However that may have been, the migration took place before the end of the Neolithic period when civilization was very little advanced; for the wheel was unknown to the Indians of America at the time of the Spanish conquest, whereas the least advanced tribes of Asia had known its use for a long time. The migrating hordes brought with them to America the art of weaving, certain dyes, the bow, the art of making fire and that of polishing stone, the harpoon, the domestic dog; and it is likely that they already had the habit of smoking opium or some other preparation, for which the Indians had, by the time of the conquest, substituted tobacco, an indigenous plant, and, farther south, coca. In short the resemblances and differences between the cultures of the Old and New Worlds prove at once that there was a common origin and that a total separation occurred at a fairly primitive level.

It is possible that the American Indians, although all of Asiatic origin, may have sprung from different groups. Some anthropologists believe that the Polynesians or the Melanesians, in small numbers, may have reached South America. That would explain certain strange analogies between the art of the Incas or the Aztecs and that of Egypt. One might add that the extreme variety of the Indian languages and the impossibility of reducing them to common roots accords with the hypothesis of several migrations unrelated to one another. Other scientists reply that the farthest wanderings of the Maoris would not have taken them to America, and that the resemblances that have been pointed out are to be explained by coincidence or the similarity of natural conditions. However that may be, and from whatever part of Asia the Indians may have come, one can say with assurance that the bond was broken at an early date and that civilization in America developed independently for several thousand years. Its agriculture consisted of the cultivation of indigenous plants— maize, beans, potato, cassava, cocoa, tobacco, and cotton—carried on without the use of a plow. In Central and South America the Indians built temples and palaces of stone; elsewhere they lived in bark cabins, tents made of buffalo skins, wooden lodges or huts of dried mud.

Before the conquests two civilizations had developed in Mexico in two different regions: in the south in the neighborhood of Yucatan, the Mayan; in the north in the region of what is today Mexico City, the Aztec. The peoples of the Mayan culture constituted a well-organized society. They were governed by a nobility who were armed with bows and spears and wore ornaments of jade, turquoise, and feathers. Their race was ancient and profoundly religious. They worshiped a God of the Rising Sun, inventor of letters, a God of Arts and of Peace, and a Fair God, the Plumed Serpent, from whom their neighbors the Aztecs derived Quetzalcoatl, the bird-serpent. The Mayan gods demanded human sacrifice and there was therefore the necessity of securing prisoners. These victims met horrible destruction at the hands of the Mayas and the Aztecs. When Cortez arrived at the palace of Montezuma, ruler of the Aztecs, the Indians told him with wonder that their master sacrificed at least twenty thousand men a year. The Mayas had invented an alphabet; they knew how to count, had conceived the idea of zero, measured the year with exactitude, and set up at the end of each twenty-year period commemorative stelae which they called *katun*. Their architecture was sublime; they built immense pyramidal structures whose truncated summits were often surmounted by temples approached by giant stairways. The rude massiveness of the figures in Mayan sculpture recalls both archaic Egyptian and modern sculpture.

The other great people of Mexico was more warlike than the Mayas. The Aztecs (and before them the Toltecs) had conquered numerous vassals who paid them tribute. The Aztec nobility, exempt from taxation, formed the court of the ruler or emperor. The emperor was succeeded by his brother or his nearest relative in the maternal line. Montezuma, last of the Aztec sovereigns, was dethroned by the Spaniards in 1520. His subjects believed him to be the most powerful man in the world and spoke with wonder of his capitol, Mexico-Tenochtitlan, built on an island in the middle of a lake, and containing a noble palace, a giant courtyard, and twenty temples of red stone. The houses, coated with blue stucco and adorned with red roses, shone in the sun. On the fragrant waters of the lake floated fifteen thousand canoes. The temple pyramids were silhouetted against the sierra; at night they glowed with fires, and the odor of sacrifice mounted toward the hideous Huitzilopochtli, God of War, voracious of victims. For the Aztecs loved roses, poetry, and blood. Why did this powerful state collapse at the first attack by Europeans? Because an empire, built like that of the Aztecs on hostile and conquered peoples, is always vulnerable; because the Spanish weapons were superior; because the Aztecs fought to secure prisoners, the Spaniards to kill; because the Aztecs believed a legend according to which the Fair God Quetzalcoatl, the Plumed Serpent, would one day return to his own people on a great white bird. The white sails of the caravels made the Mexicans think that the divine bird had alighted on the gulf.

In the region which is now Peru another civilization flourished, that of the Incas or Sons of the Sun. The empire of the Incas was an authoritarian and socialist monarchy. From his palace, built at an altitude of 13,000 feet near Lake Titicaca, the Son of the Sun reigned over millions of subjects. Military roads, garrisons, and governors insured his authority. Lands and flocks belonged to the state. An artisan could own only his tools. Of his harvest a peasant retained one-third; he had to give one-third to the state and one-third to the Inca. The officials redivided the agricultural and manufactured products. The system was severe but respected because the Inca, an enlightened despot, took care of his people. The Peruvians, like the Mexicans, possessed a calendar. The traveler can still see the astronomical tower in which the priests observed the solstices. The temples were polygons of giant stones which achieved beauty by their proportions. The prayers so closely resemble Christian prayers that the Spanish priests, when they heard them, believed that Catholic saints had passed that way: "O Pachecamas! Thou who hast existed since the Beginning and who wilt exist until the End! Thou who dost defend us from Evil and dost preserve our life, art Thou in the heavens or on the earth? Listen to the voice of him who implores Thee, give him life eternal and accept his sacrifice. . . ." The subjects of the Inca produced works of art, possessed a religion, and led a well-regulated civil life.

The Indians of North America had not, like the Aztecs or the Incas, conquered or built up empires. Many of them had remained nomads. Those of the great central plains lived almost entirely upon immense herds of buffaloes which thronged the prairie by the millions. The Indians ate the meat of the buffalo; from the skin they made moccasins, clothes, and boats; from the tendons, strings for their bows; from the horns, spoons. By drying and pounding the meat they made pemmican which sustained them in lean times. The stupidity of the buffalo rendered it relatively harmless, but also impossible to domesticate. As draft animals, the Indians used dogs. In certain localities and particularly in the Southwest (Arizona and New Mexico), the tribes from prehistoric times had been sedentary and lived in many-storeyed community *pueblos* which recall the *ksours* of the Sahara. A pueblo was an immense building made of stone rooms superimposed one upon the other in banks and ventilated from above. The Pueblo Indians cultivated maize, successfully carried on irrigation, and had domesticated the turkey; each village possessed a flock of turkeys. Before the era of the Pueblos there had been another civilization, that of the Basket Makers, who carried the art of basketry to a high point. With dyes extracted from the root of the mahogany tree, and with other essences, the Basket Makers colored the fiber of willow bark or mulberry black, red, or yellow, and made jars, sandals, sacks, and plates, ornamented with geometric designs of a singular beauty. Almost all the Indians were acquainted with tobacco; some smoked it, others chewed it or used it as snuff. Certain tribes owned pipes of stone or clay; some molded the tobacco in little cylinders of stone and thus produced the first cigarettes.

The social life of the northern Indians was simple. Some of the tribes had a chief, a *sachem*; some a council of elders. Sometimes, as in the case of the Iroquois, several "nations" formed a confederation governed by a grand council of fifty sachems and under the command of two permanent chieftains. In Dakota seven tribes had sworn not to make war against one another, and the word *Dakota* signified "those who are our friends." Among the Indians of the Plains, societies like those of the Foxes had members in various tribes. In the case of the Indians of the Rio Grande each tribe is, even today, divided into the Reds and the Whites, whose social and religious duties are different. The priests (or medicine men) had two essential functions: to heal the sick and to bring rain. The Indians loved ceremonies, dances, and palavers. They possessed dignity, courage, and unwavering stoicism in the face of death. To one another they were generous, and the tribes of the Northwest observed the custom of *Potlatch,* a festival in the course of which gifts of great value were distributed to all guests. Toward a captive cruelty was the rule. He was tortured, burned, sometimes eaten. The custom of scalping, that is to say, the removal of the hair and scalp of an enemy, was not usual in pre-Columbian times. The Indians of the Plains preferred to cut off the whole head. But the scalps were lighter and more easily transported than severed heads and lent themselves better to the ornamentation of robes or tents. The operation was carried out by making a circular incision in the skin of the head and pulling the hair vigorously. It was not necessarily fatal.

The influence of Indian civilization on North America has been rapidly effaced. Nevertheless the European colonists learned from the Indians how to cultivate certain plants; they adopted Indian foods, certain articles of clothing, and also words for certain things. *Hominy, succotash, tapioca, pemmican* form a part of the culinary vocabulary of America; *moccasin, toboggan, tomahawk, wigwam, sachem, canoe* are Indian words appropriated by Americans. Many figures of speech are translations of Indian expressions: the war path, palefaces, the Great White Father, Father of Waters (the Mississippi), the happy hunting grounds (Paradise), the pipe of peace. Used figuratively today, they once had poetic value. Moreover commerce with the Indians guided the first explorers of the continent.

The design of European civilization has been superimposed upon Indian civilization. Clearings made in the primeval forests by the herds of buffaloes became the Indian trails; the latter, followed by the first traders, were transformed into roads which were later paralleled by railways. The Indian village gave rise to the trading post, which in its turn gave way to the fort, and it to the village. Such was the history of Albany, Pittsburgh, Detroit, Chicago, St. Louis, and Kansas City. Many American

Courtesy of the William L. Clements Library, University of Michigan

Fresh fruits and vegetables—cold storage. The Florida Indians built such warehouses before the white man came, as may be seen by LeMoyne's picture, which appeared in DeBry, *America*, pt. II, Frankfurt-am-Main, 1592.

names of places, rivers, cities, states (Saratoga, Susquehanna, Arizona) are Indian words, and the beauty of their strange sound still lends an exotic charm. And finally the Indian made a contribution by bringing the pioneers closer together. For a long time he was the enemy, almost mythical and yet dangerously real, whose threatening presence saved the white men of America from the implacable hatreds of the white men of Europe.

CHAPTER III

The Spaniards in America

THE Europeans did not discover America; they stumbled upon it."
It seemed to them an obstacle in their way to the Orient. Since the
Occident had become civilized it had felt a taste and a need for the
Orient. The Romans had passionately coveted its gems, perfumes, and
dyes. The Middle Ages had turned thither for gold, satin, silk, gauzes,
drugs, and above all spices. The importance of cinnamon, nutmeg, and
pepper at a time when food was served half-spoiled is something we
can hardly imagine. A sack of pepper was a gift from one sovereign
to another. The Venetians each year purchased several cargoes of it
from the Sultan of Egypt who imported it from Malabar. The other
spices were procured from the Malaccas, whose volcanic soil baked and
rebaked these fiery condiments. The gems came from the Indies and
Ceylon, the drugs and perfumes from Sumatra and Borneo, the silks from
China. Caravans traversed all Asia, proceeding sometimes toward Malacca
where Arab merchants made purchases for Alexandria, sometimes toward
the Gulf of Persia, sometimes toward Samarkand and Bokhara across
the Mongol plains and the possessions of the Great Khan. Europeans
contended for the riches of the Orient but its geography remained a
mystery to them. All they had learned from travelers and missionaries
was that very far away was Cathay (China), Cipango (Japan), where
there were rose-colored pearls, and the Indies—the Indies of fabulous
riches, the Indies sown with gold and diamonds and rubies and sapphires.

Until the fifteenth century commerce with the Orient had been in the
hands of the Italians of Pisa, Venice, and Genoa, the Spainards of Barce-
lona and Valencia, and the Provençaux of Marseilles. Then came the
Crusades, the advance of the Turks, and the decline in seapower of the
Italian cities. The waters of the Mediterranean became unsafe. From the
idea that the earth was round—Ptolemy's idea spread by the Arabs—
there naturally arose the notion of searching for the Indies and China
toward the west by a sea route safe from the infidels. Instruments of
navigation were being improved and the seaways to the west were not
entirely unknown. Even the Romans had been to the Canaries. The
Portuguese had occupied the Azores, and their great plan was to reach
the Indies by making a circuit around Africa. To the north, beyond

fog-wrapped Thule, Scandinavian mariners, whose stories have been preserved in the Sagas, had reached Iceland and a land which they had called Greenland, although it was hardly verdant, in the hope no doubt that so flattering a name would attract colonists. It was said that certain navigators had discovered the *Antilles* or *opposite islands*—on the other side of the world. Beyond were supposed to be Cathay, Cipango, and the Indies. Here was a fine mystery to be resolved and the promise of a wonderful reward. What more was needed to tempt courageous and romantic spirits, adventurous and eager for glory?

Clements Library

America was discovered incidentally, because the maritime nations were trying to find an all water route to the East Indian sources of spices and other luxury goods. This is a picture of such an oriental market at Banta (Java). The spices are being traded in the booth (H). Original "bantam" chickens at X. From DeBry, *India*, pt. III, Frankfurt-am-Main, 1601.

Such spirits existed throughout Europe in the fifteenth century, but whereas France and England were absorbed in internal strife, Spain and Portugal had already achieved equilibrium and consolidated their monarchies. In Portugal Prince Henry gave his mariners constant support, the best maps, the best instruments, and created on the west and east coasts of Africa the Portuguese colonies which were destined to become way stations on the route to the Indies. As for Spain, in 1469 the marriage of Ferdinand and Isabella had united Aragon and Castile and founded modern Spain. Spanish feudalism had been absorbed by a centralized monarchy; the long struggle against the Moors had strengthened the position of the Catholic Church. The framework of the country seemed solid. The sailors of the Catalan ports now had as allies the excellent infantry of Castile. Where should they use their forces? In Europe the conquest of the kingdom of Granada which was drawing to a close was to settle the Moorish problem. Why not turn westward and there continue the evangelization of the planet? On their voyages Spaniards went in search of "converts as much as of spices."

Christopher Columbus, a Genoese, the son of a weaver and for a time a weaver himself, had studied cosmography and loved the sea. He understood navigation. He had will power, enthusiasm, and much imagination. After several voyages he settled in Portugal and proposed to the king an expedition to the Indies by sailing west. But the king of Portugal was at that time completely absorbed in his African project; Columbus was forced to fall back on the Spanish sovereigns. Ferdinand and Isabella kept him in suspense for a long time, sending him from *Junta* to *Junta*. Columbus demanded the rank of admiral, the vice-regency of all lands he might discover, and a tenth part of the riches found. Meticulous officials bargained with him over this hypothetical fortune. Finally he triumphed, and the port of Palos received orders to fit out three caravels for him. These three light vessels had a draught of one hundred tons for the *Santa Maria*, fifty for the *Pinta,* and forty for the *Niña*. On August 3, 1492, "the Admiral" left Spain with a crew of eighty-eight men, among whom—a symbolic detail—were Italians, Spaniards, an Englishman, and a Jew. The voyage was relatively easy and lasted five weeks. Toward the end the crew grew restive and, alarmed at sailing farther and farther from land, demanded that they put about. Columbus reassured his sailors, spoke to them of the profits that were to come, concealed the distance they had traveled, and succeeded in calming them. On October 11 the men of the *Pinta* saw a reed and some grass floating in the water. The Admiral announced that the first to see land would receive the 10,000 maravedis promised by the king and queen, plus a silk doublet. On October 12 there appeared a shore which Columbus named *San Salvador*. The grass there was as sweet as "that of Andalusia in the month of April." The whole crew sang *Gloria in excelsis Deo*. Columbus believed he was in the Indies; he had actually discovered one of the Bahama Islands.

Attracted by the astonishing spectacle, the natives congregated, some along the shore, others in canoes made of hollowed tree trunks. They were naked and unafraid, "without weapons and without laws." Columbus was astonished to find them neither white nor black. When they came aboard his ship he showed them swords. They seized the blades in their hands and cut themselves. In exchange for provisions, Columbus gave them glass beads and little bells. "It is my conviction," he wrote, "that they might easily become Christians." But he did not stay to convert them. Continuing his voyage, he discovered Cuba and Haiti (Hispaniola), each of which he mistook for Cipango. Everywhere he sought the answer to three questions: "Is there gold? Spices? And what is the religion of the country?" On this last point his mind was soon set at rest. It appeared that no heretical clergy dominated the souls of these savages. As for precious metals, each tribe offered to lead him to the treasures of the neighboring tribe. Columbus brought back paroquets, Indians with bows, spears, and gold ornaments. He told the king that he had reached Cipango and met the Sirens. He was given a triumphal reception, created Admiral of the Ocean Sea and Viceroy of the Indies. This was the zenith of his career. Subsequently he made three more voyages in the course of which he discovered Puerto Rico, Jamaica, and finally South America. Each time he set foot on the shores of a new island he believed he had found the continent; when finally he disembarked on the continent near the mouths of the Orinoco, he thought it was the Earthly Paradise. While he was exploring his domain, the first colonists he had brought over revolted against him and his brothers. The Admiral returned to Spain at the bottom of the hold with his legs in irons. Later he hung up these irons in his room as a symbol of human ingratitude. Ferdinand and Isabella, who had delivered him from his enemies, neglected and then forgot him, and in 1506 he died at Valladolid in poverty. "Weep for me," he had written, "you who love charity, truth and justice."

The discoverer did not have even the legitimate recompense of bestowing his name on his discovery. Immediately after him sailors, soldiers, and adventurers hastened on the quest for gold, pearls, and a passage to the Indies. In 1493 Pope Alexander VI, "having learned that our well loved son Christopher Colonus [*sic*] setting out in search of unknown continents had discovered peoples who believed in God and could be led into the Catholic faith, had decided for the purpose of exalting and disseminating that faith" and in order to avoid all conflict between the two Catholic powers, to divide the new worlds in advance between Spain and Portugal. And so he had traced on a globe of the world a line from the North to the South Pole, a line that passed one hundred leagues to the west of Cape Verde, and he had assigned to Portugal all countries that might be discovered east of that line; to Spain all countries situated to the west. "We, by the authority of Almighty God which was given to us in the person of St. Peter, confide to you these lands with their cities, castles, towns and villages." It is this bull of the Borgia pope that explains why Brazil today is a country in which Portuguese is spoken and Argentina a Spanish-speaking country. Meanwhile caravels and galleons were crossing the Atlantic. The voyage was hard, lasting five to eight weeks, depending on the season and the course. Two months in a poorly equipped vessel, with moldy food to eat and tepid foamy water to drink, struggling against insects and rats—that would seem long, but hope was unlimited. Captains and mercenaries set sail, drunk with heroic and brutal dreams. Catholic faith, Castilian pride, and measureless ambition were blended in their hearts. When finally the long-sought country appeared on the horizon, the heroes fell to their knees singing the *Gloria*. One of these expeditions was joined in 1499 by a Florentine, Amerigo Vespucci, who upon his return wrote a letter under the title of *Mondus Novus* which became famous throughout Europe. It was reproduced in the *Cosmographiae Introductio* of Martin Waldsee-müller, professor at Saint-Dié, who was the first to suggest that the name of America should be given to the continent discovered by Americus: "And the fourth part of the world having been discovered by Americus might well be called *Amerige,* or Land of Americus or *America* since Europe and Asia both bear the names of women." The name *America* was destined to survive, but for a long time in Spain people continued to say "the Indies."

The conquerors followed the discoverers and took part in prodigious adventures. A Spanish captain with a handful of men would suddenly fall upon an empire recalling those of Chaldea or Egypt and get possession of it as though by a miracle. Everything aided the conquest: the naïveté of the natives, who thought they saw gods disembarking, the horses of the Spaniards, which seemed to the Indians terrifying monsters, and the trustfulness of the *caciques,* or chiefs, who gave their daughters to the conquistadors. The first colonies that were founded came in contact only with uncivilized tribes; but Balboa, who took possession of the Isthmus of Darien in 1513 and was the first to see, from a high peak, the Pacific Ocean, heard the Indians talking of a fabulously rich country with palaces filled with gold, and of the Inca, Son of the Sun, arrayed in precious stones. Cortez in 1519 discovered the Aztec empire of Mexico, over which at that time reigned Montezuma, Lord of Men. Cortez had with him at the outset five hundred fifty men and sixteen horses. Having won a first battle against the Indians of the Coast, he received as tribute a helmet filled with gold dust, sky-blue cotton cloth embroidered in gold, and twenty beautiful girls. One of them, Marina, became at once his secretary, his interpreter, and his mistress. Presently he saw the capitol of Montezuma, lapped by its mountain lake, the temple pyramids aglow with sacrificial fires, the silvery palaces, and the ornaments of bright plumes sewn with diamonds and pearls. Dazzled, he decided to gain possession of the Azetc empire. It seemed an insane project, and in case of failure he knew that his heart, torn from his breast by the priest, would be offered to the God of War. But for Montezuma, the arrival of Cortez presented no less difficult problems. Was the stranger a god? Were the sails of the caravels the white wings of the sacred bird? While in doubt Montezuma received Cortez and his companions with great courtesy, placed garlands of roses around their necks, and lodged them in his own palace. There Cortez and his men made a prisoner of the unhappy monarch, a high priest betrayed by his own faith, loaded him with chains, and forced him to subserve their plans. Meanwhile the Aztecs, having killed a Spaniard, touched his flesh, and seen his blood, had lost their belief in the divinity of Cortez and the invulnerability of his men. In June, 1520, the palace was attacked, Montezuma was killed, and the Spaniards were forced to flee. The indomitable Cortez with a small force of Spaniards and the dissident Indians, who were enemies of the Aztecs, laid siege to Mexico-Tenochtitlan and, despite the furious resistance of the Aztecs, conquered it. He had given his sovereign an empire and treasures more inexhaustible than those of Aladdin.

Francisco Pizarro, one of Balboa's soldiers, had been unable to forget the description of the Incas he had heard from one of the Indians. To attack the great socialist empire of the Andes without an army was clearly impossible. He resolved to go and describe to King Charles V this prodigious prey that was lying ready. He was given only one hundred eighty men and thirty horses; later Hernandez de Soto, coming from Nicaragua with one hundred men and fifty horses, joined forces with him. This force would have been too small to be successful if it had not been aided by a tragedy in the palace. The reigning Inca, Atahualpa, was the son of one of his father's concubines, and the legitimate Inca, Huascar, was his half-brother's prisoner. This made intrigue possible. Moreover, Atahualpa, like Montezuma before him, was not sure that the Spaniard might not be a god. As for Pizarro, his fixed purpose was to emulate Cortez and seize the Inca. He succeeded at their first meeting, the Son of the Sun being so completely untouched by fear that he came surrounded by priests and not by warriors. The captive Atahualpa offered to buy his freedom by filling the room where he was imprisoned with gold to a height of nine feet. Pizarro pretended to agree. Messengers were sent racing to the temples and palaces of Peru and brought back vases, goblets, and chests of silver and gold. At the feet of the dazzled Spaniards the flashing tide mounted higher and higher. When the room was filled a fabulous treasure had been amassed. Atahualpa had kept his word. What were they to do with him? Pizarro, deciding that he was too dangerous, had him strangled, and Peru became a realm of Spain.

As for Hernandez de Soto, he was one of the first to explore North America. Having been appointed *adelantado* of Florida, he hoped to find another Peru. For almost four years he tramped through what is now Florida, Georgia, North and South Carolina, Alabama, and possibly Tennessee, pushing on even into Arkansas and Oklahoma, and discovered nothing but forests, swamps, and poor Indians who were amazed at the insatiable and furious activity of the white men. From all he asked for gold, and all replied: "Farther on!" He marched and marched, following the valley of the Mississippi, and finally he died on the shores of the great river which would one day carry riches far more amazing than those coveted by poor Hernandez de Soto. His companions, wishing to conceal his death from the Indians, threw his body during the night into the Father of Waters. Then they built a flotilla, descended the Mississippi, and succeeded in reaching inhabited territory. Meanwhile another Spaniard, Coronado, set out in search of the Seven Cities with Turquoise Gates which the Indians, with their talent for storytelling, had described to him. He did not find the Seven Cities of Cibola but wandered throughout the Southwest, going as far north as what is now Kansas. In the seventeenth and eighteenth centuries the Spaniards established themselves solidly in the region of the Pueblo Indians, giving it the name of New Mexico because the great buildings resembled from a distance the structures of the Aztecs.

Spain treated her American empire not as a colony but as a province. There were two realms, New Spain and Peru, each with its viceroy. Although the government was administered by Spain the Indians were allowed a certain autonomy. The task of assimilating them was entrusted to the church. Jesuits, Dominicans, and Franciscans established on the frontiers of the colony *missions* which were half-farms and half-monasteries. In these gracious structures of Spanish design the natives, attracted by gifts, were instructed by Spanish priests in the true religion, the arts of building and European agriculture, the breeding of cattle, and the manufacture of useful objects. The Indians were happy to be freed from their terrifying gods and from human sacrifice, and readily allowed themselves to be converted; but though they became Christians, they continued to fear Huitzilopochtli, whose cult in the form of strange practices survives even today. Whenever a mission became successful it was transformed into an agricultural and industrial colony; and the missionaries moved on to play their role at a more distant place. Thus the frontier advanced peaceably; the Indians forgot their native language and the Inquisition had great trouble in finding heretics.

It is perfectly true that the Indians were often exploited by the Spanish landowners, and numerous restrictions were imposed upon them; they were not allowed to carry firearms or to ride horseback. But because the Spaniards were few in number, because they had found highly evolved civilizations in South America, because many of them had married Indian women, and also because they believed in their evangelical mission, they treated the native population with moderation. The most astonishing peculiarity of the Spanish and Portuguese empires is the small number of men who created this great civilization. At the end of the sixteenth century, in all America there were not more than one hundred and sixty thousand Spanish heads of families, of whom only one-tenth had Spanish wives. Four thousand of these formed a landed aristocracy; they had made the country and they governed about five million Indians. In less than a century they had introduced into America the cultivation of wheat, rye, oats, all the European fruit trees, and all the domestic animals. By 1550 the beasts had become so numerous that no one knew what to do with them. Horses and pigs reverted to their wild state. It was the Spaniards who gave to California the orange, apricot, fig, and olive, gifts far more precious than the gold and pearls they carried away.

For metropolitan Spain the consequences of the conquest were disastrous: The Spanish sovereigns, deriving immense treasure from America, no longer needed the financial support of their people. This allowed them to maintain a dangerous absolutism. Between the people and the aristocracy no middle class took shape. But Spanish civilization, thanks to the conquistadors, had reached out to new lands which give it its prestige today. Even in North America there are innumerable Spanish survivals. In California, Mexico, Arizona, Florida, and Texas one finds *missions, presidios,* and *ranchos* of the Hispano-Moorish style, with their cloisters, their campaniles, their whitewashed walls, and their roofs of beautiful red tile. A whole Spanish vocabulary remains linked to a certain type of life and to the regions formerly occupied by Spain. *Lasso, corral, peon, sierra, adobe, pueblo, sombrero, desperado* have become American words. Even today a rich Californian owns a *ranch*; a poor Californian eats *tortillas*. The Catholic *monasteries* near San Francisco are numerous. Some of the American novels of our time (*Death Comes for the Archbishop, The Bridge of San Luis Rey*) describe early Hispano-American society. An indefinable charm, the grace of an old culture, an instinctive courtliness, perpetuate the memory of the *caballeros* and the missionaries in those states formerly occupied by Spain.

CHAPTER IV

The English in America

WHEN Pope Alexander VI had so generously divided the unexplored countries between Spain and Portugal, England was not even mentioned. There was nothing surprising about this omission. What was England then? A little kingdom without naval strength, torn by political and religious strife. Nevertheless, as early as the time of Christopher Columbus she had in Henry VII a king who believed that the future of his people was on the sea and who built a fleet and an arsenal to protect his adventurous merchants. Henry VII owned an interest in the expedition of John Cabot, who followed the example of the Spaniards in their search for a spice route toward the west. Instead of pepper and the Indies, Cabot found the cod of Newfoundland and the Labrador coast, but the successors of Henry VII faithfully carried on his naval program. Little by little the English merchants became aware of their strength and grew tired of respecting a treaty which they had not signed and which excluded them from the richest regions of the world. Queen Elizabeth, to be sure, had to cultivate the friendship of her good brother the king of Spain; but why should she hinder her enterprising mariners from carrying on small private wars and making off with a handsome booty?

One of these mariners, Francis Drake, in time of peace assaulted the Spanish forts, disembarked on the Isthmus of Darien, attacked the mule trains transporting gold from Peru, and brought the treasure back to England. On another occasion he seized the Admiral's galley loaded with gold, and distributed fabulous dividends to his stockholders, among whom was the Queen. The Spaniards complained, but the English, violently hostile to Papists, were not the people to give in. "Spain," Oliver Cromwell said later, "is not our enemy by accident; she is providentially so." The chronicler Hakluyt made a study of ways to embarrass the Spaniards by building forts between Florida and Cape Breton. He entitled one chapter: *How to make King Philip get down from his pedestal and make him the equal of his neighboring princes*. One of Elizabeth's favorites, Sir Walter Raleigh, and his half-brother, Sir Humphrey Gilbert, had the idea of founding a colony in North America. Gilbert obtained a charter to search for "pagan and barbarous countries" which were not yet in the possession of other Christian princes. In 1584 Raleigh equipped an expedition which landed on an island near the coast of what is today North Carolina. The land was named Virginia in honor of Elizabeth, the Virgin Queen. After an unsuccessful attempt at colonization the following year, Raleigh sent out an expedition in 1587 which left on the Island of Roanoke a little group of English people consisting of one hundred and fifty emigrants, including seventeen women. When a ship with provisions arrived at Roanoke four years later there was no trace of

Clements Library

"The arrival of the Englishmen in Virginia." An engraving showing Roanoke Island (North Carolina) in 1585, made from the drawings of John White, governor of the Roanoke colony. From DeBry, *America*, pt. I, Frankfurt-am-Main, 1590.

the colony. No one ever discovered what had become of these unfortunate people. But Raleigh said with assurance in 1602 that some day there would be an English nation in Virginia.

After the defeat of the Armada, the myth of Spanish invincibility collapsed. There was no longer any reason to respect Spain's monopoly in the New World. Nevertheless, to attack her possessions would have been a tremendous undertaking; it was simpler to settle in those regions where Spaniards had not yet come. Virginia became the style again. In 1600 the final Edition of Hakluyt's *Voyages* appeared. In 1605 there was staged in London a comedy called *Eastward Ho* which described North

America as another Eldorado. In this favorable atmosphere the merchants of London had no trouble forming companies for the purpose of colonization. The galleys of the king of Spain with their cargoes of gold bullion were sufficient lure. By 1606 two companies, the London Company and the Plymouth Company, had been formed. But the first alone survived. It was to be administered in London by a "Council for Virginia" under the control of the king, who had the right to impose certain regulations. Thus, while remaining a private enterprise, it was the bait for an empire. Toward Christmas, 1606, three of its vessels, the *Godspeed*, the *Susan Constant*, and the *Discovery* sailed from the port of London with one hundred and twenty colonists. The company had given the emigrants a sealed box which was not to be opened until they were in Virginia, and which contained the names of seven of their number who should form the local council of the company and elect the president. There was no question of a free government. The charter was the property of the company, not of the colonists. The emigrants, moreover, had only a very vague idea of what they were going to find. They believed Virginia was as narrow as Central America and intended to cross it to gain their real goal—Cathay, and then the Indies. They hoped to find a Montezuma or an Inca, and some new realm of fairyland. When, in the first week in May, they finally entered Chesapeake Bay, they saw a coast covered with cedars and cypress, wild forests and blue birds with scarlet wings. The mysterious box was opened and the council set up. It was decided to proceed up the river, which was named the James in honor of the king, and to found the first settlement about thirty miles inland in order to be safe from surprise attack by the Spaniards.

The president elected by the council of Jamestown was Edward Maria Wingfield. But the most remarkable person in the little colony was Captain John Smith, a young man of good family who had been an adventurer from the age of sixteen. With his handsome face tanned by the sun and his black beard trimmed to a point, John Smith was an Elizabethan of the great tradition. Some of the colonists hated him because they were jealous of him; but whenever it was necessary to appease the natives or to ask them for provisions, everyone turned to him. The Indians had at first welcomed the little fleet with a hail of arrows; then they had grown accustomed to the colonists and had exchanged their corn for beads and blankets. Their mood was capricious. Sometimes they came to Jamestown as friends; they accepted presents, offered gifts in return. Sometimes they brandished their tomahawks and it was necessary to fire the ships' cannon to get rid of them. But the fleet had other missions to perform. Soon Captain Newport set sail for England and the colonists were left alone.

Jamestown was no more than a miserable village of huts situated near a swamp; mosquitoes and stagnant water assured the continual incidence of malaria. During the first winter half the colonists died. John Smith, according to his own account, was very nearly killed by the Indian Chief Powhatan. He had already been bound to the stake when little Pocahontas, Powhatan's daughter, threw herself upon him and covered him with her body. This dramatic episode increased Smith's prestige; his enemies said he had invented it. As a matter of fact, he was just as capable of experiencing it as of imagining it.

All the colonists, nearly dead from hunger, fell to fighting for the meager rations. The Indians had grown tired of providing corn. It was John Smith again in that first harsh winter who saved the colony by his necessary severity: "He who does not work," he said, "shall not eat either." Newport returned with provisions in the nick of time to prevent complete disaster. He brought criticisms from the London Company. Where were the precious stones and the gold? Where was the passage to China? And what profitable cargo did Virginia propose to send? The unhappy colonists would have been much embarrassed to say. To be sure there was no lack of wood, and England needed it. And so they cut and sent timber, as well as other products of the forest. The company made a new appeal to the public, obtained funds, and in 1609 the arrival of a boatload of women, robust English servants, somewhat encouraged the men. The dreary cabins of Jamestown took on a slightly brighter aspect. But the winter of 1609-10 was terrible. Once more the colonists almost died of hunger. Why? Could they not fish and hunt? As a matter of fact, they were so ill that they lacked the strength. "Our nets were torn, the deer had disappeared, our pigs had been killed, our trading with the Indians was at an end, some of our men in flight, others assassinated, and practically all ill from the stagnant water of the James." Such was the balance sheet. The trade of grave-digger became the only active one on the plantation. In the spring of 1610 the survivors, about sixty in number, reduced to the appearance of skeletons, were about to abandon the colony and try to reach the fishing stations of Newfoundland, hoping from there to return to England, when a new flotilla appeared. Lord Delaware, whom the company had just named governor, was bringing provisions, tools, and medicines. The colony was saved.

Saved but not prosperous. There were still terrible years to come. For the shareholders who had paid in two hundred thousand pounds, it was a tremendous disappointment to find there neither Mexico nor Peru. In fact, as in the fable of *The Workman and His Children*, there was indeed a treasure in Virginia but it required much work to wrest it from the soil. An energetic governor, Sir Thomas Dale, imposed severe laws on that undisciplined country and modified the old system of communal labor, allotting to each of the colonists at least three acres, to be cultivated independently.

Salvation came in an unexpected way, from tobacco. Spaniards and Portuguese had been the first to introduce this plant into Europe. Nicot, French ambassador to London, sent leaves of tobacco to Queen Catherine de Medici and immortalized his name in *nicotine*. But it was at the court of Elizabeth that Drake and Raleigh had launched the Indian pipe. To satisfy this curious appetite for smoke England had hitherto bought tobacco from the Spaniards. Why shouldn't she produce it herself? Unfortunately the tobacco of the Indians in Virginia was too strong for the English taste. Finally, John Rolfe, a colonist, planted some tobacco imported from the Antilles which did not have the same bitterness. At once this crop became the rage. In 1617 tobacco was selling at twelve dollars a pound; it was being planted in the very streets of Jamestown. The king's government, disturbed at seeing the colony engaged in the production of a plant that was useless and "a corrupter of morals," attempted to limit the importation of tobacco by heavy duties. It was in vain. In 1616 the harvest was twenty thousand pounds; in 1627, five hundred thousand pounds; in 1662, close to twenty-four million pounds. John Rolfe, the author of this prosperity, was a widower whose wife had died not long after their arrival in Virginia. He got the idea of consolidating the local politics of the Virginians by marrying Pocahontas, "by no means," he said, "from carnal affection but for the good of this plantation, the honor of my country and the Glory of God." Responding to these noble sentiments, Pocahontas, baptized Rebecca, became a devout Christian, and followed her husband to London where she was much feted but where the winter fogs proved fatal.

Despite the success of tobacco, the development of Virginia was slow. The crossing remained long and distressing. Obviously, greater inducements were needed. A new system of generous land grants was introduced, but white workmen remained scarce and the cultivation of tobacco demanded numerous operations. In 1619 a Dutch man-of-war arrived in the harbor with twenty Negroes on board. The Virginia planters imported more. Since the Negroes did not work well except under supervision, it was not considered advantageous to employ less than twenty of them. This was an important factor in the development of the large plantation. It was also in 1619 that, with permission from the company, which wished to appear liberal, the first assembly of the colonists met—the House of Burgesses of Virginia. It first convened in the choir of the church in

Jamestown. Each meeting began with prayer. The House had its Speaker and Sergeant-at-Arms; the English excel at transporting England to the ends of the earth. Later on the governor transformed his council into an Upper House. The laws were subject to the veto of the directors of the company in London, and the crown.

In the report which Sir William Berkeley, a governor, made to the company in 1671, we read that the population was at that time forty thousand, of which two thousand were Negroes; that each year about fifteen thousand colonists or servants arrived; plus two shiploads of Negroes in seven years. The products of the colony were tobacco, a little cordage, timber, and masts for ships. Eighty English ships made the voyage each year. By 1620, the London Company had fallen into disfavor with the king; its charter was annulled and from 1624 Virginia belonged to the crown.

The settling of Virginia had been a commercial enterprise under royal patronage, but in 1620 there appeared in North America a new type of British colony. In this early part of the seventeenth century England was torn by violent conflicts. Political and religious hatreds attained a paroxysm of violence seldom equaled in that country. Three groups of churches contended for members: the Anglicans, the Presbyterians, and the Separatists, a division of the Puritans. The Anglicans accepted the hierarchies of divine right—bishops and monarchs; the low-church Anglicans were Calvinists; as also were the Presbyterians, who in imitation of Geneva maintained an established church which was governed, not by bishops, but by elders elected from each parish and united in a synod; the Separatists recognized no intermediary between them and their God and took literally the text from St. Paul: "Wherefore come out from among them and be ye separate, saith the Lord, and touch not the Unclean thing; and I will receive you." The Separatists considered as "Unclean things" both the Church of England and the Presbyterian Church. In return, both those denominations persecuted the Separatists. So some of the latter had fled to Holland, but they had found the life there uncongenial and living conditions difficult. Consequently they began negotiations with the Virginia Company to obtain a patent. Spain did not allow heretics to go to her colonies for fear of contamination; England, more of a realist, believed the heretic to be the export item par excellence. The Separatists sought a land where they might have freedom to pray in peace; the company was looking for colonists. They made a deal. Then, as the Dissenters lacked capital, they found venturesome business partners who agreed to form a company to which the emigrants should contribute their persons and the merchants their money, these diverse contributions being represented by shares of stock. To guarantee the capital it was agreed that for seven years all the products of the colony should be deposited in a central warehouse and sold by the company. Thus one hundred and two "Pilgrims," who by the way were not all Separatists, embarked on the *Mayflower* in September, 1620. The *Mayflower* ran into storms, the captain lost his way, wandered for a month along an almost unknown coast, and on December 21, after a frightful voyage, the Pilgrims, instead of arriving in Virginia, found themselves at Plymouth, where they had no concession or rights of any sort.

Before disembarking, forty-one of the men of the expedition, the so-called "Pilgrim Fathers," met in the ship's cabin and signed a pact or covenant in which they swore to remain together and to obey the laws established by common consent for the common good. The symbolic value of this pact, as was true also of the Magna Carta, was not apparent until much later. What gave it its importance was in part the equality of all believers in the independent sects and in part the absence on this coast of all established authority. In Virginia first the company and then officers of the crown exercised authority; the Pilgrims of the *Mayflower*, without having sought it, suddenly found themselves without masters. This accident transformed a religious covenant into a social contract. Having elected one of their number, John Carver, governor, the passengers of the *Mayflower* founded the town of Plymouth, whose early days were to be as difficult as those of Jamestown. Nearly half the members of the colony died during the first winter. There were times when there were only a few men able to look after the sick, cook the meals, and wash the linen; they did this in a spirit of brotherly devotion. In the end, thanks to their firm spirits, good sense, and to the help of friendly Indians who taught them how to grow corn and procure fish, the colony of Plymouth survived. In time it became comfortably established, but its growth was slow, and in 1691, when it united with the Massachusetts Bay Colony, it numbered only seven thousand colonists. This second colony did not hold the same religious principles as the Pilgrims of Plymouth, but it borrowed from them one important idea: that of assigning the lands to members of the community as freeholds. The colony of New Plymouth was finally to be absorbed by Massachusetts Bay, but its influence continued to be felt.

The group of Puritans, who in 1629 obtained a royal charter for "the Government and Company of Massachusetts Bay in New England," had among their members a number of landed gentlemen and prosperous merchants; in religion they were low-church Anglican; their leader was a well-known lawyer, John Winthrop, and the capital had been subscribed without difficulty by the members themselves. The English government, in granting the charter, had thought that the colony, like that of Virginia, would be governed from London; but the council decided to transport itself in a body to Massachusetts, which resulted in establishing an almost independent state. John Winthrop and his companions were by no means democrats. They were aristocrats or, more precisely, theocrats. They respected distinctions of class and rank. Hebraic theology, Genevese discipline, and British tradition combined to inspire in them the desire to found an authoritarian state. But the authority in their eyes, could only be religious. They believed in the letter of the Bible, in the constant intervention of God in human affairs, and in the temporal authority of the ministers of their faith. They had left their country to obey their God. "It was God who put it into my heart to incline to live abroad; it was God who made my father willing to let me go; it was God who sent Mr. Maverick, the pious minister, to me who was unknown to him, to seek me out that I might come hither." They wished to found a holy community where they would be free to worship God according to their understanding; they had no desire to accord this liberty to other sects. The church of which they dreamed was an established church, like the Church of England, but purified more completely than the latter from all odor of papism.

By the end of summer of 1630, about a thousand emigrants had arrived; many more followed. The times in England were hard. Political and religious refugees found their way either to the West Indies or to America. By 1634 Boston, which John Winthrop had founded on the bank of the Charles River, numbered four thousand inhabitants. Numerous small towns surrounded it. The communities of Massachusetts differed from those of Virginia. The soil required hard labor; tobacco did not grow well; Negroes did not become acclimated. Only small farms, cultivated by the farmer and his family, prospered, and these farms had to be grouped in villages or towns to assure common defense against the Indians. The New England town was a modification of the English manor. The farmer did not pay quitrent; he was a free stockholder and theoretically the company was to have been governed by the General Court or assembly of the stockholders. But the charter had been drawn in such a way that at the outset John Winthrop and about a dozen assistants governed alone. Then, as a result of complaints, it was decided that each town should be represented at the meetings of the Court by two delegates. And so the first assembly was formed which was later to be divided into two houses, the assistants of the governor forming a sort of Upper House, and the delegates a Lower House.

John Winthrop lived in feudal or patriarchal style surrounded by numerous servants. He was a leader worthy of confidence, self-disciplined and honest, but he was tyrannical. He considered himself, after the pattern of Calvin, as a vice-regent appointed by the Lord, and he relied upon the support of the ministers of his faith. Each Puritan congregation was independent, with a minister as its leader. All the ministers formed an oligarchy to which the authority of the Bible gave great strength. The right to vote was granted only to church members, and the clergy passed upon the qualifications of applicants. Soon, established puritanism became as odious to certain free spirits as the Church of England. William Blackstone, the oldest inhabitant of Boston, said that he had left England because he did not love the lords bishops and that now he felt no greater love for the lords brethren. The civil authority emanated from the governor, the magistrates, and those of the shareholders who accepted the church. The laws concerning sedition protected the governor against malcontents. Winthrop prided himself on having founded just this sort of state: "Now if we should change from a mixt Aristocratie to a meere Democratie: first, we should have no warr'nt in Scripture for it; there was no such government in Israell; second, we should hereby voluntaryly abase ourselves, and deprive ourselves of that dignitye, which the Providence of God hath putt upon us: which is a manifest breach of the Fifth Commandment: for a Democratie is, among most Civill nations accounted the meanest and worst of all forms of Government. . . ." He would not tolerate criticisms of the judgments of his tribunal even in the name of the law: "Whatever the sentence," he said, "the judgment is that of the Lord." John Cotton, the most famous of the preachers of that generation, shared the political ideas of Winthrop. "The doctrine of unlimited popular sovereignty was for him no other than a thistle in the Garden of the Lord." All desire for liberty was a sin. His wish was to substitute for the landed aristocracy he had known in England an oligarchy of pious theologians.

The conflicts of the more liberal spirits with Puritan theocracy was to lead to the settlement of new colonies. Roger Williams, "a pious young man filled with divine madness," arrived from England in 1631 and became a teacher of the church in Salem. He earned the hostility of the General Court by teaching that all men, being children of God, are equal and brothers; that a royal charter gives no right to the lands which actually belong to the Indians; that state and church should be separate; that to limit the right to vote in civil affairs to members of the church is like choosing a doctor for his religious convictions; and finally that all persecution for reasons of conscience is clearly and reprehensibly contrary to the teaching of Jesus Christ. "A magistrate," Roger Williams said, "is not only the Minister of God but the Minister or servant of the people." In short, he broke with the Calvinist tradition of Boston and returned to the ideas of the Pilgrims of Plymouth and to a free social contract. In 1636 the General Court exiled Roger Williams from Massachusetts and, after perilous adventures, he, together with some friends, founded a settlement on Rhode Island, to which he gave the name of Providence, in thanksgiving for the help that the generous providence of God had brought him in his distress. True to his principles, Roger Williams bought the land from the Indians, became their friend, for he spoke their language, and exercised a very happy influence over the relations of the savages with the Massachusetts Bay Colony, thus returning good for evil. Rhode Island was to be a colony of complete religious freedom, a refuge for people of sensitive conscience. Many such came there, particularly the Anabaptists. They found themselves delivered at once from the "Papist bishops and Presbyterian tyrants." Roger Williams went to England, and there became the friend of Cromwell and of Milton, and in 1663 he obtained a royal charter. To this founder of religious liberalism America owes an enormous debt.

Clements Library

An 18th century New England conception of a clergyman. From original woodcut on a 1771 broadside at the Massachusetts Historical Society.

Anne Hutchinson, an intelligent, courageous, and impassioned woman, who had caused a division in the whole Massachusetts Colony and particularly in the city of Boston by her doctrine of self-illumination and her stand against the legalism of the Puritan churches, having been expelled and excommunicated, went to a little settlement in Rhode Island known as Portsmouth. In 1643 she was killed by the Indians, an event in which the magistrates of Massachusetts recognized the justice of God.

Other discontented groups, also coming from Massachusetts, established the colony of Connecticut. The most famous of these groups was led to Hartford by "the grave and judicious" Thomas Hooker, a preacher and schoolmaster from Newton. Thomas Hooker, like Roger Williams, rejected the theocracy dear to John Winthrop. "The foundation of authority is laid," he said, "firstly, in the free consent of the people." And also: "The choice of public magistrates belongs unto the people by God's own allowance." Thomas Hooker was much too independent to agree with John Winthrop. "I should choose," he said, "neither to live nor to leave my posterity under such a government." The Fundamental Orders of Connecticut, "the first written constitution of modern democracy," which he and his friends adopted in 1639, established a free, democratic republic. But the right of suffrage belonged only to those owning property to the value of at least thirty pounds.

Other Puritans, led by John Davenport, founded New Haven on the banks of the Connecticut. They decided that divine law, as delivered by Moses, should be their code, whence came the famous blue laws which enjoined strict observance of the Sabbath, denied trial by jury, and prescribed the death penalty for adulterous couples, as well as other inhuman severities. Before long they were made less severe. In 1662 the various settlements in Connecticut united and obtained an extremely liberal charter, since the king and Parliament demanded no control over the assembly and government elected by the colony. To secure privileges without attracting attention, and to allow the churches to differ without persecuting them was the policy of Connecticut. It was successful, and Hartford became "the Cradle of American Democracy." In 1684 the charter of Massachusetts was revoked by the crown. A new one was granted in 1691, and thereafter the power slipped away from the Puritan oligarchy. A governor named by the king presided over the council, and property ownership, rather than church membership, was made the basis of suffrage. The colony's leaders tried for a long time to maintain their prerogatives. In 1702 Judge Sewall noted in his journal that one of them was sulking because in the processions in honor of Queen Anne the civil authority had taken precedence over the religious. But it was a hopeless struggle. The time of theocracy had passed. Puritanism, in the political sphere, was to give way to democracy.

CHAPTER V

The English in America (Continued)

IT WAS not only to the companies but to individuals as well that the crown granted charters. Sir George Calvert, a Catholic gentleman, had rendered service to Robert Cecil in the reign of Elizabeth. He had gone to visit Virginia. When he returned to England he had been very well received by Charles I, who, having married a Frenchwoman, showed a conciliatory attitude toward the Catholics. The king, being unable to employ Sir George in England because of his religion, created him Lord Baltimore and conferred upon him, in fee simple, the lands situated between the Potomac and the fortieth parallel. In homage to his queen, Henriette Marie, the king called the new domain Maryland. When Calvert died, without having been able to return to America, the charter passed to his son. Under the terms of the charter, Maryland was to have the character of a constitutional monarchy with the proprietor as king, head of the church, and captain general of the armed forces. He had the sovereign right to create manors and, with them, a nobility, and with the advice and consent of the freemen, he had sole authority to make laws. Baltimore began by offering a thousand acres to any gentleman who would bring five men to Maryland, and the colonists came. A Catholic and the subject of an Anglican king, he was constrained to be cautious, and he gave orders that Protestants were to be treated kindly and with justice. His wise religious policy succeeded rather well; in Maryland was to be seen the miracle of the Roman Church and the Protestant Episcopal Church living on friendly terms. In 1649, this policy was embodied in a toleration act, by virtue of which no one could be molested for his religious ideas provided he believed in the Trinity and Jesus Christ. Those who blasphemed against the divine Trinity or the Holy Virgin were to be flogged, which gave evidence of laudable moderation. Lord Baltimore maintained his difficult position until the Revolution of 1688. Following that Protestant revolt, the Church of England was established in Maryland and the Catholic Church was no longer authorized to hold public worship. This measure made the Catholics in Maryland enemies of the crown and made Lord Baltimore a Protestant. As payment for this conversion, he retained ownership of his lands; the governmental authority, however, passed to the crown.

What Charles I had done for Lord Baltimore, Charles II, after his restoration, tried to do for such faithful royalists as Clarendon, Monk, Shaftesbury, and Sir George Carteret, former governor of Jersey. In 1663 he gave them and four other favorites a vast territory south of Virginia, called Carolina. These great gentlemen conceived the strange notion of having a constitution drawn up by John Locke, who was the fashionable philosopher of that period. He drafted an amazing document in which he laid out the future classes in the state as an engineer might lay out roads. A fifth of the land was to remain in the possession of the proprietors, a fifth was to go to the new nobility who were to be created and who would have it farmed by serfs, the rest was to be in the hands of independent farmers. The purpose was to form an aristocracy. But when there were so many free lands open to colonists, why should they agree to remain on a fief as serfs or even to pay a quitrent? The proprietors struggled for a time but finally gave up, and in 1729 Carolina passed to the crown and was separated into North and South Carolina.

Lord John Berkeley and Sir George Carteret had bought from the Duke of York in 1664 the territory between the Hudson and the Delaware, which they called New Jersey in memory of the island Sir George had once governed. There they founded the city of Elizabeth, and Puritans from Connecticut founded Newark. But difficulties of all sorts discouraged the proprietors, and in 1702 New Jersey in its turn became a colony of the crown. It would appear that the founding of states was not a profession well suited to private persons.

The Society of Friends, to whom the name of Quakers had been given because they trembled with emotion when the Spirit took possession of them, was a religious group which had pushed Puritan protestantism to its logical extreme. The Friends believed that every man can communicate directly with God and that this subjective experience alone is important; that any man may be chosen by God as His interpreter and that no professional minister is necessary; that silent contemplation is the best form of prayer; that any experience in life may become "a summit" if it is the occasion of communion with the Spirit. The Quakers were pacifists; they worshiped a God of love rather than a God of vengeance; they refused to fight or to pay tithes; they dressed in an unusual manner and used "thee" and "thine" when speaking to one another. Their gravestones, bearing no names, assigned them to eternal anonymity. In short, they shocked the conformists as much by their virtues as by their beliefs. England had persecuted them; many of them emigrated to the colonies where they also were persecuted and a few were even hanged. What was to become of them? They needed a concession from the crown, but the latter could not give a charter to so hated a sect. Finally William Penn, the son of an admiral who had helped to restore Charles II, and to whom the crown owed sixteen thousand pounds, obtained from the king in 1681 a personal charter which gave him proprietary rights in a tract of land whose limits, as specified in the charter, overlapped those of both New York and Maryland, a territory almost as large as England and Wales combined. He decided to assemble the Quakers there, organize a free government, and try the "holy experiment" of a country where love and not violence should reign.

In 1682 he visited his estate, to which Charles had given the name of Pennsylvania. The beauty of the forests and rivers enchanted him. "O how sweet is the quiet of these parts freed from the troubles and perplexities of woeful Europe!" He called the capital Philadelphia, city of brotherly love. The holy experiment was a success. The Quakers' principles proved useful to them. Because they treated the Indians with kindness, the Indians were friendly to them. Because they dealt fairly, they succeeded in their enterprises. Because they were tolerant, various groups of emigrants came to them. Scotch-Irish Presbyterians, German Lutherans, English Anglicans, and Welsh settled in Pennsylvania. By the middle of the eighteenth century Philadelphia had become a little city of red-brick houses which recalled the most delightful aspects of England. Penn had hoped that his capital would be at once city and country. And so it was. Great gardens surrounded the houses. At night fireflies lighted them in luminous flight. There everything was peace, prosperity, and beauty. Although the Quakers were no longer a majority, they were elected to all important offices because the method of apportioning seats in the assembly gave them a voting strength greater than their numbers. This harmony was disturbed when Penn, a friend of the royal family, gave his support to James II, a Catholic sovereign. The Scotch and Welsh in the colony became indignant. When Penn died, his son (who had been converted to Anglicanism) lost all prestige. Between the proprietor and the assembly a conflict broke out which continued until the Revolution. The holy experiment had lasted as long as experiments usually last, but the Quakers remained, and remain today, loyal to their faith, one of the simplest and noblest in the world.

The colony of New York was Dutch before it was English. In 1609 a ship of the Dutch East India Company, the *Half Moon*, Henry Hudson, captain, had discovered a magnificent bay into which flowed a fine river which Hudson named after himself. At the mouth of the river he had disembarked on a long island of granite afterwards called Manhattan. High wooded cliffs bordered the river. The Dutch sailed as far as a point just above where Albany stands today. When they returned, their stories, and more particularly the furs they brought back, excited lively interest. Other expeditions followed that of Hudson. In 1621 the Dutch West India Company received by charter the right to exploit New Netherland, and in 1624 the village of New Amsterdam was founded on the tip of Manhattan. Two years later the island was purchased from the Indians for sixty guilders.

The development of the colony was rapid. The Dutch were enterprising, intelligent, aggressive, and accustomed to liberty. To encourage migration, the company granted vast domains to any stockholder who would bring over fifty persons or more. Van Rensselaer, one of the directors, said: "We must open the country to agriculture; that is the first step." As a matter of form, the land was legally purchased from the Indians by the payment of a few pieces of silver. It was thus that they ceded Hoboken and then Staten Island (so called in honor of the States-General of Holland). All along the valley of the Hudson there arose fine houses adorned with family portraits. The Van Cortlandts, Van Rensselaers, Beekmans, and Schuylers owned thousands of acres, and the formation of this feudal class aroused much discontent among the poor colonists. In 1643 to restore harmony the company sent out an energetic and picturesque director, Pieter Stuyvesant. He had a wooden leg (they called him old Silver Nails) and the soul of a dictator. "It may during my administration be contemplated to appeal; but if anyone should do it, I will make him a foot shorter, and send the pieces to Holland, and let him appeal in that way." When it was suggested to him that an assembly be created in New Netherland, he replied that he did not believe in electoral systems. "Each would vote for one of his own stamp, the thief for a thief, the rogue, the tippler and the smuggler for his brother in iniquity, so that he may enjoy more latitude in vice and fraud." He wished, he said, to have his authority from the company, not from a mob of ignorant subjects.

New Amsterdam had grown very fast. Boats loaded with bricks and tiles came from the Low Countries and permitted the burghers to build their solid and graceful houses. In the port the rich clothes of the Dutch merchants made a picturesque contrast to the brown skins of the Indians who came there with furs and tobacco leaf. But the English took no pleasure in seeing this Dutch enclave in their New World. In 1653 when the two countries were at war, the Dutch prepared to defend themselves and built across the island of Manhattan a wall which has given its name to Wall Street. In 1663 Stuyvesant wrote to the Dutch West India Company to send him reinforcements for want of which "the boat would sink." His tyrannical character had made him unpopular; the States-General refused to support him; many English colonists had settled on Long Island and were protesting against the actions of the Dutch governor. Suddenly Charles II claimed the territory of New Netherland on the somewhat feeble pretext of the discovery of these lands by John Cabot in 1498. It was an old story, but in 1664 an English fleet anchored in the Hudson gave it novelty. Five hundred soldiers under the command of Colonel Richard Nicolls supported the demand for capitulation. Stuyvesant saw that he was lost; his people demanded that he surrender and said that to resist was madness; the governor knew this was true. He surrendered and, without losing a man, England acquired a flourishing colony. The king gave it as a present to his brother, the Duke of York, and the city of New Amsterdam became New York, while Fort Orange took its new name from another of the duke's titles—Albany. At the same time the Duke of York received the territory which is today the state of Delaware. Originally this had been settled by the Swedes, who had established New Sweden there, and the port of Christina (Wilmington in our day).

A final colony, to the south, completed the British domain. It was founded in 1733 by a philanthropist, General James Oglethorpe. He had gone to visit a friend in debtor's prison near London, and had been so shocked by that institution that he had demanded and obtained a parliamentary investigation. As a result of this the law had been changed and ten thousand prisoners were suddenly released. Upon their discharge from prison all were entirely without funds. Oglethorpe had the idea of sending them to America. He obtained from King George II in 1732 a charter for a territory on the banks of the Savannah and applied himself to collecting money in order to found a refuge. "The trustees intend to relieve such unfortunate people as cannot subsist here, and to establish them in an orderly manner so as to form a well regulated town. As far as the fund goes, it will defray the charge of their passage to Georgia, and give them necessary tools, cattle and land." It was an experiment in paternal colonization. The philanthropists who founded Georgia wished their colony to be strictly moral. Wesley and Whitefield went there to preach. The sale of rum was forbidden, and slavery—even free Negro labor—prohibited. With their comparatively small holdings and no slaves, the Georgia planters could not compete successfully with their wealthy South Carolinian neighbors. Little by little, many of them migrated to that state. In 1737 there were five thousand; in 1742, five hundred. Finally, in 1751, the philanthropists gave up, Georgia became a royal province, and the colonists returned.

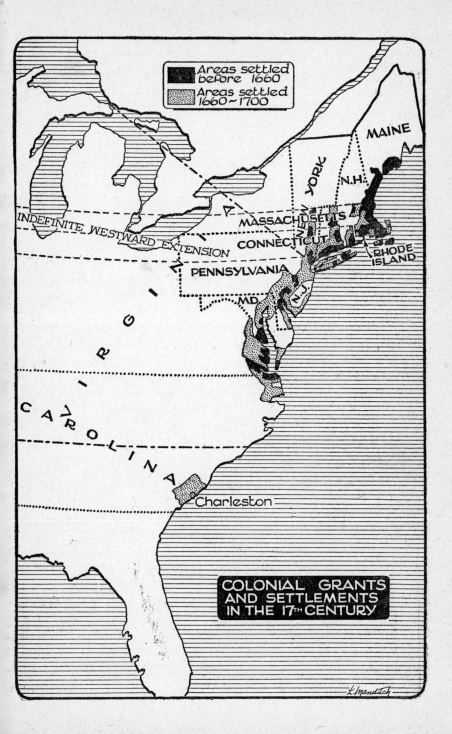

Areas settled
before 1660
Areas settled
1660~1700

MAINE

NEW YORK

N.H.

INDEFINITE WESTWARD EXTENSION

MASSACHUSETTS

CONNECTICUT

RHODE ISLAND

PENNSYLVANIA

N.J.

MD.

V I R G I N I A

C A R O L I N A

Charleston

COLONIAL GRANTS
AND SETTLEMENTS
IN THE 17TH CENTURY

L. Mandich

Thus, one after another and in various ways, eight colonies founded by chartered companies had become colonies of the crown by the time of the Revolution; three (Pennsylvania, Delaware, and Maryland) still belonged to proprietors; and two (Rhode Island and Connecticut) administered their own affairs independently. As a matter of fact, by 1750 all had a large measure of independence. All, at the bottom of their hearts, were contemptuous of a power so distant and so ignorant of their needs. All were tasting with relish in their assemblies a liberty that was to some degree rebellious. The only significant difference between them was that which distinguished the North from the South.

In the North, puritanism had given the population the morality best calculated to assure their temporal success. The Yankee or citizen of New England (the origin of the word Yankee is uncertain; one version runs that Yankee was the mispronunciation by the Indians of the word *English*, or, some say, *Anglais* as pronounced by the French) had derived from his beginnings the certitude of belonging to a chosen people: "God has sifted all the nations that He might sow in these savage lands chosen grain. . . ." The struggle against a barren soil and a severe climate, the obligation to work hard and to supplement the poverty of the land by commerce and navigation, had bred strong men, thrifty because they had to be to survive, self-satisfied, and sure that their riches, which steadily increased, were proof of divine favor. The man of the Middle Ages had worked in order to live, narrowly limited in his ambitions and his profits by the rules of his guild or corporation. The Yankee worked for the sake of working and, God willing, to make a fortune. Said Parrington, "This astonishing revolution in the ethics of work carried on its back the industrial revolution." The southerners themselves recognized the virtues of the Yankee. "Although the people," wrote Colonel Byrd, "may be ridiculed for certain pharisaical aspects of their conduct, they are none the less useful subjects by reason of their frugality, their industry, and the pains with which they avoid all scandal." They were a sturdy race, the Yankees, and one on which the country could presently build with confidence.

The South was no less necessary than the North to the equilibrium of America. There the plantation systems had developed a different independence from that engendered by puritanism, but one no less impatient of authority. Even in the Episcopal Church, contrary to the practice in England, the parishioners in Virginia had assumed the habit of selecting their own ministers. The men who met in the House of Burgesses in Williamsburg or at the tavern in Raleigh were leaders accustomed to obedience in their domains and exempt, through the institution of slavery, from all work they might consider servile. These southern leaders in 1750 resembled the country gentlemen of England. Perhaps they were even closer than their English counterparts to the old English tradition. "England changed, but Virginia did not. . . . Virginians seemed like elder Englishmen." It was as though in Virginia and Massachusetts there had developed singularly pure types of the Cavalier and the Roundhead, whose powers, for the time being at least, were to be in alliance and not in opposition. Certainly Virginia was not the whole South any more than Massachusetts was the whole North; but these two colonies represented the essence of North and South.

The Middle Colonies (those lying between the Hudson and the Potomac) were a combination of North and South, in character falling halfway between the democratic puritanism of New England and the relatively aristocratic country life of Virginia. Most of the Middle Colonies were essentially commercial, but the manner and customs of New York were very different from those of Pennsylvania. New York and Philadelphia were both rich and prosperous cities. Yet New York was more cosmopolitan; Philadelphia more urbane. Though the Quakers proved as religious as the Puritans, they showed themselves more tolerant. Philadelphia was a center of charity and culture, New York a center of pleasure, and if the rich families of New York exhibited as much tolerance as the leaders of Philadelphia society, it was more perhaps out of worldly laxity than brotherly love.

CHAPTER VI

The French in America

FRENCH sailors were among the most adventurous in Europe. Normans and Bretons had always loved danger. The men of Dieppe had been the first to found a colony on the Guinea coast; others had visited Newfoundland. "As far back as memory goes," wrote Lescarbot, "for a period of centuries, our men of Dieppe, Saint-Malo, Rochelle, and sailors from Havre de Grâce, Honfleur and other towns, have been making regular voyages to those lands to fish for cod." When the pope divided the New World between the sovereigns of Spain and Portugal, the king of France asked jokingly by what legal right the heritage of Adam had been conveyed to his dear cousins. Francis I himself had sent an explorer to North America, an Italian named Verrazzano, but the latter came back at a time when France was engaged in a life and death struggle with Spain and had no resources to spare for colonial enterprise. Finally, in 1529, after making peace with Spain, Francis I, like Henry VIII of England, fell to dreaming of galleons loaded with gold. In 1534 he aided Jacques Cartier of Saint-Malo to sail for the New World in search of a northwest passage to the Indies.

Cartier took with him sixty French sailors. He touched at Newfoundland, then continuing west entered a bay into which flowed a mighty river which he called the St. Lawrence. He landed, unfurled a banner bearing the arms of France, and sang the *Vexilla Regis*. The Indians whom he met used the word *Canada* to designate a country or city. Cartier took some of them back to France with him and they learned French and so became interpreters on subsequent voyages. Although he returned from this first voyage without either gold or news of the Indies, the king allowed him to equip three vessels and return to Canada the following year. The voyage was so long that Cartier could not return before the stormy season and had to spend the winter in a land of extreme cold. The Indians of Stadacona (Quebec) informed him that a little farther up the river there was an important encampment at Hochelaga. Today it is the site of Montreal. Cartier found there a few huts and corn fields. He wintered in a little fort which his men had built and very nearly died of cold and hunger. The sailors who returned to Saint-Malo the following spring were not very enthusiastic, and the king subsidized no further voyages. In 1541 a certain De Roberval, spurred on by the accounts of the Spaniards, got himself appointed viceroy of New France and decided to join Cartier in a third expedition. It was depressingly similar to its predecessors, and thereafter for a period of sixty years the idea of a New France slumbered. France provided amply for her citizens and inspired in them no wish to seek other countries. Those who for political or religious reasons desired to leave their native land could not obtain permission to live in a French colony. For, like the king of Spain, the French king would not extend protection in America to doctrines that he condemned in Europe. Even the wise Sully thought that distant possessions did not suit the temperament or character of France. He was mistaken.

Nevertheless, once the religious wars had subsided and Henry IV was on the throne, certain Frenchmen recalled the unexplored country where the banner of France had once been planted. A certain De Chastes, commander of the fort at Dieppe, formed a partnership with Samuel de Champlain, an explorer of great courage and experience, and secured the monopoly on trade with Canada. Champlain found Hochelega in ruins. On Chastes's death his monopoly passed into the hands of one De Monts, who made an agreement to form a company and transport at least one hundred colonists a year. He recruited volunteers, and in 1604 two ships sailed, one by way of the St. Lawrence, the other farther to the south to a region which was called Acadia. The second group, among whom was Champlain, spent the winter on an island (Sainte Croix), ran short of water, and was decimated by scurvy. When the ice and snow melted, the survivors founded the town of Port Royal on the coast. Champlain had gone to Quebec and had made friends with the Hurons and Algonquins. He provided them with French muskets to use against their enemy the Iroquois; they assisted him in exploring the surrounding country. Like all Europeans, Champlain, in marching toward the west, hoped to find the sea and the Indies. Instead, he saw an immense country of huge lakes and magnificent rivers. This New France was an empire.

The beginnings of the colony were distressing. Factions formed among the handful of men. De Monts, who was a Huguenot, lost his monopoly in France. Nothing dampened the courage of Champlain. At length Richelieu came to power. He understood that France might hope for an imperial future and accordingly founded the Company of New France, in no sense an experiment of adventurers, but a national enterprise having as stockholders the greatest names in France, including the king himself and the cardinal. At once a large flotilla was formed and sent to Canada. But it was the time of the wars with England. The ships were intercepted by privateers and the company, at the very start, lost a considerable part of its capital. A little later the colony itself was conquered by the British. But in accordance with the Treaty of Saint-Germain-en-Laye, signed in 1632, it was returned to France.

After the death of Champlain, the ecclesiastical powers became very powerful in Canada. The council that administered the colony was composed of the governor, the bishop or the superior of the Jesuits, and the governor of Montreal. The missionaries of Saint Sulpice had received from the king large concessions of land and their influence constantly increased. In 1648 the Iroquois, supplied with arms by the English and Dutch, wiped out the Hurons and threatened Montreal. At that time France had no more than five hundred men in Canada capable of bearing arms, but they beat off the Indians. During the whole period of their occupation of Canada the French were on bad terms with the Iroquois. This was partly because France had supported other tribes, but more particularly because the English of New York had developed their fur trade by agreement with the Five (later Six) Nations. The game had already been partly killed off in the forests along the Hudson. Pelts had to be obtained from regions inaccessible to Europeans; the Iroquois rendered this service and profited by it.

In 1659 Francis-Xavier de Laval, the apostolic vicar, arrived in Canada and immediately quarreled with the authorities. This disagreement, as well as the paltry returns obtained by the company, inspired Colbert, Louis XIV's great minister, with the desire to put an end to the company.

Bartering with the Indians for furs. The fur trade was an essential part of the westward movement. From Baqueville de la Potherie, *L'Histoire de l'Amérique*, 1722.

The company had brought out few colonists and had cleared but little ground. Its charter was revoked, and in 1663 Canada became part of the royal domain. A council of seven was appointed and given powers analogous to those of the Parliament of Paris; that is, both legislative and judicial. This council was to render good and loyal service. In their colonial life the French showed intelligence, great courage and devotion to the public welfare. Their faults were excessive centralization (they had too many judges, bailiffs, and seneschals, all paid by the colony) and their unhappy incapacity to achieve mutual understanding. The squabbles of officials were incessant, and each of the rival administrators made his report directly to the king, who with infinite patience read all these documents and wrote his decisions in the margin. In short, New France was still France with all its grandeurs and its weaknesses.

After the king took possession of the country the population doubled. Peasants from Normandy, Brittany, Le Perche, and Picardy came in throngs. The fur trade remained the colonists' largest source of revenue.

The same French artist's conception of the way in which the Indians used the goods they got in exchange for their furs. From *L'Histoire de l'Amérique*.

They had begun by buying the pelts of foxes and beavers from the Indians of the St. Lawrence Valley, then had gone farther west toward the Mississippi. and the Ohio. Everywhere the French and Indians got on well together. The *coureurs des bois,* often men of good family and former army officers, loved the dangers of the forest. "I cannot tell you," wrote one governor, "to what extent this life attracts our young men." In 1640, of ten thousand inhabitants, one thousand lived in the forest. Henri de Tonty, Antoine de la Motte-Cadillac, Du Luth, and Jean Nicolet, explorers and founders of cities, were all originally *coureurs des bois.* Dutch and English waited in their fortified posts for the Indians to come and sell them furs; but the

French, with remarkable daring, went out to find the Indians, made them their friends, and attached them to the colony. Each year a fleet of canoes loaded with furs came down the lakes toward Montreal. A great fair was held there, at which merchants made fortunes by selling the Indians guns, blankets, glass necklaces, and cognac.

Like the *coureurs des bois,* the French Jesuit fathers had established themselves among the Indians and had learned their language. They ran the risk of torture and death but they had no fear. "The joy one feels," said one of their number, "when one has baptized a savage, who dies shortly after and flies straight to heaven to become an angel, is a joy that surpasses all imagination." They nursed the sick, cared for prisoners, and taught the pagan infants prayers translated into their language. The Indians came and squatted in the missionaries' huts in order to hear the clock. They thought it was a living being and named it The Captain of the Days. They were filled with awe if, while it was striking, the priest said, "That's enough," and the chimes immediately stopped ringing. "What does the Captain say?" they would ask. "The Captain says, 'Get up! Go back to your own homes. . . .'" The Indians would obey. The purpose of the missionaries was, naturally, the conversion of the Indians. But the Jesuits were good Frenchmen, and all the more ready to aid the commerce of their country as its rival was heretic England.

On one point, however, they came into conflict with the *coureurs des bois.* The latter held brandy to be the best medium of exchange; they realized that it was neither very moral to corrupt the Indians nor very prudent to make them drunk, but they added that if they did not do this the English would be the only ones to profit from their virtuous forbearance. Boston rum would replace Montreal brandy, the *coureurs des bois* would get no more furs, and the Catholic missionaries would send no more Indian souls straight to heaven. Wouldn't it be better to pursue "a reasonable virtue?" Such was not the opinion of Monseigneur de Laval, who sent violent diatribes against brandy to Versailles. Colbert, at the suggestion of the king, consulted the colonists. The latter said that the quantities of alcohol sold were after all small. "Yes," replied the Jesuits, "but it only takes a small amount of alcohol to intoxicate an Indian." The debate was endless. The more serious aspect of the question was the danger to the colony represented by the pre-eminence of the fur trade. It is hardly possible to build a sound and durable prosperity on so transitory a source of revenue. A sound agricultural economy would have been of greater value to Canada.

In 1672 the king, full of hope for the future of New France, sent out an excellent governor, Count de Frontenac. He was a soldier of fifty-two who had fought in more than one war in Europe and who knew his profession. He at once won the respect of the Indians, but was saddened by the petty quarrels of the bishop and the intendant. They made the colony "a little hell." With Colbert himself Frontenac was not always in complete accord. The minister thought that all the energies of the French should be employed in developing the territory already colonized. Frontenac, on the other hand, rightly saw that from a military point of view in order to hold Canada it was essential to dominate the waterways and therefore to advance toward the Great Lakes. His plan was to build forts at strategic points commanding the mouths of these waterways. The first, Fort Frontenac, was situated at the place where Lake Ontario flows into the St. Lawrence. He gave command of it to Robert Cavelier de la Salle, a native of Rouen, for whom he had a high regard. Then in 1678 he directed La Salle to build Fort Niagara. It was a handsome structure in the style of Marshal Vauban, on the walls of which one can still read the names of Normans and Poitevins, the Frenchmen who constituted the first garrison.

Cavelier de la Salle, a Norman adventurer, dreamed, like all explorers of his time, of reaching the Western Sea. With the missionaries of Saint Sulpice, he had already gone as far as Lake Erie, and it is probable that he had proceeded from there into the basin of the Ohio. Everywhere the Indians talked to him of the Great River (the Mississippi), and he wondered whether this might not be the road to the west. But two other Frenchmen, Jacques Marquette and Louis Joliet, reached the Great River and realized that it went, not toward the Indies, but toward the Gulf of Mexico. Cavelier de le Salle proposed to follow it as far as its mouth. He built a ship, the *Griffon,* and launched it on Lake Erie, where this "floating fort" filled the Indians with amazement; later he reached the junction of the Illinois and the Mississippi; in 1682, with extraordinary courage, he descended the Mississippi to its mouth, raised there a pillar ornamented with fleurs-de-lis, and unfurled the banner of the king. The return was difficult; it was necessary to ascend the river; but Cavelier de la Salle succeeded in returning to Canada. In 1684 he went to France and urgently advised Louis XIV to create a colony at the mouth of the Mississippi which should be called Louisiana in honor of the king. Later on, by joining together Canada and Louisiana, France would acquire an immense empire. It was a vast and noble project; it would have given France practically all North America. The king understood this and entrusted four vessels to Cavelier de la Salle, but this time La Salle was unable to find the mouth of the Great River. He wandered miserably along the coast, and was finally assassinated by one of his own men.

This great man's project did not die with him. Fort Maurepas was built by the French near the Mississippi, and Monsieur de Bienville, agent of the India Company, founded there in 1718 a city which was called Nouvelle-Orléans in homage to the regent, the Duke of Orléans. A French colony began to develop; it is described in *Manon Lescaut*. In order to populate it, the company resorted to blameworthy methods: Women "of doubtful virtue" were picked up by constables and shanghaied. In order to people Nouvelle-Orléans, ancient Orléans was swept clean. "My girl," the constables would say, "wouldn't you like to go to Mississippi? I'll find you a husband worth his weight in gold. . . ." Two women on a doorstep might laugh at the passing soldiers. "There are some pretty Mississippians!" one of the latter would say, and the unfortunate women would be tossed into the cart. There were revolts, and constables were killed. Saint-Simon talks about them in his *Mémoires*. Once Nouvelle-Orléans was founded, the next step was to create a line of forts in the valley of the Mississippi to join those that Canada was constructing along the Ohio. Then the hopes of Cavelier de la Salle, of Joliet and Marquette, would finally be realized. But what power in France after Louis XIV lasted long enough to pursue such large designs?

New England resembled England, but also differed from it in more than one respect. The predominance of Dissenters, the mixture of alien races, the absence of any hereditary aristocracy, and the smallness of the fortunes made it a different and distinct type. New France, on the other hand, was a transplanted cutting from old France. In Quebec, the little French capital, a court and salons were set up. Precedence was fixed by birth and it was inflexible. Priests wore cassocks. The congregation leaving mass on Sunday in the rural parishes made a picture of provincial France. On their trips among the Indians the missionaries carried with them in valises little portable altars and embroidered chasubles. Cavelier de la Salle, attending mass in a virgin forest, wore a suit of scarlet embroidered in gold. The *coureurs des bois* alone had adopted a local costume—fur cap, buffalo-hide vest, moccasins, snowshoes; and they let their beards grow. The Indians got along well with the French, whose gaiety amused them while their gallantry aroused their admiration. They respected the missionaries because they taught them so many useful things, even how to build better forts with little towers at the four corners to guard the approaches. They had high regard for the peasants who so valiantly cleared the ground. So much work, courage, and good nature should have made the colony prosperous, and it was. But it developed too slowly to have any chance of surviving. In 1754, when the neighboring

English colonists numbered more than a million, Canada had barely eighty thousand inhabitants. This disparity, due to the bounty of France, whose citizens had no desire to leave her, and to the royal government's abhorrence of heretics, was dangerous.

CHAPTER VII

Time of the Wars

THE Europeans who had sought refuge on the new continent believed they had escaped from the endemic feuds of Europe. But the quarrels quickly overtook them. A new Hundred Years' War had broken out between France and England. The Revolution of 1688 had given the English as King William of Orange, an old enemy of Louis XIV and a Protestant. How could the king of France, an ally of the Stuarts, be on friendly terms with a man whom he considered a usurper and a heretic? For his part, William III was determined to maintain the balance of power in Europe and therefore had to oppose any effort of France to dominate Flanders either by war or by alliance. Conflict was inevitable on the European continent; in America it was no less so. There the English occupied the best part of the coast and their colonies were prosperous. But the French explorers had turned the British flank. French forts on the Ohio threatened to cut off the English colonies from the hinterland, and if the French in Canada succeeded in making connection with their fellow countrymen in Louisiana, France would become mistress of the continent. Thus local rivalries made common cause with dynastic rivalries. As for the Indians, they astutely watched these quarrels of the white man, hoping to profit by them either as opportunities for pillage or to defend their independence.

Upon the accession of William III, the Iroquois, encouraged by the English with whom they were allied, attacked the village of Lachine near Montreal in August, 1689, and perpetrated a frightful massacre. The aged Frontenac, hurriedly summoned from retirement, was sent to Quebec as war governor. He would have liked to take the offensive, descend the valley of the Hudson, and march upon New York; but not having sufficient equipment for so ambitious a project, he, in turn, instigated Indian raids against the British frontier. The massacre of Schenectady was the reply to that at Lachine. Sir William Phips, a rich Puritan of Massachusetts, determined to lead a crusade, first against Port Royal in Acadia, where he succeeded in taking possession of the city, then against Quebec. He went up the St. Lawrence with a fleet and more than two thousand men, anchored near Quebec, and sent an ultimatum to Frontenac. His representative, with eyes bandaged, was led into the courtyard of the Château Saint Louis. When the bandage was removed he saw he was surrounded by the whole garrison. Frontenac threw Phips's letter in his face, threatened to have him hanged, and said he would send no answer save by the cannon's mouth! "France recognizes but one king of England," he added, "that is the exiled King James II." Phips tried to disembark his troops but failed. He returned to Boston much discomfited, not understanding how heaven could permit this triumph of the Papists. Meanwhile in Europe Louis XIV was forced to defend himself against the powerful coalition formed by William III. In eight years of campaigning the latter did not succeed in defeating France, and at Ryswick in 1697 Louis XIV was able to sign a peace that was not too unfavorable. He was forced to recognize William III, but France retained her colonies. Unhappily it was a peace which even those who signed it considered only a truce.

Raids and massacres continued; split skulls, the scalping of women and infants, torture at the stake, the burning of villages—these make up the horrible reckoning that contrasts so strangely with the noble courtesy of many French and English officers. When the War of the Spanish Succession, known as Queen Anne's war in America, brought Queen Anne of England into conflict with Louis XIV, the Americans of New England renewed their operations against Port Royal, and for a second time took possession of Acadia. A large expedition was sent from London to Quebec. Through the fault of a bad general and an incompetent admiral this campaign was a total failure. In their church of Notre Dame des Victoires the overjoyed Canadians sang a *Te Deum*. But in Europe France was losing the war; Marlborough, a soldier of genius, was the victor at Blenheim and Ramillies. The struggle between the Whigs and the Tories, the disgrace of Marlborough, and an inspiring movement for national unity in France saved Louis XIV. The Peace of Utrecht (1713) was less disastrous than might have been feared a few years earlier. In America, France lost Hudson's Bay, Acadia, and Newfoundland, retaining only fishing rights. The French of Acadia found refuge in Louisiana where their descendants still speak French. Meanwhile Canada was saved once more and its inhabitants sang in relief: "Monsieur d'Malbrouck is dead . . ."

The War of the Austrian Succession, which in America is called King George's War (1744-48), brought no changes. Men from the New England colonies, aided by three British warships, after considerable losses seized Louisbourg, the French fortress on Cape Breton Island; but the treaty of Aix-la-Chapelle, another truce, returned Louisbourg to France to the great indignation of Boston. "Stupid as the peace," people said in England. "Immoral as the peace," the Americans said, raising the bid. Those among them who thought about the future were extremely disturbed by the French penetration of the Mississippi basin. The colonies at a critical period of their growth were hungry for lands. By the time of the French and Indian War the pioneers, in their march to the west, had already reached the crest of the Alleghenies; English fur traders were active in the region of the French forts; prominent Virginians owned large grants of land in the Ohio region. Were they going to be stopped by a handful of men? "History has been to a large extent a matter of speculation in land." In the Ohio Valley the speculators hustled history along. What scruples were there to stay them? "Who was the French King anyway? Nothing but a base Papist, and he could always be fought on lofty religious grounds. The Indians of course, being heathen, had no right to anything but conversion." The prize was worth fighting for. Englishmen, like Lord Fairfax, owned properties in the West so vast that they had not as yet even been surveyed. It was Lord Fairfax who first took with him on a surveying trip a young Virginian, George Washington, a relative of his by marriage. This Washington was a planter's son and an agreeable young man, brave and self-possessed, who enjoyed both the gay life of the great houses of the South, with its dancing, hunting, clambakes, and barbecues, and the rough life of the forests. "He is strong and hardy," said Fairfax, "and as good a master of horse as one would desire. His education might have been bettered, but what he has is accurate. He is very grave for one of his age and reserved in his intercourse. Not a great talker at any time. . . . Method and exactness seem natural to George. . . ." The wild savagery of the West attracted young Washington. Having been appointed official surveyor of the county, he spent long periods among the Indians and pioneers. In his profession he became something of a soldier and was one of the first to realize the threat to the future of Virginia represented by the advance of the French in the Ohio region. The whole commerce of the interior of the continent was carried by two rivers, the Mississippi and the St. Lawrence, and both were in the hands of the French.

The role played by France in the discovery and colonization of the American continent had been one of capital importance. Not only had

Marquette and Joliet, and after them La Salle, opened up the route of the Great Lakes and established the portages that made it possible to reach the Father of Waters through the valley of the Illinois or the Wisconsin, but a Frenchman from Belgium, Father Louis Hennepin, in 1680 had discovered and christened the Falls of St. Anthony (today Minneapolis) in the upper valley of the river. Another Frenchman, Daniel Graysolon, Sieur du Luth, had founded a post at the spot where today stands the city named in his memory, Duluth. Near the Detroit River a Gascon gentleman, Antoine de la Motte-Cadillac, had built a fort, the site of present-day Detroit. The Middle West remains dotted with French names: Prairie du Chien, Des Moines, St. Louis. The entire valley of the Mississippi is like a triumphal way bordered by monuments erected in honor of great Frenchmen, these monuments being huge cities. Farther to the north other Frenchmen had ascended the valley of the Missouri. La Vérendrye was the first white man to see the Rocky Mountains. The daring of the French explorers was deserving of admiration, but to the English colonists on the coast it was disturbing; to New York in particular, since New York communicated with Canada by waterways (the Hudson and Lake Champlain) which might become highways of invasion. The French in Canada coveted New York, which would give them an ice-free winter route. New York, well aware of this feeling, saw in it a constant danger.

The danger was all the more threatening because the colonies could never agree. Benjamin Franklin, the Philadelphia philosopher who was also postmaster general and something of a politician, having had the opportunity to observe the Iroquois Confederation, wrote: "It would be a strange thing if Six Nations of ignorant savages should be capable of forming a scheme for such a union, and be able to execute it in such a manner that it has subsisted ages and does appear indissoluble; and yet that a like union should be impracticable for ten or a dozen English colonies, to whom it is more necessary. . . ." Franklin was a wise man but wise men do not determine human affairs. If Virginia became ardent, Pennsylvania remained hesitant. To both London gave orders to take up arms if the French invaded English territory. Well and good, but what would constitute a violation of the frontier? Canada and Louisiana belonged to France, the territory to the east of the Alleghenies to England; to whom did the territory of the Six Nations belong? To the Iroquois? Then the English, who were their allies, had the right to trade there. Nevertheless the French all along the Ohio Valley nailed to the trees little panels bearing the arms of France and buried in the ground plaques with the fleurs-de-lis. In 1752 Duquesne, governor of Canada, sent one thousand men to build a series of forts and roads which would extend from Lake Erie south to the Allegheny and Ohio Rivers. Governor Dinwiddie of Virginia sent young George Washington to the commandant at Fort Le Boeuf to ask him to withdraw. The commandant, an old French soldier, Legardeur de Saint-Pierre, replied with courteous firmness that he would remain as long as he was ordered to remain.

In the following year, 1754, the French destroyed the fort built by the English at the forks of the Ohio and built a much larger one which they called Fort Duquesne. Washington was sent once more with a few hundred men to negotiate, and there occurred a distressing incident which has never been fully cleared up. A French officer, Coulon de Jumonville, sent to confer, was killed with nine of his men. The French said it was an assassination perpetrated while the two countries were at peace; Washington maintained that he had acted in self-defense. It was an unhappy beginning to his career, and the affair seemed to render war between England and France henceforth inevitable. Washington had attempted to improvise a structure called Fort Necessity, but had been forced to beat a retreat. While these events were taking place representatives of the colonies and the Iroquois met in a congress at Albany where they came to an understanding. Franklin's plan for union with a common council for defense was also discussed. This aroused jealousy and separation on all sides, but the representatives of the colonies finally accepted the plan. However, it was rejected by the colonial legislature because they refused to limit their sovereignty; their lordships of the Board of Trade rejected it because they considered that it would increase the power of the colonial governments; and common sense was overridden, as it always is so long as danger does not seem imminent.

The war had not been declared but it had begun. During the winter of 1754-55 France and England made great preparations. A French army, commanded by Dieskau, was sent to Canada; an English army, under the command of Braddock, was sent to Virginia. Each of the two countries begged the other to explain these troop movements; each replied that the sole object of its preparations was to maintain the peace. But General Braddock had been ordered to take Fort Duquesne and General Dieskau to prevent him. Braddock, an old professional soldier, was alarmed by the indifference of the colonies, which "seemed to prefer destruction to co-operation." Young Washington, who had been his aide-de-camp, said to him: "You may, with equal succeess, attempt to raise the dead as the forces of this country." When Braddock demanded transports, the only man who promised to find them was Benjamin Franklin, "one of the rare examples of ability and honesty that I have found in these provinces," said the general. Franklin, in turn, was alarmed by Braddock's optimism, which, after the fashion of Picrochole, went skimming in conversation from Fort Duquesne to Fort Niagara, from Fort Niagara to Fort Frontenac, and from Fort Frontenac to Quebec. Franklin warned him that the French had Indian auxiliaries who were skilled in ambuscade. Braddock smiled. "These savages," he said pityingly, "may constitute a formidable enemy for your American Militia; but upon the regular and disciplined troops of the King, Sir, they will make no impression whatever." When Braddock and his army had, with great difficulty, made their way into the forest, cutting a road as they went, and when they encountered there a mixed troop of French and Indians, the regular and disciplined formation of the British soldiers became the very cause of their destruction. Braddock was killed; two-thirds of his officers and one-half of his men perished. The frontier was open to the Indians.

Terror took possession of the colonies, and with reason. The Indians turned against the vanquished. Massacres and scalpings began again. Young Washington, who had emerged with honor from the Braddock affair, during which he had had two horses killed under him, was named at the age of twenty-three colonel and commander of all the troops in Virginia. But he had to undergo many vexations. The officers of the regular English army refused to obey him. The assembly begrudged him subsidies and demanded that he defend the long frontier with about fifteen hundred untrained soldiers. Exhausted by these conflicts, by criticism, calumny, and injustices, he finally resigned his commission in 1758, married Martha Custis, a widow who owned one of the largest fortunes in Virginia, and became a large tobacco planter, competent, punctilious, and energetic. In Pennsylvania the assembly voted to make war against the Indians and went so far as to promise bounties for scalps: one hundred thirty Spanish dollars for the scalp of a male Indian more than twelve years old; fifty dollars for the scalp of any Indian woman; one hundred fifty dollars for a French prisoner (but not for his scalp). This counter-savagery led a number of Quakers to resign from the assembly, and enough more were persuaded not to become candidates so that the majority at Philadelphia became non-Quaker. Despite this, a conflict broke out between the assembly and the governor of Pennsylvania. The assembly agreed to vote subsidies for the war but on condition that the lands belonging to the proprietor should be taxed like all others. The governor declared that this proposal was contrary to the charter of the colony. It was decided to send Franklin to London with the title of commissioner to present the assembly's claims to the king. Misunderstandings such as these, following upon a serious defeat, threatened England's position in America. Braddock's disaster had reduced the prestige of the army. The conflicts between English officers and English militia, between the colonies and their proprietors, created a state of mind that might one day become dangerous.

England's failures were retrieved when William Pitt came to power. He conducted the war like a despot but he won it. To Canada he sent General Jeffrey Amherst, who was forty, and James Wolfe, who was only thirty-two years old. A great man was commanding the French armies. He was the Marquis de Montcalm, an ideal type of Frenchman, courageous, simple, and generous. In the novels of James Fenimore Cooper one meets this handsome figure, a symbol of the best qualities of France. For a long time Montcalm held the Lakes successfully, but in 1758 Fort Frontenac fell, and then Fort Duquesne. In honor of Pitt, England renamed Fort Duquesne Pittsburgh. The English now had the advantage of numbers. Their colonies were fifteen times as populous as those of France. They controlled the sea and had the support of the Iroquois. Amherst had already taken Louisbourg in September, 1759, Wolfe, with an army of more than nine thousand men, laid siege to Quebec. Montcalm received no reinforcements. At grips with the European coalition, France had no troops to spare. To Colonel Bougainville, who went as Montcalm's representative to ask for aid, the prime minister replied: "When the house is on fire there's no time to worry about the stable." Nevertheless Montcalm hoped to hold the rock of Quebec. Wolfe, by a daring maneuver, scaled the cliff at night and at dawn attacked Montcalm's infantry on the Plains of Abraham. Montcalm, fighting desperately and bravely, was killed in the battle, as was Wolfe also. The following year Montreal was taken. Canada and its inhabitants, who were so completely French, were lost to France.

Thus perished the French empire in North America. This enterprise had enlisted the efforts of able men whose names even today dot the continent. But these pioneers were betrayed by the lack of colonists, by internal dissension, and, after Louis XIV, by the indifference of the mother country. There can be no colonies without control of the sea, and France at the time of the Seven Years' War did not possess a fleet worthy of her. Moreover the English colonies in America, which were very rich in all kinds of natural resources, put at England's disposal aids which France could not equal. The Treaty of Paris stripped her of almost all her colonies. She lost the entire St. Lawrence Valley and all her territory east of the Mississippi, but retained fishing rights off the Newfoundland coast, and kept the islands of St. Pierre and Miquelon. France lost India save for certain business establishments, and Senegal. Louisiana by a secret treaty had been ceded to Spain, which was bound to France by a family alliance and on whose friendship the French minister Choiseul was counting for revenge. For if Voltaire could speak lightly of "a few acres of snow" lost in Canada, and if the public in France seemed indifferent to the colonies, the king's ministers agreed to the Treaty of Paris merely as a temporary humiliation. The treaty allowed those Candians who wished to do so to return to France. The great lords made use of this provision: the farmers, the *coureurs des bois,* the clergy, and the lesser nobility remained. In 1763 they numbered about sixty thousand. From them have sprung the millions of French Canadians who, some in Canada, others in Massachusetts, in New Hampshire, or in Louisiana, perpetuate on the American continent many of the finest virtues of France.

CHAPTER VIII

Scenes from Colonial Life

IN 1763 the English colonies in North America had altogether about 1,400,000 inhabitants of the white race and about 400,000 Negroes. The Indians had been driven back into the forests, but at many points the frontier was no more than a day's journey from the coast, and the colonists remained aware of the presence on the fringe of their civilization of the savage, capricious, and fearless tribes. The Indian's traditional headdress of feathers, his shield of white leather, his black hair, and the bleeding scalps as trophies haunted the dreams of children. Among the whites distinction of class existed, but they were less precise than in England. In the South, contrary to popular belief, the first families were not all the descendants of gentlemen. Cavaliers had come in the time of Cromwell, but in small numbers; the emigrants had almost all belonged to the middle or lower classes. A planter, the head of a respected family, who sent his son to Oxford, shone at the governor's receptions, painted a coat-of-arms on his carriage, and reigned over a community of slaves, might have had as ancestor, three or four generations back, a poor fellow who had sold himself as a servant in order to pay for his passage.

In the North the governing class had at first been dominated by the clergy. Then the great merchants and shipowners had taken precedence and formed a sort of gentry. The sacred cod, dispenser of riches, figured in more than one coat-of-arms. In Massachusetts only a few families owned their own carriages, but the stagecoach and the saddle horse were in common use. When Daniel Leonard, a Boston lawyer, dared to wear gold embroidery and harness two horses to his carriage, he created a sensation. "This shocked everyone," said John Adams. "It was a novelty. No other lawyer, attorney or barrister in our province, whatever his age, reputation or rank, had yet had the audacity to own a carriage." In New York some descendants of the burghers wore powdered perukes, silk stockings, and swords; the governor entered Trinity Church followed by a Negro who presented him with his prayer book on a satin cushion. Lace cuffs and jabots were reserved for the rich, and an artisan who dressed above his station was finished. The order of precedence was observed even in the colleges, where the students were seated at commons according to their family rank. An artisan or farmer was Goodman, his wife was Goodwife. A laborer was designated by his name alone. Below him came the servants, and finally the slaves.

As a matter of fact the class system could not be oppressive in a country where one need only move west to escape from it. To every heart that longed for equality the frontier offered a primitive society where only courage and hard work counted. The indented servants who had paid for their passage by contracting to work for five years could, once the five years were up, turn themselves into pioneers. If they were successful, they founded families of landowners; if they failed, they became "poor whites," but in the South between whites, whether exalted or humble, slavery established a sort of equality. A "poor white" of Virginia was a white, as a poor beggar in Athens in the time of the democracy was nevertheless a citizen of Athens. The poor white of the South had the same sensuous imagination as his rich neighbor, the same love of gallantry, the same taste for pleasure. The mind of the South was obsessed by fear of the Negroes. Slavery had become an institution there. At the start it had not been recognized by law and was established in fact before it had legal standing. In 1755 there were in South Carolina fifty thousand blacks to sixty thousand whites; and these Negroes were not the civilized and self-controlled people of our time, but savages recently imported from Africa. The planters could not get along without Negroes, and they were afraid of them; there resulted a division of sentiment and violent race feeling. In New York the middle classes also feared their Negroes, and a slave revolt in 1712 ended in twenty-one death sentences. In New England where slaves were fewer, race feeling was less strong. In compensation poor whites there suffered from inequality of rank. The arrogance of the Boston ministers and of the great merchants was more insulting than that of an English duke because their manners were worse. The workmen complained that the gentlemen never spoke to them politely except on the eve of elections. The magistrates had tried to put a ceiling on salaries but day labor, always rare, was much in demand. A smart workman, knowing that he was indispensable, could make strong demands. Before long he was going to ask for equality of civil rights.

Although suffrage was restricted, political life was active. Each of the colonies had a legislature made up of two houses, except in Pennsylvania where there was a single house. In Connecticut and in Rhode Island the governor was elected; in the other colonies he was appointed by the crown or by the proprietors. On occasions he might buy his appointment. The son of the lieutenant governor of New York, who hoped to become governor, wrote to an English prime minister: "If my father is appointed I shall immediately pay your Lordship the sum of one thousand pounds sterling to indemnify your Lordship for his expenses." Often the position of the governor was very difficult. The local assembly voted his pay; if displeased, it would withhold his living expenses. For a century and a half the crown tried unsuccessfully to reorganize the administration of the colonies. During the troubles in England, the plantations had been forgotten, to their delight, and they had profited by this fortunate negligence to organize themselves. Then Charles II, at the time of the Restoration, had created a permanent Committee for Trade and Foreign Plantations and had tried to unite the northern colonies under one governor. In 1686 his successor, James II, had named Sir Edmund Andros governor of the dominion of New England (New England, New York, and New Jersey). In 1688 the fall of the Stuarts had led to the end of the dominion, and Parliament, which had become all powerful, had affirmed that the colonies were dependent upon it. But the Parliament of London was far away and its decisions were so slow in arriving that the colonists laughed at them. "This year," one of them said, "you complain to Parliament; next year Parliament sends someone to make an investigation, and the following year the government will have been changed."

In each New England community the center of political life was the meetinghouse with its steep roof and graceful steeple, an edifice half-religious, half-political, and a symbol of the life in these provinces. Preparation was made for the town meetings in private gatherings in the taverns or by small juntos, committees of active citizens. In 1728 Franklin composed a list of questions to be considered by the junto in Philadelphia: "Have you observed any characteristic of the laws which the legislative power ought to amend? Have you observed any recent violation of the just liberties of the people? Has anyone recently attacked your reputation, and

what can the junto do to aid you in reestablishing it?" Later on the
caucuses secretly chose the candidates which influential citizens wanted to
force on the town meeting. The electors, few in number, represented only
a small part of the population. But everyone, including those who did not
vote, was interested in the contests carried on by active citizens to defend
the charter of the colony, to resist the claims of the proprietor, or to hold
the governor in check. Independent sects, in the tradition of Plymouth,

Shipping tobacco from Virginia in the 18th century. From Fry and Jefferson,
Map of Virginia, 1775.

by their doctrine of the equality of all believers, prepared people's minds
for the idea of a republican "commonwealth," while in the forests along
the frontier, free from all restraint, a new people was growing up, composed of all races, and was forging in action a wholly American doctrine
of liberty.

In the South, the Episcopal was the most powerful church. But the
systems of great plantations created enormous parishes which, because of
the miserable state of the roads, bred indifference. Tithes were paid in
tobacco. A clergyman received a salary based on thirteen thousand three

hundred thirty-three pounds of tobacco. When tobacco fell in price the clergy was ruined. A marriage brought two hundred pounds of tobacco; a funeral, four hundred. The Middle Colonies were the stronghold of the Presbyterians, while the Congregational Church was a power in its northern domain, and was supported by taxation. For a long time it had been intolerant, and how could it have been otherwise? Had not the Puritans left England to establish "a rampart against the antichrist"? One of their ministers, Increase Mather, spoke with horror of "the hideous clamor in favor of liberty of conscience." Another, John Cotton, affirmed the theocratic character of his faith when he said: "If the people be Governors, who shall be governed?" There is a story that the Reverend Mr. Philipps at Andover, when he was asked, "Are you the minister who serves here?" replied, "I am the minister who commands here."

The devil and his creatures, witches or sorcerers, played a great role in America as in Europe during the seventeenth century. At that time everything was believed to be a sign from heaven, a judgment of God. A man struck by lightning had been punished by the Lord. When the comet of 1680 appeared, Increase Mather preached a sermon on this warning given to the world by God. His son, Cotton Mather, when he lost his manuscript of three sermons, never doubted that phantoms and agents of the invisible had been the thieves. When he had a stomach-ache he accused Satan of striking sharp blows in his middle; when he suffered from a migraine, he asked himself what sin he had committed. He was subject to visions and saw an army of devils breaking upon New England. Of course, men who believed that "the Evening of the World was near," that God had lengthened the chains that held the devil, had no time or desire for an objective study of a case. To be accused of sorcery by them was a serious matter. In the frightful Salem Witchcraft Trial (1692), nineteen absolutely innocent men and women, many of them of irreproachable and pure lives, were hanged, and one was pressed to death, for having conspired with Satan. We must add, to be quite fair, that the witchcraft madness was a world disease, that the psychological background was favorable to such delusions, that the reaction, in New England, came soon, and that as early as 1693 the governor released all such prisoners. Witches were burned all over Europe, because they were a survival of some primitive religion that Christianity hunted down. New England was no worse in this respect than Spain or France.

As for heretics, they were no better treated; to them was applied the fury of the Psalms; they were the Amalekites, children of Belial. The Quakers argued in vain for their rights as English citizens. In most of the colonies there were laws providing penalties for Quakers, and in Massachusetts, around the middle of the seventeenth century, four Quakers were hanged, one of them a woman. "Seeing that you and I are subjects of the King," one of them said, "I demand to be tried by the laws of my own nation. . . . I never heard or read of any law that was, in England, to hang Quakers." "There is a law to hang Jesuits." "If you put me to death, it is not because I go under the name of a Jesuit, but a Quaker." However that may have been, he was hanged.

The excess of evil brought its own remedy, and brought it earlier in America than in Europe. The Salem Witchcraft Trial had aroused many good people and, as was to happen later in France as a result of the trials of Le Barre and Calas, it bred some measure of tolerance. Judge Sewall, who had condemned the unfortunate "witches," five years later made a public apology. He seems to have been a kind and friendly man who had upheld conventional orthodoxy because he was a Puritan magistrate, but who had a sense of justice and sincerely repented when he realized he had made a terrible mistake. Cotton Mather himself was not altogether sure of the sanctity of this butchery.

The eighteenth-century ideas of the natural goodness of man were beginning to threaten the Calvinist doctrine of predestination. Puritanism grew milder; in many families it survived simply as a salutary discipline of conduct. During the first part of the eighteenth century all observances became less strict. Franklin seldom went to church, because Sunday was his day for reading and work. When he did go, he found the sermons dry and uninteresting. "My mother," Franklin said, "grieves that one of her sons is an Arian; another, an Arminian. What an Arian or an Arminian is, I cannot say that I very well know. The truth is I make such distinctions very little in my study." It was a novelty to hear a son of New England say that he made "such distinctions very little in my study." Boston, a city formerly closed to the sons of Belial, now had Episcopal and Baptist churches. Cotton Mather himself in 1718 took part in the ordination of a Baptist minister, and in 1726 boasted of admitting to communion in his church members of other denominations.

Then, as in England, this period of indifference was followed by a religious renaissance. It was called the Great Awakening. Traveling preachers shook the masses by their eloquence and, by arousing the parishes to the advantage of the new sects, produced a sort of religious revolution. Wesley had gone to Georgia in 1735 and there preached Methodism. An American, Jonathan Edwards, who was an eloquent preacher, had touched his parishioners in Northampton by the simplicity of his logic, the dreadful picture of hell he painted, and by his analysis of the miracle of conversion. Wesley had read an account by Jonathan Edwards of the awakening of America. Another preacher, George Whitefield, traveled through the colonies and produced amazing results. Franklin himself reported that all Philadelphia, irrespective of belief, went to hear him: "The change produced in the manners of our citizens is amazing. They were indifferent. Suddenly it seemed that all had become religious, and one could not walk in the city in the evening without hearing in each street psalms being sung by several families." The secular Franklin and the pious Whitefield got on well together. Franklin printed Whitefield's sermons and Whitefield prayed for Franklin's conversion—without result.

The personal life of the Americans was governed by the English common law. This made the husband the absolute master of the household. Administrator of his wife's property, he had the right to refuse her pocket money. In some colonies he was permitted to beat her. A few widows and old maids competently administered their own properties (Martha Custis, for example, before her marriage to George Washington), but they were exceptions. Jefferson, who was living in Paris, was shocked by the visits that women paid unattended upon men in the government; "unbelievable as it may seem," he said, "to inhabitants of a country where the sex does not endeavor to extend itself beyond the domestic line." And the same Jefferson: "In America, the society of your husband, the fond care of children, the arrangement of the house, the improvements of the grounds, fill every moment of a youthful and healthy activity." At that time women married very young and often died in childbirth. The widower remarried, for to live in chastity was grievous and to live in sin dangerous. In the South pretty Negro women sometimes submitted to the claims of the planter. But a white servant who misbehaved had her time of bondage prolonged by one year. In Virginia and in Maryland divorces were rare, since the Catholic Church and the Episcopal Church did not allow them; in Connecticut and Massachusetts, on the other hand, the law was based on the Bible, which permits repudiation. Among the Quakers, marriage required only a promise of fidelity made before witnesses. The father of a family possessed, at first, complete power over his children, but the ease with which sons could find land or a calling of their own rapidly weakened this paternal authority. As in all provincial and monotonous life, burials were pretexts for celebration, although ministers thundered against the custom.

In the South social life had great charm. The large houses afforded a generous hospitality. There balls were given to which all the planters of the neighborhood came on horseback or in barouches to dance jigs or reels or other country dances. In 1674 a tailor and another artisan were fined for racing their horses, "a sport reserved for gentlemen." In the eighteenth century there was a jockey club in Virginia. The country fairs attracted, as in Europe, booths and games of all kinds. In the clubs and taverns and in the private houses there was a great deal of drinking— brandy, rum made from various fruits, beer, and cider. Card playing was the rage. For a long time the only method of smoking was the pipe; in 1762, after his return from Cuba, General Israel Putnam introduced the cigar, but it was not until 1800 that cigars were made in America. In Virginia and around New York, rich huntsmen rode to hounds, importing their foxes from England. The taste for music was growing. In Charleston the St. Cecilia Society gave concerts and brought over French musicians. In Massachusetts the theater was not allowed until after Puritanism had lost its hold; and in Philadelphia not until 1754, because the Quakers were opposed to it.

The center of life was the home and family. The interiors of the houses were modeled after those of England or Holland, but were less elaborate: walls very simply paneled in wood, painted papers, windows with small panes. The tiles around the fireplace were apt to represent not worldly scenes but episodes from the Bible. In the center of the table would be the family Bible, often brought over from London or Amsterdam. On the walls hung family portraits. By the eve of the Revolution a great school of American portraitists had grown up in New England: John Copley, Benjamin West, and Gilbert Stuart, excellent artists whose canvases equaled those of the English school of that time and of the artists of Florence and Basle who in their day had recorded the faces of a generation of great merchants. But the colonies were not rich, and from time to time a painter had to go to work in England in order to earn his living.

The problems of education were not easy to solve. Distances, especially in the South, were an obstacle to the success of schools. Many parents realized that they were incapable of instructing their children themselves. In certain regions spelling was quickly forgotten and sometimes writing as well. In Massachusetts the Puritans could not neglect teaching because they considered the reading of the Testaments necessary for children. In 1635 the town meeting established the Boston Latin School. In 1642 a Massachusetts law made parents responsible for having their children taught to read. In 1647 another law decreed that every community of fifty families should have a school in which reading and writing were taught, and every town of a hundred families or more should have a grammar school, that is, a secondary school that prepared for college. The law was not always observed, but little by little the number of grammar schools increased. Daughters of schoolmasters opened dame schools where girls and small boys learned the alphabet, the catechism and sometimes to read and write. For boys there were elementary schools. Franklin went to a grammar school and then got his true education by himself with remarkable success. In the other colonies the charge of education was left to the parishes. Too often all that was required to secure the right to teach was to rent a room, put seats in it, and procure a mahogany cane to inspire slow minds. The South initiated the methods of the English: elementary schools for the poor; tutors for rich children, who completed their education in college, sometimes in England. George Washington had been taught by a sacristan and later by a schoolmaster. He knew a little Latin, trigonometry, drawing, and at the age of fourteen he drew up the plans of his neighbors' property. Later the library of Lord Fairfax, a cultured man who had known Addison and Steele, completed his education. He read *Tom Jones* and current novels. His culture closely resembled that of an English gentleman. Jefferson had been sent to board with a clergyman and had acquired an excellent knowledge of the Latin classics. He had read Voltaire's *Essay on Customs* and Montesquieu's *Spirit of the Laws*. Patrick Henry had almost no schooling, but his father had taught him Greek, Latin, mathematics, and ancient and modern history; he read Livy once a year. The quality of the average speech delivered in the colonies shows that, for the better minds, lack of schools did not entail lack of culture.

Harvard College was founded in 1636. The General Court that year voted four hundred pounds to establish a college, and the following year selected for its location Newtown, whose name was changed to Cambridge in order to put the institution under the patronage of the great English university. In 1638 "it pleased God to excite the heart" of a Mr. John Harvard, a young Charlestown minister and a friend of letters, to leave half his fortune, which was in all seventeen hundred pounds, for the creation of a college and its library. He started the latter by a gift of two hundred sixty volumes. These rules for admission were agreed on: "When a student shall be capable of understanding Cicero (or any other classic Latin author) on sight, and also of speaking or writing in Latin in prose or in verse, then only admit him to the college." Neither an examination in English nor a knowledge of history, geography, or mathematics was required. At college, in addition to Latin the students were to learn Greek, Hebrew, and take part in theological discussions. A Dutchman who visited Harvard at the time it was starting wrote: "We found there eight or ten young men sitting in a circle and smoking tobacco. The smoke filled the room. . . . We asked them how many professors they had and they replied: 'Not one. There is not enough money to pay for them. . . .' " This state of affairs did not last. The charter of 1650 created a corporation which from that date on administered the college. The latter became rich through gifts and legacies.

Later the South had its own college, William and Mary, founded in 1693 and named in honor of the English sovereigns. James Blair, commissary for Virginia, had gone to England to seek support for this college, intended to form religious souls. The answer he frequently received was: "Damn your souls! Make tobacco." But he brought back from his trip a charter and a gift from the royal couple. Yale was founded in 1701 as a rival to Harvard, and in 1747 the Presbyterians in their turn started the College of New Jersey, which later became Princeton University. Among the first universities were also the Academy of Philadelphia (later the University of Pennsylvania); an Anglican college in New York, King's (today Columbia University); a Baptist college in Providence (Brown); and Rutgers. Dartmouth, which had at first been a school designed to convert the Indians, was transformed into a college thanks to funds collected in England by one of its graduates, and was given the Count of Dartmouth's name because he was the first president of the Board of Trustees.

At the start American culture could only be imported from England. Boston had Bibles, grammars, books of theology, and textbooks of navigation sent over from London. The South gave a little more attention to belles-lettres. The first original writings were memoirs (those of John Smith, William Bradford, the journal of John Winthrop, his history of New England, later the journal of Judge Sewall, which draws so clear a picture of rural life) and theological essays (those of Thomas Hooker, John Cotton, Increase Mather, and Roger Williams). Cotton Mather and Jonathan Edwards formed a second and third generation of religious writers. The *Magnalia Christi Americana* of Cotton Mather is a religious history of New England and an effort to show the beneficent action of Providence on the inhabitants of these colonies. Later, political preoccupations took precedence over theological controversy. The epoch that produced a Benjamin Franklin had no place for a Cotton Mather.

Franklin, sensible, witty, and moderate, was the great writer of his period and was a sort of American Voltaire, but a Voltaire combined with Sancho Panza. If he did not have the mad poetry of *Candide,* he possessed gifts of irony and satire, and his common sense amounted to genius. The puritanism of New England (where he was born) left no trace in his character. It has been said of him that he was much less interested in saving his soul from eternal fire than in saving his neighbor's house from burning up. Men's actions, not their beliefs, seemed to him the measure of their value. He shared with Voltaire a taste and respect for the sciences. In politics he was open-minded, reasonable, humorous, witty, incapable of hating his adversaries, and always ready to accept a fair compromise. Carlyle, who detested him, dubbed him the Father of all Yankees. But is that accurate? A true Yankee possesses a respect for culture, thriftiness, and business acumen, which Franklin had too, but also a certain affectation of virtue which was very foreign to Franklin. Franklin took great liberties in words and in deeds and had a lively sense of humor. He did not fear platitudes when they were also truths, nor did he fear epigrams: "Keep your eyes open before marriage," he advised, "and half shut afterward." Or again: "There are more old drunkards than old doctors." He contributed to American culture, not only by his works, but by creating the first public libraries, improving stoves and lamps (both helpful for reading), and in facilitating the circulation of magazines when he was postmaster general.

The first American newspapers were newsletters written by hand. Then John Campbell, who sent news to several people, found it more convenient to print his letters under the title of *The Boston News-Letter*. On April 24, 1704, Sewall notes in his journal: "I gave Mr. Willard the first newsletter which has ever crossed the river." Other journals were started in Philadelphia and Boston; one of which was the conservative *Boston Gazette,* the other the *New England Courant,* which was very radical and was edited by James Franklin, Benjamin's brother. James Franklin was a fearless and imprudent young man, who published satires against the Mathers and got himself arrested several times. Later Benjamin Franklin bought the *Pennsylvania Gazette.* The *New-York Gazette* was controlled by Governor Crosby, a corrupt and dictatorial man; when he came into conflict with his managers, the latter started a rival paper, *The New-York Weekly Journal,* which was published by John Peter Zenger, a German. The governor in a rage ordered that the *Journal* be burned by the public executioner. The mayor declared the order illegal. Zenger was arrested and prosecuted for libel. At the trial there appeared for the defense, to the great surprise of all, Andrew Hamilton, an illustrious and venerable lawyer from Philadelphia, who eloquently defended the freedom of the press. The verdict was: "Not guilty." Zenger was acquitted in a tumult of applause, and when Hamilton returned to Philadelphia he was received with high honors, flag-draped windows, and the thunder of cannon. The word *liberty* was evidently dear to Americans.

CHAPTER IX

Colonial Economy

THE first point to be noted about the economic life of the English colonies in America is their unmistakable prosperity. Growth in population is its most striking index. In 1640 the colonies had twenty-five thousands inhabitants; in 1690, two hundred thousand; in 1770, about two million. Thus the population had increased tenfold between 1690 and 1770. This prevents us from lightly condemning British methods. Some would reply that the success had been won, not thanks to those methods, but in spite of them. This point deserves further examination.

Second point: This prosperity came chiefly from agriculture, hunting, and fishing. Cities were few; only five of them in 1790 had more than eight thousand inhabitants (Philadelphia was the first); and they represented together only 3.3 per cent of the population. More than nine-tenths of the Americans worked on the land. The others were merchants, shipowners, sailors, miners, and artisans. Factories remained few and unimportant; England discouraged their growth. In the eyes of the English the colonies were lucrative enterprises, "plantations" destined to supply them with (a) products they lacked; wines, so that England could get along without France; spices, so that she could get along without Portugal; wood, so that she could get along without Sweden; furs, pottery, whale oil, saltpeter, pitch, hemp, and so forth; (b) a market to absorb their manufactured goods. The conversion of raw materials into finished products was to remain the business of the mother country.

This conception was bound up with the mercantile system that declared a country's prosperity to consist in obtaining a favorable trade balance. The proper thing was to sell to foreign countries as much as possible and buy from them as little as possible. The plantations in America and other places allowed the cultivation on British soil of products that England otherwise would have had to buy abroad; the supporters of this system therefore fostered the colonies, but only on a condition that they should not go beyond the role assigned to them. The plantations were not to aspire to produce anything but raw materials. A colonist who became rich was not allowed to invest his money in manufacturing. The Navigation Act of 1651 required that the exports of the colonies to England should be carried in English ships. The Staple Act of 1663 decreed that all imports from foreign countries into the colonies should first pass through an English port and there pay duty. Thus English commerce with the colonies was protected against all competition from outside. The Act of 1660 reserved certain products—tobacco, sugar, cotton, indigo, etc.— exclusively for the English market. In the eighteenth century this list was added to: naval stores, tar, pitch, etc., in 1706; rice, 1706-30; furs in 1722; molasses in 1733; iron, lumber, hides, etc., in 1764. Wheat, fish and rum were not on the list, but could not be exported except via an English port, which prevented, for example, any direct exchange between the colonies and the French or Spanish Antilles or between the colonies and Portugal.

Did the colonies on the whole suffer from these restrictions? They had in return the protection of the English fleet and the English market for their tobacco. In 1620 a proclamation had prohibited the planting of tobacco in England. But the effects of the mercantile system varied in different regions. The South, whose products were tobacco, rice, and indigo, all necessary to England, could easily exchange them for the manufactured goods she needed. The southern planters had agents in England with whom they carried accounts, to whom they entrusted their sons when they went to study at Oxford or Cambridge, and whom they commissioned to buy an embroidered waistcoat, a shawl, or the latest books. There was, however, a danger even to the planter in this British monopoly. Jefferson said that debts became hereditary from father to son for generations, so that for the London merchants the planters became a sort of private property. Thus the South did not grow rich, but it managed to live. In the North the mercantile system appeared more dangerously absurd. The North produced wheat, meat, and fish, which England did not need. How then should the Yankees pay for the textiles, furniture, clothes, and shoes they required? By exporting precious metals? The colonies did not produce them. By obtaining credits? The English were forbidden to extend them. By sending exports to other countries? This was the only way, but the Navigation Acts made this trade difficult.

In fact the so-called "triangular" trade was the only operation open to the northern colonists. A Boston merchant would buy wheat, sell it in Portugal in exchange for a cargo of wine, exchange the wine in England for cloth and hats, and finally import the cloth and hats to America. This operation was allowed on the condition that it pass through a British port both coming and going. Or again, the American merchant might buy molasses in the Antilles, convert it into rum at Boston, exchange the rum for slaves in Guinea, and import the slaves to the Antilles against a new cargo of molasses. Finally, one could exchange wheat for sugar in the Antilles, and the sugar for manufactured products in England. These complex operations led to the formation in the North of powerful commercial houses such as Hancock and Faneuil in Boston, Delancey in New York, and Logan in Philadelphia. To these great merchants and ship-owners who had their own vessels it was a temptation to disregard the English laws and trade directly with Europe, or even to sell their molasses in the French or Spanish Antilles in contempt of the law. This contra-band assured such big profits that all practiced it. The colonials had no scruples because they considered the acts unjust; the English customs inspectors either accepted bribes or just stayed in England where they drew their pay without ever visiting their posts. America prospered despite mercantilism, but that was because the system was never seriously enforced.

At the beginning colonial agriculture learned a great deal from Indian agriculture. The Indians, with primitive implements, had been able to clear the ground, fertilize it by burning roots, and had even learned to rotate crops. They were the sole authority on the cultivation of corn, a grain unknown to Europeans. John Smith describes them digging holes and planting in each four grains of corn and two beans. In New England, besides corn, the farmers grew wheat, oats, and rye, but European observers warned them that they were ruining the soil. In addition, they planted orchards of apple trees, imported farmyard animals which multi-plied quickly, and made a success of dairy farming. In the North the small independent farm produced not only food for the farmer and his family but linen for the household and wool for clothes. In the South there was no lack of small farms, but the cultivation of tobacco had led to the formation of great estates, situated on river banks to facilitate the shipment of crops. Tobacco exhausted the ground quickly, and when the planters tried to fertilize with the manure of their animals, the English smokers complained of a disagreeable odor. Hence the neces-sity every two or three years of clearing new fields; hence also the exten-siveness of the plantations, a great part of which remained sterile or unused. Of three thousand acres, six hundred would be cultivated and the rest lie fallow. Toward the middle of the eighteenth century the exhaustion of the ground induced planters to try other crops. Rice did well in the marshy lands of South Carolina. A woman named Eliza Lucas, as a result of deaths in the family, found herself at the age of sixteen in charge of three plantations. After a number of attempts she succeeded in acclimating indigo, flax, hemp, and mulberries. Never before had a girl played so great a role in the economic life of a country.

The labor question was a grave problem in a constantly growing country. From the Indian nothing could be expected; he clung to his independence, and the harshest of masters could not profitably exploit him. Immigrants (Germans fleeing from the Palatinate, Irishmen fleeing from poverty) were fairly numerous, but these farmers or artisans came for the purpose of starting establishments of their own; they left their native lands to be free, not to serve new masters. Thus labor immediately became dear. An English traveler noted that the price of a cake was higher in Boston than in London, although milk and flour were cheaper. Young girls who agreed to be housemaids married at twenty, and the new couples set out for the frontier. The solutions were: for the pioneers in the West, mutual aid and neighborliness; for the whole coast, indented servants; for the South, at first indented servants and later slavery. The indented servants were so called because they signed contracts of from four to seven years, written in duplicate on a large piece of paper, the halves of which were separated by a wavy cut or indent. They were either volunteers who agreed to the arrangement to pay their passage, or people kidnaped by traders, or those condemned for minor crimes. Here is an example: A man had made an agreement with the captain of a vessel to transport him, his wife, and their five children to America for the sum of fifty-four pounds. He died during the crossing, having paid sixteen pounds on account. On arrival, since the contract could not be carried out, the captain sold the widow for twenty-two pounds, the three older boys for thirty pounds each, and the two younger ones, who were under five, for ten pounds, thus making a profit of one hundred twenty-two pounds. The papers carried advertisements like this: *"Arrived from London; an assortment of English servants, men and women, for sale. Reasonable prices. Time allowed for payment. Apply to Captain John Ball on his ship."* The "reasonable prices" were from fifteen to twenty pounds for a period of four or five years. At the end of this time white servants were free and their masters were required to give them, upon departure, a suit of clothes, a small amount of money, and enough corn for one year. Several colonies granted fifty acres of land to these "freed" men, of whom many became prosperous colonists.

Slavery would never have existed in America if it had not been an ancient African institution. In Guinea prisoners had always been sold as slaves, and the tribal chiefs found it quite natural to hand them over to white captains. When the Treaty of Utrecht allowed the English to trade with the Spanish colonies, it became a considerable branch of commerce in which the most respectable shipowners of Liverpool, Saint-Malo, and New England took part. Small ships of fifty tons made the voyage from Boston (or Salem) to the slave coast. The business was profitable. One bought eight thousand gallons of rum in the Antilles; with that one procured in Guinea thirty-five Negro men, fifteen Negro women, and several boys and girls, plus a little gold dust. This barter of alcohol for human flesh and blood produced a handsome profit. It has been estimated that between 1750 and 1800 the slave traders carried away from Africa from fifty to one hundred thousand blacks a year. However, only a small part of this number was imported into the colonies. Crowded between decks, constantly in chains (for the crew was too small to take any chance of revolt), the Negroes died of dysentery, filth, and smallpox; 8 to 10 per cent perished during the crossing. The survivors were turned over to merchants, who sold them singly at a commission of 10 per cent. Georgia was the only colony where slavery was positively forbidden by law; and this was changed in 1746. In the North (for economic and not moral reasons) the Negroes were seldom anything but domestic servants, but in the South the cultivation of tobacco, rice, indigo, and later cotton led to such growth of slavery that soon the planters were dismayed by this enormous "foreign body" beside which they had to live. Hence the increasing severity of the slave laws. Nevertheless, many of the masters were humane; between blacks and whites ties of affection were formed; the strange poetry of the Negroes and their instinctive romanticism reacted upon the Southerners, while the slaves forgot Africa and became, after their fashion, Americans.

From the very beginning of colonial life fisheries had played an essential role in American economy. Fish were becoming scarcer along the European coasts; the Catholic countries, because of their numerous periods of fasting and abstinence, could not get along without them; and so European fishermen were venturing farther and farther from home. Sailors on the American coast found themselves in a particularly favorable situation. The cod became one of the great mediums of exchange in New England. Whaling, so well described by Melville in *Moby Dick*, furnished employment for a whole fleet. Ships of some two hundred tons, with crews of fifty men, could kill these monsters, cut them up, and extract the whale bone, blubber for candles, and oil. More than four thousand seamen made a living at this dangerous and adventurous calling.

It was also the time of the pirates, the privateeers, the freebooters, the buccaneers, and the smugglers. The Antilles, with their deserted islands and innumerable creeks, afforded hiding places. On the streets of New York or Newport, people would point out pirate captains walking at large with diamond-studded daggers in their belts. The pirate's trade was a poor one. The risks were greater than the rewards. As for the contraband trade with the Spanish and French Antilles, it was carried on by the most upright American shipowners, all determined to observe to the letter the laws of their assemblies and to violate without scruple those of the Parliament in London.

Clements Library

One source of New England's wealth in colonial times—the codfish. From H. Moll, *Map of North America*, 1715.

Industry remained principally domestic; on the farms the women spun and wove wool while the men molded pots and forged tools. A number of sawmills had been set up in New England and the Middle Colonies. Shipbuilding was a prosperous industry, having for clients not only local shipowners but those in England as well, for ships cost less per ton in this country. By 1760 America was launching as many as four hundred ships a year. In 1775, of six thousand English merchantmen more than two thousand had been built in America. In 1776 Massachusetts was estimated to have one ship for every one hundred inhabitants. The fur trade played both a commercial and a political role. It was the rush for furs

that led to the first development of the West and brought the French and
English into violent opposition. New England possessed a few textile
mills and a few foundries, but these industries were embryonic.

Because American economy in the eighteenth century was a colonial one,
America lacked currency. England did not permit the colonies to issue
money. The latter attempted to get around this difficulty by making
legal tender of warehouse certificates, in particular those for tobacco,
which had a more stable value than other produce. A French traveler
heard the citizens of Virginia saying: "This watch cost me three barrels
of tobacco; this horse fifteen, and I've been offered twenty for it." In time,
all the colonies tried the experiment of paper money, but around the middle
of the century an act of Parliament forbade the further issuance of bills
of credit. In Massachusetts an attempt was made to found a land bank
which should issue notes secured by real estate, personal security, and
merchandise. This idea delighted the debt-ridden farmers but enraged
the rich merchants of Boston who demanded that the governor suppress
it. On advice of the latter, London decided to apply to the colonies the
Bubble Act against speculation and to suppress the land bank. This made
its founders furious. Already, even in this almost primitive economy, the
free-money men were confronting those who believed in a rigidly controlled currency. In his *Factors in American History*, Pollard wrote: "Each
colony had its East and its West, its merchants and its farmers, its creditors
and its debtors. The debtor has always desired an abundant, inexpensive
money with which to pay his debts, silver or paper in preference to gold,
banks to give him credit and assemblies that favor giving legal currency
to paper money."

In 1760 Franklin published a booklet entitled *Information for those
Desirous of Coming to America.* In it he described with exactness and
common sense the economic situation of the colonies:

The truth is, that though there are in that country few people so miserable
as the poor of Europe, there are also very few that in Europe would be called
rich; it is rather a general happy mediocrity that prevails. There are few
great proprietors of the soil, and few tenants; most people cultivate their
own lands, or follow some handicraft or merchandise; very few are rich
enough to live idly upon their rents or incomes, or to pay the highest prices
given in Europe for paintings, statues, architecture and other works of art. . . .
Of civil offices, or employments, there are few; no superfluous ones, as in
Europe. . . . It can not be worth any man's while who has a means of living
at home, to expatriate himself, in hopes of obtaining a profitable civil office
in America. . . . Much less is it advisable for a person to go thither, who has
no other quality to recommend him but his birth. . . . It is a commodity

that cannot be carried to a worse market than that of America, where people do not inquire concerning a stranger: "What is he?" but "What can he do?" . . . In short, America is the land of labor, and by no means what the French call *Pays de Cocagne*.

Whom did Franklin advise to come to America? Poor young men or those of modest fortune, who knew how to work on a farm or had some other trade. Such men would be sure of finding work, fertile ground at ten guineas per one hundred acres, and friendly neighbors. The poorest could begin by being servants; in few years' time they would have the means of gaining their independence. North America was not Peru; it had few attractions for rich travelers, but to the unfortunates, if they were brave and hard-working, it offered more resources than Europe.

CHAPTER X

Conclusion

THE inhabitants of the New World had not created a civilization; they had transferred from beyond the oceans the civilizations of the Old World. In their minds, as in those of Europeans, centuries of culture and experience were alive. In South America the culture and experience were Spanish; in Canada they were French; in New England, as in Virginia, they were essentially English. It is true, other races were mixed with the first Anglo-Saxon colonists. Germans, Swiss, Scots, and Irish formed a tenth part of the population. But language, laws, and ideas came from England: "Was not Elizabeth our Queen?" wrote one American. "And Shakespeare our poet? And Drake our hero and protector when the Spanish Armada bore down on our fathers' shores?" Family and social life were governed by English customs. Colonial furniture, when it did not come from England, was often a copy of English furniture; the architecture was an adaptation of the Georgian style. The first university town took the name of Cambridge. "I hear," said Burke, "that they have sold as many Blackstone's *Commentaries* in America as in England." The rights of the colonists were guaranteed by charters from the English kings and by the traditional liberties of England. Magna

Carta was to become as precious a memory for Americans as for Englishmen.

In 1763 many Americans were patriotic Britons, proud of belonging to a nation that had just won a great war and conquered Canada. There was no question of rebellion. What had Franklin said in London? That the colonies would never unite "against their own nation who protects and encourages them; with which they have so many connections and ties of blood, interests and affections, and which, it is well-known, they all love much more than they love one another." Franklin literally loved the English people, and this too was the sentiment of many Americans. The colonists participated in English culture as today the French in Algeria or Tunisia participate in French culture. From their Anglo-Saxon forebears they had inherited a taste for public discussion, the habit of orderly debate, and a natural aptitude for parliamentary government. When they said "home" they meant the Old Country which had given, to many of them, flesh and blood and, to all, their powers and rights.

But if the colonies remained thoroughly English, an attentive observer would have noticed, by 1763, a weakening of the bond. Distance had produced its effects. When problems are urgent no one can wait six weeks for the solution. The colonists had been forced to govern themselves. "The ocean remains," Burke said; "no pump can dry it up." Life on the frontier had produced men who were jealous of their independence. How were they to be coerced when they could not even be reached? Many of the colonists were not of English origin, and even in English families the children had been born in the colonies. They commenced to consider as foreigners all those who did not share their tastes and interests. Braddock's officers no longer seemed compatriots to the American officers. In two hundred years England and America had both changed. "The Englishman became a Whig; the American became a pioneer." The two languages themselves were no longer completely identical. To fit new situations Americans had had to coin new words (*backwoodsman, log cabin, halfbreed*), "a language succulent and nervous." Certain archaic expressions like *stock, cattle, fall* for *autumn,* preserved in America since the time of the Pilgrims, seemed ridiculous to English visitors. They are nevertheless to be found in Shakespeare. The expression "I guess," in the sense of "I suppose," became for the English the very symbol of Americanism; they could have found it in *Henry IV*. When Franklin went to France he was told to use "the language of the United States." When Hutchinson talked to George IV about corn: "Corn? What is corn?" said the king. "Indian corn," Hutchinson replied, "or, as the writers say, Maize." American neologisms, like *antagonize, immigrate, belittle, influential*, shocked English purists. Johnson talked with contempt of "the American dialect." Small matters, but they produced among the English an impression of quaint provincialism; among the Americans an uneasy sensitiveness.

The religious and philosophic ideas of the colonists differed in certain respects from those of the English. The Dissenters had fled England in order to find tolerance and liberty. They were terrified as soon as anyone talked of "establishing" the Church of England in America. Episcopalian clergymen went to England to be ordained, but Congregational ministers were rebels against authority. When the Bishop of London talked about a colonial Episcopate, Samuel Adams thundered against these tyrants, the bishops, and conjured up the specter of papism. The cynicism of the dandies and fops of London aroused the indignation of the Puritans. "Chastity is certainly not the style in England," one of them said, and went on to ask how a corrupt aristocracy could govern honest Protestants. Franklin himself, on one of his rare bad days, said that compared to such people every Indian was a gentleman. The stories they heard about the clubs, about the card playing and gambling, about the debauches in London or in Bath, shocked many Americans. As for the English who came to America, they had the habit of treating Americans as the nobles at the court of Versailles used to treat the *bas bretons.* "America is not a community of civilized creatures," one of them said. Witherspoon, a Scotsman who became president of Princeton College, wrote: "I have heard in this country, in the assemblies, in the tribunals, in the lecture halls, and I read every day in the press, faults of grammar, improprieties and gross expressions that no person of equal rank in Great Britain would employ." This mutual criticism was not calculated to strengthen the bond. An English officer who said, "A British soldier can beat six Yankees," made stout enemies for England of all Yankees within earshot. James Otis complained of the London gossips who talked haughtily of "our colonists" as though the citizens of the colonies belonged to the citizens of the mother country. But the English, on their side, were exasperated when an Adams spoke of the colonies as an experiment of Providence "for the edification of the ignorant and the emancipation of humanity, still enslaved everywhere on earth."

Politically America was more radical than England. In England a very ancient class system was evolving slowly toward greater equality. In America, the forest and the Indian had established immediate equality. All the radicals of the world had found a meeting place in a land where ancient hatreds no longer pursued them. In the time of Cromwell the Levelers had found refuge there. Their descendants were not disposed to accept the authority of a king who tended toward absolutism, nor that of a Parliament in which only the great English landowners were represented. The Nonconformists had separated from the Church of England to assure themselves of freedom of conscience; they might well one day separate from England to assure freedom of their persons. In the beginning theocracy had replaced autocracy in America; when, in its turn, it had been forced to relinquish the civil power, it left behind a democracy. In England the number of voters was small because only landowners could vote and they were few in number; but in America, except for servants and slaves, almost everyone was a landowner and inequalities of suffrage seemed less bearable. In addition, the English troubles of the seventeenth century, by weakening the central power in London, had strengthened the peripheral power in America. The charters had made several colonies states within the state. English officials were little respected there. Many of them did not even come to live in America; they drew their salaries and stayed at home. The governors themselves were severely judged. "It was not Virginia that needed a Governor, but a Court favorite that needed a post." The type of man that England thought best suited to this office was, in point of fact, the one most calculated to displease. "It is impossible for the dignity of the throne or the peerage to be represented in an American forest." It was inevitable that the Puritan Yankee and the English Tory should be at swords' points. Moreover, almost all the governors were Anglicans, a fact that shocked the Puritans. The authority of England was irritating, not because it was exercised tyrannically, but because it was exercised intermittently and seemed a foreign body, useless and disturbing, in an organism that was already autonomous.

But of all the misunderstandings the most serious was the economic one. England, in establishing the colonies, had expected from them the products which she lacked: spices, wines, silk. She had pictured their production as supplementing her own. But what did the colonies send? Fish, which she hardly needed; tobacco, which disappeared in smoke; wheat, naval supplies, furs, and a few masts for ships. It was a great disappointment, and the tropical possessions in the West Indies were much better thought of in the mother country. On his side, the colonist was irritated to see restrictions imposed on his commerce and prohibitions pronounced against his industries. Franklin said: "Great Britain would, if she could, manufacture and trade for all the world; England for all Britain; London for all England, and every Londoner for all London." The colonies had trouble in seeing themselves as "markets destined to enrich all the merchants of the City"; they wanted to exist for themselves; they thought their interests were just as important as those of some English shire. They did not pause to consider what they owed to England—the capital that had given them their start, the British fleet that made their continued existence possible. They were like those children who at adolescence criticized their family, forgetting the sacrifices of their parents, and if they are reminded of these reply: "They did no more than their duty. They brought me into the world, didn't they? What else could they do but raise me?" Ingratitude? Perhaps, but it is a law of

Clements Library

Vital factors in the growth of America: the sawmill which produced the lumber for houses, and the blockhouse which provided security. Here is Colonel Skene's sawmill near Skenesboro, New York, as pictured in Thomas Anburey's *Journal*, 1793.

nature. Arrived at a certain degree of maturity the fruit detaches itself from the tree, the child from its family, the colony from its mother country.

Did the defeat of France and the annexation of Canada by the crown combine to give the colonies the impression that henceforth they would have less need of England to defend them? At the time of the Peace of Paris English diplomats had pointed out this danger. Having successfully applied in Europe the balance-of-power policy whose formula is "divide and rule," they asked themselves whether it might not be wise to establish in America this same balance, and whether the presence of the French in Canada might not be useful in enforcing the obedience of the colonies. It was for this reason that some of them suggested that the king of France be left in possession of Quebec, and that England should take Martinique and Guadeloupe in exchange for Canada. There were ministers in France in 1763 who detected in the colonies possible allies against England; Choiseul believed that from there one day would come the shock that would upset the British Empire. But the great majority of Englishmen did not believe in this danger. On the American continent there remained an enemy—the Indian. Let the colonists make it their business to hold him in check; the British fleet would protect them from the Bourbons. As for a union of the colonies against England, Franklin laughed at this idea. Even at Albany he had not been able to make them unite in the face of an immediate and pressing danger. How should they unite against their own country? It would require, Franklin said, the most outrageous tyranny and oppression to make them do it. "The waves do not rise but when the wind blows."

In 1763 the colonists were faithful subjects of the king and never dreamed of denying him their loyalty. But once in a while they had the uncomfortable feeling that they were citizens of the second class, governed by the crown, not for their own good, but for that of more privileged subjects. Did they exist only to provide a market for British industry, and to afford sinecures for court favorites? Discontented spirits began to say so. In the eyes of an English minister, colonial commerce was a small question bound up with a thousand others. In the eyes of the colonists it was the condition of their existence. Nevertheless, even among the malcontents there was hardly any talk of the combined American colonies as a nation. They were more conscious of the things that separated them than of the things that united them. Communication between them was difficult. Bad roads, forests, and Indians were the obstacles. Quarrels about the frontier divided them: Maryland, Pennsylvania, Virginia, Connecticut and New York vied with each other for land. But without their realizing it, the bond that united them was already strong. A planter on the Potomac looked very different from a Boston merchant and their interests might perhaps diverge. On the other hand, a pioneer on the Virginia frontier and a pioneer on the Pennsylvania frontier resembled each other. Scotch farmers on the extreme fringe hardly knew to what colony they belonged. All had engaged in the same struggle against the forest; all had the same love of independence; all felt the same impatience at certain official attitudes. "To have had common glories in the past, to possess a common will in the present, to have accomplished great things together, and to wish to accomplish more, these are the essential conditions for being a people," says Renan. Americans did not yet know that together they had accomplished a great thing; on the day when they realized it, they would feel the desire to accomplish more.

GEORGE WASHINGTON

The original study from life by Rembrandt Peale, painted in
Philadelphia in the autumn of 1795. Peale's subsequent seventy-
six paintings of Washington were all based on this work.
Courtesy of the Historical Society of Pennsylvania

Book Two

AT THE CROSSROADS

CHAPTER XI

Post-War Problems

A PEACE, even a victorious peace, creates as many problems as it solves. The Peace of Paris (1763) raised more than one problem for America. France had been eliminated from the immense basin of the Mississippi; but the French, as much by their alliance with the Indians as by their forts and outposts, had hitherto maintained order in that region. Who henceforth was to play that role? It could only be the British army. General Amherst sent a mission to occupy the French forts. It encountered the opposition of the Indians. Pontiac, a chief of the Ottawa tribe, became the center of resistance. Highly intelligent, he realized that the English represented a greater danger to the Indians than had the French. The latter, because they were not numerous, desired only a little land. But the Indians knew the inexorable march of Anglo-Saxon colonization, the advance of farmers in a massive migration. Pontiac secretly planned an uprising, and for a time the Indians were successful. An attack on the fort at Detroit failed when the English commandant at Detroit was informed of it, and the fort was besieged. The French, at Amherst's request, informed the Indians that peace had been signed between them and the English and that no help could be expected from them. "Dear children," said the French commandant of Fort de Chartres, "forget all your hostile purposes. Shed no more of the blood of your English brothers. Our hearts and theirs are now united; you cannot strike one without injuring the other." This plea induced Pontiac to make a peace. But it was accepted by the tribes only after prolonged clashes, raids, and massacres. The problem of pacifying the West had not yet been solved.

What would the English government do with the immense territory it had acquired? Many colonials hoped that this domain would be opened to them and that farmers, speculators, and trappers could make their fortunes there. That was the *laissez-faire* solution. It was not without danger; first of all, for the Indians. If the crown abandoned them to the greed of the land speculators the Indians would be robbed. What revolts and massacres would follow before the affair could be settled! But this was not the only objection. The colonies had never reached an understanding among themselves as to what part of the hinterland belonged to each of them. The rectification of frontiers and the ensuing quarrels would be endless. Those colonies without a share in the hinterland would be jealous of the others. The hunters and the speculators would have contradictory interests. Moreover the experience of two centuries had inspired in the ministers of the crown a desire to govern this new empire more energetically than the original colonies. To the latter, at a time when America was of interest to no one and the mother country was torn by revolution, had been "imprudently" accorded privileges that rendered them more independent than the rest of England. This evil was not to be allowed to spread, and in the case of the new territories provision was to be made for stricter administration. In October, 1763, the government announced that three new provinces would be created: Quebec, East Florida, and West Florida. As for the territory bordered by the Alleghenies, the Mississippi, and the Great Lakes, it was to become an Indian reservation. No one was allowed to make a homestead there or to buy or sell land without special license, and those living there were ordered to leave. The colonists were enraged. The West was their hope, their future, their conquest. In England Burke protested against an attempt to make a lair for savage beasts of land that God "by explicit charter had given to the Children of Men." He might have added that if the government of George III did not allow malcontents the chance of becoming pioneers, he would turn them into rebels.

As a matter of fact, this decree was treated like all those having to do with America; it was not strictly enforced. Certain groups obtained large domains carved out of the western "Indian reservations." Washington acquired thirty-three thousand acres in the Ohio Valley, and with the Lees he had an interest in another enterprise. In 1773 a company in which Benjamin Franklin and William Johnson were active received the approval of the Board of Trade for its request for a grant of two and one-half million acres between the Alleghenies and the Ohio. The Privy Council had agreed to the proposal when the Revolution put an end to the plan. It was this wise lack of consistency in the English administration, this "salutary neglect," that rendered it bearable to the colonists. The customs collectors, had they done their duty, would have exasperated the merchants of the coast; but they did not do it. Many of them remained in England, drew their salaries at home, and lived in peace. Before a more rigid law-enforcement policy was adopted in the late sixties, to collect two thousand pounds in duties cost His Majesty's government seven thousand pounds. This negligence might be "salutary" for the colonies; it was onerous for the crown. But to establish an efficient system of customs would have run the risk of spoiling everything. "At bottom the great problem of the decade that followed the Peace of 1763 was that of reconciling centralized imperial control with the already existing colonial autonomy."

When, after 1763, England began to demand more of the colonies, many blamed the new king, George III, and his autocratic ideas; but the problem went deeper than that. "Great Britain adopted a new imperial policy because she had conquered a new empire." At the time of the chartered companies and the proprietors, the government in London had tolerated rather than protected colonial enterprises. The first colonists defended themselves; they cost the mother country very little. The war against France had been an entirely different matter. The administration, defense, and organization of the new conquests came to an enormous total. A French population in Canada and the necessity of guarding a long frontier against the Indians required the presence in America of at least ten thousand men. But expenditures for the colonies had already risen to four hundred twenty thousand pounds, and the quitrents produced barely sixteen thousand pounds. To this the colonists replied that one could not ask plantations still in swaddling clothes to guarantee the costs of their support. "As long as he is still in his childhood," said J. Wilson, "a subject cannot be expected to fulfill all the duties of his allegiance. One must wait before demanding this accomplishment until he arrives at the age of discretion and maturity."

This argument lost cogency if the infant in swaddling clothes demanded the enjoyment of the liberties of a full-grown man. And so one might excuse some irritation on the part of the mother country, especially since the latter's debt had risen sharply as a result of the war. In 1764 when Grenville, the new chancellor of the exchequer, with his prolix skill explained his budget to Parliament, he announced that the increase of capital debts amounted to seventy million pounds and that it would be necessary to raise three million in new taxes. Two solutions were possible: to raise the property tax in England, or to increase the revenues from colonial customs. The landed gentry who constituted the Commons would feel a natural and lively preference for the second method. Grenville made his choice accordingly. His colleagues, not without sanctimonious satisfaction, heard him propose duties on foreign coffee, on Madeira wine, on indigo, on sugar and molasses entering the colonies, to which was added an absolute prohibition on the importation into the colonies of foreign rum. The Sugar Act was intended both to increase revenue by

putting an end to the shameless smuggling and to protect the planters in
the British West Indies against those in the French and Spanish Antilles.
This budget, which would cost his audience not a penny, was warmly
received by Parliament and there was general agreement there that Mr.
Grenville was a great financier.

The reception was less hearty on the other side of the ocean. The colonies
had one particular objection to the Sugar Act: that the English authorities
intended to enforce it. A horrible innovation. Up to this moment smuggling had been tolerated. Armed patrols, inquiries, and requisitions
appeared unbearable. And in 1765 Grenville repeated the offense. It was
necessary, he said, to defend the colonies by collective and permanent
measures. Who was able to organize this military and naval defense?
The colonies themselves? Thirteen governments had never organized
anything, and Franklin admitted that union was necessary but impossible.
His Majesty's government? Then it would need new resources. What
resources? The treasury suggested a stamp tax. Would the Americans
object? Their agents in London were consulted by Grenville, who
inquired of them with what sauce the Americans would like to be eaten.
As for himself, he thought that a stamp tax was the easiest to digest, but if
the Americans preferred some other condiment, he was ready to study
their preference. Franklin suggested a return to the old method of the
English kings who used to ask the colonies themselves to vote the necessary sums. "Can you think of any mode of taxation more convenient to
them?" asked Grenville. "Can you agree on the proportion each Colony
should raise?" Franklin had to admit that he could not. Nothing
remained for Parliament but to vote the Stamp Act, which it did in
February, 1765.

This act decreed that stamps sold by appointed agents should be used
in America for all documents, licenses, announcements, journals, alma-
nacs, playing cards, etc. Was this decree legal? The agents of the colonists
took their stand on the right possessed by every British subject of not
being taxed except by his own consent. "But," Grenville replied, "no one
contests this right. The colonies are represented by Parliament, Council
for the Empire, which has voted this tax." This was the principle of
virtual representation which applied as well to all those Englishmen,
very numerous at that time, who had no vote. The English of the Middle
Ages had said, "No taxation without representation," and from this
phrase Parliament had been born. The English of the eighteenth century
contented themselves with: "No taxation without *an act* of Parliament."
This was a step backward, and the colonists might object that those Englishmen who did not have a vote were represented indirectly by voters from

the same shire, having the same interests as themselves, whereas the colonists were not represented at all. If the empire was to be represented by Parliament, why were there not in Parliament members elected by the empire? To which Dr. Johnson, the self-appointed defender of the ministry, replied: "We do not put a calf into the plough; we wait till it is an ox." "Well and good," the colonists replied in their turn, "but then why make the calf pay?" The thesis of the colonists was that of the Middle Ages: taxes must be consented to in Parliament by the states of the realm and there was no American *state* in the British Parliament. Moreover, the colonies had received their charter from the king and not from Parliament; they owed allegiance, said their representatives, to the sovereign alone, which was once more a strange appeal to the ideas of the Middle Ages.

In Westminster the debate about the Stamp Act was one of the most languid Burke had ever listened to. In fact the affair passed with so little noise that the city hardly knew what the House had done that day. Only when Townshend asked "if our American children planted by our care, nourished by our indulgence, and protected by our arms will be so ungrateful as to refuse to aid their old parents bound down by the heavy burden of debts," Colonel Isaac Barré, an Irishman who had fought with Wolfe at Quebec, leaped to his feet: "They planted by your care! No, it was your oppression that planted them in America. . . . They nourished by your indulgence! They have nobly taken up arms for your defense. . . ." The House was awakened for an instant by this fine outburst of oratory, then dozed off again until time to vote, and the Stamp Act passed by two hundred votes to forty-nine. Nevertheless a wise man might have foreseen that this law was pregnant with disaster. It threatened for the first time to unite the colonies. Until then different sections had had different interests. A duty on molasses irritated the merchants of the North; a duty on tobacco, the planters of the South. But this flood of stamped paper was going to exasperate North and South alike, and irritate lawyers and journalists whom a prudent government never molests. Nevertheless, seen from London, the measure seemed trivial. Franklin himself, who disapproved of it and who knew the unfavorable sentiment in the colonies, did not dream of resisting it. Undoubtedly he knew that his fellow citizens would be irritated. But what was there to do? He was overcome by the spectacle of British power. How could one think of a rebellion? The ports which were the centers of colonial life were at the mercy of the English navy. Franklin thought so little of the possibility of resistance that he himself selected as distributor of stamps for Philadelphia one of his friends, Mr. Hughes.

He was far from imagining the tempest that the Stamp Act would raise in America. It was not that the burden was crushing. Stamps varied in price, depending on the importance of the document, from one penny to six pounds. It was the principle of the measure that shocked Americans. They had always admitted the right to impose customs duties because that was a regulation governing the *external* commerce of the colonies; they refused to pay *internal* taxes voted by a Parliament in which they were not represented. In Philadelphia, Franklin's enemies, with the unscrupulousness characteristic of enemies, seized this occasion to attempt to ruin his prestige. They circulated a rumor that in order to get him to endorse the Stamp Act the crown had promised him a government post. They talked about setting fire to Franklin's house, and his wife courageously declared that she would defend it, if necessary, with gunfire. In Virginia the great planters, who had hitherto dominated the House of Burgesses in Williamsburg, were jealous of their rights, but they would have contented themselves with a moderate protest if there had not been in the assembly, which met in May, 1765, young representatives of the frontier, pioneers of an aggressive type. Among these was Patrick Henry. This young lawyer of twenty-nine had been a trapper, a trader, a farmer, all unsuccessfully. Suddenly, because he possessed natural eloquence of the classic type, he had become successful as a lawyer. A great reader of the Bible and of Livy, he patterned himself on these vehement yet simple models. In 1765 he proposed five resolutions concerning the Stamp Act and submerged the assembly "in the torrents of his eloquence." The "old families" listened to him with irritation. When he said: "Tarquin and Caesar each had his Brutus, Charles the First his Cromwell; and George the Third . . ." cries of "Treason!" interrupted him. The loyal subjects of His Majesty had no liking for such violent language.

But all the representatives of the frontier and of "the poor whites" supported Patrick Henry, and the five resolutions were passed by a majority of one vote, despite the opposition of Peyton Randolph, the speaker, whom Thomas Jefferson, then a young man, heard say on the way out: "I would have given five hundred guineas for a vote!" The next day Peyton Randolph succeeded in having the fifth resolution, which was the most violent, expunged from the record of the debate. Soon copies of the "Virginia Resolves" were circulating in Boston, Philadelphia and New York. They said in substance that His Majesty's subjects in the colonies owed no obedience to business regulations which had not been voted by their own assemblies. Boston was enthusiastic. Until then Massachusetts had taken the lead in protesting against the new English policy. If the rich Anglican planters of Virginia joined them and drew up incendiary proclamations, then it became possible to hope for union. A circular letter was addressed by Massachusetts to the other colonies, asking them to send delegates to a congress that was to be held in New York to beseech the king for justice. For Parliament, and not the king, appeared as the villain in this play. Nine colonies responded to the appeal; in three others the governors refused to convoke the assemblies to choose delegates. By "humble supplication" the congress reminded His Majesty of the first principles of finance. Grenville and the Commons would have been little troubled if the "humble supplication" had not been accompanied by a vigorous resolution placing an embargo on all English merchandise until such time as the Stamp Act should be repealed. To supervise the enforcement of this measure, an underground movement was formed, calling itself the "Sons of Liberty." It had been Colonel Barré in his speech in Commons who had first given this name to Americans. The Sons of Liberty pledged themselves to use all means to combat unjust laws and in particular the abominable Stamp Act.

The violence of the movement might seem surprising. But interest reinforced principle. For the rich businessmen of the ports, who had made their fortunes by smuggling, the Sugar Act had been a disaster, and they hoped to get it abrogated. The farmers of the frontier would not excuse England for the creation of the Indian reservation. The planters of the South saw in England a nation of creditors and, like the farmers of the frontier, they were enraged by the law concerning the western lands which destroyed both acquired rights and hopes. Intellectuals, like John Adams, saw in the imposition of a stamp tax on journals a means of controlling the press, education, and thought. And so most men of prominence were in favor of resistance. Through their efforts, the young men and artisans were aroused. Very quickly these radical elements escaped from the control of the moderates. The moderates, in a comfortable position because of their wealth to keep up passive resistance, could wait quietly in their handsome houses until the ruin of her commerce induced England to propose a settlement. But young lawyers, without clients, small merchants who had no merchandise to sell, exhibited less patience. Houses and effigies were burned; persons of importance, stamp collectors and members of the Anglican clergy, were maltreated by the crowds and, as they said, "forced to be free." The Sons of Liberty gave the name of Sons of Despotism to anyone who did not think as they did. The house of Thomas Hutchinson, the lieutenant governor, together with the treasures and documents it contained, was gutted. Thomas Hutchinson was an honorable man, the scion of an old consular family, the historian of his province, a courteous, conscientious, and thoroughly respectable magistrate; but his sentiments were those of an English Tory. He loved his king; he was devoted to the principle of imperial unity; and he considered the British Parliament the ideal of all assemblies. These ideas for a time had assured his popularity. Suddenly they were no longer the style, and Thomas Hutchinson, like his Tory friends, no longer possessed any understanding of the rebellious America that surged around him. He condemned it, hated it, and considered it mad. The people of Boston on the other hand decreed him a reactionary, and to cure him of his errors set fire to his house. More than one among the comfortable doctrinaries who had unleashed this movement began to rue what they had done.

Happily for the American moderates, the English moderates were also tired of this struggle. The merchants of London were painfully aware that the factories lacked work. And why this conflict? To sell stamps? But stamps were not being sold. Rockingham, who had replaced Grenville as minister, started to talk of abrogating the Stamp Act. Grenville protested: "Great Britain protects America; America is therefore bound to yield obedience." He asked when Americans had been emancipated. "I ask," Mr. Pitt interrupted, "when they have been reduced to slavery?" An academic debate on the rights of Parliament did not interest the City. "We don't understand your policy at all," said the merchants, "and we see that our business is suffering. Find a remedy or go to the devil!" This was illuminating and irrefutable. Franklin was called to the bar of the House of Commons to give his opinion. He would have liked a complete overhauling of colonial administration and the right for the colonies to have representatives at Westminster. But finding no support in England for this project he advised the abrogation of the Stamp Act pure and simple. "Suppose," one of the members asked him, "that the Stamp Act is retained; will the bad humor of the Americans go so far as to make them purchase poor merchandise elsewhere in preference to ours?" Reply: "Yes, I believe so. . . ." Question: "What has hitherto been the pride of the Americans?" Reply: "To follow British styles." Question: "What is their pride now?" Reply: "To wear their old clothes until they can make others themselves." It is hard to tell whether it was Franklin's testimony that won the day for the Americans. Be that as it may, the clarity of his exposition, the simplicity of his replies, and their moderation enabled Parliament to save its face. The Stamp Act was rescinded and Franklin, who a year earlier had been the traitor of traitors, became a popular hero in America. King George III, who had a high regard for his own majesty, hesitated a long time before signing this capitulation. But the ministers represented to him the grave discontent of the City; Parliament by a declaratory act maintained its theoretic rights; the king gave in; and in the spring of 1766

America celebrated this victory in all its taverns by innumerable toasts to liberty. Fireworks, banquets, barbecues showed that the colonies were happy at the reconciliation. Everywhere the imperial flag was unfurled. At that moment it would not have required much skill to cement the union anew through reform. Franklin had indicated in outline the form it should take: The American colonies might become a free dominion within the framework of the British Empire. But Franklin in his objective fashion sought to ignore the passions of the time, and passions may not be ignored.

CHAPTER XII

Second Round

AMERICAN public opinion had won the first round, but English public opinion remained unsatisfied. Were Americans Englishmen or were they not? Or were they Englishmen when it was a question of protection and Americans when it was a question of taxation? "We are English," the Americans replied, "but we will not submit to internal taxation." To many Englishmen this position seemed preposterous. Whether the taxes were internal or external, it was a question of paying legitimate expenses, and it was hard to see why a free citizen should prefer to die rather than pay for a stamp but would agree to live and pay customs duties. The Sons of Liberty cried out against oppression. "Who's oppressing them?" England asked. Can you imagine, Englishmen asked themselves in good faith, a more conciliatory administration than the English administration in America? In what way was it a monstrous injustice to urge the Americans to participate in the costs of their own defense? Did not the English pay much higher taxes than the Americans? Had the colonies ever proposed any other method? To the Tories nothing seemed more ridiculous than this campaign, supported in England by the Whigs, in favor of a liberty which (they said) no one was threatening.

In 1767 the chancellor of the exchequer was Charles Townshend, a charming and paradoxical man, as witty as he was indiscreet, "who belonged to every party and cared for none," who in one debate sustained two opposed theses with equal talent, "who beat Lord Chatham in language, Burke in metaphor, Grenville in presumption, Rigby in impudence, himself in folly, and everybody in good humor." Parliament was growing tired of the "insolence" of the colonies. Concessions had but increased their intransigence. Boston refused to indemnify the Loyalist victims of the riots; the Assembly of New York refused to quarter the English troops as the Quartering Act demanded. Lord Chatham, himself a great friend of the colonials, condemned their attitude, saying that they had made it impossible to say a single word in their defense. Townshend in a speech that was much relished by the House said in effect: "We have had enough of this. The Assembly in New York must be suspended until it is ready to enforce the law. Since the customary reprisal of the Americans is to refuse to vote their governors' pay, we must assure the latter's salaries by taxes levied upon the Americans. What taxes? Since the Americans prefer, no one knows why, external taxes, well and good. They shall have external taxes. We will put duties on glass, paint, paper and tea. And to collect these new taxes we will establish in America a corps of resident tax collectors."

No sooner proposed than voted. This time the British Parliament believed itself on firm ground. The wildest American radical had never disputed Parliament's right to levy customs duties. No doubt. But the naming of paid collectors by the mother country was going to remove from the colonial assemblies all authority over these officials. This was the first grievance. The new law authorized these collectors to enter any house, store, or cellar to seek out contraband merchandise. This was the second grievance, and it was the more serious. For the American was master in his house and was horrified at the idea of any violation of his home. In fact, the presence in Boston of these commissioners, armed with writs of assistance and supported by armed patrols, quickly aroused opposition. Every smuggler became a malcontent. In 1768 the ship *Liberty* belonging to John Hancock, a shipowner of Boston, arrived from Madeira loaded with wine. John Hancock, a graduate of Harvard, was one of the Boston merchants who recited Vergil and Homer. "If modesty's a fault," said his American biographer, "Hancock was innocent of it." And Thomas Hutchinson said: "His ruling passion was fondness for popular applause. . . . His natural powers were moderate and had been very little improved by study. . . ." John Hancock loved the excellent wine of Madeira, on which the tax was high. The customs man who came aboard was seized and locked up, and the wine was unloaded without payment of duties. The English commissioners seized the ship; the crowd attacked their houses. The commissioners and their families had to seek refuge aboard a man-of-war. The seizure of his ship gave John Hancock a not unpleasing prominence, and although he was rich he became a popular hero. When he was prosecuted John Adams, who defended him, raised the question of the validity in America of the Townshend law: "My client, Mr. Hancock, has never given his consent to this law: he did not himself vote for it, and he never voted for anyone who could have represented him in this debate. . . ." Two English regiments received orders to occupy the garrison in Boston. Their red uniforms brightened the streets and irritated the crowds. In that city of fishermen they were called "lobster backs." Their military bands on Sunday scandalized the sons of puritanism and liberty. The citizens refused to speak to the soldiers. Once more the atmosphere was charged with storms. Now the customs service was bringing in thirty thousand pounds a year; it cost thirteen thousand, and the expenses of the two regiments more than absorbed the difference. Bad finance and bad policy.

The radicals in Boston were now wondering whether Townshend's acceptance of the principle of external taxes had not concealed a trap. But this time the argument was harder for them to sustain than in the case of the Stamp Act. On what pretext could they oppose what the colonists had accepted for one hundred fifty years? John Dickinson, a dignified and honest Whig lawyer and the author of *Letters from a Farmer in Pennsylvania*, a series of simply but effectively written articles, found a way of doing it. He explained that the danger of the tax was not so much in the tax itself as in the intention of those who levied it. Taxation designed to regulate commerce was legitimate; taxation intended to produce revenue and to pay officials was not. Samuel Adams, a favorite orator in the Boston town meetings, maintained that Parliament itself was subject to a superior power, which was the British Constitution, and that no law was valid if it contravened this Constitution and the Magna Carta. If anyone had raised the objection that the British Constitution did not exist, he would have replied that the greatest strength of the British Constitution was that it did not exist except in human reason and in the nature of things. Now by virtue of natural law every man should be consulted before being taxed. Benjamin Franklin, who possessed a clear and honest mind, which is dangerous in time of revolution, thought these distinctions not very clear. He would have found it simpler to say: "Either Parliament can make all laws for America; or it cannot make any." This formula had the advantage of stating the true problem, which was that Americans at the bottom of their hearts no longer wanted to accept *any* law from England, and thus of forcing America and England to seek some new formula of imperial union. But Franklin and a few others were the only ones to see this larger aspect of the question.

The colonists had already made the discovery that in the eyes of the English merchants a refusal to trade constituted the strongest of arguments.

It was this embargo that had led to the abrogation of the Stamp Act; they made use of the same method to deal with the new taxes. In 1769 the imports from England to New York fell from four hundred eighty-two thousand pounds to seventy-four thousand pounds. Pennsylvania and Maryland reduced their purchases by half. The South took longer to give up its old and cherished habits; but little by little, through the influence of men like George Washington, who had conceived a deep-seated hatred for England during the last war, the planters began to understand that here was a means of reducing their heavy indebtedness to their agents in London.

In Boston the tension mounted dangerously. The General Court of Massachusetts, which had sent circular letters to the other colonies, urging common action for the defense of their liberties, received an order in the king's name to annul this resolution. When it refused the governor dissolved the assembly. Troops were ordered to Boston from Halifax. On the evening of March 5, 1770, a fire alarm drew into the streets of Boston a large crowd, composed in part of young boys. It had snowed; a snowfight began, and soon the motionless red sentries became targets. One of the soldiers peppered by snowballs called for help; the guard turned out; the crowd attacked. Shots were fired, and when the scuffle was over four bodies lay on the snow. This is one account of what was called the Boston Massacre. As a matter of fact it was an unfortunate episode, responsibility for which was divided, but the orators of the town meetings raised such an outcry that Governor Hutchinson was compelled to withdraw the English troops from the city. Horace Walpole wrote: "You have seen the accounts from Boston? The tocsin seems to be sounded in America. I have many visions about that country and fancy I see twenty empires and republics forming upon vast scales all over that continent, which is growing too mighty to be kept in subjection to half a dozen exhausted nations of Europe." Seven months later the captain who had given the order to fire and his men were tried in Boston. John Adams, although he belonged to the party opposed to England, had the courage to defend these innocent soldiers and secure their acquittal by the jury. It was a fine example of intellectual and civic honesty.

Incidents multiplied in all the colonies and kept irritation alive. The boycott was extended; in 1769 English exports to the colonies had dropped by over half a million pounds. Once more London rebelled and addressed a petition to Parliament. Lord North, who was the prime minister, paid great heed to the feelings of the City. He proposed to Parliament that it abrogate the detested law. But as a point of honor he was unwilling to admit that he was giving in to a collective pressure which was "inadmissible" and, the noble lord went so far as to say, "illegal." The Townshend taxes should be ended, well and good, but it was not because of the American rebels or commercial pressure, certainly not: it was because they should never have been enacted. To demonstrate quite clearly that Parliament was not renouncing its rights, a tax, a single one, was to be retained, and that so light that it could not cause the colonies any distress; just one small tax on tea. What the unhappy premier failed to see was that the point of honor, on the other side of the ocean too, was the only thing that mattered. American merchants decided, in July, 1770, to resume the importation of English merchandise—except tea. "That England had insisted on this detail for the purpose of maintaining her rights, and that America had refused to give in in order to demonstrate her liberty, constitutes a singularly high tribute paid by two eminently practical peoples to the prestige of abstract ideas."

It was evident that Lord North hoped to follow a policy of appeasement. This policy found allies in America. The great merchants who had unleashed the movement five years earlier because their trade with the West Indies was menaced had seen without pleasure the populace become active and violent. "They had been able to hope that America would govern herself as long as they had believed that they were America. But if home rule was to become mob rule, they would still prefer the King and Parliament," wrote Schlesinger. Even the most liberal, John Hancock among them, decided to let controversies lie. Some went so far as to import English tea; others imported great quantities of contraband Dutch tea, which was cheaper and permitted a combination of profit and loyalty to their community. During two or three years it seemed possible that everything would be smoothed over. "The people appear to be weary of their altercations with the mother country, and a little discreet conduct on both sides would perfectly reestablish a warm affection and respect towards Great Britain for which this country was once remarkable." But the radicals were biding their time and at their head was Samuel Adams, whom Governor Hutchinson, his victim, called sometimes the "Machiavelli of chaos," sometimes the "incendiary in chief."

Samuel Adams, the oracle of the people of Boston, was the son of a businessman who after a long period of prosperity had been partially ruined by a decree of the British government against a bank in which he was interested. This was the first grievance against England. The son had succeeded in mismanaging the paternal business and in 1762, at the age of forty, had decided to consecrate his talents henceforth exclusively to the interests of the community. Of his financial integrity there was no question. The glitter of gold never seduced him. Samuel Adams ate little, drank little, slept little, thought much, and asserted even more. In his youth he had loved clubs, discussions of principle, and political skirmishes. Another name that Hutchinson gave him was "master of the marionettes." Indeed he used to spend entire days talking to the shopkeepers and artisans in the doorways of their places of business or in the taverns, and this long-standing familiarity gave him great influence over their opinions. Samuel Adams had no equal in proving to the happy citizens of New England that they were miserable slaves suffering from British tyranny. He loathed the little aristocratic and servile clique that gravitated around the governor. The appeal to loyalty left him unmoved. He saw in the actions of the government of George III a deliberate effort to despoil Americans of the liberties they had acquired: The first step would be to free the governor from all control by paying him directly from London; the second, to empower the governor to name the councillors; the third, to prohibit town meetings. That done, absolutism would be installed over a people hitherto free.

To combat this usurpation, Samuel Adams was ready to make use of any weapons. His enemies said that he was intellectually the most dishonest of men and that he did not know it. It may be that he did know it and did not care. He sincerely wished to defend liberty, but he was incapable of granting it to those who did not think as he did. He condemned intolerance and practiced it without remorse, nor did he have any great scruples in vilifying the servants of the crown. In his young manhood he had chosen as subject for his Master of Arts thesis at Harvard: "Whether it be lawful to resist the supreme Majesty if the Commonwealth cannot otherwise be preserved?" and decided in the affirmative. Trained in Puritan scholasticism, he conceived the world as the theater of an eternal battle between liberty and tyranny. Tyranny could not be conquered except by the sovereignty of the people; liberty could not be saved except by equality. Samuel Adams was not willing to admit even parliamentary government, and saw in the town meeting, where he had won his own triumphs, the one true democracy. The idea of a reconciliation with England filled him with horror. How could he live without that hatred? Between 1770 and 1773 the British government remained inactive, and Samuel Adams also should have grown calmer. But he could not give up this struggle, for the struggle was within himself. On the contrary, it was during this period that he was most active in spreading his propaganda against "our implacable enemies." When the people of Boston saw the light of his solitary candle late at night, they would say: "There's Samuel Adams writing against the Tories." He composed pamphlets and articles under twenty different names and wrote innumerable letters, all proving that it would be much better for the affairs of the colonies if they were administered by the colonies themselves. With a genius that would have done credit to a professional agitator he organized town committees of correspondence whose duty it was to maintain constant contact between radical farmers and the workmen in the cities. In 1773 the House of Burgesses in Virginia initiated a project of the same kind, appointed a committee for inter-colonial correspondence. This agitation continued and spread. All that was needed was an incident to provoke a crisis.

In May, 1773 the East India Company, crushed by debt and close to bankruptcy, had accumulated in London a stock of seventeen million pounds of tea. In an attempt to save the company, and also as a means of suppressing the sale of Dutch tea, the British government agreed to exempt that company, and that company alone, from all export duties from England. Moreover, the directors of the company decided to dispense with middlemen and sell directly to the public. In this way their tea would be much cheaper than that of the Dutch company and they would regain their lost market. It is difficult to imagine a more stupid project or one better calculated to provoke disturbances in an already nervous mercantile community. It enraged the merchants who also had stocks of tea and, in particular, John Hancock, who had become since his trial a sort of political boss. The East India Company did not have a good reputation. In the East Indies it had fomented wars, stirred up rebellions, and dethroned princes to increase its profits. What plot was it hatching in America? If it secured the monopoly of tea, it might subsequently extend this method to spices and to silk. "But, thank God, we are not Sepoys, nor Marattas, but British subjects who are born to liberty." The moderate John Dickinson himself in *Two Letters Concerning the Tea Tax* protested with extreme violence against the ministers who attempted to restore the fortunes of a bankrupt company at the expense of American liberties.

At the same time this was not solid ground from which to launch a decisive attack upon England. How could one convince the masses that a reduction of ninepence in the price of tea was an intolerable persecution? At least the stage needed to be set. Chance and Samuel Adams did the trick. When the company's first ship, the *Dartmouth,* was tied up at a dock in Boston, a large meeting organized in the Old South Meetinghouse brought together an excited crowd. Samuel Adams and Josiah Quincy denounced England, George III, Parliament, the government, and the company. "This meeting," said Samuel Adams finally, "can do nothing more to save the country." On the evening of December 16 a group of young men held another and gayer meeting, with much drinking of punch. They dressed themselves up as Mohawk Indians. When the punch had produced its effect and the bright-colored feathers had been donned, the Mohawks ran down to the dock, boarded the *Dartmouth,* and threw the tea overboard, defying King George III to interrupt their "tea party." A few leaves of this historic tea, washed up by the tide on neighboring beaches, are today preserved in a glass bowl in the Boston Museum. Next morning the moderate middle classes severely condemned this expensive masquerade. "The Indians," they said, "never behaved in such savage fashion." No reasonable businessman approved the destruction of eighteen thousand pounds of tea. In the other colonies the act was censured. Franklin said that he hoped this unjustifiable act of violence would be punished. John Adams approved of it, saying that the destruction of the tea had been absolutely necessary, but on the whole the reaction was such that, had the British government been skillful, it would have found in this incident an opportunity for reconciliation.

But the government of King George III possessed more arrogance than skill. It took a strong line. "The bets are down," said the king. "The Colonies must now triumph or submit." In April, 1774, Parliament voted five laws which America called the five "intolerable acts." The first completely closed the port of Boston until reimbursement should be made for the tea, which was to have the result of depriving Bostonians of their livelihood, and thus turning even peaceloving ones into revolutionists. The second revised the charter of Massachusetts, gave the king the right to appoint the members of the council, and prohibited town meetings. The third transferred to England the criminal trials arising out of the application of these laws. The fourth concerned the quartering of troops not only in Massachusetts, but in all the British dominions in North America. The fifth, called the Quebec Act, accorded religious liberty to the Catholics of Canada and substantially extended the limits of the province of Quebec, which, in the eyes of the citizens of New England, was a monstrous attempt to establish autocratic government in the colonies, perhaps even to win French Canada over to the side of the crown, thus instituting on the American continent a balance of power. Finally General Gage was named governor of Massachusetts. He was a soldier who believed in strong measures and he had said to George III: "They will be lions whilst we are lambs, but if we take the resolute part, they will undoubtedly prove very meek." More than one British newspaper had condemned the tea auctions advertised by gunfire. The *St. James Chronicle* published a little poem:

> O Boston wives and maids, draw near and see
> Our delicate Souchong and Hyson tea!
> Buy it, my charming girls, fair, black and brown.
> If not, we'll cut your throats and burn your town.

The measures enacted by the Tories could not but delight American radicals, whom they furnished with what they had hitherto most lacked—legitimate grievances. From the beginning of the affair, Chatham and Franklin had advised the Bostonians to pay for the lost tea and put an end to the incident. This attempt at appeasement had exasperated and enraged Samuel Adams: "Franklin may be a great philosopher but he is a bungling politician."

In the British Parliament there was a man who denounced with luminous intelligence the stupidity of the government's intransigent attitude. This was Burke. He said one should go beyond the narrow aspects of the controversy. No one, he added, would doubt the possibility of a commodity like tea supporting a duty of threepence. But no commodity would support a duty of threepence or of one penny so long as passions were aroused and two million men were determined not to pay it. The sentiments of the colonies, he said, had once been those of Great Britain. They were the sentiments of Mr. Hampden when the latter was called upon to pay twenty shillings. Would those twenty shillings have ruined Mr. Hampden? No, but the payment of so much as one-half of those twenty shillings, in the way in which they had been demanded, would have made him a slave. What had been the attitude of the colonies prior to this new fiscal policy? They had been peaceful and loyal. Why interfere with something that was going well? Why not, on the contrary, cultivate the friendship of the Americans? Why sacrifice their affection for the vain pleasure of levying symbolic imposts? If one insisted on making enemies, let it be at least for serious reasons. But to appear at once as tyrants and as petty and stupid tyrants Burke considered an insensate attitude. "Return to your old principles," he pleaded. If America was to be taxed, let her tax herself. He would not, he said, go into the discussion of reciprocal rights. He would not enter into these metaphysical distinctions, the very name of which he hated. Leave the Americans as they were and these distinctions would perish with the unhappy quarrels that had given them birth. If, however, they pressed too hard, the boar would turn against the hunter.

CHAPTER XIII

Toward Independence

THE five "intolerable acts" aroused the indignation of Americans. It was worse, they said, than the treatment of Carthage by the Romans. One could search in vain through the archives of Constantinople for a case of equal injustice and brutality. Revolutionary spirits skillfully exploited the maladroitness of Lord North. All the colonies rushed to the succor of the city of Boston, "starved" by the closing of the port. The people of Connecticut gave sheep; those of the Carolinas, rice. It was decided that a Continental Congress, made up of delegates from the various colonies should meet in Philadelphia to study the means of common resistance. Both John and Samuel Adams, together with John Hancock, were delegates from Massachusetts.

John Adams bore small resemblance to his cousin Samuel. Son of a Massachusetts farmer, he had gone through Harvard, where he had been outstanding in intelligence. One hundred years earlier his insatiable ambition would have made him a minister of religion. Toward the middle of the eighteenth century the study of law seemed a surer path to power. An assiduous reader of the classics, with a thorough knowledge of Cicero and Montaigne, he believed he had mastered the art of government and wished to practice it. He was not lacking in civic courage. "I have accepted," he once wrote to his wife, "a seat in the House of Representatives and thereby have connived to my own ruin, to your ruin, and the ruin of your children. I give you this warning that you may prepare your mind for your fate." Abigail Adams, a woman worthy of this heroic and grandiloquent husband, signed her reply: *Portia.*

John Adams, unlike his cousin, did not have the faculty of making crowds love him. Samuel was a democrat in manner as well as in doctrine; John's enemies described him as a self-made aristocrat. Honors and titles delighted him, as did ceremonies, provided they revolved around him. A Puritan realist and enthusiast, "always protestant and never reformed," he believed that human nature is essentially bad. In his political projects he never forgot original sin, of which he had his own share in the form of vanity. He said of himself that it was "his cardinal sin and cardinal folly." Sensitive to criticism, he had a need to succeed, to get ahead, to dominate. As soon as anyone vied with him for first place, he believed he was being persecuted. He desperately regretted having been born in a colonial province where he would never have an opportunity for great accomplishments. Despite his solemn and at times pompous manner, there was violence in his temperament. On the day following the Boston Tea Party he expressed admiration for "the dignity, majesty and sublimity" of this incident, but regretted not seeing as many corpses floating in the harbor as there were leaves of tea. The Stamp Act had seemed to him a personal offense: "This execrable project was set on foot for my ruin." The struggle between England and the colonies was in his eyes a fight between Satan and John Adams. "He is," said one Englishman, "the most ungracious man I ever met." But this rudeness had its advantages. He was so certain of his own superiority that fear of public opinion had no influence on him and he said openly all that he thought. His friends called him "honest John Adams," and even his enemies did not question his intellectual integrity. "I am persuaded," Franklin said, "that he means well for his country, is always an honest man, often a wise one; but sometimes, and in some things, absolutely out of his senses." In Congress he was to show more wisdom than folly.

It was the first time he had left Boston. He was surprised by the activity and prosperity of New York, but he lost none of his arrogance. "I have not seen a single gentleman here," he said. It is true that certain New Yorkers had had the bad taste to refer in his presence to the citizens of New England as Goths or Vandals, and to make malicious allusions to the hanging of Quakers. When he arrived in Philadelphia, riding in the carriage of John Hancock, the Maecenas of this campaign, the crowd wanted to unharness the horses and pull the great men's carriage themselves. John Hancock, eager for any sort of triumph, would gladly have let them do it. Samuel Adams declared that he would get out of the carriage and walk rather than allow his fellow countrymen to degrade themselves to the level of draft animals. John Adams admired the symmetry and cleanliness of the city, but he added: "Philadelphia with all its trade, and wealth, and regularity, is not Boston. . . . The morals of our people are much better; their manners are more polite and agreeable. Our language is better, our taste is better, our persons are handsomer. Our spirit is greater, our laws are wiser, our religion is superior, our education is better."

Those delegates from New York and Pennsylvania who favored resistance begged John Adams to be prudent and never to mention the extreme measures desired by Massachusetts. There was a powerful group in New York who were terrified at the thought of civil war; in Philadelphia there were Episcopal clergymen who depended on favors from London. So much weakness enraged John Adams. "When Demosthenes asked the people of Greece to form a league against Philip, did he propose simply a Non-Importation Pact?" he asked. But, like his colleagues from Massachusetts, Adams maintained his reserve in order not to frighten the other delegates. Most of the latter were suspicious of anything that smacked of rebellion. A group of moderates tried to secure the adoption of a prudent resolution written by Joseph Galloway of Pennsylvania, proposing a permanent grand council of colonial delegates, to meet at least once a year and to be "an inferior and distinct branch of the British Parliament." They failed. The group from Virginia, which included George Washington, Richard Henry Lee, and Patrick Henry among others, supported the men from Boston. "Shall we, after this," wrote Washington, "whine and cry for relief when we have already tried it in vain?" Little by little this party gained ground. "Adams, with his crew, and the haughty Sultans of the South, juggled the whole Conclave of the Delegates," said one discontented moderate.

For the many prominent men who were loyal Englishmen at heart, this was a difficult situation. They had no wish to abandon the unfortunate Bostonians; they had no desire to sacrifice their relations with the empire, their business affairs, and their tranquillity to the passions of radicals who actually were distasteful to them. Their only hope was that "if they showed their fists perhaps George III would respond by holding out his hand." To satisfy those who favored platonic protestation, Congress drew up a declaration of rights and grievances and adopted a petition to the king, written with vigor and dignity, which asked for a return to the Statute of 1763. But to satisfy the radicals, the moderates had to endorse the Continental Association, which recommended to the colonies that they break off all commercial relations with England. What would the prime minister do? Lord North wished to "extend an olive branch"; the king insisted on showing the sword. Consequently Lord North proposed to Parliament that it relieve from all taxes those colonies that voluntarily agreed to contribute to the defense of America (this was the olive branch); while the sword, represented by General Gage's little army, was suspended over Boston.

In Massachusetts, a provincial Congress had taken over control from the assembly, and many inhabitants were giving it their allegiance. It had created militia forces of *minutemen,* that is, those ready to serve at a minute's notice; and it set up depots of arms and ammunition. In April, 1775, General Gage was informed of the existence of one such powder magazine at Concord, a charming little town near Boston. A Colonel Smith was ordered to proceed secretly to Concord with six to eight hundred men during the night of April 18. It was hoped that thus Adams and Hancock, who were at the home of a friend near there, would be arrested. But nothing remained secret from the underground organizations. Several messengers hastened through the countryside to give the alarm. Paul Revere, a small engraver and one of the Sons of Liberty who had taken part in the Boston Tea Party, became famous for his midnight ride. He aroused the captains of the militia, and so at Lexington the English found themselves faced by about forty militiamen. Shots were fired, the first of the war, and eight minutemen were left on the field. The retreat was dreadful for the English. In ambush behind rocks and trees there waited militiamen enraged by the death of their friends. As in the case of Braddock, the rigid order of the English was their undoing. When Major Pitcairn finally reached Cambridge he had lost two hundred forty-seven men in killed and wounded.

The smell of powder and blood delighted Samuel Adams: "What a glorious morning is this!" The wise Franklin himself gloated. "A most vigorous retreat," he wrote to Burke. "Twenty miles in three hours. . . . Scarce to be paralleled in history. . . . The feeble Americans could scarce keep up with them. . . ." It should be said that the disdainful attitude of the army of occupation had greatly irritated the Americans. One of General Gage's officers had written that if two regiments could not put to flight all the militiamen of Massachusetts, the regiments would deserve to be decimated. And Lord Sandwich had said in the House of Lords: "Believe me, My Lords, the very sound of a cannon would carry them off as far as their feet could carry them. . . ." It was time to come down a peg, but strangely enough after these incidents English opinion became bellicose. Walpole was amazed by it: "The war with our Colonies, which is now declared, is a proof what influence jargon has on human actions. A war with our own trade is popular!"

A second Continental Congress met at Philadelphia in May, 1775. A number of political personalities were gaining prominence throughout the colonies. John Adams proudly wrote that a conclave of cardinals assembled for the election of a pope could not offer better specimens. And he was right. Qualities of style and of thought in this assembly would have done honor to a British Parliament of the best period. The important men of the First Congress were reunited here, plus several others; the Adamses were present and the Lees of Virginia and John Hancock and Washington and Jefferson and John Dickinson, "A shadow, tall but slender as a reed, pale as ashes." Franklin and Morris, the first a liberal, the second a conservative, represented Pennsylvania. As a matter of fact, the "representation" was only approximate; the number of abstentions had been enormous; Samuel Adams had been elected by less than one-tenth of the voters of Boston. "The American Revolution, like so many revolutions, was the work of an active minority which persuaded a hesitant majority to a cause for which the latter had but little stomach." Up to this time the majority of Americans had been loyal subjects of the crown, and even those who at the bottom of their hearts had hoped for a complete break had not dared to say so. From this moment on, when economic warfare had become civil war, the advocates of violence in both camps carried the day. As one American historian has said, Galloway and Chatham could easily have reached an understanding; Samuel Adams and Lord North could not. It was then that men in America began to be labeled Tories or Patriots. But these words for a long time had no precise meaning. If Tory meant being faithful to the king, then nine-tenths of the Americans were Tories as late as 1775; if Patriot meant one who favored a break with England it was, in the eyes of the English and their friends, a debatable definition. Samuel Adams would have said of Joseph Galloway that he was an enemy of American liberty; Joseph Galloway would have said of Samuel Adams that he was a rebel. But Joseph Galloway would have called himself a loyalist; Samuel Adams would have chosen the fine name of patriot. Disinterested authorities believe that at that time there were in the colonies one-third ardent loyalists, one-third uncommitted, and one-third radicals.

After Lexington, a spontaneous truce intervened. Each of the adversaries tried to prove that the other had been the first to fire. The Congress in Philadelphia carried on its debates amid administrative difficulties. How was it to govern thirteen colonies which were jealous of one another and no one of which was willing to participate in the costs? General Gage, on his side, wrote reports and did nothing. The British government sent seven thousand men under the command of Generals Howe, Clinton, and Burgoyne. General Howe was the brother of Viscount Howe, who had been killed fighting on the side of the Americans at Ticonderoga, and of Admiral Lord Howe, a great friend of Franklin. The general was distressed to arrive as an enemy in Boston, a city which he loved and in which his brother's memory was venerated. But this was no time for memories. To the radicals, General and Admiral Howe became "the two hateful brothers dedicated to the annals of infamy." As for the American militia after Lexington, they came and camped around Boston, bottling up Gage's army in the city. In the month of June the latter discovered that the Americans had fortified two hills close to Cambridge on the other side of the Charles River—Breed's Hill and Bunker Hill. The circle was growing tighter. Gage thought he would have no trouble in breaking out. He led veteran soldiers against men who, for the most part, had never been under fire and who were short of powder. The thin red line bristling with bayonets climbed bravely under Howe's orders to the assault of Breed's

Hill.* It was a massacre. The Americans, protected by a barricade, held their fire until the last moment, then shot at point-blank range. When bullets gave out, they used screws and nails. In three assaults the English lost more than a thousand men out of three thousand five hundred, and a large number of officers. Finally they turned the position and the Americans abandoned the hill, but it was a disastrous victory. The American General Greene said that they had a great deal more land they would willingly sell at the same price.

When the Congress in Philadelphia received the news of Bunker Hill it had just chosen a commander-in-chief. This is always a difficult problem for a coalition army. Each important colony thought that it had the right to command. John Hancock, the proud Whig merchant, in a vague way colonel of militia, was a candidate. But his colleague from Massachusetts knew him too well to support him. Adams would have loved to be chosen himself: "O that I was a soldier! I would be, I am reading military books." Only to make Adams a soldier would take time, and meanwhile he thought it wiser, in order to maintain the union of the planters and merchants, to choose a Virginian. Now there was one who seemed indicated in all respects; that was George Washington. He possessed military experience, the authority that comes from fortune and birth, and a magnificent presence which compelled respect. Washington was not the man to ask for a post, but he came to the sessions in a colonel's uniform for no reason except, perhaps, as a discreet reminder of his services and to indicate that he was ready to fight. During the debates he listened gravely and said nothing, a wise policy for a general. His noble and majestic face inspired respect, almost fear. When John Hancock heard Adams propose: "A gentleman who comes from Virginia . . . a gentleman who is designated by his experience . . ." his eyes betrayed his resentment. Washington, as soon as he heard his name, left the meeting hall and hurried to the library, which proves that though he might be modest, he was not unadroit. He was unanimously designated. His short speech of acceptance was perfect. He said he felt unequal to this task but would do his duty; he would accept no salary save for the reimbursement of his expenses.

It was an excellent choice. There was never a man better suited to command than Washington. He had energy, decisiveness, and authority. He had mastered his own nature and achieved complete self-control. "I have no resentments," he said. Nevertheless he did retain one, an inextinguishable resentment against England. From his expedition with Braddock and

* This is known as the Battle of Bunker Hill, although the engagement actually took place on near-by Breed's Hill.

from the arrogance with which career officers treated the Virginians, he kept an unhappy memory which from the first conflicts had thrown him into the camp opposed to England. He was not by any means a radical, but he thought that the gentleman of Virginia should lead the way along the path of honor. In 1774 he had said: "I will raise one thousand men, subsist them at my own expense and march myself at their head for the relief of Boston." The administration of a great property had made him a careful and methodical man. He even possessed those little human weaknesses without which his majestic manner might have frightened away friends. He loved young people, cards, and pretty women. "He can be sometimes completely impudent," wrote one of them, "the sort of impudence, Fanny, that you and I love so much." The English themselves could not help admiring him: "There is not a king in Europe," said one of the London papers, "that would not look like a valet beside him." Above all he possessed those qualities essential in a leader, grandeur of mind and force of character; he had no animosities, no pettiness, no small vanities. He was neither depressed by reverses nor intoxicated by success. In a word, he deserved to command others because he had learned to govern himself.

Washington made the trip from Philadelphia to Boston on horseback in fifteen days. On the way he learned of the Battle of Bunker Hill, and his first question was: "Did the militia fight?" "Yes." "The liberties of the country are safe." On July 3 he took command at Cambridge. What sort of army did he find? About seventeen thousand men, commanded by hastily commissioned officers. Nathaniel Greene had been an ironmaster; Benedict Arnold, a druggist and bookseller; John Sullivan, a lawyer. Israel Putnam and Horatio Gates had fought in a war, but it was a very small war. The soldiers lacked arms and uniforms, but not enthusiasm. They wore on their caps the motto: "Liberty or Death," and many wore it in their hearts. Others wanted to go home, and every day there were desertions. The age of the soldiers varied from eighteen to sixty. Sometimes a boy and his grandfather would be serving together. Washington, by instinct, had no love for militia. He said that you never knew how they came or where they went; they ate your provisions, emptied your arsenals, and deserted you at the critical moment. Their lack of discipline shocked his military mind. The men were unshaven, talked in the ranks, and treated their officers as equals. "Each of them acts like a general and not one of them like a soldier." He begged Congress to give him a regular army: "To bring men to be well acquainted with the duties of a soldier requires time. To expect the same courage from raw and undisciplined recruits and from veteran soldiers is to expect what never did and perhaps never will have happened." But Congress remembered Cromwell and feared a dictatorship. Nothing remained for Washington but to make the best of the material at his disposal. He imposed severe discipline and succeeded in raising the prestige of the officers. But he never had a high opinion of these improvised armies.

What could the English generals do? Carry out an expedition into the interior? That would mean running the risk of losing contact with the fleet and, since the British forces were small, the lines of communication would be exposed. Shut themselves up in Boston? To do that they would have to hold the city. Washington laid siege to it and cut it off from the surrounding country, while numerous American privateers blockaded it by sea. Food supplies gave out; there was no meat. An egg was a rarity. Fortunately for Howe, the Americans were short of cannon and ammunition. To remedy this they made an expedition against Fort Ticonderoga, which commanded Lake Champlain and the road to Canada. The operation was easy. The English garrison, consisting of forty-eight men, were completely ignorant of the Battle of Lexington and thought they were at peace; one hundred twenty cannon were part of the booty. This victory made an expedition against Canada possible, and Washington considered it feasible. Would not the French Canadians, who had been so recently conquered, be natural allies for the colonies? But he found the Canadians hostile to this idea. The Quebec Act, which had given them religious peace, had been violently attacked by American Protestants. The Canadians were determined not to fight for either of the two adversaries. In vain two American armies, one led by Benedict Arnold, the other by Montgomery, tried to take Quebec. It was a total failure.

On the other hand, Washington in March, 1776, had a great success at Boston. Thanks to the cannon from Ticonderoga he was able to take possession of Dorchester Heights, one of the hills that dominate Boston. Howe had to retake it or evacuate. A frontal attack, like that at Bunker Hill, would have been a slaughter. General Howe did not wish useless bloodshed. He decided to embark his army and take it to Halifax. The Boston loyalists besought him to take them with him; they knew that the rebel troops would not feel indulgent toward them. To leave their city and their homes was sad, but "neither Hell nor Halifax could be more uncertain shelter than Boston." Howe agreed to take them on condition that they would bring only what was essential. And so in the streets of Boston there was to be seen, struggling toward the harbor, a pitiful procession of fugitives who belong to the oldest families of the city, pushing before them in handcarts or wheelbarrows their children and their possessions. Many wept. The Whigs, hidden behind their shutters, watched with glee the Tories hurrying toward the fleet, as though "the Devil himself were at their heels." At the docks the ships were loaded pell-mell with soldiers, baggage, women, and children. One hundred seventy sailing vessels, a veritable forest of masts carried away the English and their partisans. At the same hour Washington made a triumphal entry into Boston at the head of his troops. Most of the loyalists who left that day were never to see their country again.

CHAPTER XIV

The Declaration of Independence

THE colonists were now at open war with the mother country, but they had not broken the legal tie nor declared their independence. There would be certain advantages, however, in doing so. Independence alone would enable the Americans to secure from the neutral countries recognition as belligerents, to demand for their prisoners the treatment due to soldiers, and finally to prosecute the loyalists, legally if not justly, and to seize their property. But many of the colonists still hesitated, some through loyalty to the crown, like Franklin's own son, Governor William Franklin; others because their business depended on their being citizens of the British Empire; and still others because they retained a hope that their English friends, Burke, Chatham, and Fox, would achieve a compromise. For despite the hostilities there remained many Englishmen who were well disposed toward America. The Duke of Richmond said in the House of Lords that the action of the Americans was "perfectly justifiable in every possible political and moral sense." The noble-minded tolerance of the English permitted free expression of opinions such as this.

It was King George III who forced the colonists to cross their Rubicon. He was neither wicked nor stupid, and had a rather high conception of his duties. He was a hard worker and dreamed of being a good despot. But there is no such thing as a good despot. In order to dominate Parliament and the press he had corrupted them. The gangrene of this corruption had spread to the ministers, the army, and the navy. Thus the king, to reinforce his personal power, had weakened his realm. In his eyes the

American affair was a matter of honor. Moreover, he was playing a game the stakes in which transcended America. He was attempting to establish an absolute monarchy in his realm; if he failed in the colonies, the Whigs and constitutional monarchy would triumph in England. In his speech from the throne in October, 1775, he said that England would never renounce her colonies, that she would exact respect by force of arms, but that she would treat with indulgence her erring children if they sought the king's pardon. The unhappy sovereign could not understand how little disposed George Washington, with a thousand like him, would be to seek amnesty in the role of prodigal sons. This was the first blunder.

The second was to announce a policy based on strength at a time when the British Parliament had no strength. The English army in 1775 had numbered at most fifty thousand men, of whom twelve thousand were in Ireland and had to stay there, others in India, the West Indies, and Canada. England was opposed to obligatory service. In order to send soldiers to America, George III had to buy them from the petty German princes. From the Duke of Brunswick, the landgrave of Hesse-Cassel and a few others he bought the services of thirty thousand German soldiers for seven pounds apiece. In addition the landgrave and the duke were to receive seven thousand pounds a year each. These mercenaries could not be expected to fight with enthusiasm; in fact, many of them deserted and founded American farm families. But one can understand the fury of the Americans that their sovereign should send foreigners to fight against them. Even in England clear minds could see the threat to British liberties in this attack upon American liberties. "In order that Parliament may be free," Burke said, "it is necessary that the colonies be free"; and he added that the establishment of a military government in America would entail the same consequences for England. Bodies of armed troops, he said, who had learned to despise parliamentary assemblies, who had exacted high tribute without the consent of those who paid, who had not been subject to the ordinary tribunals in the country in which they served—such men could not be transformed by a mere voyage to such an extent as suddenly to respect in Great Britain the things they had been taught to despise in America. Burke's view was right; liberty is not divisible.

The speech from the throne had been an insult to Americans; the sending of foreign mercenaries was a provocation; the taking of Boston was an encouragement. After this, public sentiment which had hitherto been reserved swung over in favor of a break. The publication of a pamphlet brought about the crystallization of resistance. This pamphlet, called *Common Sense,* was the work of Thomas Paine, an unknown Englishman. This stranger, who was destined to arouse America, had up to that time made a lamentable failure of his life. Twice he had had small administrative posts and both times he had been discharged. His wife had left him. At a time of complete despair he had met Franklin, who was struck by the young man's magnificent eyes and gave him a letter of introduction. He arrived in Philadelphia in 1774 possessed of many grievances and a literary style. While Congress was sitting, he had spent his time in the streets of the city gathering news and sounding out public opinion. Finding the latter too indifferent, he had undertaken to arouse it by this pamphlet. The thing that made its success was the writer's direct and simple manner. Legal discussions were commencing to bore the public. The author of *Common Sense* paid no attention to the law. Did America, the America of the little people who worked in shops or on farms, benefit by remaining bound to England? It was a question for common sense, and common sense, Paine said, answered: "No."

"Has a government that is jealous of our prosperity," he wrote, "the right to govern us? Whoever replies no to this question is a partisan of independence, for independence simply signifies 'shall we make our own laws or leave this duty to the King who is the greatest enemy of this continent?'" If anyone were to reply that hitherto the colonies had prospered under this regime, he would retort: "You may as well say that hitherto a child has thrived on milk and so it will never be necessary to give him meat. . . . It is to the obvious interest of America to withdraw resolutely from European disputes. . . . No greater absurdity can be conceived than that of three million people rushing to the harbor each time a ship arrives to find out what liberties have been left them. . . . Liberty has been a fugitive in all quarters of the globe. Oh Americans! Receive this fugitive and prepare a refuge for humanity!" Paine went much farther even than Samuel Adams. He condemned all forms of government: "Society, in every state, is a blessing, but government even in its best state is an evil. . . . Of more worth is one honest man to society than all the crowned ruffians that ever lived. . . . The distance at which the Almighty has placed England and America is a strong and natural proof that the authority of the one over the other was never the design of Heaven. . . . There is something absurd in supposing a continent to be perpetually governed by an island." The effect of the pamphlet was prodigious. In London, Tom Paine was so hated that it became the style for English gentlemen to wear the initials T. P. in nails on the soles of their shoes so that they could stamp on them. In America, *Common Sense* became the Bible of the village radicals; one hundred twenty thousand copies were sold in less than three months. The radicals exulted; inveterate Tories were converted; and Washington himself called it "sound doctrine and unanswerable reason."

The opinion of Washington about Tom Paine and that of Tom Paine about Washington were not destined always to be so favorable.

On what grounds could a declaration of independence be based? For a long time the propaganda of the colonists had made use of legal arguments borrowed from the British tradition. "No taxation without representation. . . . No virtual representation. . . . We depend for our charters on the King and Parliament." These medieval theses did not seem completely adequate. The intellectual atmosphere of the times suggested a better base—that of natural law. In 1688 when the English Whigs wished to replace James II, the legal king, by William III, they had been forced to demolish the doctrine of divine right. Locke assumed the task, and in his *Treatises on Government* replying to the *Patriarcha* of Sir Robert Gilmer, he had demonstrated that every subject possesses certain natural rights and that if these are violated the social pact, the *covenant*, between the sovereign and his people is broken. This idea naturally appealed to Americans. It reached back to their origins, to the covenant of the first Pilgrims. It enabled them honorably to break one covenant, establish another, and to prove that they were independent of George III by virtue of "the laws of Nature and of Nature's God."

Washington had forcefully expressed himself in favor of independence, and his entry into Boston gave him great prestige. Virginia followed him, partly for political reasons, partly for economic ones. New England was completely in accord. "Is not America already independent?" asked Samuel Adams, "Why not say so?" New York, Pennsylvania, Maryland, and North Carolina were hesitant. Finally, on June 7, 1776, Richard Henry Lee of Virginia proposed to Congress the following measure: "That these united colonies are, and of right ought to be, free and independent states." It was decided that the preparation of a declaration of independence should be entrusted to a committee of which John Adams, Thomas Jefferson, Benjamin Franklin, Roger Sherman, and Robert Livingston were to be members.

Jefferson was a delegate from Virginia who had made a name for himself in the Congress. A man of thirty-two, already famous in his own section, he feared "the morbid violence of discussions" and remained silent during the meetings, but in committee and in conversation he was "prompt, frank, explicit and decisive." Moreover he wrote with clarity and had published a little treatise on America's rights which had attracted attention: "The God who gave us life," said Jefferson, "gave us liberty at the same time." Passionately attached to his principles, in discussion he showed the most exquisite urbanity. Convinced, but not fanatic, he was sufficiently modest to accept a compromise. On occasion he was paradoxical in conversation; in action he exhibited common sense. These qualities had resulted in his being chosen one of the committee; they had the further result of prompting the committee to entrust him with drawing up the Declaration. Adams, who also could have done this work, was the first to say: "You shall do it. First: you are a Virginian, and a Virginian ought to appear at the head of this business, Reason second: I am obnoxious, suspected and unpopular; you are very much otherwise. Reason three: you can write ten times better than I can." This coming from John Adams was high praise for the masterly pen of Jefferson. The latter set to work. Some emendations were made in his text by John Adams and Franklin. On July 1, nine states voted for its adoption, and three others the next day, leaving only New York. On July 4, after minor corrections, the Declaration was adopted unanimously by the delegates of twelve states. New York followed suit on July 9. Couriers bore it immediately to the four corners of the new nation.

The Declaration of Independence was addressed to the whole world: "When in the Course of human Events, it becomes necessary for one People to dissolve the Political Bands which have connected them with another, and to assume among the Powers of the Earth, the separate and equal Station to which the Laws of Nature and of Nature's God entitle them, a decent respect to the Opinions of Mankind requires that they should declare the causes which impel them to the Separation." There followed a statement of the principles on which the Declaration was based: "We hold these truths to be self-evident: That all Men are created equal; that they are endowed by their Creator with certain unalienable Rights; that among these are Life, Liberty, and the Pursuit of Happiness." This part of the Declaration, inspired by Locke, has served as a basis for all democratic movements in the world, beginning with the French Revolution. It affirms that the object of all government is to guarantee the rights of man; that all government derives its powers from the consent of the governed; that if a government fails to guarantee these rights, the duty of the people is to modify or abolish it. The rest of the document, of less permanent value, was a long list of grievances: the denial of representation, oppressive laws, acts of war. King George III was violently attacked, somewhat to the displeasure of John Adams: "I never believed George to be a tyrant in disposition and nature." But Jefferson loved tirades and fiery eloquence. The document ended: "We, therefore, the Representatives of the UNITED STATES OF AMERICA, in General Congress assembled, appealing to the Supreme Judge of the World for the Rectitude of our Intentions, do, in the Name, and by Authority of the good People of these

Colonies, solemnly Publish and Declare, That these United Colonies are, and of Right ought to be, Free and Independent States."

English historians have said that the Declaration of Independence is not an original document, that it owes most of its ideas to Locke, and that America has derived from England the doctrine that freed her from England. This is only partially true. Jefferson was always the first to say that he did not consider it, in any manner, his duty to invent entirely new ideas or to express sentiments that had never been expressed before. On the contrary, what had been asked of him was to express in a simple and clear fashion those ideas which had been adopted by a great number of Americans. In this he succeeded. The originality consisted not in the ideas but in the fact that these ideas for the first time became the charter of a nation and passed from the domain of theory into that of practice. Moreover there was in the Declaration of Independence something more than a paraphrase of the treatises of Locke. The realists in Congress would have contented themselves with the classic enumeration of the rights of man: life, liberty, and the ownership of property. For "property" Jefferson substituted "the pursuit of happiness," a term which had been used in the Virginia Bill of Rights, with which he was naturally familiar, and it is this substitution that gives the document "a note of idealism and makes its appeal an eternally human one." It was these words that gave the masses, who were still deprived at that time of political rights, the hope that the Revolution was made for them as much as for the middle classes.

CHAPTER XV

Military Operations

IT WAS the cannons' turn to speak. For the war in America the British government had a not unreasonable plan. England had control of the sea and so could take possession of the harbors and waterways. Of these latter the most important was the valley of the Hudson, the key to the campaign. If the English got control of that they could cut the colonies in two, thus rendering the administration of the new nation difficult and resistance impossible. Hence this plan: General Howe was to go by sea from Halifax to New York, take possession of this port, and proceed up the Hudson River; an army coming from Canada by way of Lake Champlain was to reach the river at Albany. By the juncture of these two forces the colonies would be divided. Meanwhile a third army, commanded by Sir Henry Clinton, was to land at Charleston and rally the southern loyalists. The fate of Clinton's army was quickly decided; for it was not even able to get ashore at Charleston, where it was welcomed by gunfire. "We never received such a drubbing in our lives," said one of the English sailors. This fleet, badly damaged, beat a hasty retreat, and at New York joined Howe's, which had come from Halifax.

Washington, who understood the importance of the Hudson Valley just as well as the English, had moved his army from Boston to New York by land and established his headquarters in that city in April, 1776. Forts Washington and Lee had been built to defend the entrance to the valley at the point where the George Washington bridge now stands. Washington's army numbered less than twenty thousand men; Sir William Howe's army was about thirty thousand strong, and the fleet gave him the advantage of mobility. The commander of this fleet was Lord Howe, a crusty but kindly man, taciturn and timorous, whom his men had nicknamed Black Dick. The two Howe brothers were Whigs and had never approved the colonial policy of George III; they kept hoping against hope that the affair could be settled without too much bloodshed. This state of mind influenced their actions from the start. When they arrived in New York they disembarked their troops on Staten Island; Washington's army held the southern point of Manhattan. Lord Howe was the bearer of a message from George III, a message which the king thought conciliatory and which the Americans thought offensive, for it offered Washington and his friends an amnesty from which John Adams was excluded. The letter was addressed to *George Washington, Esq.,* for the king did not recognize the title of General, Commander-in-Chief of the American forces. Lord Howe, hoping for peace, wrote: "George Washington, Esq, etc——" and told the officer who delivered the letter to say that "etc.——" could signify anything, including *Commander-in-Chief.* Washington smilingly replied that "etc.——" could indeed signify anything, including an insult. He transmitted the letter to Congress, which judged it unacceptable, and conciliation ended there.

Howe was in an advantageous position, for he had the means of landing his army wherever he wished in Washington's rear. What could the latter do? Nothing. He had neither enough troops to guard all the coast nor troops mobile enough to be rapidly transported to a threatened position. It was madness to try to defend New York, but such were the orders of Congress. Because the heights of Brooklyn commanded the city, Washington had detached some of his men and posted them on Long Island. This was a dangerous position for the Americans; they were dependent upon water transport for their communications and the enemy had control of the sea. On August 27 Howe dispatched half his army, under cover of night, across Long Island to take Brooklyn from the rear. He attacked at daybreak with complete success and the Americans lost two thousand men. They retreated, fighting as they went, but Washington's position on Manhattan was hardly better. How could he prevent the English from landing on the northern end of the island? Terrified New Yorkers meanwhile were imploring him not to abandon them. Luckily for him the Howes, who were more and more eager to make peace, sent one of their prisoners General Sullivan, to "sound out" Congress, and this allowed the army in New York a time of respite.

Congress also would have liked peace, but it distrusted the English and demanded first of all that the independence of the United States should be recognized. Howe did not have the authority to deal with this question and the parleys halted there. There was nothing left but to fight. The English fleet landed troops on the east shore of Manhattan at the place where 34th Street is today. On that day Howe could have cut off the retreat of a part of the American army, but he stopped for luncheon at the house of Mrs. Murray on Murray Hill, and during this time four thousand Americans under Israel Putnam were able to escape. Then Washington placed the larger part of his army on the right bank of the Hudson, and by a series of skillful maneuvres eluded the attacks of Howe, who attempted each time to turn the American position by landing and found each time that the Americans had withdrawn farther to the north. Finally Howe abandoned his plan, returned to Manhattan, and attacked Fort Washington. There he seized about three thousand men as well as cannon and ammunition. Fort Lee was abandoned in time, and what remained of the American army beat a retreat across New Jersey.

What remained of the American army? It was not much. Many of the men had come to the end of their period of enlistment and, discouraged by the propaganda of the New Jersey loyalists who told them the war was lost, chose to return to their homes. It was then that Thomas Paine wrote the fine and glowing phrases that were to become famous: "These are the times that try men's souls. The summer soldier and the sunshine patriot will, in this crisis, shrink from the service of his country; but he that stands it *now*, deserves the love and thanks of man and woman." Lee, whom Washington had left with seven thousand men on the Hudson farther to the north and whom he now ordered to join him, carefully

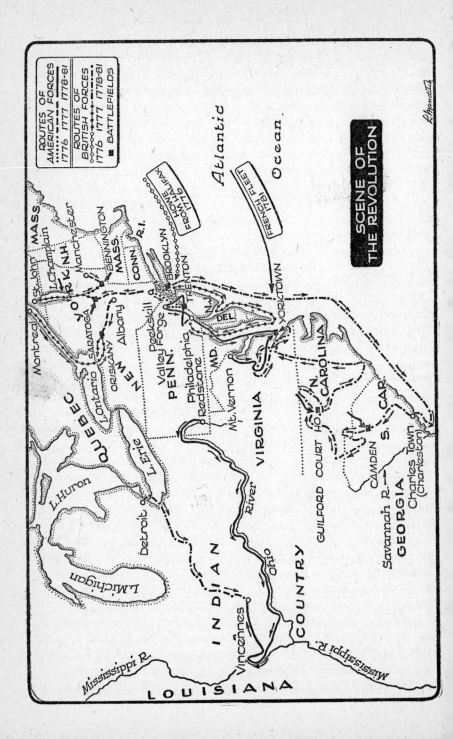

ROUTES OF
AMERICAN FORCES
1776 1777 1778-81

ROUTES OF
BRITISH FORCES
1776 1777 1778-81
■ BATTLEFIELDS

Atlantic

Ocean

HOWE HALIFAX
JUNE 1776
FROM

FRENCH FLEET
1781

SCENE OF
THE REVOLUTION

Montreal
St. John's
L. Champlain
MASS.
N.H.
Manchester
SARATOGA
BENNINGTON
MASS.
CONN.
R.I.
YORK
NEW
ORISKANY
Albany
L. Ontario
BROOKLYN
TRENTON
N.J.
DEL.
YORKTOWN
Peekskill
Valley Forge
PENN.
Philadelphia
Redstone
MD.
Mt. Vernon
VIRGINIA
GUILFORD COURT HO.
N. CAROLINA
CAMDEN
S. CAR.
Charles Town
(Charleston)
Savannah R.
GEORGIA

L. Huron
L. Michigan
L. Erie
Detroit
QUEBEC
Ohio
River
INDIAN
COUNTRY
Vincennes
Mississippi R.
LOUISIANA

refrained from moving and viewed without displeasure the difficulties that encompassed Washington, whom he considered feeble and incompetent. Soon Washington had no more than four thousand men with him. He crossed the Delaware and took refuge in Pennsylvania, close pressed by Howe and his army. If Washington had not taken all the boats across to the west shore, Howe would have been able to take Philadelphia within a few days. Congress had already left the city and fled to Baltimore. But it was only a postponement. Howe believed that whenever he wished he could take possession of the capital and that then the war would be over. But there was no hurry, and since Christmas was approaching he left for New York where he wished to spend the holidays, leaving his headquarters at Trenton under the protection of the German mercenaries. Washington, informed by his spies of Howe's movements, conceived the idea of an audacious stroke. He knew that Christmas was an important celebration for the Germans and that certainly on that day the river bank and the city would be poorly guarded. Moreover it was snowing; the Delaware was filled with drifting ice. No one would suspect an attack. On Christmas day Washington crossed the Delaware and seized Trenton. Then, when Lord Cornwallis was sent to drive him out, instead of fleeing and recrossing the Delaware, Washington allowed the enemy to advance and then boldly took up his position athwart the English lines of communication at Princeton. Cornwallis, in a panic, fearing to be cut off, beat a precipitate retreat. The skillful tactics of Washington had earned him his first victory. The colonel of militia was not a bad general.

But all these campaigns were not *the* campaign. The plan in London remained unalterable. Sir John Burgoyne was to come down from Canada with an army; Sir William Howe was to proceed up the Hudson with another army; and Colonel St. Leger, with a smaller force, was to come down the Mohawk. They were to meet at Albany and the war would be over. Lord George Germain, Secretary for the Colonies, in his office at Whitehall, approved the plan. But he did not take into account the fact that it is impossible, from a distance of five thousand miles, to foresee what difficulties there may be in an operation which involves penetrating virgin forests and crossing unexplored and hostile country. Finally, the failure of the campaign was assured when Burgoyne's army left Canada for Albany to meet an army which was not on its way to Albany.

For Howe, as the result of a misunderstanding due to delayed dispatches and inefficiency in London, had decided to take Philadelphia. It was a natural strategic mistake for a European to make, for whom the capital of a nation is its heart. But America was a body with thirteen hearts. During the spring of 1776 Howe had hesitated. He was ill informed about the condition of Washington's forces. To venture into New Jersey might mean to risk the re-enactment of the Cornwallis fiasco at Princeton. He tried in vain to draw Washington onto open ground, failed to do so, and thus squandered a large part of the year 1777. Finally in July he mysteriously embarked his army, leaving Clinton in New York. Where was he bound? Washington greatly feared that he was going to reoccupy Boston, which was very poorly defended at that time. At last, after five weeks of waiting, he learned that Howe had landed on the shores of Chesapeake Bay. And so it was Philadelphia that the English general was once more threatening. And he was going there by sea. Washington was delighted at this news. He had already sent General Gates with a small army against Burgoyne. As soon as it became clear that Howe was at a distance this task became easy. "Now let all New England turn out and entirely crush Genl Burgoyne!" wrote Washington. While this operation was going on Howe would take Philadelphia, but he would lose the campaign.

Sir John Burgoyne was something of a soldier, something of a politician, something of a dramatist, something of a courtier, and a perfect man of the world. He had pulled many strings to secure this command in place of General Carleton, and since he was the son-in-law of Lord Derby and well thought of at court, he had succeeded. On the success of his expedition he never entertained a doubt. How could civilians beat a professional soldier? After all, the journey by sea was not dangerous, and the passage through the forest which was to follow was very short. The army seemed adequate, seven thousand men plus six hundred or seven hundred Indian auxiliaries. Burgoyne, who was a gentleman, distrusted his savage allies. Before setting out he gathered them together and harangued them for three hours. He told them he was counting on their good behavior. No murders, no scalps, no pillage. Burke later on in the House of Commons made great fun of this speech: "My gentle lions, my human bears, my tender-hearted hyenas, go forth! But I exhort you, as you are Christians and members of civilized society, to take care not to hurt any man, woman or child. . . ." The Indians were surprised, disappointed, and offended and, as soon as things began to go badly, they disappeared with the arms, blankets, and provisions that they had been given. The English had been so sure that it was going to be nothing more than a simple military promenade that several officers had brought their wives and Burgoyne his mistress, who was also the wife of one of his officers.

At the start everything went well. Burgoyne took possession of Ticonderoga, which commanded the route through Lake Champlain. He captured prisoners and seized twenty-eight cannon. This news excited the enthusiasm of the king: "I have beaten them," he cried. "I have beaten the Americans!" But the English Colonel St. Leger, who was coming from Oswego to join Burgoyne, was stopped by the Americans and retraced his steps. The moment the English army entered the forest, its huge convoys became difficult to defend against pillaging Indians, whether enemies or friends. In this wild country bare of fields and houses it was impossible to find food for the men. Lines of communication became so long and difficult that a pound of salted meat, delivered in this forest, cost the British government thirty pounds sterling. The extremely sparse population turned out to be hostile. At the end of a month Burgoyne's troops were hungry and discouraged. The course of wisdom would have been to strike obliquely towards New England where at least he would have found a civilized country. But the orders of the War Office were explicit. He must proceed to Albany and there meet Howe. While the unhappy Burgoyne, through adherence to discipline, was hurrying to destruction, Howe was at sea with his army sailing toward Chesapeake Bay.

Soon Burgoyne's situation became desperate. An American army under General Lincoln cut off his retreat toward Canada; another American army, commanded by General Gates, barred the road to New York. When he attempted to attack, Gates, and especially Benedict Arnold, stopped him dead. He shut himself up at Saratoga and awaited his fate. What could he do? He had no provisions; he wasn't receiving any. His Indians had long since left him; his German mercenaries accepted defeat unregretfully. On October 17 Burgoyne capitulated. Five thousand men laid down their arms. Gates had promised them the honors of war and permission to embark at Boston for England. Congress disavowed him. Burgoyne's army wandered for a long time along the roads and finally through the fields of Massachusetts. When, later on, peace had been signed and a move was made to repatriate the army, it was discovered that it no longer existed. Many of the soldiers had become colonists. The virgin continent possessed such powers of assimilation that it transformed into citizens those who had come as enemies.

CHAPTER XVI

France Enters the War

THERE was one European power which was attentively observing the revolt of the English colonies and on which Burgoyne's capitulation was to have a great effect; this was France. She had been painfully humiliated by the Treaty of Paris. Great Britain had made the mistake of inserting in it a clause that a proud people could not forgive —the obligation upon France to dismantle the Forts of Dunkirk and the right of England to install a commissioner in that city. French statesmen were hoping, not for military revenge, but for a weakening of England. This feeling was stronger, moreover, among the ministers and soldiers than at court and among the people. All cultured Frenchmen were at that time Anglomaniacs. Voltaire and Montesquieu had made English ideas fashionable. Intellectuals went to London to win their diplomas as thinkers. Le Tourneur's *Shakespeare* was the rage. To all appearances the two countries were reconciled; actually each government was pursuing the other with a meticulous and Machiavellian hatred. England was secretly encouraging the Corsicans to revolt; Choiseul, the French prime minister, was delighted at hearing of a riot in London. "Never," he said, "will the English cut as many of their own throats as I could wish." Since 1768 he had been observing the beginnings of an American revolution, and had rubbed his hands over it. His agents in America sent him reports on its progress. Meanwhile he was quietly rebuilding the French fleet. At the end of the Seven Years' War this had numbered only forty-seven ships of the line and ten frigates in deplorable condition; by 1771 France already had sixty-four ships of the line and forty-five frigates in good order. The mastery of the seas was quietly changing hands.

Louis XVI succeeded Louis XV and Vergennes succeeded Choiseul. Vergennes was not a genius, but he possessed experience, common sense, prudence, and patriotism. That is enough to make a statesman. He did not want war, but he believed that anything which weakened England strengthened France, and that the rebellious colonies ought to be discreetly encouraged. This policy alarmed his colleague Turgot, minister of finance, who thought that a war would ruin the country. The young king did not support Vergennes in this matter. Louis XVI was what George III wished to be—an absolute monarch. Why should he support rebels? Moreover the foreign policy of France was tied up, through the Family Compact, with that of Spain; and the latter, because she lived on her American colonies, could not approve colonial revolution. "If you are determined at all costs to free some country from the English yoke," said the Spaniards, "why don't you free the Irish Catholics?" King Charles III of Spain thought that it did not comport with the dignity of two monarchs openly to support a people against their sovereign. Nevertheless, it was to his advantage to encourage the insurrection and supply arms for it, but in secret. "We must hope," the Spanish minister wrote, "that the Americans and the English will exhaust each other." It is a hope that numerous peoples have entertained at all epochs in history whenever two other nations were at war.

To aid the colonies without going as far as war, this was Vergennes's program. But how was it to be carried out? Every action of the French government was spied upon by Lord Stormont, the English ambassador. It was necessary to find some individual, who might at need be disavowed, and charge him with the task of secretly furnishing supplies. There was a man who seemed especially made to play this role, a man rich in ingenuity, poor in capital, daring in action, and a steadfast friend of liberty. This was Caron de Beaumarchais, a writer of genius and an adventurer by profession. In London Beaumarchais had met an American, Arthur Lee, who had talked to him about the needs of his fellow countrymen and the ease with which this great nation could pay, in tobacco and other commodities, for what it bought. Arthur Lee was an accomplished and dangerous liar; but Beaumarchais, who did not know this, immediately saw the possibility of a glorious and profitable transaction. On his return he made his report to Vergennes, and it was decided that Beaumarchais should found a fictitious business houses: RODRIGUE HORTALEZ ET CIE.; and that the French government and the Spanish government should each contribute one million pounds to the imaginary Hortalez, who was to make use of this capital to buy uniforms, cannon, and powder for the Americans. It is easy to imagine the joy that the author of the *Barber of Seville* would derive from the task of creating out of whole cloth and lodging in a fine hotel in the Faubourg du Temple a Spanish merchant as powerful as he was fictitious. Life became a comedy madder than any on the stage. Actually, Beaumarchais, the secret agent, was more active than secret. Lord Stormont, who had got wind of the affair, went to Vergennes and inquired whether France was supporting the enemies of England. Vergennes replied with imperturbable gravity that there could be no question of that.

Meanwhile the United States Congress and its Committee of Foreign

Correspondence (which was functioning as the State Department), learning of the favorable sentiment in France, began to think about making use of it. But certain delegates were hesitant. They still belonged to the English tradition. To seek an alliance with an enemy of England was high treason. And then the French—Papists and friends of the Indians! But necessity made a quick end of their scruples. Clothing, arms, and money were lacking. It was decided to send Silas Deane, a member of Congress from Connecticut. Why Silas Deane, who was not a diplomat and did not know a word of French? Because he was rich and lived in luxury that amazed the colonists and led them to believe that a court would not amaze him. Vergennes received the American envoy, told him that, since France was at peace with England, he could not officially act, but that he would close his eyes to everything that was done unofficially. He urged Silas Deane to negotiate with Rodrigue Hortalez, that is to say, with Beaumarchais, to whom the French arsenals would deliver excellent cannon, first effacing, to be sure, from a sense of decency and prudence, the king's arms. The mythical Hortalez evinced incomparable energy, delivered materials of war sufficient to equip about twenty-five thousand men, but was never paid. In vain the unhappy Beaumarchais, who had risked in this enterprise not only the governments' two million pounds but his own small personal fortune and that of his friends, demanded the promised tobacco. Nothing, or next to nothing, came. Arthur Lee, who had become a personal enemy of Beaumarchais, told the American Congress that there was nothing to pay, that the material furnished was a gracious gift from the French government, and that the pretended claims of Beaumarchais were only a comedy designed to fool England. Congress believed Arthur Lee. The more Beaumarchais cried out and lamented, the more America replied with a knowing smile: "Oh yes indeed, we realize that you have to say these things and that we're not supposed to pay any attention! . . ." A scene worthy of *The Marriage of Figaro*. The misunderstanding was not cleared up during Beaumarchais's life and he died in poverty in 1799. Thirty-six years later his heirs obtained, with great difficulty, a small part of the sum which, all jurists agreed, was their due.

After the Declaration of Independence, Congress appointed Franklin, Jefferson, and Deane as its official representatives in France. Jefferson declined and was replaced by Arthur Lee. Franklin, who was very well known in France, was an excellent choice and he accepted. He said he was old and not good for anything but, as the merchants say of their remnants, they could have him for whatever they chose to give. He was instructed to secure a commercial treaty, a loan, and an alliance—a delicate piece of negotiation. "In short," Franklin said, "what is required of me is to say to France: 'help us and we will feel no obligation toward you.'" But his mission was aided by his prestige. Everything contributed to it: his fame as a scientist, his reputation as a sage, the simplicity of his appearance, his wit in conversation. The philosophy of Poor Richard was that of the French middle class. His experiments with lightning were well known. "We have seen him disarming tyrants and gods," was written under his portrait by Carmontelle, and Turgot resorted to Latin in order to praise him: "Eripuit caelo fulmen sceptrumque tyrannis." The Academy of Sciences made him one of their members; he regularly attended its meetings. He met Voltaire and the two famous ancients embraced before an enraptured public. In vain the English ambassador sought to create the illusion that Franklin was unpopular in his own country and was more of a refugee than an ambassador. At court and in the city there was talk only of "the great Franklin."

The Franklin legend answered the sentimental and intellectual needs of the French people. It was the time of the *Nouvelle Héloïse* and the dairy at the Trianon, the time when a simple and rustic life was the style. As a matter of fact there was nothing rustic about Franklin, and he was more subtle than simple. But he knew how to play to perfection the role expected of him. Once he saw the success of his fur cap and spectacles he wore them everywhere. Having inadvertently received a delegation without his wig, and having observed the prodigious effect of this negligence, he turned the accident into a rule, and gave up the wig. The Parisians thought he was a Quaker; he was careful not to deny it. Ancient republicans were the style; the Americans seemed like contemporaries of Cato and Fabius. In theory the king of France was an absolute monarch; in practice, he depended on a public opinion; it was the opinion of those small groups in Paris and Versailles who, though they had no rights, no vote, no arms, imposed their ideas upon the ministers. Now these groups were the ones that idolized Franklin. The young nobles admired him, just as they exalted Voltaire and Rousseau. In France of this time, seething as it was with ideas, people talked of "independence in the camps, democracy in the chateaux, philosophy in the ballrooms and virtue in the boudoirs." America became the promise of that liberty which they hoped for and awaited. "New England has more sages than Greece." Congress was the Roman Senate. Every young man wanted to fight for the insurgents. Grimm talks of the enthusiasm that impelled youngsters to leave father, mother, and brothers and go to the aid of an Esquimo or a Hottentot if it were in the name of liberty. This intellectual atmosphere in France, as much as reasons of state, determined the actions of Vergennes.

Volunteers came in throngs. Many things drew them toward America: the nobleness of the cause, their rancor against England, desire for adventure, the virgin forests, the beautiful Indian girls, the hope of rapid advancement. Silas Deane, a vain and thoughtless man, began by accepting all those who presented themselves. By 1776 he was deluged. "The rage for enlisting in the service of America continues to increase and consequently I am submerged with offers, many of which come from persons of high rank." The commissioners were no longer able to answer all the letters. When Franklin arrived, he had great trouble in discouraging so many zealous friends, each of whom thought he was a Caesar. "You have no idea the pains people take, without personal interest, to recommend candidates." Many officers, who had been accepted by Silas Deane and to whom he had, without authority, promised commissions, were ill received by Congress when they arrived in America. They were disappointing and disappointed. The Americans were justly irritated to find themselves commanded by Europeans who did not even speak their language. The volunteers, who expected to be greeted with grateful enthusiasm, were filled with consternation at the coolness of their reception. But the best of them, as always happens, triumphed over troublesome prejudices.

Such was the case of the young Marquis de Lafayette. This nineteen-year-old officer belonged to two of the great families of France, one by birth, the other by alliance, for at the age of sixteen he had married Marie-Françoise de Noailles, daughter of the Duke d'Ayen and granddaughter of the Duke de Noailles. He had very quickly felt oppressed by his wife's family, which was all powerful at the court of Versailles. His father-in-law had made him an officer of the Noailles Regiment. At court he did not appear to good advantage, for he had more intelligence than wit. The queen had not been able to refrain from laughing at his awkwardness in the hunting field. He wanted to escape from surroundings for which he did not feel fitted. Later on, Jefferson was to say of him that he had a voracious appetite for popularity; this was because he had missed success at the outset. But he was impelled by other and more noble sentiments. It was at Metz that he had first heard the Duke of Gloucester, who was the brother and enemy of the English king, talk about the American Revolution. The Duke said that right was on the side of the colonies; at Metz he made two converts, the Count de Broglie and the young Lafayette. Broglie conceived at that time the idea of making America the scene of France's revenge against England, but he was too important a personage to go in any capacity save that of commander-in-chief. Lafayette with two of his friends, the Viscount de Noailles and the Count de Ségur, went to Silas Deane and asked to be accepted for service.

Silas Deane had not yet enlisted recruits of such quality, and he was so dazzled that he promised a commission as Major General to a boy. But when the Duke d'Ayen learned of his son-in-law's plans, he raised a great uproar. Moreover the French government, if it wanted to maintain its fiction of neutrality, could not allow members of three such noble families to enter the service of the rebels. Noailles and Ségur bowed. Lafayette secretly bought a ship, *La Victoire*, fled to Bordeaux, then to Spain with other officers, and ordered the captain to set sail for North America. For his young wife, who was pregnant at the time, he left a letter: "I hope that for love of me you will become a good American." In June, 1777, after fifty-four days at sea, he landed at Georgetown in South Carolina. From there he proceeded to Philadelphia where, after having been forced to wait with his friends in the street in front of Independence Hall, he was coldly received by a member of Congress who treated him as an adventurer. "We have asked nothing from you." It was discouraging, and many of the French officers were filled with bitterness and decided to return to France. Lafayette, however, wrote to Congress that after the sacrifices he had made for the cause, he believed he had the right to request two favors; that of serving without pay and at his own expense and that of serving as a volunteer and ordinary soldier. The tone was proud; moreover Congress had just received a letter from Franklin recommending kind treatment for these young men whose influence might in future be useful. Soon the Marquis de Lafayette was a major general in the United States army. He was not yet twenty years old.

He joined Washington at the time when Howe was marching against Philadelphia, and took part in the confused and indecisive battle of Brandywine, where he conducted himself well and was wounded. When, after the loss of the city, Washington established his winter quarters at Valley Forge, not far from Philadelphia, Lafayette followed him. Washington had at once been attracted to the young man and had adopted him. They were born to understand each other. Neither of the two men was brilliant, and their caution was a bond; both had good manners; both had a sense of honor. The foreigners who had joined the American army before Lafayette had criticized everything and thereby displeased the officers. When Lafayette was shown men in rags and his opinion was asked, he replied: "I am here to learn, not to teach."

This attitude was all the more appreciated inasmuch as the army was in a pitiful state. The winter at Valley Forge had been frightful. Many of the soldiers had no shoes and the roads were stained with streaks of blood from their feet. Often bread was lacking. The continental dollar had fallen so low that it took a wagonload of bills to pay for a wagonload of food. Many of the soldiers deserted; some of those who remained were without clothes. There was a regiment consisting of but thirty men and a company composed of a single corporal. Add to this the quarrels of the politicians, the intrigues of the generals, the swindling of the contractors. Sometimes even Washington's patience was exhausted by the complaints of armchair strategists, who blamed him for not acting and demanded the immediate opening of a battle front. Adams himself, who had had him made commander-in-chief, criticized him now and at the end of a dinner cried: "My toast is: A short war and a violent one!" Washington replied with great dignity that it was much easier to remonstrate from the fireside in a comfortable room than to seize some barren and frozen hillside or to sleep beneath the snow. The time came when even he was doubtful of victory—for reasons of morale rather military considerations. He said that at a time when unity was so essential, distrust and jealousy controlled men's minds and partisan passions ruled the day. This, he added, gave rise to gloomy reflections and presaged nothing good. But he quickly regained his confidence: "We should never despair. Our situations has before been unpromising and has changed for the better; so I trust it will again. If new difficulties arise, we must put forth new exertions and proportion our efforts to the exigencies of the times."

Naturally the great desire of Congress was to secure a treaty of alliance with France. French public opinion strongly favored it, and there was criticism of Vergennes's slowness. But the latter still hesitated. The affairs of the colonists were going badly. Franklin might say all he liked to the contrary and might retort, when someone said to him that Howe had taken Philadelphia: "No, Sir, Philadelphia has taken Howe," it was still hard to keep up one's confidence. "When I hear such talk," Lord Stormont laughed, "I make no reply. I leave that to General Howe and I am sure that, sooner or later, it will be as good a reply as has ever been made." This was also the feeling of Spain, which would have liked to give the Americans "just enough support to nourish their hopes," but no more. The news from America chilled Vergennes's enthusiasm. Was it wise to expose oneself to the danger of a war with England in order to go to the aid of the vanquished? Who was this Benjamin Franklin? In the event of victory, an ambassador; in the event of a defeat, a traitor. But suddenly, with Burgoyne's capitulation, hope changed sides. The news was brought to France in November, 1777, by a brigantine that made the crossing from Boston in thirty days. Franklin communicated it to his friend and contractor Beaumarchais, who showed such eagerness in rushing to spread it that his carriage upset and he dislocated his arm. The *Times* of London itself was forced to admit the authenticity of the news: "General Burgoyne has surrendered to Mr. Gates," said the *Times*. For a rebel, even a victorious one, cannot be a general. This success of the insurgents decided Vergennes. No chance must be given England of making a peace of reconciliation with the Americans. On December 17, 1777, Franklin was informed that Louis XVI had decided to recognize the independence of the United States and to sign a treaty of commerce and friendship. In exchange for this alliance, France demanded no special return. She did not want to take anything that the Americans might regret in the future; she did not desire any territory. The only condition was that neither ally should make a separate peace. "Such was the bounty of the King," the American commissioners acknowledged, that nothing was proposed to them that they could not accept in a spirit of perfect understanding.

CHAPTER XVII

Rochambeau and Victory

IT WOULD have been to England's interest to prosecute the war vigorously and bring it to a quick conclusion. But the England of George III was not that of Pitt. It would have been easy for Sir William Howe to wipe out Washington at Valley Forge, where he had gone into winter quarters with eleven thousand hungry and half-naked men, one-fifth of whom deserted before the winter was over. Howe did not do it. Why? Perhaps because as a Whig liberal he had scruples; perhaps because of the bitter memory of Bunker Hill; perhaps because he hoped that the revolutionary movement would fall to pieces of itself; perhaps because Philadelphia, where he had a charming mistress, had become this Hannibal's Capua. And yet what easy prey his adversaries offered! The authority of Congress was weak, its administration deplorable. Eloquence cannot create resources. An orator in a town meeting is not a financier. The continental dollar was so far depreciated that some Americans, Tories by interest and perhaps by conviction, preferred to sell their powder, butter, and meat to the English. Intrigues further weakened what remained of the armies. General Gates, intoxicated by his success against Burgoyne, schemed against Washington with the Irishman Conway, whom Congress had made a brigadier general and who, like all brigadier generals, thought that he was really meant to be a major general. Conway carried on a campaign for Gates in the lobbies of Congress. He said that Washington had won only one battle, and that on a snowy night against a few drunken Germans. Washington confronted those who wanted to replace him with his customary impassivity and dignity, and Gates was eliminated. Lafayette, who had at first been taken in by Conway, wrote to Washington: "I have discovered that he is dangerously ambitious. He has done everything to destroy my confidence in you and my affection for you. . . . If you were lost to America no one would be capable of holding the army together for six months. . . ." It was true. In this time of misery and doubt, Washington was the Revolution. Without him it would have collapsed.

In England Howe was criticized for his inaction. "Anyone but Howe would have defeated General Washington," people said. "Anyone but General Washington would have defeated General Howe." At length, in the spring of 1778, Howe was recalled by London and Sir Henry Clinton succeeded him. The Tories of Philadelphia gave Howe a touching farewell celebration. There was a tourney of officers costumed as Turks, a triumphal arch surmounted by a statue of Fame, and classical and country dances. War in ruffles. Sir Henry Clinton was less sensible than Sir William Howe to the delights of Philadelphia. He decided to take the army and the fleet back to New York. This time the army made the journey by land across New Jersey. Washington, whose strategy seemed to be to have none, to follow the English and to harry them, attacked Clinton's army at Monmouth without decisive result. Clinton gained New York with his ten thousand men, and Washington established his headquarters at West Point on the Hudson River. From there he could keep watch over Clinton and await the arrival of his new allies.

The first French fleet was commanded by Count d'Estaing, a newly appointed admiral who had made his career in the army. He was a man "of brilliant conceptions and feeble execution. His vision was large and his activity small." His orders were vague; he was "to take such action as would be advantageous to the Americans and would glorify the King's armies," and to spend the winter in the West Indies. But what action? In a maneuver planned in consultation with the American General Sullivan, he tried to take Newport. It was a failure for which, as always happens among allies when they are unsuccessful, the French blamed the Americans and the Americans the French. The loyalist fifth column circulated stories that the French were coming to establish the New Bastille, that the teaching of English would be forbidden, that Samuel

Adams had been forced to abjure Protestantism, that a ship full of con-secrated wafers and chasubles had arrived in Boston, and other absurdities in which, as was fitting, the witless took delight. Lafayette, overjoyed at the arrival of his compatriots, exerted himself to straighten out misunder-standings, but his position was a delicate one. In the eyes of the French army he was a subaltern and a deserter; in the eyes of the American army he was a general and a hero. "You must find it absurd," he said timidly to D'Estaing, "to see that I have become a sort of general. I admit that it makes me laugh myself."

Clinton had decided, after long hesitation, to go and fight in the South. After the Burgoyne affair the North dismayed him; he knew New Eng-land was hostile. On the other hand, Tory refugees who had come from the South to New York assured him that the Carolinas and Georgia were only waiting for the arrival of the English to rise against Congress. But the refugees had mistaken their personal resentment for the sentiment of their native sections. As a matter of fact the English, despite the bril-liant victory of Cornwallis over Gates at Camden, were never able to pacify the South where the patriots kept up a redoubtable guerrilla war-fare. D'Estaing had long since left for the West Indies. Victory and peace seemed farther away than ever.

At the end of 1778, Lafayette had asked for and obtained a leave of absence to go to France. He wished to reawaken enthusiasm for the American cause, which defeats and Count d'Estaing's unfavorable com-ments had inevitably dampened. Washington willingly let him go, be-lieving that he was more useful as a propagandist than as a soldier. He was well received at Versailles. The queen herself was eager to see him and hear him speak of "our good Americans." His presence alone and the emotion it excited were the best propaganda. To Maurepas and Vergennes he convincingly explained the situation in America. The French minis-ters at that time were thinking of an invasion of England, and all through the summer of 1779 a fleet was concentrated at Le Havre and Saint-Malo. This project miscarried, but everywhere else there were French squadrons at sea, and what Lafayette asked in the name of the Americans was both possible and easy. He requested that a body of four or five thousand sol-diers be sent to the aid of the United States. Versailles raised two objec-tions: The Americans did not seem to be in agreement with one another, and French troops had not been well received. Moreover Spain, to which France was bound by a Family Compact and which was engaged in a war against England, having a colonial empire itself was not much in sym-pathy with the colonists' cause. Lafayette replied that so far as he was con-cerned, Washington was enough to inspire confidence and that if he,

Lafayette, were to command the French, they would be well received. In the end he persuaded the ministers and they decided to send six thousand men to be placed at the personal disposal of General Washington to use as he saw fit. But since Lafayette was too young and inexperienced, command of the expedition was given to the Count de Rochambeau. Lafayette, however, was to precede the troops and announce to Washington the success of his mission (February, 1780).

Because the minister of the navy was Monsieur de Sartines, "whose watch was always slow," Rochambeau and his army were at Brest long before the transports. The latter arrived by such slow degrees that Rochambeau finally decided to wait no longer and left with fifty-five hundred men but without his cavalry. He had two fine regiments and officers who bore the greatest names in France: Montmorency, Custine, Chartres, Noailles, Lauzun. In July, 1780, the convoy arrived without losses within sight of Rhode Island; at Newport the troops were well received. "The French officers of all ranks made themselves agreeable by that courtesy which characterizes the French nation." As a matter of fact, the people of Newport were a little afraid they would make themselves *too* agreeable. The Duke de Lauzun had the reputation of paying court to every woman he met. In Newport he was lodged in the home of a beautiful Puritan woman. He was sensitive enough to understand the difference between such a hostess and Madame du Barry. These handsome soldiers, well dressed, well armed, who paid in gold for what they bought and who created such an impression of strength and ease, aroused great hopes. But Rochambeau had not come from France to enable his officers to dance in Newport. As D'Estaing had formerly done, he asked himself: "What is the most useful thing for me to do?" Lafayette, who was acting as liaison officer, advised the capture of New York. Rochambeau was not anxious to take advice from a boy. He was fond of Lafayette, but he talked to him as a father to a son rather than as one general to another: "The warmth of your soul," he said to him, "has somewhat affected the soundness of your judgment." Which was true, but hardly polite. Finally Rochambeau had an opportunity to see Washington himself at Hartford. The French general staff were delighted by the American commander-in-chief. He seemed to them frank, dignified, a little sad, and very impressive in manner: "A true hero." Lafayette served as interpreter. The two generals, Rochambeau and Washington, agreed to ask the king of France for reinforcements. To win the war they would need thirty thousand men and control of the sea.

Upon his return from Hartford, Washington met a painful surprise. The most important strategic position for the American army was West Point. There a passage between high banks made it possible to control all shipping on the Hudson. Washington had entrusted the command of this position to Benedict Arnold, a civilian who had proved himself a military leader since the beginning of the war and who had contributed more than anyone else to the defeat of Burgoyne. Washington was unaware that this excellent soldier had become a bad citizen. He had been court-martialed for rather trivial reasons, and although he had been acquitted, he had retained a feeling of resentment. He thought he had been unfairly treated by Congress. Moreover, having married a Philadelphia woman with loyalist sympathies, he now secretly sided with the English. Using an English secret agent, young Major André, as intermediary, he negotiated with Clinton and proposed to turn over West Point. A heavy iron chain barred the river. It was agreed that on an appointed day, under pretext of making repairs, Arnold should replace one of the links of the chain with rope, which would allow the English fleet to break through. But Major André, on his way back from one of his interviews with Benedict Arnold, was caught by the Americans. He was carrying papers that proved Arnold's treason. André was hanged as a spy. Arnold, warned in time, succeeded in escaping, and became Clinton's adviser. "You can win the war very quickly," he told the English general, and actually in January, 1781, the Americans seemed lost. The English fleet under Rodney was blockading them. The American soldiers, not being paid, or clothed, or fed, were becoming discouraged. "These people are at the end of their resources," wrote Rochambeau, and he urgently requested reinforcements and money.

France's response was generous. It was brought by the ship *La Concorde* on May 16, 1781. Six million pounds in gold was sent to Washington, thus enabling him at length to pay his army. Moreover, Admiral Count de Grasse had left for the West Indies with a large fleet, and through all the summer he would be at Washington's disposal. There was urgent need of preparing plans for this campaign at once. Washington suggested an attack on New York, which remained, in his eyes, the strategic center of the colonies. Rochambeau hesitated; he would have preferred a campaign against Cornwallis, who was winning Pyrrhic victories in the South against Greene and was being drawn farther and farther from his bases into a hostile country by an adversary who was skillful, mobile, and always out of reach. Cornwallis persistently begged Clinton to come to his aid. Clinton, however, believing that Washington was preparing to attack New York, ordered Cornwallis to retire to a port in Virginia so as to be under the protection of the fleet, to secure this port with a small garrison, and to send reinforcements to New York. Benedict Arnold, who was now in command of a British army, urgently counseled the two English generals to concentrate their efforts, remarking that a team pulling in different directions would not get far. Finally Cornwallis obeyed orders and assembled his army of about seven thousand men in the port of Yorktown at the mouth of the York River in Chesapeake Bay. The French army had set out from Newport toward New York, and Clinton was more than ever convinced that New York was to be the point of attack.

Unfortunately for him, the advice of Rochambeau was adopted. The French had been informed of the impending arrival of Admiral de Grasse in Chesapeake Bay. The fleet would be able to support the army there. The defenses of Yorktown were much less formidable than those of New York. At length the decision was made. The French army and the American army, now united, crossed New Jersey on their way to Virginia. For the American veterans it was familiar territory; for Washington a pilgrimage to the scenes of his only victories; for the French an expedition through a countryside whose autumn foliage delighted them. In Philadelphia they were given a triumphal reception and learned that twenty-eight ships of the line had just arrived in Chesapeake Bay and had landed three thousand men who had joined Lafayette. Cornwallis had expected Rodney's fleet; he saw Admiral de Grasse's instead. Soon sixteen thousand men were besieging Yorktown. An English fleet under Admiral Graves tried to break the blockade of the city. The combined strength of the two French squadrons, the one from Newport and the one under Admiral de Grasse, gave the French such naval superiority that Admiral Graves was defeated in Chesapeake Bay and had to beat a retreat toward New York. There remained only one hope for Cornwallis: the arrival of Clinton with an army to relieve him. But Clinton delayed. He finally embarked on October 19. That was the day when Yorktown surrendered. Some historians have blamed Cornwallis for not having attempted a sortie. "I thought," he said, "it would have been wanton and inhuman to sacrifice the lives of this small body of gallant soldiers." The English army filed past between two lines of victors, one French, the other American, in respectful silence. Washington and Rochambeau allowed no civilian to be present at this ceremony in order not to humiliate the brave soldiers. Cornwallis had asked to be put on the sick list and did not appear. The general who took his place started to give his sword to Rochambeau; the latter, with a courteous gesture, pointed to Washington. But the real victor of the day was Admiral de Grasse. The sequel to this story is a strange example of the instability of human affairs. Cornwallis, the vanquished, was to remain a respected man in his own country and to become governor general of India, then viceroy of Ireland; while Admiral de Grasse was to lose his fleet soon after in the West Indies and die in poverty and disgrace.

CHAPTER XVIII

The Making of the Peace

THE capture of Yorktown was not an event of such importance that it must inevitably have led to peace. A great country like England, which had as yet thrown only a small part of its resources into this war, could easily have continued the struggle if it had been willing to accept the necessary sacrifices. But English public opinion was becoming hostile to this campaign. Great orators—Chatham, Burke, Fox—were making it unpopular; the Whigs called Washington's army "our army" and discouraged enlistments; Dr. Johnson and Edward Gibbon, whom the ministry employed to defend its policy, did not have the same prestige. The merchants wept for their lost clients and hoped for a reconciliation. After all, what did it matter whether the colonies were independent so long as they were still markets? "Strike, but buy," the merchants of the city said to America. American privateers had done, and continued to do, much damage to British commerce. In the single year of 1777 more than four hundred and fifty English ships had been captured. A single ship-owner, Nathaniel Tracy, had gained more than three million dollars in prizes. John Paul Jones, the American sailor who had brought Franklin the news of Burgoyne's surrender, covered himself with glory in many a battle. Congress, for its part, favored peace provided it was an honorable one. In 1779 it had decided to send a plenipotentiary to Paris, and hesitated for some time between John Adams, Jay, and Franklin. The last had been much maligned in Congress, as had been the case throughout his career, and John Adams inspired more confidence than did Jay in New England, which wanted its fishing rights adequately safeguarded during the peace negotiations. And so Jay was appointed minister to Madrid, and Adams was instructed to prepare plans for the peace, but he was to act in accord with Franklin and Jay. In addition to the fishing rights and independence, the thorny points were: the western frontier of the United States, the navigation of the Mississippi, and indemnity to the loyalists. The last was particularly delicate because England could not honorably abandon her loyal subjects who had lost everything for her, while in the eyes of the colonists these worthies were traitors, justly stripped of their possessions.

The choice of John Adams was not altogether a happy one. Adams had valuable qualities of education and honesty, but his character was not that of a diplomat: "He not only suspected of wickedness those who differed from him, but he was sure they were wicked." He distrusted the charm of the French, their courtesy, their adroitness. For the first time in his life he did not feel at ease. He believed the French considered him a bigot and a fanatic. Not speaking a word of their language, he could not make them accept his superiority. He discovered, not without surprise, Franklin's popularity in Paris, but he had never liked his colleague. "Franklin loves his ease, hates to offend, and seldom gives any opinion till obliged to do it. . . . It is his constant policy never to say yes or no decidedly but when he cannot avoid it." Adams, for his part, preferred brutal frankness which seemed to him more republican. To acknowledge that the United States owed a great deal to the alliance with France was distressing to Adams's pride. He said that the war had been already won, that the weather had served to destroy the English. "I think," Franklin wrote, "an expression of gratitude is not only our duty, but our interest. . . . Mr. Adams, on the other hand, seems to think a little apparent stoutness, and a greater air of independence and baldness, will procure us more ample assistance." If one listened to Adams, the colonies owed nothing to France and France owed everything to the colonies. At the moment of Rochambeau's departure, he feigned a great indifference to the military aid of France and said that America could quite well win the war all by herself. Vergennes was angered, and wrote to La Luzerne, his minister in Philadelphia, that Adams's pedantry, arrogance, and vanity made him unsuitable for negotiations. Adams, for his part, had taken a dislike to France and the French. He said of the French: "They are not a moral people." He suspected Vergennes of aiding the loyalists in order to maintain the seeds of division in America. Vergennes did all he possibly could to deal only with Franklin, without whom a break would quickly have occurred between America and her ally. Adams left Paris and tried to negotiate a loan in Holland. On that occasion he failed, and it was necessary for Vergennes to forget his grievances and, thinking only of the common cause, to borrow two million from the Dutch himself in order to give it to the Americans.

When Congress learned from Franklin and La Luzerne of Adams's unpopularity in Paris, it decided to have him joined by other commissioners, Jay, Laurens, and Jefferson, "to oppose him in those vagaries which his too ardent imagination and his stubborness never failed to produce." Laurens was captured by the British and Jefferson stayed at home, but Adams was none the less irritated: "Congress," he said, "surrenders their own sovereignty into the hands of a French minister. Blush, blush, ye guilty records! Blush and perish!" The instructions of Congress to its commissioners were that they should make the frankest and most confidential communications on all subjects to the ministers of "our generous ally, the King of France"; that they should not undertake anything at all in the negotiations for the peace or the armistice without their approval; and finally that they should be governed by their advice and opinions. The advice and opinions of the French government were simple. The government wanted peace. The war had been, and still was, costly to France, whose finances were already compromised. France had no territorial ambition: she wanted neither to get back Canada nor to see it annexed by the United States. But she had made commitments to Spain, and the latter refused to make peace until Gibraltar was restored to her. Meanwhile the United States was giving very little thought to Spain, and none at all to Gibraltar. It wanted independence, an indemnity or in place of that Canada, a settlement of the western boundary question and of the fishing rights. As for England, since Yorktown she had, at heart, accepted defeat. Lord George Germain had gone to take the news of the surrender to Lord North at 10 Downing Street. A friend asked him afterwards: "How did he take it?" "How did he take it? As he would have taken a ball in the breast. For he opened his arms, exclaiming wildly as he paced up and down the apartment during a few minutes: 'O God! It is all over!'" The king began by saying that he hoped no one would think that these events would alter his principles. The poor king never suspected that in saying that he had given an excellent definition of folly. But "facts are stubborn things." In February, 1782, a motion in favor of peace was defeated in Parliament by a single vote. Lord North's ministry was replaced by Rockingham's ministry, a Whig cabinet in which Fox was foreign secretary.

Lord Shelburne, minister of the colonies in the new Whig ministry, was an old friend of Franklin and the most liberal of men. The astute and courteous Franklin sent a note of congratulations and a secret negotiation began between the two men. The English offered the colonies their independence on condition that the peace between France and England should honor the Treaty of Paris. "This seems to me," said Franklin, "a proposition of selling to us a thing that is already our own, and making France pay the price they are pleased to ask for it." England desired a peace of conciliation with the United States in order to keep as clients those whom she had lost as subjects. Franklin insinuated that the reconciliation would be more complete if England would give up Canada and Nova Scotia. On this subject Shelburne was very definite! "Why Canada? Under the guise of reparations? We do not wish to hear any talk of reparations. . . . To prevent future wars? A more amicable method can be found. . . . As the source of indemnity for the Loyalists? No independence without indemnity. . . ." At this point Jay, who had arrived from Madrid (May, 1782) and had taken part in the argument, replied: "No peace negotiations until there is official recognition of the principle of independence." This recognition was not expressed until later on in the speech from the throne of December 5, 1782, and the phrase was painful for the king to pronounce: "Did I lower my voice when I came to that part of my speech?" he asked anxiously. Lord Shelburne was now prime minister, and the negotiation had been made easier by the defeat of Spain at Gibraltar and that of Admiral de Grasse in the West Indies. England had become once more mistress of the seas. France's promise not to make peace before restoring Gibraltar to Spain fell by force of circumstances. Vergennes tried to persuade the English to exchange Gibraltar for Florida, but failed.

There remained only one means of satisfying Spain: to find a compensation for her in America. Spain had large interests there and she had watched, not without uneasiness, the birth of the United States so close to Spanish Mexico. If the American colonies were freed from England and had at their disposal the immense territory situated between the Alleghenies and the Mississippi, what developments might not follow? Count Avenida wrote to the king of Spain: "This federal republic is but a pigmy in the cradle. A day will come when it will be a great and even a formidable colossus on this continent. Freedom of conscience and the facilities for increase in population which are given by immense territories, as well as the advantages of the new government, will attract the farmers and artisans of all countries. In a very few years we shall observe to our regret the tyrannical existence of the colossus." And so Vergennes suggested a division of the Indian territories into English and Spanish zones of influence. This greatly displeased Jay, who wanted a frontier for the United States on the Mississippi. Moreover the irascible Jay was irritated by the phrase "plantations or colonies" used by England in her negotiations with Vergennes. "What do these words matter?" said Vergennes. "Am I not dealing with an English King who traditionally uses the title of King of France?" Jay had no confidence in Vergennes, and in this he was wrong, for Vergennes was honestly trying to reconcile his duty toward France with his commitments to two allies who were not in agreement. Shelburne had always hoped to negotiate directly with the Americans; he found in Jay a collaborator with the same sentiments. Franklin felt certain scruples which were moreover justifiable, for the allies had undertaken not to negotiate separately. John Adams, who hated the French more than the English, and Benjamin Franklin more than the French, swayed the balance, and Franklin had to accept the principle of a secret and separate negotiation.

On the question of independence there was no longer any disagreement. England gave up the territories between the Alleghenies and the Mississippi. And this river was to be the dividing line between the United States and the Spanish possessions. Navigation of the Mississippi was to be open to both Americans and English. England was to keep Caanda. The frontier between the United States and Canada was somewhat vaguely drawn. The Americans were to retain fishing rights on the banks of Newfoundland and the Gulf of St. Lawrence. All private debts on both sides were to remain due and were to be paid in undepreciated currency. There remained the question of the loyalists. England demanded that their civil rights and confiscated property be restored. The Americans protested. But there were historic precedents: Neither Cromwell nor Charles II had refused an amnesty to their political adversaries, and the effects of this clemency had always been happy. Vergennes, when he had been consulted earlier, had advised, to Adams's great displeasure, that the Tories be well treated after the war. Franklin, usually conciliatory, was not so on this point. He raised the question about those who had in good faith bought the property of the Tories and were now in possession of it. He pointed out that the poverty of Congress prevented it from paying its own soldiers, and that it would be scandalous to indemnify enemies when one was unable to repay one's own friends. Finally he said that the measures against the Tories had been taken by the individual states and that Congress had no power in the matter. Shelburne was stubbornly insistent; for him it was a question of honor. The English still occupied New York; he offered to turn over the city to the Americans in return for an overall indemnity for the loyalists. But the commissioners refused to buy what the recognition of independence had already given them. Finally Shelburne, who was anxious to come to terms, had to give in; the Americans simply promised "to recommend to the States" measures of reparation. It was an empty promise and the English knew it very well, but it saved their face.

When the preliminary articles had been signed, it became necessary to inform Vergennes. This was not a pleasant task; it was assigned to Franklin. Vergennes welcomed him and merely remarked, without acrimony, that this haste in signing showed a lack of courtesy toward the king of France. Franklin made what excuses he could. He called Vergennes's attention to the fact that it was said in the preamble that these articles were provisional and would not become binding until peace was signed between

France and England. Vergennes made no other accusation than that of incivility. The devil of it was that Franklin at the same time had to present, on behalf of Congress, whose resources had run dry, a new request for a loan. This time Vergennes could not refrain from scoring a point and calling attention to the contrast between the secret negotiation and this new appeal for funds. Franklin had a ready wit and extricated himself by a skilled and graceful letter: "I have just learned," he wrote, "that the English are congratulating themselves on having caused a division between us." It was not altogether without reason that the English congratulated themselves; but Franklin, after having expressed his regrets at being guilty of neglecting the proprieties, added that it seemed to him desirable to maintain silence about "this little misunderstanding," which was calculated to delight an adversary. And so Vergennes forgot "the little misunderstanding" and loaned another million pounds. Franco-American relations remained good. The French prime minister, with engaging maliciousness, insisted on the American commissioners being present at all negotiations with Spain and England and would not sign the preliminaries of the peace until after they had done so. By the treaty France regained St. Pierre and Miquelon and some concessions in India and Africa. Spain got the Floridas. All this was unimportant. The United States was the only real beneficiary of the war.

The treaty was signed in September, 1783. At this time an English army was still in occupation of New York. It waited before withdrawing until the last loyalists, both in that city and in Charleston, had been assembled for evacuation. These unfortunates were the chief victims of the war. England was losing only a few colonies; the loyalists had lost everything. Finally on November 25, 1783, the last English vessel left the port of New York. The English consoled themselves by predicting the most gloomy future for the United States. The Americans, they said, would bitterly regret having left the empire and would humbly ask to be taken back. Josiah Tucker, Dean of Gloucester, declared that the differences in interests, manners, and customs among the American states were so great that they could never be united under one government of whatever sort. On the other hand, Burke wrote to Franklin: "I congratulate you as the friend of America; I trust, not as the enemy of England; I am sure, as a friend of mankind."

CHAPTER XIX

Conclusion

THE American War of Independence transformed Europe as well as America. It has been said that the most important event in nineteenth-century English history was the taking of the Bastille; one might say with equal justice that the most important event in the European history of this same century was the Congress at Philadelphia. Before the War of Independence George III and his ministers were dreaming of the possibility of establishing an absolute monarchy in England, of undermining Parliament through corruption and canceling traditional British liberties. The defeat of this policy in America entailed the defeat of the Tories in England; it brought into power the Whigs, who had opposed the war; it allowed Burke and Pitt to maintain the principles of 1688; it saved parliamentary government. In France the American war, by completing the financial ruin of the monarchy, paved the way for its downfall. The example of the young republic, its Bill of Rights and its vocabulary, together with the reports of Rochambeau's young officers, supplied the first men of the French Revolution with the framework of their doctrine. That this doctrine was destined in France to become something very different from what it had been in America was clearly to be seen in 1793 and later in the time of Bonaparte; it is no less certain that during the closing years of the old regime Frenchmen had sought ideas and models in the United States.

The thirteen colonies after the war had become thirteen states. But these thirteen states remained thirteen countries, jealous, sometimes hostile, loosely bound to one another by a Congress that had no authority. Many of them did not want any closer bond. But influences stronger than their wishes had been in operation in the course of the war years. To the men of the thirteen states the struggles against a common adversary had given common memories and common glories. The war had mixed together in the armies men of North and South, East and West, who had learned to know, and often to admire, one another. It had brought about many marriages between Americans from different regions who otherwise would never have met. It had shown a Puritan from Boston, for example, that a Virginian who was loyal to the Church of England was not necessarily a devil in human guise. Most important of all, through the necessities of action, it had raised to national leadership the best men in America, who were among the best men in the world. Because these men had been forced to improvise everything, because they had suddenly found themselves bereft of the political, military, and economic systems of England, they had been forced to learn everything and to understand everything. Necessity had proved a good school for leaders. The United States in 1783 was not yet a country, but it had produced men capable of founding one.

Was this cause which the gods had favored the cause of justice as well? This is a question to which for a long time it was difficult to give an impartial historical answer in England or America. "The tendency," wrote the Englishman Pollard, "was to regard the period as an American golden age, followed by no fall of man. Humanity, as nearly as possible, reached perfection in George Washington: the chosen people had emerged from Egyptian bondage with its Ten Commandments; and the rights of men were its Book of Revelation." Actually modern American historians no longer profess this political Manicheism. They admit that the controversy between England and America was not the controversy between Good and Evil. Legally, if one appealed to the principles of the Revolution of 1688, which proclaimed the sovereignty of Parliament but not universal suffrage, the revolt of the colonies was not defensible; on the other hand, it was if one appealed to the doctrine of the Middle Ages, that of taxes freely consented to by the states of the realm, or to natural law. Between loyalists and patriots there had been differences of opinion and of character, but not of moral values. It was victory which gave the rebels of 1776 their historical prestige as liberators.

Now this victory might well have eluded them. In fact it would have eluded them without the support of France. Washington believed on several occasions that he could not win the war. In times of doubt he showed the most stoic courage; but if the armies of Rochambeau and the fleet of Admiral de Grasse had not come to his aid, he would today cut a very different figure in history. The support of the Bourbons emphasizes the character of the war; it was neither a political revolution like the French Revolution nor an economic one like the Russian Revolution. The members of Congress were defending liberties, but they were those liberties that they had always had. Only a few men like Jefferson caught sight on the distant horizon of a progressive and humanitarian policy. The others, Boston merchants or southern planters, or even radicals like Samuel Adams, simply hoped that American citizens after the war would find themselves as free as they had been before George III. They did not dream of enlarging the suffrage or of freeing the slaves. Their revolt had been that of a group of influential citizens who, because of distance, prosperity, and the immensity of their lands, had acquired the habit of independence and were unwilling to admit the sovereignty of a distant state, or for that matter any sovereignty whatsoever. "Americans may be defined as that part of the English-speaking world which has instinctively revolted against the doctrine of the sovereignty of the State and has, not quite successfully, striven to maintain that attitude from the time of the Pilgrim Fathers to the present day," wrote Pollard.

If the revolt of America had not succeeded at the time of the War of Independence, it would inevitably have broken out anew later on and would have triumphed. The prosperity and rich resources of the country would have continued in countless ways to attract emigrants. The frontier would have bred a larger and larger number of vigorous citizens impatient of absentee authority. Sooner or later the war would have begun again and the increasing population of America would have assured her victory. The only alternative would have been some form of completely independent dominion status within the framework of the empire. But then a day would have come when that empire's center of gravity would have shifted to the American continent. This solution would not have been so good as that provided by the victory of Washington and Rochambeau. For on the day of Yorktown something great was born. We have said at the beginning of this history that, on a continent set apart, freed from the survivals and servitudes of the Old World, humanity was to have the opportunity of trying a new experiment. That was true; but the Pilgrims, willingly or not, had brought with them many of those servitudes. Their sentimental, ideological and political ties with old Europe had retarded them on the paths of enterprise. The breaking of these bonds was to allow them to carry on the experiment more freely and better to adapt their institutions to the novelty of the situation. Without the War of Independence America, as we know it today, would not have existed, and this would have been a great loss. The hope of the world was one day to be centered in this immense power, freed from the feuds of Europe. Without a clean break this freedom would not have been possible. It is true, as modern historians say, that the precise object of the quarrel in 1776 was not very important, and that if sages like Franklin and Burke had been heeded, the war and the separation could have been avoided by a reform of the empire. But the finest human experiment would then have been distorted through the weight of the past, and the triumph of the sages, fortunate in its time, would have been deplorable for ours.

The war had settled several capital questions. Who was to govern America? America herself or a mother land? Victory replied: America alone shall govern America. Were hereditary rights to play their customary part on the new continent? Victory answered: There will be no place on the new continent for an aristocracy of birth. Other problems remained to be solved. Was America to be governed by a plutocracy, the middle classes, or the people as a whole? The departure of the Tories had eliminated a certain number of large fortunes, but the southern planters and many Northern merchants, by associating themselves with the Revolution, had saved both their fortunes and their prestige. Once England had been eliminated, different groups of Americans would come into opposition. The aristocratic and agrarian civilization of the South, the aristocratic and mercantile civilization of the North, and the democratic civilization of the frontier would each in its turn seek to impose its ideals on the new community. Victory assured the United States of the right to give American solutions to its problems, but it did not provide those solutions. Who believed at that time in a close union of the thirteen states? Patrick Henry no doubt had said, "I am not a Virginian; I am an American." But he was the exception, not the rule. The citizen of Baltimore felt himself to be a citizen of Maryland; the citizen of Boston, a citizen of Massachusetts. They had united *against* England; they had still to unite *for* America.

THOMAS JEFFERSON
Painting by Mather Brown, London, 1786.
Courtesy of Mr. Charles Francis Adams

CHAPTER XX

The Critical Period

VICTORY is a test which, like defeat, is a measure of the strength of nations. Military leaders who have been respected by the political leaders during the war are objects of suspicion when peace is made. Victorious generals have power. What would happen if they chose to use it for their own ends? The Continental Army refused to be demobilized until the question of pay was settled. To the officers, Congress had promised half-pay for life; to the men years of back pay were due and money was lacking to discharge the debt. "All this comes of our being a republic," the malcontents grumbled. "Too many cooks spoil the broth!" Washington had to intervene personally to prevent a rebellion. In June, 1783, a crowd of mutinous soldiers in Philadelphia so alarmed Congress that the latter fled to Princeton where the college gave hospitality to the discomfited legislators. They had such a dread of a *coup d'état* that the formation of a social organization of veteran French and American officers, the Cincinnati, terrified them, especially when they learned that it was to be hereditary. John and Samuel Adams talked with horror of this "new and insidious form of nobility." The future was to show the vanity of their fears, but they were justified at the time by the weakness of the government.

Washington took leave of his troops in New York on December 4, 1783. The officers of his general staff met in a tavern. He embraced many of them in the French fashion. Then in silence they accompanied him to his boat and from the New York shore watched him recede toward New Jersey. Many wept. He proceeded on horseback to Annapolis where Congress was in session, and there solemnly resigned his powers as commander-in-chief. Like all ceremonies in which Washington took part this one was full of dignity. To show the primacy of the civil power and the sovereignty of the Union, the deputies remained covered. The general made a short speech. He rendered his detailed and accurate accounts, he commended the country to God and the armies to Congress. A few days later he was in Mount Vernon; he modestly thought to finish his days there. As for the army, Congress ordered that it be demobilized with the exception of twenty-five men to guard the arms and equipment at Fort Pitt and fifty-five at West Point. To pay the soldiers, certificates were printed, but their depreciation was rapid and more than one beneficiary sold them dirt cheap.

The Confederation had been launched on the ocean of time. How could it stay afloat? And once the danger was past, would not the American league fall apart as of old the Hellenic leagues had done as soon as the Persians withdrew from Greece? The thirteen states seemed as different from one another as Athens from Sparta, Argos from Thebes. The only bond between them was the Articles of Confederation. Now what did those Articles provide? A Congress in which each state possessed one vote and in which the opposition of three states could prevent the passage of an indispensable measure. "The idea of sanction," Madison said, "is essential to the idea of law as the idea of coercion to that of government." The federation, possessing no court of law, could not enforce the common decisions. Since the President or Congress had no real authority, the country was without a leader. Theoretically Congress had the right to print currency, borrow money, organize a postal service, and regulate Indian affairs and disputes between the state; in practice, it was powerless. Perhaps this impotence corresponded to the secret desires of the federated states. Burke had said that the Americans scented on every breeze the approach of tyranny. A shipowner in Boston certainly had no desire to delegate large powers to an assembly where he might be beaten by a southern coalition; a Virginia planter entertained the same feelings in regard to the Yankee merchants. A new regime must prove itself before acquiring the prestige of legitimacy. The Confederation had won the war; it now had to survive the peace.

The weakness of Congress mollified fears; it also created dangers. This assembly had issued paper money, the continental dollar. What value could this dollar have when the states, the sole owners of the real wealth, would not accept responsibility for it? "It's not worth a continental" became a customary expression of contempt in America. A barber found it cheaper to paper his shop with these dollars than to buy wallpaper. Although the war had only cost the Americans one hundred four million dollars, measured in gold, a quite bearable debt for a rich country, confidence was lacking. Commerce and industry were in danger of ruin, not only because of the monetary anarchy, but because the economic framework of the country had been for two centuries that of the British Empire and now Great Britain treated American merchants as foreigners. The infant industries that had been created in America during the war possessed neither capital nor reserves. The states called *united* declared commercial wars on one another. New York raised trade barriers against New Jersey; Connecticut boycotted New York. Within the same state one class opposed another. The debtors were hoping for inflation; the creditors feared it. In the North an alliance had been formed of the very powerful commercial and maritime interests with the most eminent members of the liberal professions (such as John Adams) and also with the officers of the Order of the Cincinnati. All these notables were aristocrats by instinct. They believed in a property qualification for suffrage; they hoped to unite wealth and authority. On this point the patricians of the North were in perfect understanding with the planters of the South. In the other camp were the farmers, the pioneers, the radicals of the type of Patrick Henry or Samuel Adams, and also the agrarian philosophers who, like Jefferson, saw the salvation of a state in a prosperous rural life and in popular suffrage. This populist and agrarian party dominated the legislatures of several states, and for this reason did not want a central government to become too powerful.

In 1786 "the friends of order" were alarmed, but also aided in their designs, by a sort of rural uprising in western Massachusetts. The debt-burdened countrymen, thinking themselves ill treated by the magistrates, began a little civil war. A veteran of Bunker Hill, Daniel Shays, put himself at the head of the farmers, who were demanding that paper money be issued and protesting against the seizure and sale of their goods. Between one and two thousand plebeians followed this tribune. They made armed attacks on the courts of justice and a United States arsenal. General Knox wrote to Washington that they maintained that the lands of the United States, having been defended against confiscation by the English through the efforts of all, should henceforth be the common property of all. This dreadful situation, Knox added, frightened all men of principle and of property in New England. "Our government," he said, "must be modified and strengthened." The patricians, becoming frightened, raised a militia which put down the disturbance, but the latter had stirred up the whole country. Washington wrote that in every state there were combustibles which a spark would suffice to ignite. The sage of Mount Vernon had been distressed to see the victory of liberty marred by these disorders: "Good God!" he said. "Who, besides a Tory, would have foreseen such things, and a Briton predicted them?" Should we interpret these popular disorders, Washington asked himself in all honesty, as the effects of British propaganda or of genuine grievances? "The most important thing of all," said the rich, "is to protect our lives and our properties."

It was what the poor had said, too, when they revolted. Jefferson alone approved of Shays. He did not think that the farmers, angered by implacable creditors, were "dangerous anarchists." "God forbid," he wrote, "that we should have twenty years without rebellion." For Thomas Jefferson, a studiously paradoxical politician, loved to say that the tree of liberty needed to be watered from time to time by the blood of patriots and tyrants.

It was far from true that nothing went well during these so-called critical years, but the post-war Americans saw only their woes, and they suffered from them. They were irritated and harassed by grievances. For example, the treaty provided for the immediate evacuation by the English of all the territories that had been ceded. This was done on the coast, but not in the region of the Ohio posts. Why? A thousand official reasons were given. The true one was that the English merchants in Canada were reluctant to give up the fur trade. Meanwhile the American farmers in the West, who had to transport their products to the markets, ran into the English if they tried to go by way of the Great Lakes and the St. Lawrence; the Spaniards, if they tried to go by the Mississippi. They felt stifled and dreamed of expelling all foreigners from their continent.

On the whole the desires of the citizens of the new country seemed simple. To the east they wanted to be isolated from the European continent. To the west they wanted to be free to spread over the American continent. But how could they be isolated from Europe when they needed to export and import? How could they spread in America without an understanding with England and Spain? And how could they come to an understanding with England without first disengaging themselves from the treaty of alliance with France? To the post-war Anglophiles, like Jay and John Adams, this Franco-American treaty was a heavy burden. It might one day involve them in a struggle in which they were not at all concerned. John Adams had said that it should be their first principle to maintain a strict neutrality in all future European wars. If by misfortune it should become necessary to make an exception to this neutrality, at least let it not be to the profit of France. In Adams, Francophobia was a matter of temperament; as for Jay, the descendant of the Huguenots, he could not pardon the French for the revocation of the Edict of Nantes and in Biblical fashion he visited the sins of the fathers upon the children even to the third and fourth generation.

When John Adams went to London as minister of the United States and was officially received by the king, he said with emotion that he hoped to restore "the old good nature and old good humour" between the two countries of the same blood, the same language, and the same religion. The king made a bantering reference to his sentiments toward France, his ally. "I must avow to Your Majesty," Adams said, "that I have no attachment to any but my own country." George III replied: "An honest man will have no other." But if in France John Adams had

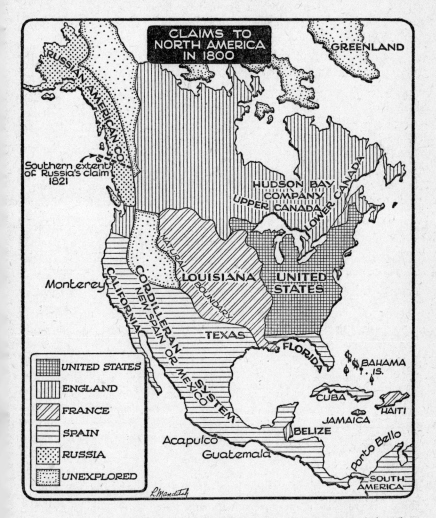

hated the French, in England he quickly came to hate the English. They had less respect for him than he had for himself. "An Ambassador from America! Heavens! What a strange combination of words!" said the English press. The British government looked down on Congress and thought it was in no position to make commitments in the name of the states. "You should have thirteen ambassadors," the Foreign Office said ironically to John Adams. The English, who had not forgiven the rebellion, treated the Americans with a meticulous and offensive politeness. This was unwise, for there remained between the two countries so many ties that the heart of America might have been an easy and profitable sentimental conquest for England. But pride often triumphs over wisdom and even over self-interest.

One of the most difficult problems for the Confederation had been the division of the immense territory that extended to the west between the Appalachian Mountains and the Mississippi. Seven states possessed by charter unlimited rights to westward, and wanted to exercise them. But the states that didn't possess such territories, Maryland in particular, had protested. If a few privileged states, Maryland said, were permitted to absorb all the additional territory to the west, the equilibrium of the Confederation would be upset. What Maryland had proposed from the beginning was to hold the Northwest Territory in common, and have it administered by Congress until such time as it was sufficiently populated to form new states. Maryland had refused to sign the Articles of Confederation until this solution was adopted. New York agreed in 1781, and, thanks to the influence of Jefferson, Virginia and the other states with special rights followed suit. A decision of capital importance. If the Northwest Territory had not belonged to the country as a whole, the development of the continent would have been effected by a few states opening up virgin territories and these states, becoming disproportionately powerful, would have been a menace to the others. On the other hand, the possession *in common* of an immense territory united the thirteen states, imposed collective duties on them, and gave Congress its first real authority. The national sovereignty of the Confederation was henceforth actual. Maryland, at the time when she was holding out, was accused of egoism and stubbornness. As a matter of fact, this little state by its obstinacy laid the foundations of a great country.

How should these lands be distributed to the pioneers? In 1784 Jefferson devised a plan, known as the Ordinance of 1784. He divided the Western Territory into sixteen states which should become parts of the Union as soon as the density of their population justified it. All of them should be republican in government, and agree to remain part of the United States forever. The first draft excluded slavery after 1800, but this proposal was deleted. Jefferson gave his states strange names: Sylvania, Michigania, Metropotamia, Illinoia, etc. This was the time when American cities were being called Ithaca, Syracuse, Corinth, and Sparta. The ordinance was passed but never went into effect. In 1785 it was decided to sell the lands to the public. The whole Northwest Territory was divided into blocks six miles square called townships, and each township into thirty-six sections. In each township one section—Section 16—was to become the property of the public schools. The principle of this measure was sound, but to sell the lands it was still necessary to assure the buyers that they would be protected, defended, and governed. In March, 1786, certain citizens met in Boston and founded the Ohio Company of Associates, which offered to buy immense territories for a million dollars payable in continental certificates. They retained a skillful negotiator, the Reverend Manasseh Cutler, an effective lobbyist, to represent them in Congress and to secure the establishment of the territorial government. The Reverend Manasseh Cutler was not much impressed by the disinterestedness of Congress; he was able to arrange the concession desired by his group only by drawing into the affair some very prominent men and compensating them handsomely, if indirectly. One and a half million acres were finally granted to the company in 1787.

The Northwest was temporarily given a governor (who was, as though by accident, General St. Clair, president of Congress), three judges, and a secretary, to be appointed by Congress. For the future it was decided: (a) that territories containing more than five thousand but less than sixty thousand free male inhabitants should have the right of governing themselves by elected assemblies, but not the right of being represented in Congress; (b) that with more than sixty thousand inhabitants, a state government might be set up and the new state admitted to the Union on equal footing with the original states; (c) that slavery should be prohibited; and (d) that civil and religious liberty and trial by jury should be guaranteed to the inhabitants of the territories. This Ordinance of 1787 is one of capital importance. Through it the federal principle triumphed over the colonial principle on the American continent. Every new populated district that entered the Union was to become, after a trial period, a member of the Union. No nation had ever applied to its future annexations principles as generous as these. It is only fair to add that the problem was wholly different from that of the colonial empires. The new states were to be peopled by men of the same race and the same civilization as the old states. It was a case of transplanting rather than of conquest.

CHAPTER XXI

The Constitution

THE Revolution, which had given the colonies their independence, had been the work of a group of prominent men, cultured and liberal, whom the radical masses had supported with the necessary power. The troops had often terrified their leaders. "Despite such misleading names as the *Boston Tea Party,* the Revolution was a revolution and it had all the usual accompaniments of a revolution: violence, demagogy, contempt for vested interests, opportunities given to rancour and greed," observes D. W. Brogan in his *Government of the People.* The persistence of this revolutionary state of mind disturbed all those—the merchants, financiers, security holders—whose interests demanded quiet, respect for contracts, and the re-establishment of order. Experience had shown that Congress, as constituted by the Articles of Confederation, was powerless to govern a nation. An assembly can control; it can act only through the person of an executive; but Congress had no true executive. "You talk, my good Sir," wrote Washington, "of employing influence to appease the present tumult in Massachusetts. . . . Influence is not government. Let us have one by which our lives, liberties and properties will be secure." Yes, there was need of a central government. But would it be possible to secure the acceptance of one by states that were so jealous of their independence? Certain men thought so and made an effort to create this government. They were among those who had made and won the war. They belonged to that class of moderate reformers who inspire revolutions, start them, but seldom finish them. In America they undertook to halt the revolution in its first phase. The strange thing is that they succeeded and that in the United States moderates created and governed the republic.

A local controversy was the starting point of the movement for the Constitution. In 1785 the commissioners of Virginia and Maryland met to discuss certain questions relative to the navigation of the Potomac. They quickly discovered that Pennsylvania and Delaware also had interests to safeguard, and Virginia proposed that all the states should send delegates to Annapolis in 1786 "to consider how far a uniform system in their commercial regulations and other important matters may be necessary to the common interest and permanent harmony of the several

States." Only five states were represented at Annapolis, but good observers believed that the abstentions had as purpose the preparation of a larger plan. Actually what the leaders wanted was a convention charged with reforming the central government. As Edmund Randolph said later in his opening speech at the Federal Convention: "The Conferation was made in the infancy of the science of constitutions . . . when no commercial discord had arisen among states; when no rebellion like that in Massachusetts had broken out; when foreign debts were not urgent . . . when treaties had not been violated; and when nothing better could have been conceded by states jealous of their sovereignty. But it offered no security against foreign invasion. . . ." At the same time, fearing that they might not be supported by the mass of debt-burdened citizens who hoped for relief through disorder, the reformers had at first made use of questions of commerce and navigation as a screen and had made the unsuccessful meeting at Annapolis an excuse for convoking a new convention "for the sole and express purpose of revising the Articles of Confederation, in such a way as to render them adequate to the exigencies of government and the preservation of the Union." In short, the purpose was to give the country a constitution, but the word was not mentioned so that no one would be dismayed.

This convention assembled in Philadelphia in May, 1787, with a slowness that was explained by the difficulties of travel. It was, as Jefferson said, an "assembly of demi-gods." John Adams and Jefferson himself were in Europe (the former as minister to England, the latter to France), but aside from them each of the states had delegated its most notable citizens. Of these fifty-five men, twenty-nine had been students at various colleges or universities, and among the twenty-six others were men of the caliber of Washington and Franklin. George Washington was unanimously chosen as president; he was seated on a dais and his authority, combined with the dignity of his bearing, lent the deliberations incomparable distinction. He early set the tone of the convention by saying: "If, to please the people, we offer what we ourselves disapprove, how can we afterward defend our work? Let us raise a standard to which the wise and the honest can repair; the event is in the hand of God."

The most intelligent man at the convention was probably the young delegate from New York, Alexander Hamilton; but the stiffness of his manner kept him from eloquence and his ideas from popularity. Born in the West Indies, he had nothing in his character that responded to the democratic instincts of Americans who had been molded by the life of the frontier. Hamilton warmly admired the British government, including the aristocracy. He was a partisan of federal unity even at the cost of states' rights. "We must annihilate," he said, "the state distinctions." He would have liked to put all militia under the orders of the central government, unify the debts, and create a true national sovereignty. He had no confidence in the common sense, intelligence, or good will of the masses. His was a strong and pessimistic mind, and he believed that force and self-interest alone control men's actions and that institutions survive only if it is to the interest of the rich and influential classes to maintain them. "The voice of the people," he said, "has been said to be the voice of God; but, however generally this maxim has been quoted and believed, it is not true in fact. The people are turbulent and changeable; they seldom judge or determine right." Because he was clearheaded he realized that only a republican government would be acceptable to Americans, but he hoped that at least the executive power might be as strong as possible.

James Madison, the delegate from Virginia, had hardly more illusions about humanity than Hamilton. "If men were angels," he said, "there would be no need of government at all." But he managed to refrain from such cutting statements as Hamilton's. Also, he had much greater authority than the latter, and became known as the Father of the Constitution. He was a small man, pale, timid, erudite, and witty, who blushed whenever anyone stared at him; but he had thoroughly studied the history of federal government (particularly in Greece, Switzerland and Holland) and George Washington had the greatest esteem for him. Madison was not a member of any party, and for this reason he was accused of opportunism by the fanatics; but the clarity of his ideas, his moderation, and the charm of his character contributed much to the success of the convention. Like Hamilton, he thought that the essential role of a constitution is to safeguard the rights of the minority against the strength of an oppressive majority. To accomplish this he put his faith in the means that had been tested by time—trial by jury, *habeas corpus,* and frequent elections. He believed that no human mind, however intelligent it might be, could redo in a few weeks the work of generations. It was the strength and the virtue of the Philadelphia convention that it made use of known methods which had been tested either by other countries or by the states of the confederation.

John Dickinson, the author of *Letters from a Farmer,* struck the keynote of the discussion when he said: "Experience must be our only guide. Reason might mislead us." Very different from most revolutionary assemblies, this one was realistic and objective. The men who composed it almost all had large economic interests to defend. Among the fifty-five delegates, not one represented the small farmers or the city workmen, which would seem to us a mistake and an injustice, but at that time it does not seem to have shocked anyone. Neither Patrick Henry nor Samuel Adams was present. It has been observed that fourteen of the delegates (Washington among them! had made investments in land, that forty of them were creditors of the Confederation, that fifteen of them owned slaves. At the same time it would be most unfair to explain their decisions by their personal interests alone. The distinguished men who met at Philadelphia had at heart the future of the country which they had jointly founded. The gravity of their mission filled them with a quasi-religious feeling. The enterprise was new; it was great; it demanded reflection and solemnity. And so the founders provided themselves with a setting of silence and mystery. All the sessions took place behind closed doors. The members pledged their honors not to reveal the discussions. Being a little doubtful of the aged Franklin, who at eighty was not always master of his tongue, two of the members accompanied him to his house each night. Sentinels were placed at the doors of the conference and no secretary was present at the discussions. This procedure saved the convention and assured the quality of its work. Often violent conflicts brought the delegates into opposition with one another. If these disagreements had been made public all compromise would have become impossible. That excellent document, the Constitution of the United States, is the offspring of wisdom and secrecy.

The first problem that any confederation has to solve is the conflict between the large and small states. Hitherto each state had one vote in Congress. The large states considered this method unjust and demanded that representation should be proportional to population and to direct taxation. They supported a plan proposed by the delegation from Virginia, which provided for two Houses, one elected by popular suffrage, on the basis of population, and the second to be elected by the first; the executive and the judiciary to be chosen and named by the Houses; the national legislature to have the right to decide on the constitutionality of the laws voted by the states. The little states rallied to a plan proposed by New Jersey, which possessed most of the faults of the Articles of Confederation: a single House, with equal representation for all the states; no sanction for the decisions of the federal government except the employment of force and judicial review; a committee chosen by the legislators to be the sole executive power; and a judiciary appointed by the executive. For several weeks the two groups contended fruitlessly. "The gentleman from New Jersey," said a representative of Pennsylvania, "is candid. . . . I will be equally candid. . . . I never will confederate on his principles." And a delegate from Delaware cried: "Gentlemen, I do not trust you!" In June the heat became atrocious and tempers flared. The situation seemed so desperate that Franklin, the skeptical Franklin, proposed prayers at the beginning of each session as the only means of restoring some measure of amiability. The newspapers ironically referred to Independence Hall as Unanimity Hall. Finally, toward the middle of July, the weather became somewhat cooler and a compromise proposed by Connecticut was adopted: two assemblies of which one, the House of Representatives, would give the states a representation proportional to their population; the other, the Senate, to be made up of two senators from each state whatever its importance. The ground had been cleared; the founders could now build.

The Constitution of the United States is essentially a compromise between the necessity of creating a republican government in order to keep the support of the people and a desire to provide against demagogy in order to retain the confidence of the notables. In the plan as it was adopted equal powers were balanced against each other. The president was to play the roles that in England belonged to the king and the prime minister. Some even desired that he should be called His Majesty the President. Hamilton had suggested that the president be appointed for life, and at the bottom of his heart he would have preferred a king. His notes for a speech have been preserved in which he says that if a government is in the hands of a small number it will tyrannize over the larger number; if it is in the hands of a large number, it will tyrannize over the smaller number. Therefore it must be in the hands of both, and the two must be distinct. However, if they are separate, they need a mutual control, a brake. But since a monarchy obviously had no chance of being accepted, Hamilton rallied without argument to the idea of a republic. At the start people talked about "the throne of the president" and Patrick Henry, who watched the scene as a bitter and hostile critic from the corridors, sneered at this court etiquette. In actual fact, the president of the United States was (and remains) much more powerful than the king of England. He was to be chosen by a special body of electors, selected in each state as the legislature should decide and equal in number to the total number of senators and representatives of that state in the United States Congress. The fact that George Washington was the first president helped to invest the office with an immense and merited prestige. A vice president was to be chosen at the same time as the president. The candidate who received the largest number of votes was to be president, the second largest vice president. If no candidate received an absolute majority of the electors' votes, the House of Representatives was to choose the president. In the event of the death (or impeachment) of the president, the vice president should assume the duties of that office. To give some employment to the vice president, he was made president of the Senate. In the mind of the founders this latter body was to serve as a privy council, and no ministerial cabinet was provided for. But the practice was different.

The two Houses were to represent the nation. Certain timorous spirits would have liked to remove both from popular election. "The people," said Gerry, "are the dupes of pretended patriots." But Hamilton himself recognized that it was essential that at least one of the Houses (the House of Representatives) should be directly elected by the people. At that time there was no question of universal suffrage. In the America of 1787 the property qualification for voting was no great handicap because of the great number of small property owners. Two states had already done away with the property qualification. The thesis accepted by the founders was that a citizen without property, having nothing to lose, would let himself be tempted by the most absurd experiments and would be at the mercy of demagogues. Madison admitted the same uneasiness. He wondered whether the interests of property would be adequately safeguarded in future elections, and added that in England if everyone could vote the ownership of lands would be compromised and an agrarian law would be passed. He insisted on defending what he called "the permanent interests" of the country. Furthermore, although the new Constitution admitted the principle of popular sovereignty, it did nothing to assure the people as a whole of their civic rights. It was later, through amendments, that universal suffrage was established in the United States. Election to the Senate, which was to take the place of the House of Lords, was left to the legislatures of the states.

There was a long discussion as to whether, in calculating the number of representatives from each state, slaves should be taken into account. The South demanded it. "The Northern delegates maintained that slaves, as chattels, ought no more to be reckoned as part of the population than houses or ships." "Has a man in Virginia," exclaimed Paterson, "a number of votes in proportion to the number of his slaves? And if Negroes are not represented in the states, to which they belong, why should they be represented in the general government?" Finally a compromise was adopted: The slaves, although they did not have the right to vote, should be counted to the extent of three-fifths of their number in calculating the number of seats for each state. This was absurd, but all compromises are absurd, being designed to mollify feelings and not to satisfy the intelligence.

The founders believed that the success of the British Commonwealth was due to the separation of powers; and so they took great precautions to separate completely the executive and the legislative functions. Contrary to the English system, in which the ministers were members of Parliament and responsible to the House of Commons, the custom became established for the president of the United States to choose his cabinet members outside of Congress and the department heads did not appear before the House or Senate, nor could Congress dismiss them. As the president was replaced every four years and the representatives every two years, there might result from these laws two years of conflict between the executive and the legislature. In this case the president had the right of veto over the decisions of Congress, but Congress could by a two-thirds vote override the veto. At a time of crisis this method could be slow and dangerous; actually at such a time the executive took the necessary initiative. In event of dispute concerning the interpretation of the Constitution or the constitutionality of the laws voted by the states, a Supreme Court, to which the judges were appointed during good behavior by the president with the consent of the Senate, decided as last resort. Justice was elevated above the majority rule. *Vox justitiae, vox Dei.* This was a genuine safeguard for the minority against a demagogic majority; but later frequent complaints were to be heard about the tyranny of the judiciary power in America. Congress also had the right to create federal courts; they were to give the federal laws that sanction which the laws of the Confederation had always lacked. Finally it was agreed that Congress should choose a territory ten miles square which was to constitute the District of Columbia and on which the federal capital was to be built.

A problem full of danger was the division of authority between the federal and state governments. The powers and functions of the federal government were enumerated in the Constitution. It had the right to raise taxes for the payment of debts and to assure the defense of the United States; to borrow money; to regulate commerce between the states and with foreign countries; to coin money; to establish a postal service; to declare war; to raise armies and militia. All the powers not enumerated were reserved to the states. Thus the position of Congress was very different from that of the British Parliament. The latter, not being limited by any written constitution or any enumeration of powers, possessed all rights, including that of changing the form of government. It was the nation. The Constitution of the United States, on the other hand, could not be changed except by amendments proposed by two-thirds of Congress or by a national convention called by Congress and agreed to by three-fourths of the states in their legislatures or special conventions. That meant that changes would be carefully considered and rare. Would not this rigidity of the Constitution, adapted to a certain way of life and thought, be a handicap when great and unforeseen changes took place? Perhaps. But the founders wanted a rigid Constitution in order to preserve the country from the excesses of Congress. The people delegated to Congress only a part of their powers. It was to them that appeal had to be made in the last resort. The Constitution was proclaimed in the name of the people of the United States: "We the People of the United States, in Order to form a more perfect Union, establish Justice, insure domestic Tranquility, provide for the common defense, promote the general Welfare, and secure the Blessings of Liberty to ourselves and our Posterity, do ordain and establish this Constitution for the United States of America."

The final scene was simple and moving. A secretary read the definitive text of the Constitution, then Franklin arose and, since his voice was weak, Wilson read his speech for him. Franklin admitted that he did not approve of all of the Constitution, but he added that he did not think himself infallible, that an assembly possessed of passions and prejudices could not produce anything that was perfect, and that it was surprising to consider how close the system that had been adopted came to perfection. He begged all the members to sign in order to show their unanimity. There were, however, a few abstentions. Meanwhile the people in whose name the Constitution was being proclaimed knew nothing about it. It had to be submitted to Congress, and to the conventions in each state.

Then began a very lively opposition. The nation split into Federalists and anti-federalists. The anti-federalists said that the lawyers, the savants, and the rich men had reached an understanding for the purpose of making poor illiterate people swallow this pill, the Constitution. The creditor class was in favor of a strong central state; the debtors expected more charity from the original states. The radicals of 1776, Samuel Adams, Patrick Henry, showed small enthusiasm for the Constitution. Some went so far as to express the fear that if a territory were to be given to the government it would fortify itself there and become a dictatorship. The people of Pennsylvania were in favor of ratification; in Massachusetts, John Hancock, the governor, had an attack of gout which would not end, said those who knew him well, until that wily statesman was sure of the direction of popular sentiment. Washington and Madison had some trouble in winning the support of Virginia; and to convince New York, Hamilton, with the aid of Madison and John Jay composed closely reasoned essays which have been collected under the title of *The Federalist*. North Carolina and Rhode Island were the last states to ratify the Constitution, and only did it against their better judgment. Even a man as moderate as Richard Henry Lee, while recognizing the good qualities of the Constitution, criticized it for omitting the most important of factors, a true representation of the people. Every man who reflects, he said, could see that the change proposed was a change of power from the masses to a small number. But he did not take into account the possibility of amending the Constitution, a possibility which was one day to meet his objections.

From France, Jefferson wrote that he would not consider the Constitution complete until there was added to it a bill of rights. In this he was right; individuals should be protected against partisan passions, and it is proper that the essential rights of the citizens should be inscribed in every constitution. As it was, the document drawn up by the assembly had very rare qualities. Its authors had profited by the experience acquired by the states; they had taken account of the Articles of Confederation and of their proved faults; they had used the test of realism. Success was to show their wisdom. No doubt this success was due in large measure to the privileged situation of the United States and to its incomparable riches. But all things considered, and after more than one hundred fifty years of experience, it is permissible to say that the Constitution of the United States, supplemented by the Bill of Rights, has proved itself wise and efficacious, and that it carries in itself the means of its own transformation when the nation shall judge that necessary. No work of man is perfect. That of the founders approaches perfection as closely as the circumstances allowed.

CHAPTER XXII

The Birth of the Parties

THE first election put into office the men who had forged the Constitution. The electors chosen by the nation unanimously selected George Washington as the first President of the United States; John Adams became Vice President. In April, 1789, Washington journeyed on horseback from Mount Vernon to New York, where the inauguration was to take place. When he rode through Trenton young girls, dressed in white, threw flowers in his path. In New York he made an appearance on the balcony of Federal Hall, remodeled by the French architect L'Enfant, at the corner of Wall and Nassau Streets, above a sea of welcoming faces, and took the oath on a Bible presented to him by the chancellor of New York, while women waved their handkerchiefs and men their hats. The President was pale and grave. He understood his difficult role. He had to invest the presidency with an air of majesty without giving offense to republican hearts. His natural dignity stood him in good stead and for a long time set the pattern for inaugurations in the American tradition. Henceforth every four years the newly elected president was to appear to take the oath of office before a vast throng who regarded this ceremony with the same respect and emotion as the English do the coronation. Thus are memories and rituals made the foundation of enduring states.

President Washington showed the same substantial characteristics as Washington the commander-in-chief. He was methodical, hard-working, and deliberate. He carefully read all documents for which he had to assume responsibility, and pondered at length before acting. The office of President was so new that the smallest details of conduct were important. He quickly realized that the President must not be too accessible. He composed a list of questions about these problems and submitted it to Jay, Madison, John Adams, and Hamilton. "The President, in all matters of business and etiquette, can have no object but to demean himself in his public character in such a manner as to maintain the dignity of his office, without subjecting himself to the imputation of superciliousness or unnecessary reserve. Under these impressions, he asks for your candid and undisguised opinion." Adams advised a frankly royal protocol with chamberlains and masters of ceremonies; in his private life the President might remain a simple human being, but his public life, to insure respect, should be surrounded with a halo of splendor and mystery. Hamilton, on the other hand, advised the avoidance of excessive pomp which would quickly arouse irritation in an equalitarian country; nevertheless, he thought that the President should never accept invitations, and should not himself entertain guests, except rarely on the great anniversaries of the Republic. Should he be called "Mr. Washington"? "Sir"? Mr. President"? "Excellency"? Some senators had suggested as the official title: "His Highness the President of the United States." This smacked too strongly of Cromwell, and the House of Representatives chose: "The President of the United States." Washington was satisfied. "Happily that question is settled," he said. "I hope there will be no more talk about it." As for John Adams, he was principally concerned as to what his place should be when the President came into the Senate:

"Where shall I be then?" he asked. "I beg the gentlemen of the Senate to reflect upon my situation." Had it been the intent of the Constitution, John Adams wondered, to make of the President and Vice President the two consuls of Rome? The two kings of Sparta? In that case, might he not take his seat on the same large chair as the President under a canopy of crimson velvet? And how should the Vice President be addressed? Someone suggested "His Rotundity," but "His Intelligence" would have been more to the point.

Although the Constitution had not provided for a ministerial cabinet, the President needed collaborators. It was stated that he might consult the heads of the principal executive departments, but these departments at first were few in number. A Secretary of State (Jefferson) was charged with foreign and domestic affairs; Hamilton had the Treasury; General Henry Knox, War; Randolph was Attorney General. In addition, Samuel Osgood was the first Postmaster General. Between this presidential "family" and the British cabinet there was nothing in common. The British Prime Minister consults his colleagues; the President of the United States has no colleagues; he, and he alone, is the executive. If all his ministers are opposed to a measure which he favors, his single opinion outweighs all theirs. Jefferson was still in France as minister when Washington decided to make him Secretary of State. Jefferson did not want this office, but he accepted it. "It is not for an individual to choose his post," he wrote to the President. "You are to marshal us as may be best for the public good."

In Hamilton and Jefferson, whom Washington had just made colleagues, were incarnated two opposed and contradictory political philosophies. No historian has been able to speak of these two men without drawing parallel portraits because in this case the parallel is in the nature of their beings. Hamilton represented the party of resistance; Jefferson the party of movement. Jefferson, the rich planter, the owner of numerous slaves, was a democrat; Hamilton, the illegitimate child, the man without fortune, without slaves, was an aristocrat. Hamilton, who had French blood and a wholly French logic, admired the British tradition; Jefferson, who had no French blood, admired Diderot and Rousseau. Hamilton, a pessimist like all aristocrats, believed that man preys upon man; Jefferson, an optimist like all democrats, maintained that man is born good and is corrupted by society. Hamilton thought a strong government necessary; Jefferson, that a government should govern as little as possible. Hamilton, who appeared fiery and headstrong, hated disorder; Jefferson, who seemed nonchalant and kindly, said: "I like a little rebellion now and then; it is like a storm in the atmosphere." Hamilton

wanted the world to be governed by "the rich, the wise and the good";
Jefferson wanted the world to be governed by the common man. Hamilton considered the people "a great beast"; Jefferson, a thinking body.
Hamilton, cynical, impatient, and sometimes contemptuous, attached no
importance to public opinion: "Men," he said, "are reasoning rather than
reasonable animals." Jefferson had confidence in man and in public opinion. Hamilton wanted to make the United States an industrial country;
Jefferson, an agricultural country. Hamilton wanted to found the state
on the loyalty of the privileged classes; Jefferson, on the affection of the
masses. Jefferson clung to the independence of the original states; Hamilton would willingly have weakened the states to strengthen the federal
government. The strangest thing was that Hamilton, who believed himself a realist, was a romantic; and Jefferson, who thought of himself as an
idealist, was a realist. For Hamilton sought the support of bankers; Jefferson, that of farmers; and in this world there are more farmers than
bankers.

The two men were no less different in manner than they were in doctrine. Hamilton, small, slender, elegant, wore white silk stockings and
sometimes a lace jabot. He powdered his reddish-blond hair and wore
it tied at the back of his head in the French fashion. His handsome,
violet-colored eyes were both austere and fascinating. From childhood he
had been a great reader of Plutarch and had dreamed of military glory.
A soldier during the Revolution, he retained a military tone and bearing. Washington had made him "the pen of the army"; Hamilton
would have preferred to be its sword. Beneath the frivolous appearance
of a roué, he was an impassioned worker. His tenacity, moral courage,
and generosity should have taken him to the top, but he was handicapped by his arrogance of mind. He astonished men by his superiority;
he shocked them by being so sure of it. He lacked the experience of taking part in a Boston town meeting. The American world, he said, was
not made for him; and he himself was not made for the American world.
Jefferson, on the contrary, was negligent in dress and awkward in movement. His glance was evasive—because of shyness, his friends said; because of disingenuousness, said his enemies. At first sight he seemed
kindly rather than combative. But he had strong convictions. Although
on his mother's side (she was a Randolph) he belonged to the Virginia
aristocracy, he held the political ideas of his father, a pioneer and farmer.
During his youth, spent in western Virginia, he had seen his father's
friends clear the ground, defend it against Indians, and govern themselves. It was to these apprentice years that he owed his confidence in
democracy. Hamilton despised his adversaries; Jefferson esteemed his to

the extent of placing a bust of Alexander Hamilton on the mantelpiece at Monticello. Hamilton was intransigent and pursued his chosen course against wind and tide; Jefferson, in case of a squall, shortened sail to save his ship. Hamilton counted on his actions to attract partisans to his cause; Jefferson patiently built up his party, flattering one, caressing another, writing thousands of letters, and attaching to himself in every American community the men who could serve him. In a word, Hamilton was a doctrinaire and Jefferson a politician.

While Jefferson was still in France, Madison, in response to his complaint that there was no bill of rights in the Constitution and in accordance with suggestions made by the state ratifying conventions, got the first Congress to vote a series of amendments that constituted the most complete guarantee of human liberties that had ever been given to a society. Much more extensive than the English Declaration of Rights, the American Bill of Rights assured religious tolerance by forbidding Congress to make any law to establish any religion or to prohibit the practice of any. Religious beliefs thus became a question that concerned the individual alone. Among other guarantees were freedom of speech, freedom of the press, and freedom of assembly, as well as the right of people to bear arms. This splendid document was as important as the Constitution itself and afforded the most efficacious protection against the growth of tyranny. The first Congress also passed a Judiciary Act which established the federal courts. About the creation of a Supreme Court all were in agreement, but many thought that below this the state courts would be adequate. Others believed that one could not trust the state courts, always influenced by local considerations, to render impartial judgment in those cases in which federal laws were involved. And so it was decided to create federal courts.

At the Treasury, Hamilton's first concern was to draw up a balance sheet, which he did in the form of a report to Congress that has remained famous as a model of style, clarity, and intelligence. This balance sheet showed that the federal government owed abroad about twelve million dollars; at home, forty-two million dollars; and that the debts of the states amounted to twenty-one million five hundred dollars. Hamilton maintained that all these debts should be funded at par, including the debts of the states, because they had been contracted for the common cause and the federal government should pay the interest. Thus the credit of the new republic would at once be based upon respect for obligations. What Hamilton did not say aloud was that this would also satisfy the propertied classes and win their support for the state which had thus become their principal debtor. The plan was open to criticism; it inflicted a heavy charge upon a young state that had no resources. Was it even equitable? A large part of the domestic debt consisted of certificates of pay issued to the army. Now these certificates, sold by the soldiers for whatever they would bring, had greatly depreciated. At the first rumors of redemption at par, speculators had rushed through the states on horseback and in carriages to buy them up at the lowest price possible. If these obligations were repaid at par, who would profit? The soldier? Or the speculator? Hamilton would not allow the rights of the bearer to be challenged "for," he said, "security of transfer is an essential element of the public credit." Sound finance perhaps; less sound morality. Hamilton himself was honest; some of his friends had fewer scruples. The profit for the speculators in this operation was to be tremendous. Jefferson described with horror the relays of post horses and the fast sailing vessels which the financiers and their agents had used to buy up all this paper, at 25 per cent or even 10 per cent of its value, before the bearers learned that they were to be reimbursed in full. Immense sums, he said, had been taken by fraud from the poor and ignorant. The men who had been enriched by the dexterity of a leader, Jefferson added, would naturally become partisans of the man who had made their fortune and who had made them instruments of his enterprises. Madison fought energetically in favor of the original owners but was defeated.

Concerning the federal government's assumption of the states' debts, the controversy was no less heated. Each member of Congress formed his opinion on this point by calculating the amount of debts owed by the state he represented. A state that was heavily indebted found the measure excellent; a state which had lain outside the zone of military operations and thus had expended practically nothing for the war exhibited no special enthusiasm at assuming new liabilities. South Carolina showed her wounds—ravaged plantations and burned houses; Maryland, relatively unscathed, advised her to bear her burden nobly; South Carolina was willing to share the nobility *and* the burden. Finally there was a vote in an atmosphere of fury and confusion, and Hamilton was defeated thirty-one to twenty-nine. But Hamilton was a resourceful man. He needed only two votes. To get them he had something to barter; it was the choice of the site for the federal capital. Each state, and especially Pennsylvania and Virginia, hoped to possess that capital both for honor and for profit. Now Pennsylvania and Virginia were among the states most opposed to Hamilton's financial measures. In the course of a dinner with Jefferson, Hamilton proposed a deal: he would get some northern votes for a capital on the banks of the Potomac if representatives from Virginia would vote for the assumption of the states' debts. The bargain was sealed. During the construction of the new city Philadelphia should be the provisional capital. Members of the government there found themselves mingling with a local society that was in no respect democratic. English influence preponderated. The queen of the city was Mrs. Bingham, a rich and beautiful woman, bold in conversation, who had lived in Europe, been feted at Versailles and London, and who prided herself on having a salon. When the French Republican, Brissot, came to Philadelphia, he was shocked by the elegance of Mrs. Bingham's receptions and the way in which she used her charm on behalf of the Federalists. Meanwhile in August, 1790, Congress, thanks to the support of Virginia, voted all of Hamilton's measures. To pay the interest on the debt he counted on import duties, an excise tax on distilled liquors and on the sale of the western lands.

Alexander Hamilton's dream was to reconstitute in America a governmental, economic, and financial edifice modeled on that of England. One of the elements of this structure was to be a Bank of the United States patterned after the Bank of England. This creation hardly seemed indispensable. The state could encourage the development of private banks already in existence. Hamilton thought the state would be stronger if commerce and future industry depended on it for credit. But here again opposition was lively. Was the creation of a bank a constitutional measure? It did not figure among the powers of the federal government enumerated in the Constitution. "The Constitution," said Hamilton, "authorizes the Government of the United States to make all laws necessary for the powers enumerated. . . . A bank is necessary to regulate commerce, borrow, print money. . . ." This was the theory of implicit powers, a convenient but dangerous one, for it allowed one to make of the Constitution almost whatever one liked. To this Jefferson replied that a bank might be convenient, that it might or might not be useful; that was a question open to debate; in any case it was certainly not necessary, and consequently it was not constitutional. "Beg pardon," replied the Hamiltonians, "*necessary* does not mean *indispensable*; necessary often means *useful*." Washington decided this lexicographical discussion in favor of Hamilton, and a bank with a capital of ten million dollars was established on February 25, 1791. The Treasury was to subscribe two million dollars and did not have it. Hamilton solved this problem by a truly Hamiltonian device. He drew imaginary bills on Dutch banks and handed over these drafts to the organizers in payment for the government's shares; the public subscribed the rest of the capital. Then, the bank being founded, the Treasury borrowed two million dollars and withdrew the drafts. The comedy was ended.

The following year the monetary system of the country was organized.

The dollar was given a fixed value in gold and the decimal system was adopted for coinage. At the same time the value of silver in relation to gold was declared to be 1 to 15. This system was unsound. No one could believe that the relative value of the two metals would not change. If it changed, the cheap money would automatically drive out the good. This is what happened later on when the discovery of new silver mines made the value of this money drop. Immediately gold fled the country, while silver poured in. Hamilton, always a partisan of personal government, would have liked to see on the first coins the likeness of the President in whose administration they were issued. But Jefferson thought that this idea smacked distressingly of monarchy, and on gold coins an eagle with wings spread was substituted for the imposing profile of George Washington.

"You say that our antagonisms began with the Federalists and anti-Federalists," John Adams wrote later. "Alas! they began with human nature; long before the Revolution Whigs and Tories were already disputing savagely." It was true; but in America the Tories during the Revolution had ceased to be conservatives in order to play the part of loyalists, and this had led to their disappearance. After the Revolution the class that desired an extension rather than a limitation of governmental powers became the Federalist party. And the party in opposition was called anti-Federalist, not because it was hostile to the federal government, but because it insisted that the powers of the government should be limited. The anti-Federalists soon chose to call themselves Republicans; in their eyes it was a way of accusing their adversaries of being, if not monarchists, at least monocrats. The Federalists, and in particular Hamilton, favored the capitalistic proprietors, shipowners, big merchants, and rich lawyers and sought support from them. The Republicans spoke in the name of the farmers, the planters, and also the small artisans. They maintained that the methods of Hamilton, especially the creation of a bank, encouraged speculation and corruption. The debate was as much economic as political. Those who wished to maintain an agricultural America were Jeffersonians; those who wished to lay the groundwork for an industrial America were Hamiltonians. The majority in the South and in the West were for Jefferson; the big cities of the coast, for Hamilton. But temperament also played its part. There were Federalist farmers; there were Republican merchants.

Taking a general view, one might say that the Republicans were democrats; the Federalists, aristocrats. Or more precisely still, that the Republicans represented the citizen against the powers; the Federalists, power in the control of prominent persons. It appears that in every free state these two conceptions must be opposed to each other, and that it is a sign of health that they should be so opposed. But experience has shown that it is not possible to have them live side by side in the same government. Washington thought that the President should be above the parties and that he had the right to take his collaborators wherever he found them. His heart was with Hamilton; it was Hamilton whom he asked to draw up the first drafts of his speeches. The results obtained by Hamilton, re-establishment of public credit, the prosperity of business, seemed to Washington great and praiseworthy achievements. Jefferson, on the other hand, would have preferred less prosperity and more equality. He had returned from France thoroughly imbued with French philosophy. He was "positively electrified at the prospect of the French Revolution." In France he had seen the beginnings of the clubs and societies which sustained the Revolution. With patience and skill he began to organize in the same fashion the Republican party in the United States. He had no doubt, moreover, that if the struggle between the Republicans and the Federalists should become a battle of the land against the city, the Republicans, in a country that was still largely agricultural, must in the long run triumph over the Federalists.

CHAPTER XXIII

The French Revolution

IN 1789 surprising news arrived from France. On July 14 the people of Paris had stormed and then destroyed the ancient royal fortress of the Bastille; on August 4 the French nobility in an excess of abnegation had given up their traditional privileges. Was France, like America, going through a moderate revolution? And had the example of the young republic served to guide the ancient realm? Franklin's long stay in Paris, his popularity, the legend that had grown up around him, the stories brought back by Rochambeau's officers and by travelers, had certainly helped to inspire in the French a passionate desire for change. Since there existed a continent where virtue, simplicity, and liberty were triumphant, why not imitate it? At Lafayette's house as well as in Jefferson's quarters there had been long and fiery discussions. The Night of August

Fourth had been the work of an influential group of young noblemen to whom the American war had given great prestige, and at whose head were the Viscount de Noailles, brother-in-law of Lafayette. After the capture of the Bastille, the key of that fortress had been sent to Washington "because it was American principles that had opened its gates." The Declaration of the Rights of Man had been modeled on the American declarations. France had given Lafayette to America; the latter reciprocated by giving France Jefferson, who advised his friends in Paris to be radical in ideas and moderate in action, a combination familiar enough in Anglo-Saxon countries but hard to maintain in Latin countries. "You are replacing Franklin?" the French ministers had asked Jefferson. "I succeed him; no one can replace him," Jefferson had replied. It was truer than he knew.

The news from France at first filled Americans with enthusiasm. They were proud of being imitated, proud of these young officers who were their spiritual sons, proud to learn that when news of Franklin's death (April 17, 1790) reached France, the Café Procope had been draped in black, the chandeliers hung with crepe and over the door the inscription: FRANKLIN IS DEAD. Many hoped that this revolution, like that of the United States, would be stopped in time and would remain in the hands of its original leaders. They were disturbed when they learned of the increasing violence. No doubt there was an excuse—the threat of invasion. But American clergymen protested against the treatment inflicted on the French clergy and all Americans condemned the massacre of innocent citizens by unauthorized tribunals. To England and later to America came refugees, fleeing the guillotine, and these decried the regime. Burke, the former defender of the American Revolution, began violently to attack the French Revolution. Thirty thousand copies of Burke's *Reflections on the French Revolution* were sold to right-thinking people; one hundred thousand copies of *The Rights of Man* to the "song singing" multitude.

The Rights of Man was a pamphlet by Tom Paine who, though he knew no word of French, had become a deputy at the Convention. Tom Paine made fun of the pity expressed by Burke for the victims of the Terror. "He pities the plumage," said Tom Paine, "and forgets the dying bird." Paine's thesis was that the French Republic, since it was a democracy, had all rights, even that of disregarding law. "What a whole nation decides to do, it has the right to do." But the idea that there cannot be a constitution superior to the wishes of the people was diametrically opposed to the doctrine of the American Founding Fathers, and the reaction was violent. The young Boston lawyer, John Quincy Adams (son of

John Adams), ably replied to Paine under the signature of "Publicola."
He recalled the rights of minorities. If a majority is not bound by any
law, human or divine, and knows no regulation but its own good pleasure, what security, he asked, could the citizens of a nation have and how
could their inalienable rights be guaranteed? Meanwhile John Adams,
Publicola's father, made use of the example of revolutionary France to
condemn all democracy. Remember, Adams warned, that democracy
never lasts long. Soon it becomes exhausted and turns against itself. There
has never been a single democracy, he declared, that did not end in
suicide.

Came the Terror, and America was split in two. The French Revolution, one American said, drove a bloody furrow across American history
as across French history. It not only split the parties; it shaped them,
gave them their frontiers, their passwords, and their bitterness. Half the
country saw in it a struggle between an oppressed people and a tyrant
and took the part of the people against the tyrant. The other half saw
a struggle between the elite and the populace, between religion and
atheism, and took sides with the elite and religion. When the revolutionary army victoriously resisted invasion, the American masses were de-
lirious. Among the more radical the manners of the Revolution spread.
People said: "Citizen Adams . . . Citizen Jefferson . . ." Democratic societies were modeled after the French clubs. King Street in New York
became Liberty Street. Meanwhile the Federalists were emphasizing the
cruelty of the Jacobins. Gouverneur Morris, who had replaced Jefferson as United States ambassador in Paris, was conspiring to save Louis
XVI and trying to arrange for the king's flight. Washington had been
forced to advise prudence: "It has been said in France that you are
favorable to the aristocracy and hostile to the Revolution." In America
it was not only the classes, but the states as well, that were divided by
this conflict. A great majority in the South were for France, less through
Jacobinism than through hatred of the English. New England was
against France, through a mixture of puritanism and Anglophilia. The
word *Jacobin,* a derogatory epithet among the ruling classes, became an
expression of praise in the vocabulary of the opposition. In Philadelphia
a crowd assembled and sang the "Marseillaise" under the window of
Mrs. Bingham, the priestess of Federalism. In Boston all those who did
not love Beacon Street were labeled Jacobins. In Charleston rich planters
wore tricolor cockades, and the descendants of the Huguenots took revenge for Louis XIV by celebrating the execution of Louis XVI. These
quarrels became still more violent with the arrival of Citizen Genêt, the

diplomatic representative to the United States of the New French republic.

Before the Revolution, Citizen Genêt had been an official of the monarchy. His father, director of a subcommittee in the Department of Foreign Affairs, had been well acquainted with Franklin and John Adams. The latter, in fact, had once taken little Edmond Genêt with his own son, John Quincy, to the zoo. Edmond Genêt had succeeded his father in the offices of Monsieur de Vergennes. At the time when events and his career had demanded it, his political ideas had changed and he had made himself conspicuous by his revolutionary zeal; Paine, the oracle of the assemblies on American questions, together with the poet Joel Barlow, had conceived the idea of sending him to America. Genêt was a nephew of Mme. Campan, lady in waiting to Marie Antoinette, and Paine had hoped to arrange for the king and queen of France to leave for America with him. It was clear that if these two unfortunates remained in Paris they would be guillotined. Tom Paine foresaw that this execution would create a distressing impression abroad, even in a friendly country; he hoped to substitute exile in place of the death sentence. His efforts were in vain; meanwhile Edmond Genêt had been appointed and had sailed. His mission was to demand the fulfillment of the Treaty of Alliance of 1778, which provided that in case of war the United States should aid in the defense of the West Indies and that the ports of each of the two countries should be at the disposal of the navies of the other. Genêt was to equip privateers to destroy British commerce and to attempt to reconquer France's colonial empire—Canada, Louisiana, and Florida. It was a vast program, but Citizen Genêt was not intimidated by large plans.

When he landed in Charleston, saw the tricolor cockades and was feted by the Huguenots, Genêt lost his head. He believed he was the idol of the country, the Franklin of this new War of Independence, and even before presenting his credentials he began his campaign. He opened recruiting offices, bought ships for privateering, and hired former American officers to organize an army for the capture of Florida and Louisiana. Praiseworthy energy, but it was to encounter unforeseen obstacles. Part of the people of the United States were wholeheartedly with Genêt; the government, however, was alarmed by his conduct. In a war between France and England, Washington wished to remain neutral. This was not easy. The Treaty of 1778 was explicit; France had already carried out her part, even to victory; Jefferson, recalled in his country by Washington to serve as Secretary of State, maintained that America in its turn could not evade its responsibilities. Hamilton and his friends said that the treaty had been concluded between the United States and the king of France, that the king of France no longer existed, and that those who had cut off his head were in no position to claim his diplomatic heritage. Jefferson replied that the treaty had been concluded, not between the United States and Louis Capet, but between the American nation and the French nation. Washington believed the treaty valid, and in this he was in accord with Jefferson; he thought neutrality desirable, and in this he was in accord with Hamilton. But could the President make a declaration of neutrality when, according to the Constitution, all decisions regarding peace and war belonged to Congress? Jefferson demanded that Congress should be consulted, for he had no doubt that the response would be favorable to France. Hamilton succeeded in persuading Washington to address a proclamation to the citizens of the United States requesting them not to become involved in the hostilities. The word *neutrality* was not used, which calmed Jefferson's scruples, but though the word was absent the fact was not.

Naturally Genêt was furious. A friendly government, nay, an allied government, was preventing him from fulfilling his mission! Jefferson subtly endeavored to draw a distinction between the Secretary of State, who was forced to prohibit and to criticize since such was the will of the President, and Citizen Jefferson, who was willing to listen to the confidences of Citizen Genêt. The latter violently declared that he would appeal over the President's head to the American people. He actually succeeded in rousing the crowds in Philadelphia; engravings were published showing "The Death of G—— W——" in which one could see Washington being guillotined. Some people, like John Adams, feared that an uprising organized by Genêt might attempt to force the government's hand and to induce it to fight on the side of France; Hamilton, completely anti-revolutionary though he was, laughed at these fears. Genêt remained drunk with what he conceived to be his popularity. "I live in the midst of constant celebration. The aged Washington will never forgive my success and the enthusiasm with which the whole city throngs to my house." Dinners at four dollars a plate were given in his honor, in the course of which he sang the "Ça ira." He believed he was strong enough to overthrow the American government, and he established Jacobin clubs wherever he went. But he was much mistaken, and already his Republican friends themselves were growing tired of his excesses. "He will involve us in his shipwreck," they said, "unless we abandon him." Jefferson groaned: "Genêt makes my position terribly difficult"; and he now accepted the noninterventional policy of the President, although this was "a difficult pill for our friends to swallow."

Since Citizen Genêt continued, all too successfully, to arm privateers, his recall was requested and agreed to (1794). His successor, Citizen Fauchet, arrived bearing orders to arrest Genêt and send him back to France to be tried there. Washington refused extradition, thus saving Genêt's head, and the latter became a naturalized American, married the daughter of the governor of New York, and then, having lost his wife, married the daughter of Postmaster General Osgood and ended his days in 1834 as a wealthy country gentleman with an estate on the Hudson. Jefferson had resigned in December, 1793, and retired to Monticello. It was only an apparent retirement. Excellent party leader that he was, Jefferson, from the seclusion of his hermitage, was preparing future victories. He had correspondents in all the important communities and he sustained their zeal by a flattering friendship and innumerable letters. He organized clubs and committees. He watched over and criticized the policy of the administration. In retiring he had said that he was tired of the zeal with which Hamilton, whose influence remained dominant, was soliciting "kicks for American breeches from English boots." Washington himself thought that it had become necessary to straighten out Anglo-American relations. The United States cherished numerous grievances: The English, ten years after the peace, had not yet evacuated the posts of the Northwest; some English officials in Canada continued to treat Americans as enemies and to stir up the Indian tribes of the frontier against them. Since England had been at war she had paid scant attention to the rights of neutrals and had seized all cargoes having any connection whatever with France, which in fact permitted her to seize any American cargo. The shipowners of New England were exasperated. "Free ships make free goods," they said. But the arguments of strength triumphed over considerations of logic. Finally, American sailors, on various pretexts, had been seized, carried off, and forcibly enrolled in the Royal Navy.

Washington judged it necessary to open negotiations with England, and sent to London Chief Justice Jay, a fierce Anglophile who could not pardon France either for being Catholic or for being revolutionary. Jay was not lacking in intelligence or honesty, but he was so susceptible to flattery that in a negotiation he could be denied everything provided it was done to the accompaniment of "praise for his person." "Every man has his weak side, and Mr. Jay's weak side was Mr. Jay." He was so pleased with London that he stayed there about a year, after which he brought back a treaty that caused an uproar. Jay had accepted the English doctrine concerning contraband of war. There was no mention in his treaty of the right of search or the impressment of American sailors, or the indemnities that had been demanded. All that Lord Grenville had conceded was the promise to evacuate the Northwest before June, 1796, plus a few small concessions in the West Indies. It was so brilliant a success for British diplomacy that this very fact rendered it dangerous. The Federalists dared not publish the Jay Treaty and their opponents christened it the Grenville Treaty. The Senate, which discussed it in secret session, refused to ratify one of the clauses. Hamilton had to support it in public, but privately he spoke of it as "the work of an old woman." A senator from Virginia gave a copy to the editor of a paper who published it. There was an immediate outcry. Jay was burned in effigy. Then the public forgot, and some even said in a spirit of contradiction that it was not such a bad treaty. But the Republicans made use of it in the elections to attack the Federalists, who, they said, had betrayed America's French friends to the profit of her English adversaries.

During Jay's sojourn in London the American General Wayne had given a vigorous lesson to the Indians at the Battle of Fallen Timbers and had taken possession of the present-day Toledo. A few days earlier, Washington had been forced to call out the militia to restore order among the farmers of Pennsylvania who had revolted against Hamilton's taxes, especially against the tax on whiskey. The western farmers, all of whom distilled their own liquor, had protested against this levy. They had always made whiskey from their excess corn and rye; they had no other way of exporting their surplus; they refused to pay a tax to which they were unaccustomed, and this refusal in their eyes was just as virtuous an action as the revolt against the British Parliament had formerly been. The rebels were the same; they had simply changed tyrants. Although the rebellion was neither very violent nor very long, Washington wished to make an example of it and to show the strength of the federal government. He succeeded quickly and without bloodshed, but in the ensuing campaign the Republicans made use of the resentment of the farmers. In January, 1795, Hamilton resigned. He could not live properly on the $3,500 salary and had to reopen his law office. He continued to write, to inspire, and to fight, but he remained profoundly pessimistic. A stranger at heart in the nation he had helped to found, an aristocrat by instinct in a society naturally democratic, he did not believe in the future of the work accomplished by his friends and by himself. He said that every day proved to him more and more clearly that the American world was not made for him. He was right: The American world had not been made for him, but in large measure modern America was made by him.

CHAPTER XXIV

The Decline of Federalism

I N 1792 Washington had been re-elected; there had been no opposition. In 1796 he refused to be a candidate. Opposed in principle to the idea of a third term, he had moreover been made indignant by his treatment at the hands of unbridled partisans. The almost religious respect which at first had been accorded him had been followed by violent abuse. Jefferson, in a letter to a friend which was interpreted—against his denial—as referring to Washington, wrote of "apostates" who, after having been "Samsons in the field and Solomons in the council," had allowed the courtesan England to cut their locks. Some said that he had never been a general; others that he had misappropriated state funds! When Congress was about to give him a vote of thanks, a representative named Giles said that he hoped gentlemen would compliment the President privately, as individuals; at the same time, he hoped such adulation would never pervade the House. "I must acknowledge that I am one of those who do not think as much of the President as some others do." Washington complained with justice that he was attacked in terms so excessive and indecent that they would hardly have been merited by a Nero, a notorious defaulter, or a common pickpocket. Worn out and discouraged, he would, he said, have preferred the tomb to another term as President.

Once he had made this decision, he announced it to the public in an eloquent farewell message. It was said to have been drafted by Hamilton, and he did indeed collaborate, but the ideas were Washington's. He warned his country "in the most solemn manner against the baneful effects of the spirit of party." He advised in foreign policy "not to give in to passions nor in international relations to continental catchwords." "Observe good faith and justice toward all nations. . . . Permanent inveterate antipathies against particular nations and passionate attachments for others should be excluded. . . . The nation that indulges toward another an habitual hatred or an habitual fondness is in some degree a slave. . . . Europe has a set of primary interests which to us have none or a very remote relation . . . it must be unwise in us to implicate ourselves by artificial ties in the ordinary vicissitudes

165

of her politics or the ordinary combinations and collisions of her friendships or enmities."

Washington being, by his own wish, eliminated from the contest,
John Adams became the logical candidate of the Federalists. Hamilton
remained the head of the party but he was young, unpopular, and
aggressive; he had no chance of being President and he knew it. His
love of England also would have sufficed to make him distasteful to
the electors. John Adams, on the contrary, though he admired British
institutions, now passed for an Anglophobe, and he had really become
one as he was also a Francophobe, a Europaphobe, and an Adamsophile.
On the Republican side, as the frail and timid Madison did not wish
to run, Jefferson had a clear field. He said he did not want to return
to public life; his enemies doubted his sincerity, but it was a fact that
he loved his retirement in Monticello. Nevertheless he agreed to be
a candidate. The strange method of selection which did not permit the
electors to specify respectively a President and a vice president, but
obliged them to vote at random for two men, fostered schemes and
intrigues. Hamilton, who did not like Adams, hoped that Thomas
Pinckney, the other Federalist candidate, would be elected President.

Aaron Burr was (beside Jefferson) the Republican candidate. Son
of a president of Princeton and grandson of the great preacher Jonathan
Edwards, an able soldier during the Revolution, Burr had returned,
like Hamilton, to the practice of the law and had taken part in the
political life of New York state with brilliant success. He was a man
of much charm, adored by women. All the nameless children of New
York were attributed to him. Aaron Burr was one of the first to discover the advantage to be gained by making use of the strength of the
Tammany Society in New York elections. At the time when the
loyalists were ranging themselves under the banners of St. George,
St. Andrew, and St. Patrick, the opponents of England, the Sons of
Liberty, had founded as a joke the Society of the Sons of Tammany.
Tammany was a celebrated Indian chief, and it was as an ironical
reflection on the British saints that the rebels canonized him. Later
the Tammany Society in New York had become a demagogic group
principally opposed to the propertied classes. Aaron Burr made use of
it against the Federalists. When the election came Burr had thirty
votes; Pinckney fifty-nine; Jefferson sixty-eight; and Adams seventy-
one. And so Adams was elected, but by a margin of only three votes,
for which he was never able to console himself. Hamilton's maneuvers
had failed to elect Pinckney; Adams had been saved by the prudence
of his New England friends, who had voted only for him and had

thrown away their second vote. "Who would have thought," he said indignantly, "to see such a character as Jefferson, and much more, such an unknown human being as Pinckney walk over my head."

His presidency did not begin under favorable auspices. The Federalist majority had been much reduced. Jefferson, the Republican Vice President, was regarded as an intruder by the Federalist administration. Within the party itself, Adams was on bad terms with Hamilton, who was still the leader behind the scenes. He had retained in his cabinet three men who had been with Washington at the end of his presidency, and of whom it was said "that they did not exceed mediocrity except in respect of mendacity." On the day of the inauguration, Adams was struck by Washington's evident joy: "Washington seemed to me to enjoy a triumph over me. Methought I heard him say: 'Ay! I am fairly out and you fairly in! See which of us will be happiest.' " Nevertheless Adams himself was happy enough that day. He had always had an insatiable appetite for ceremonies in which he played the principal part. There was, of course, that paltry majority of three votes to spoil his pleasure. But if his party had treated him ill, could he not triumph over parties and become President of the whole country as Washington had wished to be? He little imagined that his own cabinet members distrusted him and that one of them had described him as: "A man of great vanity, pretty capricious, of a very moderate share of prudence, and of far less real abilities than he believed himself to possess."

An unjust portrait. Adams was very intelligent and, despite his pride, sincerely devoted to his country. But his Calvinism and his political experience combined to give him a sorry opinion of human nature. He thought that self-interest and not ideas actuated men. He did not believe in equality. Every democracy, he said, carries within it an aristocracy as clearly defined as that of France, Rome, or England. If you give power to the multitude, he added, there will be no limit to its demands. The new aristocracy will take your places and treat their former comrades just as severely as you formerly treated them. A republic, according to the new President, should observe the golden mean and stick to the middle of the road between tyranny and anarchy, the extremes which always threaten human societies. In a word, Adams was a realist. He feared the influence of the rich and powerful minority as much as that of the poor and active majority; as much, but not more. He maintained that the role of the statesman is to defend the state against exploitation on one hand and greed on the other. It was an equitable attitude, but not a popular one, and John Adams had few friends.

At the very start, Adams found himself faced by a Franco-American crisis of major importance. Monroe, who had succeeded Gouverneur Morris as ambassador to Paris, had been received at the bar of the Convention and had given warm expression to the sympathy of the United States for the French Revolution. The State Department had rebuked him for this demonstration, which was inconsistent with neutrality, and eventually recalled him. There followed a great uproar in France where the notorious Jay Treaty had already evoked lively indignation. The Directory refused to receive Charles C. Pinckney, Monroe's successor, when he arrived in Paris early in December, 1796, and a number of American ships were seized by French men-of-war on the high seas. It was in fact, if not in law, a break in diplomatic relations. Adams, who desired peace, decided to send to France a special mission composed of John Marshall of Virginia, Elbridge Gerry of Massachusetts, and Pinckney. Meanwhile the Federalists were advising preparation for a war against France, the building of ships and the raising of an army. When the three envoys arrived in Paris, Talleyrand, minister of foreign affairs, sent word that the Directory was seriously annoyed at the United States and might perhaps refuse to receive the mission, but that, in the meantime, qualified persons would call upon them. The "qualified persons," who were designated in the official documents by the letters X, Y, Z, were Messieurs Hottinguer, Bellamy, and Hauteval. At first they insinuated, then stated quite openly, that the mission would not be received unless it gave the Directory "a small mark of consideration," a loan, a gift, which was fixed at two hundred and fifty thousand dollars and which should be without prejudice to the loan that was to follow. The three Americans replied furiously: "No! Not sixpence!" A reply which, as the story of the XYZ affair circulated in the United States, took on this more heroic form: "Millions for defense, not one cent for tribute!"

The publication of the report of the XYZ affair enraged America, and not without reason. More than ever the Federalists preached war; Hamilton believed that the Directory itself was going to declare it. The Jeffersonians begged that all France should not be held responsible for a few dishonest citizens. An improvised Navy Department was given urgent orders to build a fleet. The Treaties of Alliance of 1778 were denounced; Congress authorized the raising of an army, and Washington was summoned from his retirement to take command. Adams hoped to do what he liked with the old man, but he encountered the firm will and meticulous precision of Washington. The general was old, but he did not let himself be influenced. He nominated as major generals, in order of preference, Hamilton, Pinckney, Henry Knox, and Henry Lee. The choice of Hamilton exasperated all his enemies and Adams as well. Thus personal rivalries resulted in weakening the Federalist party. Hamilton was all the more anxious for war since he thought that it would unite the country, make public enemies of the Jeffersonians, and deliver America from French influence. But Jefferson, who saw the trap and was playing the game of politics himself, sent word secretly to warn Talleyrand that a war would lead to the immediate ascendancy of English influence in the United States. Talleyrand understood, played for peace, and won; for Adams, who wished to avoid war at all costs, suddenly decided to send a new minister to France. He had consulted neither Hamilton nor his cabinet, and both were infuriated. Only one hope remained for the Francophobes: the defeat of the Directory and its General Bonaparte by reactionary Europe. At Marengo, Bonaparte destroyed this hope as well, and on September 30, 1800, a commercial treaty between France and the United States put an end to the quarrel. All the rest of his life Adams said that he wished no other inscription on his tomb but this: "Here lies John Adams who in the year 1800 took upon himself the responsibility of peace with France."

Meanwhile in 1798, at the height of the crisis, the Federalists had obtained the passage of laws designed to strengthen the country in time of war. Among these measures was a Naturalization Act that required fourteen years' residence (instead of five) in order to become an American citizen; an Alien Act which authorized the President to deport any alien he considered dangerous; and a Sedition Act which provided punishments for persons who opposed the execution of the laws, wrote, uttered, or published false or defamatory articles about the President and the government, or incited to revolt. A general xenophobia, as well as the revolutionary activities of certain refugees, had inspired these measures. America was tired of importers of hatred, and innocent foreigners suffered the results of this exasperation. When the Directory requested visas for a delegation from the French Institute which wished to visit the United States, John Adams replied: "We have too many French philosophers already, and I really begin to think, or rather to suspect, that learned academies have disorganized the world, and are incompatible with social order." Even the English chemist Priestley had been accused of dissolving church and state in his laboratory retorts. Hamilton did not approve of this sudden intolerance in a liberal country. "Let us not establish tyranny. Energy is a very different thing from violence." But his Federalist friends forgot that the effects of violence soon rebound upon the heads of those who practice violence. They denounced their adversaries as Jacobin atheists and anarchists; they threatened New England, if Jefferson ever came to power, with the horrors of the guillotine; they made use of the new laws to arrest their political enemies. These excesses were to lead to the destruction of the party.

The Republicans, not being a majority in Congress, were unable to prevent the passage of the Federalist measures. But in those states where they were powerful, these measures had been declared unconstitutional. Virginia and Kentucky passed resolutions affirming the right of the states to annul laws of the federal government when the latter exceeded its powers. In respect to the Alien Act the resolutions were in error, for immigration was within the competence of the federal government; but the Sedition Act infringed liberties guaranteed by the Constitution. Actually the protest was a campaign measure designed to put the Republican party in the saddle in time for the presidential election of 1800. An appeal to the jealousy of the states might be effective, and it was. In Virginia, people went so far as to talk of the "Federalist terror." The Federalists, for their part, showed themselves incapable of understanding that party struggles are inevitable in a free country, and that if they are kept within reasonable limits they may even be useful. They wanted to annihilate their adversaries; the wise course would have been to learn to live with them. But for that there was need of political experience, which time alone could give the young republic.

Adams thought he was certain to be elected President a second time in 1800, as Washington had been. He was the only one who thought so. He had become embroiled with his own party leaders, and Hamilton considered him a traitor. The party itself had lost popularity in the country at large, where Jefferson's strong organizations dominated public opinion. The division in the ranks of the Federalists was to assure the success of the Republicans. Hamilton made great efforts to keep Adams from being chosen as the party's presidential candidate, but he failed. A campaign of extraordinary violence began. Hamilton and his friends represented Jefferson, the gentleman farmer of Monticello, as a man with a knife between his teeth, "an atheist in religion, a terrorist in politics." If the Republicans won, so went the Federalist propaganda, the families of New England must expect to see their houses burned, their daughters violated, and the bonds of marriage dissolved. When the electors met, Jefferson and Burr each had seventy-three votes; Adams sixty-five. The Constitution provided that in such cases

Congress was to choose the President, and Congress was Federalist. Aaron Burr should have withdrawn at once in favor of a much older and more famous man whom the country wished to see President. But it was only the influence of Hamilton, who feared Burr even more than Jefferson, that resulted, after thirty-six ballots, in a final victory for Jefferson. This contest had seemed so absurd to everyone that soon an amendment was passed to make the election of President and Vice President two distinct operations. Contrary to the precedent established by Washington, Adams, who was furious at his defeat, did not wait to welcome Jefferson or to take part in the inauguration. Perhaps he is not the only President of the United States who has hated his successor, but he was the only one to show it so naïvely.

CHAPTER XXV

The Time of Jefferson

SOME historians think that the election of Jefferson was a second American revolution. This is an overstatement, but it is true that with Jefferson a new political philosophy came into power. Washington and Adams had had faith in liberty, not in democracy. Jefferson, on the other hand, believed in the American people. Raised by his father, who was a farmer and pioneer, "he loved his backwood neighbors and he, in turn, was loved by them." In those surroundings he had formed three ideas concerning the policy of the United States, and to these he passionately clung. The first was the superiority of a decentralized government. Every movement to consolidate the central power at the expense of the states seemed to him "Toryism in disguise." He believed local government was best because men have a clearer understanding of small affairs in which they are personally interested than of large matters in which they can easily be led astray. "Our country is too large," Jefferson said, "to have all its affairs directed by a single government. Public servants at such a distance, and from under the eye of their constituents, must, from the circumstances of distance, be unable to administer and overlook all the details necessary for the good government of the citizens; and the same circumstance, by rendering detection impossible to their constituents, will invite the public agents to corruption, plunder and waste." The second idea was his belief in the superiority of an agricultural civilization over an urban one. "Those who labour in the earth are the chosen people of God if he ever had

An anonymous anti-Jefferson cartoon of about the year 1800. Jefferson, about to burn the Constitution of the United States on the altar of Gallic despotism, is prevented by an American eagle.

a chosen people. . . . Corruption of morals in the mass of cultivators is a phenomenon of which no age, nor nation, has furnished an example." His third idea was the result of his feeling of alarm at the powers given to the Supreme Court by the Constitution: "The great object of my fear is the Federal Judiciary. That body, like gravity, ever acting, with noiseless foot, and unalarming advance, gaining ground step by step, and holding what it gains, is engulfing insidiously the special governments into the jaws of that which feeds them." All power withdrawn from the permanent control of the people seemed to him a usurpation.

But if the new President differed from his predecessors in doctrine, he remained in manner a cultured and genial Virginian. Eighteenth-century philosopher and nineteenth-century politician, he showed consummate skill in putting the philosopher at the service of the politician. An aristocrat by birth, appearance, and education, he affected a democratic simplicity which bordered sometimes on slovenliness. He received the British ambassador in bedroom slippers out at the heels, which shocked that diplomat. But this was not carelessness, far from it; he had no respect for the British, wanted to show his independence, and knew that this anecdote would be repeated and serve him well among his constituents. He said he was aware that he made no distinction between writing to the most powerful or the most humble person in the world. This was true, but it was strange that he found it necessary to say it. He forced himself to show great evenness of disposition. Under the apparent calm, however, there blazed a fiery nature: "I have sworn upon the altar of God eternal hostility against every form of tyranny over the mind of man." He distrusted the rich, the powerful, the proud; his affection went out to the humble and even more to the farmers and workmen. The mighty returned his distrust. In Philadelphia at the time of his vice presidency the "best families" did not receive him. Nevertheless he was pleasant to meet. He had no sense of humor but he did have subtlety and taste. His intellectual curiosity was boundless. His memory was encyclopedic, but it was an elementary encyclopedia and often ill informed. He had a smattering of all the sciences; he knew a little Greek, a little Latin, a little French. He boasted of having learned Spanish in nineteen days aboard ship with no other master than *Don Quixote*. Possessed of a mania for mechanics of the most bizarre kind, he had filled his house at Monticello with devices of all sorts; a weather vane showed the direction of the wind inside the house, a counterweight opened the door, a system of pulleys brought bottles from the cellar to the master's table. He had taste. Monticello, which he had designed, was charming; and later he was to make the University of Virginia, with its curving brick walls, the finest architectural unit on the continent and one of the finest in the world. He was so fond of reforming that he undertook even to revise the Gospels and to combine all four into a single continuous narrative.

His popularity surprised men like Hamilton, and even Washington, for he was neither an orator nor a soldier. It was due to the fact that the masses instinctively knew Jefferson had confidence in them. Optimism is the most American of sentiments. In regard to human nature, Jefferson was an optimist, Adams a pessimist; and that is why Americans voted for Jefferson.

Major l'Enfant, a Frenchman, had drawn up the plans for the new federal capital to be built on the bank of the Potomac. His vast and orderly project provided for a capitol where Congress would meet, a beautiful house for the President, avenues, squares, monuments. But in 1800 the site of Washington was a lake of mud, the capitol was unfinished, and the city consisted of nothing but a few Negro cabins. Nevertheless, it had been decided to hold the ceremony of inauguration there, and a few days before March 4, with his customary simplicity, Jefferson had come to stay in the Conrad Boarding House. When the day came he went to the capitol on foot "wearing a suit of cloth woven in America." The Chief Justice, John Marshall, one of Adams's men who hated Jefferson, administered the oath on the Bible. Then the President read his inaugural address. The "best families," who had feared to find in him a Robespierre or a Marat, must have heard with relief his appeal for reconciliation. All were asked to abide by the laws, work for the common good, and remember the inviolable principle "that although the will of the Majority is in all cases to prevail, that will, to be rightful, must be reasonable; that the Minority possess their equal rights, which equal laws must protect." "All difference of opinion," he added, "is not a difference of principle. . . . We have called, by different names, brethren of the same principle. We are all republicans; we are all federalists."

Just what did he mean? The two parties asked that question in vain. Probably that the whole country was for the republic against monarchy, and for the federal government against disorder. The President proclaimed tolerance for all, even those who were hostile to the Union; equal justice for all; liberty of the press; liberty of thought; support for the states in defense of all their rights; commercial peace and honest friendship with all nations; a lasting alliance with none. "Sometimes it is said," he went on, "that Man cannot be trusted with the government of himself. Can he then be trusted with the government of others? Or have we found angels in the form of kings to govern him? Let history answer this question." Jefferson thought that a good government was one that allowed men to perform their work freely. He hoped to repay the debt and to this end wished to reduce expenses, eliminate unnecessary personnel, and avoid war. He said he was in favor of a rigorously frugal and simple government and the application of all possible economies to the payment of the national debt. He added that he was hostile to the multiplication of officeholders and salaries when they had no other purpose than to satisfy partisans.

When the ceremony was over Jefferson returned, still afoot, to the Conrad Boarding House. In all probability, he had already decided on the makeup of his cabinet. For Secretary of State he chose Madison. The two men came from Virginia and Jefferson had a father's protective love for Madison. Not that the difference in their ages was great; Jefferson was fifty-eight; Madison, fifty. But the President was tall and vigorous, the Secretary of State small and frail. In the Treasury Jefferson placed Albert Gallatin, a naturalized Genevese and a friend of Madame de Staël and of Baring, the English banker. Gallatin, after being elected to Congress, had revealed a true genius for finance. His incorrigible French accent made this transoceanic Necker a hard orator to understand, but the clarity of his ideas far outweighed this defect. The principal concern of the Democratic-Republicans was to annul the last Federalist laws. The Sedition Act, which was temporary, died of itself; the Naturalization Law was amended and the period reduced from fourteen years to five. The tax on whiskey was repealed, to the great joy of the frontier farmers, who loved Jefferson more than ever. Gallatin estimated that the federal revenue would be about $10,600,000 a year, and that by reducing the expenses of army and navy there need be no more than $3,500,000 expenditure, which permitted a yearly reduction in the debt of $7,000,000. At the end of a few weeks Jefferson went to live in the presidential mansion, which had been ironically named "the Palace," and which Abigail Adams had inaugurated in the midst of plasterers. "The Palace" was not finished, and in particular had no stairway. At his reception Jefferson decided to do away with all right of precedence. Guests went in to the table *pêle mêle* (it was a word he had brought back with him from France). He believed "all human beings are perfectly equal, be they fellowcountrymen or strangers, great lords or simple mortals, and should be treated as such." This resulted in angry ambassadors seeing their chairs snatched away from them by more vigorous congressmen. But the food was worthy of Virginia, the hospitality that of the South, generous and inexhaustible, and the conversation was brilliant. Since Jefferson was a widower, the charming Dolly Madison, wife of the Secretary of State, played the part of First Lady.

"We are all republicans, we are all federalists." The phrase sounded well in the speech; in practice it was necessary to pay heed to the feelings of the party. Now the party wanted offices. Up to the last instant Adams had filled all vacant posts with Federalists and these "midnight nominations" tied Jefferson's hands. "Officials seldom die and never resign," he said. What the friends of the new order required of him was a purge of the whole administration, a difficult action for Jefferson, who had just proclaimed and commended reconciliation. "Mr. Jefferson's plan," said the malcontents, "was to conciliate the North by the dispensation of his patronage, and to rely on the South to support his principles." The pressure became too strong for him to resist and he had to dismiss, as the Constitution allowed him to do, officeholders whose only crime had been to have opinions. This was the first application of the "spoils system," which was to become one of the sores of American political life. Jefferson used it only in moderation.

The most important act of Jefferson's administration was the acquisition of Louisiana. This immense territory, much more extensive than the state which today bears that name and comprising a large part of the valley of the Mississippi, had been ceded by France to Spain in 1763. The latter had granted Americans the right of navigation on the Mississippi and the right to store merchandise at New Orleans. These two rights were indispensable to the Americans of the Ohio River Valley, that is to say, the farmers of the West for whom the river highway was the only possible commercial outlet. And so their anxiety was aroused when they learned in 1802 that Spain by secret treaty had returned Louisiana to France in exchange for Tuscany. Bonaparte, then at the zenith of his glory, seemed a much more dangerous neighbor than feeble Spain, and the Americans were alarmed. They had reason to be. Talleyrand, who knew America, was urging the First Consul to rebuild a French empire, to unite by way of the valley of the Mississippi the bonds between Louisiana and Canada, perhaps even to reconquer the latter and wipe out the Treaty of 1763. As preparation for this enterprise, and to assure a base, General Leclerc had been sent to Santo Domingo, where the Negro Toussaint l'Ouverture had established a dictatorship in defiance of France. Leclerc vanquished the black Bonaparte, but subsequently died himself of the yellow fever that ravaged his army. Jefferson, the friend and admirer of France, was nevertheless the first to understand that if the latter occupied the mouth of the Mississippi the United States would have no choice but to throw herself into the arms of England. He instructed James Monroe and Robert R. Livingston, his minister to France, to open negotiations with France and to offer an undetermined sum for New

"The Mississippi at New Orleans." From Captain Basil Hall, *Forty Etchings*, London, 1829. The flatboats brought the produce of the Mississippi valley to the port, where it was transferred to the ocean-going vessels in the background of the picture. Before railroads all such produce for export had to pass through this bottleneck. This is why the United States had to acquire Louisiana, and why New Orleans became a great commercial center.

Orleans and West Florida; if France refused, they were to secure, if possible, the cession of the island of New Orleans; failing that, the negotiators were to ask for a territory on the left bank of the Mississippi; if that also failed, perpetual right of navigation and storage. Finally, if all failed, Monroe and Livingston were immediately to start conversations with England.

The American envoys were astounded when Talleyrand answered them by saying: "Buy New Orleans? Why New Orleans? Would you not prefer all Louisiana?" The fact was that the expedition to Santo Domingo had disgusted the French with that climate; the First Consul needed money and at the moment when he was beginning a war with England he had no wish to make himself vulnerable by dispersing his armies, especially on a distant continent where England, mistress of the seas, would have all the advantages. There was a brief period of bargaining, and the Americans purchased an empire for the sum of sixty million francs. It was a strange adventure for Jefferson: "This parsimonious lawyer had spent on the authority of his executive power alone a sum equal to three-fourths of the Debt which Hamilton had assumed for the States with the authorization of Congress; the champion of a literal interpretation of the Constitution had acquired foreign territories and granted American citizenship to their inhabitants, acts which were not mentioned among the powers enumerated in the Constitution." He was quite well aware of the lack of consistency in his position. But he also saw that the future of the country depended on the negotiation. The acquisition of Louisiana more than doubled the area of the United States. It assured Americans of free navigation on the Mississippi, that is, of the economic future of the West. It enormously increased military security. To the westward the frontier was so vague that the entire continent might well become American. Before ratifying, Jefferson would have liked to see an amendment made to the Constitution, giving him the legal power to sign. But Livingston and Monroe were pressing him. Talleyrand and Bonaparte might change their minds. He signed, and the Senate ratified his decision.

One might say it was Thomas Jefferson who made the United States a continental power. Not only did he give the country Louisiana, he was also the first to send an American expedition by land toward the Pacific. The west coast had been reached on many occasions by Spanish, English, and Russian navigators. It was known that a great river, the Columbia, discovered in 1792 by Captain Gray, flowed down from the high mountains to the ocean. The name Oregon had been recorded even before that. Since 1783 Jefferson had been dreaming of occupying the territory "from one ocean to the other" granted to the first colonists by the royal charters, and of dispatching an expedition from the Mississippi to the Pacific. At that time the necessary money could not be found. But in 1803 when he was President he obtained from Congress $2,500 "for a literary project." This strange description was intended to avert the suspicion of England, who also had designs on that region. The exploration was entrusted to two young men, Lewis and Clark. Meriwether Lewis had been Jefferson's secretary, and the latter had recognized his courage, perseverance, knowledge of the Indians, and honesty. The journey was as romantic as any that could be imagined. Lewis and Clark proceeded up the Missouri, crossed the Rocky Mountains, descended the Columbia River, and finally heard the waves of the Pacific breaking at the mouth of the Columbia. This trip was to be of inestimable importance later on in establishing America's claim to this region.

It was written that Jefferson's greatest successes should be achieved in violation of his principles. This pacifist made a war, carried it on at four thousand miles distance from America, and won it. A tiny war. The Barbary pirates of North Africa, from the time of the late Middle Ages, had been exacting tribute from all the sailors of the world except those that were strong enough to defend themselves. Since the day when the independence of the United States had been declared, the British fleet had ceased to protect United States merchantmen and the Barbary privateers had dealt savagely with them. What was to be done? It would be necessary to pay tribute to the Sultan of Morocco, the Bey of Algiers, the Bey of Tunis, and the Pasha of Tripoli. It was humiliating and moreover useless, for the demands of the privateers increased each year. The United States had reached the point of spending almost two million dollars. Jefferson decided that enough was enough, and sent a small squadron into the Mediterranean against the Pasha of Tripoli. The American frigate *Philadelphia* was stranded, its officers and sailors taken captive by the Barbary pirates and reduced to slavery. Lieutenant Decatur, having made fast beside the frigate, blew it up to keep the Pasha from getting possession of it. Then a small expedition by land, led by the United States consul at Tunis, took possession of Derna (in memory of which a street in Boston is still called Derna Street). The Pasha became terrified and asked for terms. It was in the course of this campaign in the Mediterranean that the American navy (which showed great enterprise and heroism) first earned the respect of European navies and became aware of its own strength.

The Louisiana affair was not yet settled. The Creoles of New Orleans thought it had been agreed that Louisiana should become a state, and indeed it would seem that Jefferson's ideas would not permit him to impose external authority upon another people. But Congress refused to admit Louisiana and made it a territory. This resulted in a feeling of great bitterness. On the other hand, Jefferson thought that West Florida and Texas had been part of his purchase. Spain and France denied it. Shadowy negotiations had taken place and these were displeasing to the purists of the Republican party. One member of the party, the eloquent and rebellious John Randolph of Roanoke, loudly attacked Jefferson, and another, Aaron Burr, conceived the extravagant notion of making a personal empire for himself in Mexico or Florida. Since 1805 Burr had no longer been Vice President. As the brilliant and cynical boss of New York he had for several years entertained boundless political hopes. The election of 1800 destroyed them. The vice presidency, attended by Jefferson's ill will, proved a blind alley. He tried to find a way out by running for governor of New York. Opposed by Hamilton, who called him a "dangerous man," he was defeated. He provoked Hamilton to a duel and deliberately killed him. Thus the pistol of an adventurer cut short the life of a man of genius, honor, and courage who had, perhaps, imperfectly understood eighteenth-century America but who had made a brilliant contribution to nineteenth-century America. Hamilton died insolvent, leaving a widow and children. The duel, which had been almost a murder, put an end to Aaron Burr's political career. Seeing that he was done for in his own country, he threw himself into desperate and shameful enterprises. He asked the English for a million dollars as the price of detaching the western territories from the Union; he tried to get money from the Spaniards, and then conspired with General Wilkinson to attack Mexico. Wilkinson denounced him and Jefferson had him arrested for treason. Aaron Burr, tried by a Grand Jury, was acquitted, thanks to Chief Justice John Marshall, who eloquently recalled the definition of treason and showed that it did not apply to this affair. But if Burr was not a traitor, his career was finished and he had to go into self-imposed exile in Europe. There he lived for a time by his wits and on gifts from women. Later he returned to the United States, married a rich widow, and resuming his original profession became once more a prosperous lawyer.

Meanwhile Napoleon and Great Britain were vying for the domination of the world, and this titanic struggle stirred up eddies in all oceans of the globe. To recruit their sailors the English had recourse to "impressment"; on all the oceans they stopped ships, searched them, and if they found English, Scotch, Irish, or Welsh merchant seamen, they arrested and enrolled them. Soon they were subjecting American ships to the same treatment. It is true that some deserters from the British fleet had been given false American passports; but also many

Americans were falsely accused of being English or Irish and were forcibly enrolled. When the State Department complained to the Foreign Office, the Foreign Office replied that the man in question could not be found, or that he was at sea, or that he was dead. The most serious incident occurred when the American frigate *Chesapeake* was summoned to halt by the English frigate *Leopard* on the pretext of searching for a deserter. When the captain refused, the *Leopard* opened fire, killing three men and wounding eighteen. This insult to the American flag in time of peace (1807) stirred up wholehearted, unanimous, and legitimate indignation. Exasperation at the attack on the *Chesapeake* united Americans of all parties. "The affair of the *Chesapeake*," Jefferson said later, "put war into my hand. I had only to open it and let havoc loose." But Jefferson did not like war; the tone of his proclamation was so moderate that the irascible John Randolph could say that it had rather the air of a note of apology. The situation at sea became intolerable for neutrals. The British government's Orders in Council forbade all commerce with European ports. Napoleon's Decrees (Berlin, 1806; Milan, 1807) prohibited all commerce with the British Isles and ordered the seizure of all ships coming from England or her colonies. Between the Orders in Council and the Decrees, what was to become of the Yankee shipowners? It is a great compliment to their skill to record that in these difficult circumstances their prosperity remained unaltered.

Jefferson thought that he could secure respect for America by means of what he called "peaceable coercion." By this strange and paradoxical formula he meant the old method of breaking off trade relations. "Our commerce is so valuable to them," he said innocently of the French and English, "that they will be glad to purchase it, when the only price we ask is to do us justice." A member of Jefferson's own party, John Randolph, protested against this "milk and water bill." "It is too contemptible," he added, "to be the subject of consideration or to excite the feelings of the pettiest state in Europe." It must be admitted that facts bore Randolph out. Monroe, sent to London to negotiate, achieved nothing. An American embargo on all foreign commerce (December 22, 1807) did much more harm to America than to France or England. Moreover, American shipowners disregarded it. Freight rates were so high that they were willing to run any risks. The result was that in 1808, by a decree from Bayonne, Napoleon ordered the seizure of all American vessels found in French ports. "For," he said ironically, "these vessels cannot be American; if they were, they would respect the embargo; they are, therefore, camouflaged English ships."

The Federalist shipowners began to ask if their interests were to be sacrificed indefinitely to the agrarian pacifism of the "charlatan" in Washington. "I will lift the embargo," Jefferson told Paris and London, "if the Orders in Council and the Decrees are abrogated." Canning replied, with courteous mockery, that "His Majesty would be happy to see the lifting of the embargo which caused the American people such hardships," but he retained the Orders in Council. In New England anger rose to the point of sedition and in certain town meetings there was even talk of secession. Three days before the inauguration of his successor, James Madison (March 1809), Jefferson had to capitulate. He lifted the embargo. As the first four years of his administration, including the purchase of Louisiana, had been brilliant, so the last four years had been undistinguished. John Randolph compared them to the lean kine in the Bible who came after the fat kine. Toward the end Jefferson himself was beginning to wonder whether the country could avoid war. "Perhaps," he wrote to a friend, "perhaps the whale of the ocean may be tired of the solitude it has made on that element, and return to honest principles; and his brother robber on the land may see that, as to us, the grapes are sour. . . . I think one war enough for the life of one man; and you and I have gone through one which at least may lessen our impatience to embark in another. Still, if it becomes necessary we must meet it like men, old men indeed, but yet good for something." He was happy to hand on the office to Madison, whom he had chosen as his successor and imposed upon the party. Never did prisoner delivered from his chains, he said, feel relief equal to his when he was freed from the manacles of power.

CHAPTER XXVI

War's Labor Lost

A GREAT expert in constitutional law, of subtle and honest mind, far better informed than Jefferson, Madison had shone from youth onward as a second-magnitude star of singular brilliance. But his frail constitution, which had prevented him from fighting in the War of Independence, made him timid. From childhood he had believed himself destined to an early grave; he was to live to the age of eighty-five. A small blond man with blue eyes, always clad in black, with powdered hair gathered at the nape of his neck, he spent his life reading and writing. His friends loved him; he was unknown to the masses. Although witty and sometimes Rabelaisian in private, he seemed so insipid to those who did not know him well that they thought it impossible even to invent a scandal about him. Without his wife and without Jefferson he would never have been President—and would have found that easily bearable. At forty-three he had married a young widow, the pretty, plump Dolly Todd, who was as skilled in politics as her husband was the reverse. He had met her in Philadelphia, where she and her mother took in a few boarders, among them the redoubtable Aaron Burr, who had one day introduced to her the "great little Madison." He fell in love with her and married her. At the time when he was Secretary of State, she paved the way for his election to the presidency by giving Congress such excellent and sumptuous dinners that the unusual mortality that year among senators was attributed, by public opinion, to these culinary triumphs. On the day of his inauguration, Madison trembled so much that it was hard to hear what he said. Moreover he did not say much. Jefferson, on the contrary, seemed radiant. As for Dolly Madison, at the reception that followed the ceremony, she had the air of a queen in her white gown with a long train, her rope of pearls, her turban imported from France, and her bird of paradise plumes. Madison, for his part, looked exhausted. A friend who saw him standing, pale and swaying, said to him: "I wish with all my heart I had a little bit of seat to offer you." "I wish so too," Madison replied, and added with the melancholy humor that was characteristic of him, "but I would much rather be in bed."

The Republican party at that time was so divided by foreign policy and the embargo that Madison had great difficulty in forming a cabinet. He kept Gallatin in the Treasury, but as Secretary of State he had to accept Robert Smith, whom he did not like and who began the administration with a diplomatic disaster. It was agreed between the State Department and David Erskine, the British minister, that the United States should once more authorize commerce with England, and in return the Orders in Council would no longer be applied to the United States. This was a triumph for the new President, and the whole country sang his praises. But Erskine had exceeded his authority and was disavowed by Canning: The Orders in Council were retained, and Madison was sadly compelled to re-establish the embargo. To cap the climax of misfortune, Erskine was recalled and replaced by "Copenhagen" Jackson, who was celebrated in the diplomatic corps for his brutality and insolence. In Washington, Jackson surpassed himself and was so disagreeable that the gentle Madison refused to deal with him, and he in his turn was recalled. Meanwhile the ships were once more tied up at the harbor quays and the Yankee sailors were protesting. Congress tried a new policy: It authorized the reopening of *all* commerce, but decided in advance that if either France or England abandoned the offensive measures, then commerce with the other would be suspended. It was a premium offered to the first one to give in. Napoleon cunningly accepted and promptly announced to the American government that he would revoke the Decrees of Berlin and Milan. Although John Quincy Adams thought, not without reason, that this was nothing but "a trap to catch us in a war with England," Madison, bound by his declaration, was forced to act and once more suspended commerce with Great Britain. This meant running the risk of war, and the President asked Congress for the means to put the country in a state of defense, but Congress was thinking as much of the coming election as of the enemy, and the administration was not sustained. Madison replaced Robert Smith as Secretary of State by Monroe, who knew England well and who hoped to remain at peace with her.

The American navy had violently resented the humiliation of the *Chesapeake* affair and was hoping for revenge. Its wish was granted when Commodore Rogers, who was on patrol in his frigate *President* in the neighborhood of New York encountered an English ship, tried to stop her in order to search for an "impressed" sailor, fired, killed nine men and wounded twenty-three. The score was now even. The English, suddenly less uncompromising, agreed to return the sailors taken from the *Chesapeake,* or at least the two still living, and to indemnify the families of the dead. But the elections had introduced into Congress a group of young men called the War Hawks, who were deliberately hoping for an open break. Why? Because they represented the frontier states and they saw in an Anglo-American conflict a chance for expansion. In the Northwest there were still questions to be settled—that of the fur trade; that of the Indians who continued to attack American farmers and who were thought to be armed by the British. Perhaps even a conquest of Canada might be possible. To the people from the South, the annexation of the Floridas seemed desirable to protect the shores of the Mississippi and the Gulf. Had not the conquest of Spain by Napoleon released the Spanish colonies from their allegiance to a defeated sovereign? "Nature has decreed the union of Florida and the United States." A small uprising aided nature, and western Florida gave herself to the United States. Madison hesitated. Ought he to take this province that was offering itself? Public opinion allowed no refusal.

Of this public opinion the West now formed a part which it was necessary to take into account. Since the promulgation of the Northwest Ordinance, three new western states—Kentucky, Tennessee, and Ohio—had been admitted to the Union. Others were in process of formation. The movement of migration toward the West was uninterrupted. New cities— Cincinnati, Cleveland, Pittsburgh—were developing. Countless rafts floated down the Ohio loaded with the meager possessions of families on their way to settle lands sold to them by real-estate companies whose advertising had attracted them. There were men like Daniel Boone who could only live as the advance guard of human society with free space before them. In 1769 he had left North Carolina for the blue grass of Kentucky. Later he had left there for the Missouri and eventually went as far as Kansas. But men like Boone were not the only type in the West; in their wake followed the planter and the land speculator. By 1810, Kentucky, Tennessee, and Ohio were inhabited by established citizens who were building houses instead of cabins, laying out cities, endowing colleges, and founding churches. And so in the West there arose the elements of two new political parties. On the fringe was born the democracy of Ohio, more equalitarian, ruder, more picturesque than that of Jefferson, dominated by men who wore coonskin caps and short hair instead of powdered wigs. In the new cities a self-reliant and individualistic middle class arose with unlimited hopes and ambitions. The two groups had one desire in common; they wanted land, always more land, the planters in order to push forward and clear it, the middle classes for purposes of sale and speculation. But in their rush toward the West they encountered the Indian and they believed that behind him, arming him and exciting him to resistance, were the British in Canada. And so all these men of the West, impatient of obstacles, declared in favor of a rapid expansion in the country, even at the cost of a conflict. The most violent among them raised the war cry: "Canada! Canada!" There they would find unlimited open spaces. This desire became an obsession. To conquer virgin lands they were ready once more to brave the British Empire.

Young Henry Clay, congressman from Kentucky and, at thirty-four, Speaker of the House of Representatives, an eloquent man with charming manners, and an aggressive nationalist, was one of the most vigorous champions of this warlike policy. In southerners like John C. Calhoun, the brilliant orator who represented South Carolina in Congress, he found allies who responded by crying "Florida!" when Clay shouted "Canada!" But if the War Hawks of the South and West were fiery, the Federalists, and the Yankees in general, for the most part condemned this agitation. What, they asked, were the United States' grievances against England? She was arming the Indians? That had not been proved. She "impressed" sailors? She had made apologies, the offenses were mutual, and there had been British deserters on American ships. As to the conquest of Canada, it was a large enterprise, and the Yankees, having tried it several times, retained an unpleasant memory. But the young War Hawks had no doubt of success. "The militia of Kentucky alone," said Henry Clay, "are competent to place Montreal and Upper Canada at your feet." Calhoun maintained that this conquest could be carried out in four weeks: "Is it nothing to extinguish the torch that lights up savage warfare?"

It is only fair to remember that for the men of the frontier the Indians represented a real and terrifying danger. As formerly in Pontiac's time, a powerful chief, Tecumseh, and his brother, the Prophet, had succeeded in uniting a number of tribes. On November 7, 1811, General William Henry Harrison, governor of the Indian Territory, crushed them at Tippecanoe, and found that they had been armed with English muskets. At this news the warmongers exulted. A member of Congress who had seen his three brothers killed by Indians talked sternly of "the power that seizes every occasion to intrigue with the savages and encourages them to mutilate our women and children." President Madison mediated a long time. Finally he gave in. His enemies lost no time in pointing out that this was the year when the question of his re-election was to be decided, and he knew that he had no chance without the support of the young partisans of war led by Clay and Calhoun. However that may be, on June 1, 1812, he sent Congress a war message that was nothing but a long list of British offenses, at the head of which in the place of honor, stood the "impressment" of sailors. Although all these grievances were old stories, war was declared on June 18. Five days later the British prime minister, who of course knew nothing about these discussions in Washington, withdrew the Orders in Council. Most reasons for fighting were gone, but the battle had begun.

In England the situation was grave. Napoleon seemed very close to defeating her; the workers were complaining of unemployment and there were riots; the farmers had become threatening; the colossus was tottering. But America went to war without army or navy. She had about seven thousand men, badly commanded and without a general staff, and sixteen ships against the immense British fleet. Her financial situation was no better. The Bank of the United States had disappeared the preceding year through non-renewal of its charter. Gallatin decided to issue paper money himself, and to finance the war in this way and by borrowing, rather than to increase taxes in a country that was already full of discontent. But loans were not easy to place when the North, the richest part of the country, was opposed to the war. Six-per-cent bonds could not be floated at better than 80, and only then by accepting in payment bank notes that were depreciated to 65 per cent of their value. The morale of the nation was poor. New England thought it wrong to attack England at the moment when she was defending the liberty of the world against Napoleon. New England was surprised to see the agricultural population of the West so determined to defend the honor of American sailors when the American sailors themselves had declared that they were satisfied. New England could not understand why war should be declared in 1812 when the principal pretext was the *Chesapeake* affair, which had taken place in 1807 and which, moreover, had been satisfactorily settled. The truth was that the real motives were quite different from the ostensible ones. When Henry Clay discoursed about the rights of sailors, he was thinking of the wishes of the pioneers. The war was a sectional one, and when election day came it was by a sectional majority of the West and South that Madison was re-elected.

The war had hardly been declared when the two adversaries began talking about peace. The Americans simply asked that England should renounce "impressment" on their ships; the English said they were ready to stop visiting American ships *in fact* but not to renounce *in principle* "an ancient practice which was among their customs." A subtle and fruitless distinction. Shipowners of New England said that they did not want to be protected; the War Hawks condemned them for their cowardice and swore that they should be protected in spite of themselves. The invasion of Canada was a lamentable fiasco. Canada had no troops, barely four regiments, plus militia and Indian auxiliaries. It numbered only a half-million inhabitants, against over seven million in the United States. But the United States had only a tiny regular army, grown indolent through inaction. The New England militia refused to mobilize for "Mr. Madison's War." That of New York went as far as the frontier and arriving there stopped dead, saying that they would defend their own land but not invade Canada. They watched the defeat of an American army on the other shore of the Niagara without making any move to help. When at last they opened fire, it was to show "a preference for the General's tent as target." There was a moment when it seemed likely that Canada would invade the United States. English troops occupied Detroit.

On the other hand, the United States covered itself with glory at sea. In London there had been talk of "a few fir built frigates manned by a handful of bastards and freebooters." But the frigates *Constitution, United States,* and *President* had a firepower superior to any other vessel in the world, and they inflicted terrific blows on the British fleet. Now all America was repeating the phrase "fir built frigates." Decatur, the hero of Tripoli, took an English frigate prisoner. The American privateers took

BROTHER JONATHAN Administering a Salutary Cordial to JOHN BULL.

Courtesy of the American Antiquarian Society, Worcester, Mass.

Caricature by Amos Doolittle, 1813, depicting Perry's Victory on Lake Erie. In submitting it to a newspaper the artist remarked: "Although many caricatures extant are of no use, and some of them have an immoral effect, I flatter myself that this will not answer that description. At the present time, it is believed, it will have a tendency to inspire our countrymen with confidence in themselves."

so many prizes that English insurance companies were demanding a premium of 15 per cent for a single Channel crossing. Naturally these successes, however brilliant they might be, could not decide the issue of the war. But on the northern lakes other and more decisive naval engagements were being fought. The control of the lakes was necessary to assure the service of communications and supplies in those uninhabited regions. Oliver Hazard Perry, a young American officer, built a fleet on Lake Erie and in September, 1813, gained a naval victory there so complete that it enabled General Harrison to take Detroit, destroy Tecumseh's Indians, and make safe the northern frontier.

As long as British resources were being absorbed in Europe the war languished; but in 1814, when Napoleon had been defeated, England became stronger and more active in America. She devised a plan for invading the United States from three sides: by way of Niagara, Lake Champlain, and New Orleans. In the north, at the battle of Lundy's Lane, the now well-trained American army put up a good fight. On Lake Champlain Commander MacDonough, United States Navy, scored a decisive victory over the British fleet and put an end to an invasion that might have been dangerous, for it was threatening New York by the classic corridor of the Hudson. In revenge, on the Atlantic coast, the English succeeded in a most effective raid against the American capital. The city of Washington was defended by no more than a few gunboats. A small expeditionary force of four thousand five hundred men arrived from Bordeaux, landed on the shores of Chesapeake Bay, and advanced overland on Washington. Madison called out the militia; less than one-tenth of the men summoned appeared; they were hastily assembled at Bladensburg, seven miles from the capital. Few of these militiamen had ever tasted fire; after a few shots they fled in disorder toward Washington. Their excuse was that the British, lacking bullets, had launched rockets at the American positions; these did little damage but were startling and most effective. This rout was called not the Battle of Bladensburg but the "Bladensburg Races." Only four hundred sailors were left to delay the enemy and save the militia from massacre, but they could not save the city. Madison, his wife, and cabinet had to cross the Potomac in haste, Dolly Madison carrying the silver spoons and the portrait of George Washington by Gilbert Stuart. Admiral Cockburn found the presidential dinner still hot and ate it. The next day he burned the public buildings in the city in reprisal, he said, for the burning by the Americans of the Parliament of York (Toronto). In the Virginia fields Madison was received with insults by the people, who believed him responsible for this disaster, but he remained unmoved. When, later on, the President returned to Washington, it was necessary to repair and entirely repaint "the Palace" which had been ravaged by fire; after that it was popularly called the White House; although that was not its official designation until much later. In New England this war produced unforeseen results. The embargo had made the development of industry necessary. In 1805 there were four thousand five hundred spindles for cotton spinning in the United States. In 1815 there were one hundred and thirty thousand. Countless privateers enriched the shipowners with their prizes (more than one thousand three hundred). Army contractors sold food and leather at very high prices to the British troops in Canada. But "Mr. Madison's War" remained unpopular among the Yankees. The annexation of the West, some said, by destroying the equilibrium of the Union had released the eastern states from their allegiance. They must either break away or demand new laws. The legislature of Massachusetts invited the other New England states to a convention which met at Hartford. Madison was alarmed and thought secession close at hand. But the conspirators did not go that far. The moderate Federalists won the day and confined themselves to suggesting amendments to the Constitution. For example, in no two successive administrations was the President to come from the same state. It was a direct attack upon Virginia, Mother of Presidents, and upon Madison. But the agitation quickly died.

As to the British expedition to New Orleans, it was brief and inglorious. In Tennessee there was a General Andrew Jackson who had had a very strange career. A Major General of the militia of Tennessee, he had never had occasion in his forty-five years to go to war. When the chance came, first against the Indians, then against the English, this amateur acquitted himself very well indeed. In December, 1814, some eight thousand to nine thousand veteran English soldiers under General Pakenham landed in Louisiana. The Englishman thought he could take New Orleans without trouble. But Jackson, who had been made major general of the army and commander-in-chief in the South, recruited men, built trenches, and when the attack came on January 8, 1815, it was received as at Bunker Hill. Pakenham was killed; the English sustained about two thousand casualties; the expedition was done for and Jackson, nicknamed Old Hickory by his soldiers because of his toughness and endurance, became the most popular man in the country. Peace had been signed fifteen days before he won his victory, but he did not know it and he had given his country reasons for pride which for a long time made this war, in the eyes of America, a second War of Independence.

It was the unique characteristic of this conflict that the peace negotiations were begun almost on the day of the declaration of war and were never interrupted. The emperor of Russia himself took a hand in the proceedings. His country invaded by Napoleon, he did not wish England to be distracted from the European war. Finally in 1814 the American negotiators met the British negotiators at Ghent. The Americans were John Quincy Adams (son of John Adams), more Puritan than the Puritans, a Protestant of Protestants, and a determined champion of New England's rights; Henry Clay, "the gallant Harry of the West," prince of the War Hawks and apostle of expansion; Gallatin, the straightforward and conciliatory Swiss; James A. Bayard of Delaware, whom John Quincy Adams called the Chevalier; and Jonathan Russell of Rhode Island. Adams went to bed at dusk; Henry Clay at dawn. Adams insisted, in the name of the fishermen of Nantucket and other places, on fishing rights in Newfoundland, and cared very little about the Mississippi; Henry Clay would gladly have abandoned Newfoundland, and was interested only in the Mississippi. All the American delegates were at one in demanding the abandonment of "impressment"; all the English delegates were at one in refusing this. They, for their part, demanded an end to the American fishing rights in Newfoundland, a vast Indian reservation in the Northwest, and a rectification of the frontier on the basis of the territory they then held. Henry Clay swore that he would not agree to cede the Indian territory; Adams that he would die for the fishing rights; both that they would maintain, in the matter of the frontiers, the *status quo ante bellum*. The negotiations seemed hopelessly involved. But Wellington, whom the British government proposed to send out to win this war in America, replied very wisely that without control of the lakes he could do nothing. The general's prudence was a useful lesson for the British government, which decided to give up the idea of territorial acquisitions. And the Indians? They would not be used again. And the fishermen? They were to be passed over in silence. The rights of neutrals at sea? Too dangerous a subject. The Mississippi? Not a word. The treaty contained nothing more. And so there was no reason at all for not signing it, which was done on Christmas Eve, 1814. The English invited the Americans to dinner and served them roast beef and plum pudding. The orchestra played *God Save the King* and *Yankee Doodle*. The sentimental feeling that united the men of both nations that evening was perhaps the single element of reality in this agreement. But that was nothing to scoff at. And "impressment"? It disappeared completely in the nineteenth century; with Napoleon defeated it was no longer necessary, life aboard warships became less hard, and voluntary enlistments sufficed to maintain a fleet. Thus the question settled iteslf as soon as the statesmen ceased to discuss it, as is the way with questions.

The reactions of nations are as unpredictable as those of individuals.

It is hard to imagine a more absurd and fruitless conflict than the War of 1812. The pretext for it was a determination to assure the freedom of the seas; it was concluded by a peace in which this was not even mentioned. It had so completely divided the country that President Madison was afraid of secession. It ended in such a spirit of unity that the famous Hartford Convention dissolved without making any demands. And what had been the reason for this sudden change of attitude? A victory gained by an amateur general fifteen days after peace had been signed. The art of government is not easy. It only becomes so in certain brief and happy periods when economic prosperity engenders political euphoria. The United States was about to enter such a period.

CHAPTER XXVII

The Era of Good Feeling

THE Peace of Ghent coincides with the end of a world. In the United States as in Europe the nineteenth century begins in 1815. During the eighteenth century abstract doctrines about man brought into opposition the Hamiltons and Jeffersons of all countries. After 1815 who cares about universal man or natural rights? The Western world is entering the era of nationalism. In the eighteenth century Americans were sharply divided into pro-English and pro-French. After 1815 they are all unanimously pro-American. Europe had interested them as long as she was battling for political philosophies. But what did the citizens of Kentucky or Ohio care for the dynastic rivalries or colonial ambitions of the old nations of Europe? More than ever the United States felt itself independent and autonomous. During the war, the East had given birth to industries; the South had regained her wealth through the growing of cotton; to the west, a whole continent awaited development. The unity of the country was assured by its common prosperity. It was manifested in striking fashion in the two elections of Madison's successor, who had been his Secretary of State, James Monroe. In 1816 Monroe had all the states for him except three: Massachusetts, Connecticut, and Delaware. In 1820 he was elected unanimously except for one vote, and that single ballot was withheld only through principle—in order that Washington should remain the only President to have been elected unanimously. Was an era of national union to follow that of partisan and sectional strife? For several months one might have thought so.

Monroe deserved to be the beneficiary of this national unity. Like Jefferson and Madison he was a Virginian, but neither the East nor the North held it against him. Jefferson said of him that he was so honest you could search his soul and not find a single blot. He was conscientious and modest; he dressed in the old fashion: silk breeches, buckles, pumps. Adams described him as "investigating by the midnight lamp the laws of Nature and nations." He was inaugurated, as was fitting, on a day of delightful calm. In his inaugural address he spoke "of the present happy state, the increased harmony of opinion which pervades our Union." Henceforth Americans loved one another. Or at least they seemed to. Political programs were no longer sectional but national and, furthermore, nationalistic. An army of ten thousand men was raised with two major generals, one of whom was Andrew Jackson; new warships were added to the fleet. The Republicans (and particularly those from the West) now took up once more the projects of Alexander Hamilton. Suddenly accepting the activities of a central government, they created a second Bank of the United States (the charter of the first had expired in 1811); they voted a protective tariff to help the infant industries of the East; to satisfy the western voters who lacked means of transportation, they undertook the construction of roads and canals which "would bind together all the States of the Republic" and incidentally make the fortune of the land buyers. Thus the Republicans, disguised as Federalists, substituted for the ancient colonial system of England something that they called the American system. The idea was simple. America could and should be henceforth sufficient unto herself. New England would produce the manufactured products needed by the South and West, and the agriculturists would find markets for their products in the industrial states. The American system was accepted for the time by the whole country. Monroe made a trip to the former Federalist sections; the warmth of his reception proved that grievances had been forgotten. A Boston newspaper said that this trip inaugurated "the era of good will." The phrase pleased the President and he made frequent use of it.

Naturally the idea that the American system would satisfy all America was nothing but a beautiful dream. Sectional interests continued to be in disagreement on many points. The South and the East both sought the commerce of the new western states and vied with each other for it. The natural access to this region was the Mississippi. Around the beginning of the century the steamboat with which Americans had been experimenting for a number of years, had been made commercially practicable, and had greatly increased the usefulness of the river. In 1807 Robert Fulton, to everyone's great surprise, had succeeded in going up the Hudson River as far as Albany—a distance of one hundred fifty miles—in thirty-two hours. This was revolutionary. Up to that time the flatboats that supplied the service on the Mississippi and Ohio between New Orleans and Pittsburgh had gone upriver by the expensive method of towing. It required three or four months and the fare for one passenger was $160. As soon as the steamboats were powerful enough to proceed against the current, the price of passage fell to $30. By 1825 there were on the Mississippi and Ohio one hundred and twenty-five steamboats, picturesque floating hotels.

To compete with New Orleans the ports of the East had only one resource: to open a direct means of communication with the Great Lakes. Then they would be able to drain off the commerce of the northern part of the new states. In answer to this need the Erie Canal was constructed from Buffalo on Lake Erie to Albany on the Hudson River. It was built by the state of New York, and inaugurated in 1825; Governor Clinton solemnly threw a bucket of water from Lake Erie into New York Harbor to symbolize the marriage of the waters. The success of the canal was complete. The freight charges from New York to Buffalo were reduced from $100 a ton to $15, and the time of the trip from twenty days to eight. Thus the prosperity of Buffalo was assured, and it became a great port of transit on the shore of Lake Erie between Detroit and New York. Utica, Syracuse, Rochester, Buffalo, Cleveland, Detroit, and Chicago entered a boom period. The canal also made the defense of the country's northern frontier much easier. After this success every port in the East wanted to have its canal and to compete with New York. But all did not fare so well, for they encountered the competition of a new means of transportation—the railroad.

President Monroe had resolutely decided not to select a Virginian as Secretary of State. The East and the West would have accused him of perpetuating the Virginia dynasty. But Henry Clay expected to be offered the post and was profoundly wounded when John Quincy Adams was named instead. Nevertheless it was a good choice. John Quincy had Puritan firmness, the Adams pride, a certain knowledge of Europe, and he was well fitted to represent America in a time of nationalism. His relations with England were not troublesome. The storm of 1812 had cleared the air. The 49th parallel became the frontier between Canada and the United States as far as the Rocky Mountains, and it was agreed that the Oregon Territory should be occupied by a condominium for ten years. It was with Spain that thorny questions remained to be settled. In Florida, Spain still remained theoretically sovereign. However, weakened as she was in Europe, she had great trouble in maintaining order in her colonies. Runaway slaves found a refuge there, as well as marauding Indians who harried Georgia from this retreat which they thought inviolable. General Jackson, in the course of a victorious expedition against the Seminole Indians, was led to pursue the enemy into Spanish Florida, and there he hanged two British subjects who were accomplices of the Indians. Spain protested; Monroe and his cabinet, at heart, approved Jackson, but they dreaded a war begun by a violation of the frontier without congressional authorization; John Quincy Adams, aided by the French minister, Hyde de Neuville, succeeded in combining firmness with a conciliatory attitude. To the Spaniards he said: "Put your house in order or sell it to us." King Ferdinand of Spain finally agreed to sell Florida and her claims to the Oregon Territory to the United States for five million dollars. That night John Quincy Adams thanked "the Dispenser of all good things."

But the whole Spanish empire in America was threatened with ruin. During the occupation of Spain by Napoleon, South America had enjoyed a *de facto* liberty; it had traded directly with the United States and with England; and the latter, who had never forgiven Spain for her monopoly of commerce with South America, had been at great pains to disseminate on that continent ideas of liberty and separatism. The restoration of Ferdinand VII in 1814 had put an end to these dreams of independence; in 1816 the king of Spain had reconquered a large part of his empire. But certain men—San Martín, Bolívar, O'Higgins—had resisted, had fought on, and had founded republics in Venezuela, Chile, and La Plata. These events had been greeted with enthusiasm by many Americans who, like Henry Clay, saw "the glorious spectacle of eighteen millions of people struggling to burst their chains and be free"; with horror by the monarchic governments in Europe which constituted the Holy Alliance, and which at the Congress of Verona (1822) even talked of helping the king of Spain to conquer his colonies.

Adams did not fear Spain, even if she succeeded in re-establishing her authority in South America. For centuries she had been a peaceful neighbor. But if she lost her empire, he feared to see her supplanted on the American continent by some power that would be stronger and therefore more dangerous. The czar, with strange solicitude, had offered the United States a place in the Holy Alliance, an invitation which Adams had declined, saying: "For the repose of Europe as well as of America, the European and American political systems should be kept as separate and distinct of each other as possible." But Russia was in occupation of Alaska and was talking about colonizing the west coast of the American continent.

England also had certain undisclosed ambitions in regard to that coast which disturbed the Americans. "You claim India," John Quincy said to the English ambassador, "you claim Africa, you claim . . . There is not a spot on this habitable globe that I could affirm you do not claim." On the other hand, England and the United States were equally reluctant to see Spain cede Cuba to France in return for the support she had given. Moreover, England had no desire to lose her markets in South America and no special love for the policy of the Holy Alliance. Consequently in 1823 Canning suggested to the United States a joint declaration in which the two Anglo-Saxon nations should say that they did not aim at the possession of the former Spanish colonies themselves but that they could not watch with indifference their transfer to any other powers. John Quincy Adams did not approve the idea of a joint declaration, which again seemed to commit America to one of the European camps. He succeeded in persuading Monroe to make a declaration of principle, but to make it alone.

A message to Congress on December 2, 1823, enunciated what was called the *Monroe Doctrine* and what was mainly Adams' doctrine. This message said: (a) that the American continents henceforth were not to be considered grounds for future colonization by European powers; (b) that the United States would not take part in any war between the European powers; (c) that, on the other hand, it could not view with indifference what happened in America, and that any attempt on the part of monarchic powers to establish their political systems on this continent would be regarded as dangerous; (d) that it would not intervene to deprive the European powers of colonies they already possessed; (e) that any intervention against the independence of the republics of South America would be considered by the United States as unfriendly. The doctrine had no aggressive characteristics. To wish to see no other powers intervene in South America implied that the United States itself would refrain from annexation. Moreover in the eyes of Johny Quincy Adams and Monroe, it was not a statement of doctrine but a declaration concerning definite contemporary events. It was later that this document became a charter of the country's foreign policy.

The Monroe Doctrine was one of the aspects of the nationalism which at that time welded a constellation of states into a nation. The doctrine of Marshall, who made the Supreme Court the guardian and interpreter of the Constitution, was another aspect of the reinforcement of the central power. John Marshall had been named Chief Justice by John Adams in 1801. For thirty-four years he dominated the Supreme Court by the firmness of his character and the clarity of his intelligence. Born like Jefferson in western Virginia (the two men were cousins), he had the same charming simplicity of manner but not the same political ideas. Jefferson read Rousseau; Marshall, in his youth, had been strongly influenced by Pope. Believing in the necessity of reinforcing the Union in order to counteract the centrifugal force of sectionalism, he undertook to make the Supreme Court an instrument of unification above the President and above Congress. The Constitution charged the Court with the duty of supervising the enforcement of the laws. But what should the Court do if a law voted by the states or by Congress seemed to it contrary to the Constitution? Had it the right to declare this law void and to refuse to enforce it? It was the doctrine of John Marshall that this was not only its right but its duty. This theory, which has been given the name of "judicial review" gave the Supreme Court immense power. It made a third political body, and this compelled the Presidents to exercise extreme prudence in their selection of the judges who would wield such power. Between Jefferson and John Marshall there was a bitter and lasting struggle. But in the last analysis, this conflict was useful to the country. Each of the two men limited the powers of the other, and from their strife wisdom was born.

The first encounter was the case of Marbury *vs*. Madison, which permitted John Marshall to affirm the supremacy of the Court's authority. Marbury was a justice of the peace in the District of Columbia, one of John Adams's "midnight appointments." Madison, who was Secretary of State, had refused to approve Marbury's commission, and the latter protested, citing the Judiciary Act of 1789. Marshall decided that the relevant article of the Judiciary Act of 1789 was unconstitutional. "A legislative act, contrary to the Constitution, is not law. It is emphatically the duty of the Judicial Department to say what the law is." Jefferson, disquieted by such pretentions, tried to strike at Marshall by impeaching Judge Chase, one of the members of the Supreme Court, but could not secure a condemnation by the Senate; and Marshall continued, long after Jefferson, through the administrations of Madison and Monroe, a work that was as great as that of the founders, for it was he who gave to the Constitution its quasi-religious authority. In the affair of McCulloch *vs*. Maryland, the question to be determined was whether the state of Maryland had the right to tax banknotes issued by the Baltimore branch of the Bank of the United States. Marshall showed that laws passed by the states can be annulled by the Supreme Court if they are contrary to the federal Constitution. The national government had not been created by the states nor was it sustained by them; it emanated directly from the people and nothing was superior to it. Finally, in the case of the Trustees of Dartmouth College *vs*. Woodward, it maintained the sanctity of contracts by forbidding the state of New Hampshire to modify the original charter of the college.

An important decision, for it protected numerous private foundations from legislative abuse. It has been said that toward the end of his life John Marshall became the most reactionary man in America. Perhaps, but in the course of his long career he had imposed upon his country that respect for law which is the foundation of all liberty.

In this era of good will, nationalism, and unity, one subject threatened a profound division of the nation; that was slavery. About the time of the founding of the Republic, this institution had seemed doomed. The prod-

Clements Library

A primitive cotton gin in operation 30 years before Eli Whitney's patent. The *Universal Magazine*, July, 1764, published this picture showing the operation of a "mill to separate the seeds from it (the cotton)".

ucts hitherto grown for export in the South—tobacco, rice, and indigo— could no longer be sold at a reasonable profit. Many of the great estates lay fallow. Slaves had no work to do. Liberal planters of that time had suggested the total abolition of slavery. Why could not cotton be grown profitably in the United States? At the end of the eighteenth century England had learned to spin and weave this product in great quantities by machine. The climate of the South was favorable to cotton but the work necessary to separate the fibers from the seeds (ginnage) was so prolonged and costly that it made the price prohibitive. A slave could barely clean one pound a day. And so the plantations were vegetating in 1793 when a young student named Eli Whitney from Westboro, Massachusetts, went to spend his vacation in the South, heard talk about these difficulties, and conceived the idea of a machine. He talked about it to the overseer of the Greene family, with whom he was staying, and the latter commissioned him to build a model. When the machine was tried out, it became evident that with its aid a single man could gin as much cotton as fifty by hand. Through this very simple device, cotton growing became profitable and it developed with prodigious rapidity. In 1791 the United States exported less than two hundred thousand pounds of cotton; in 1810 ninety-three million pounds. Now this form of agriculture lent itself to the employment of slaves. It required manual labor throughout the year for simple opera-tions. It was easy to oversee because the bushes were low. From that time the number of slaves mounted rapidly (seven hundred fifty-seven thou-sand in 1790, about four million in 1860). Their price increased; before Whitney's invention a good Negro was worth about $300; after it, around 1830, the average value was about $800; and in 1860 the market was to reach a peak of $1,800. For the southern planters slaves became, not only a property of immense value, but a necessary condition of their wealth. In South Carolina and in Georgia King Cotton reigned, and controlled poli-tics as well as economics.

The northern states which had condemned slavery and prohibited it within their boundaries had looked on with disapproval when the South obtained, at the very beginning of the Republic, twenty supplementary seats in Congress thanks to a black population that did not vote. Great care had been taken in admitting new states so as to maintain an equal balance between slave states and free states. Ohio and Vermont, free states, had counterbalanced Kentucky and Tennessee, slave states. The line of demarcation between the two types of state had been the one formerly drawn by Mason and Dixon, to separate Pennsylvania from Maryland and its prolongation toward the west by the course of the Ohio. At the time of the Louisiana Purchase, planters had transported their slaves there. New states had been created, some slave, others free. But always the bal-ance had been maintained. Both camps demanded it; neither could allow the other a majority in the Senate. When the territory of Missouri in its turn asked to become a state, plantations employing slaves had been es-tablished there. James Tallmadge of New York stipulated that Missouri be admitted only on condition that no new slaves be brought in and that children of the Negroes should be free. The South protested. In the North old Federalists saw in this a means of stirring up sectional strife and put-ting their party in the saddle again. The aged Jefferson showed great alarm: "This momentous question, like a fire bell in the night, awakened and filled me with terror. I considered it at once as the knell of the Union." This was ringing the knell a trifle too soon, but Jefferson was right in scenting grave danger for the future. Provisionally a compromise was accepted. Maine (which had just separated from Massachusetts) was admitted as a free state, while Missouri was let in as a slave state, which made it possible to keep an equal balance in the Union and in the Senate. Furthermore, it was agreed that slavery should henceforth be forbidden in the Louisiana Territory north of latitude 36° 30', except in Missouri. Good will had triumphed; but one could prophesy that ill will was to have its turn.

CHAPTER XXVIII

The Era of Ill Feeling

SOMETIMES good will is accompanied by bad politics. Lulled by the charm of Virginia, Mother of Presidents, purged of rival parties by the elimination of the Federalists, official America slumbered in deceptive bliss. Jefferson had given rise to Madison, who had given rise to Monroe, who had given rise to John Quincy Adams. With a regularity like that of succession to the throne in a stable monarchy, twice in a row the Secretary of State had succeeded the President. The alternation of the presidency between the South and the East could not fail to irritate the West, which was growing, now amounted to more than one-third of the Union, and wished to be governed by energetic, democratic men of its own kind, rather than by learned sages from Boston or Virginia, Fathers or Sons of the Constitution though they might be. The unanimity of Monroe's elections had been deceptive. Since it seems inevitable that men should hate one another in some fashion, factional struggles had been replaced by animosities within the governing class. There is a story about a call William H. Crawford paid on Monroe in the course of which the Secretary of the Treasury threatened the Chief Executive with his cane, crying: "You damned infernal old scoundrel!" The President had snatched up a pair of fire tongs to defend himself. Such, on occasion, was the era of good feeling.

When the time of the presidential election of 1824 approached, John Quincy Adams began to glance longingly at the White House. Did he not have every right to it? Was he not an Adams, John, son of John, Secretary of State by the grace of Monroe, future President by the grace of God? The parties were dead; only persons counted. His appeared small, bald, neglected. He was awkward and arrogant in public, a mediocre orator, but by no means displeasing in private. Cold, distrustful, calculating in his relations with his colleagues, in family life he revealed himself as affectionate and simple. The surface was unpleasant: sanctimonious unction, virtuous defamation of character. He who dug deeper found robust honesty, patriotism, unshakable firmness, and a volcanic nature. His rages were like fireworks. He arose at five o'clock in the morning, read two chapters of the Bible, translated a little of the *Iliad,* then went for a swim in the Potomac and returned to read the papers before breakfast. He prided himself on his ability to write, kept a private diary, and learned by heart the fables of La Fontaine and recited them while riding horseback. Dazzled by the brilliance of his own culture he was, like his father before him, annoyed to find himself confronted by rivals whom he considered unworthy.

This was not the unanimous feeling of the various sections of the country, all of which wished to present their "favorite sons." The East was proud of having the most eloquent of Americans, the inspired orator, Daniel Webster. The West had made an idol of Henry Clay, a Virginian who had come at an early age to Kentucky, had grown up with his state, and represented it in Washington. Clay's charm was irresistible and he had been the first to succumb to it. He liked to please, and the first idea awakened in his mind by a controversy was that of a compromise. A Jeffersonian and pacifist at the beginning of his career, he became quite sincerely a patriot and expansionist at the time of the war of 1812; in 1824 he was the partisan of a strong central government which would shower its paternal gifts upon the West in the form of roads, canals, and subsidies. A seductive and persuasive orator, he had the reputation of being an excellent leader of men "but one who did not know where to lead them." The South had two favorite sons: Crawford of Georgia, a member of the cabinet for almost ten years, a man of superb presence of whom it was said that he was "the reputation of a reputation"; and, more important still, John C. Calhoun. This ascetic planter from South Carolina, thin, fiery, bereft of a sense of humor but not of driving power, represented the new South, that of the "cotton belt," which was much harsher and more realistic than the Virginia of Jefferson. His somber blue eyes and angular features foreboded violent actions, but in 1822 the policy of John Calhoun was not very different from that of Henry Clay.

The dark horse in this presidential race was General Jackson, hero of New Orleans and other places; his state, Tennessee, had proposed his candidacy two years earlier. That Jackson was a remarkable man, no one doubted, but some said he was a great democrat, others "a despot and a demagogue." His life had been extraordinary. Of Scotch stock, born in South Carolina like Calhoun, he had spent his childhood in the backwoods Waxhaw settlement. His father had died before his birth, his mother before he was grown. Red-headed, aggressive, and lighthearted, he thrived on combat. To earn a living he had been apprenticed to a master saddler; then at sixteen he had opened a school, barely knowing how to read and write himself. At twenty he had made himself a lawyer, although he had very vague ideas about the law. At twenty-one he had been made district attorney of the frontier town of Nashville, Tennessee. It was not a bad choice. On the frontier a public prosecutor had to arrest wrongdoers with his own hands. The law, without strength, was impotent. Jackson was brave, a good horseman, a good shot. In Nashville that meant a good prosecutor. He was respected. Men are always able to recognize a leader. Jackson was given command of the firemen and the militia; later he commanded armies. Despite his duels, his picturesque oaths, his rages, he read the Bible and possessed the dignity and courtly manners of the South. He believed in romantic love and had married Rachel Donelson Robards, a woman deserted by her husband. After the marriage he suddenly discovered that his wife's divorce had never become final. He was living in sin. For a man of his type it was a dreadful misadventure.

This inadvertently adulterous couple would have become the laughing-stock of Nashville if fear of Jackson's pistol had not silenced the gossips. When the divorce had been duly obtained Jackson had the ceremony performed again, this time legally, but the episode poisoned his political career. As congressman, senator, general, he was ever on the alert for insults. It is well known that he killed one man for this reason—Dickinson, the best shot in Tennessee. Such was the past. It had left is marks on Jackson. The man inspired instant liking. With his tall figure, his gray curls, his blue eyes, his fierce, soldierly face, he made a fine impression. His orthography was altogether personal, his grammar fanciful; of Latin he knew only five or six words, which he had caught on the wing. But he shone through his courage, honesty, and sincere love for the common man. "I have confidence," he said, "in the virtues and good sense of the people." Incapable of conciliating individuals, he knew how to make the masses love him. Without the insistence of his friends he would never have thought of the presidency. "No sir," he said. "I know what I am fit for. I can command a body of men in a rough way but I am not fit to be a President." But he quickly realized that no favorite son had the support of the country. Adams lacked friends; Clay, principles; Crawford was unpopular; why not Jackson? Up to his time a caucus, an informal meeting of members of the two Houses of Congress, had laid the plans for the election and chosen the candidates. But public opinion was tired of King Caucus and the newspapers were demanding his abdication. In 1824 King Caucus chose Crawford; it was the surest way of ruining his chances.

Although he recognized him as a possible and dangerous rival, John Quincy Adams had a fondness for Jackson. Before the election he gave a ball in his honor. Between the tall and cadaverous general and the short, stout Secretary of State, Mrs. Adams looked as though she were receiving between Don Quixote and Sancho Panza. Jackson was wearing pumps for the first time in his life. All evening he was most assiduous in his attention to Mrs. Adams. The rivals seemed on excellent terms. Came the vote: ninety-nine for Andrew Jackson of Tennessee, eighty-four for John Quincy Adams of Massachusetts, forty-one for Crawford of Georgia, and thirty-seven for Henry Clay of Kentucky. No candidate had obtained an absolute majority, and so it became the duty of the House of Representatives to make the choice. Clay withdrew. But in favor of whom? His choice would decide the election. He entertained himself by watching the bowing and scraping of his adversaries of yesterday, all of whom now called themselves his friends. But with his own future and his "American System" in mind, he had long since made a secret agreement with Adams. When the House voted, John Quincy Adams had thirteen states for him; Jackson, seven; Crawford, four. A single vote had given John Quincy Adams the state of New York and an absolute majority. It was that of Stephen van Rensselaer. This old man, honest and irresolute, at the moment when the ballot box was coming toward him had asked God to inspire him and had bowed in prayer at the end of the table, his head between his hands. When he had opened his eyes, the first thing he saw lying on the floor was a ballot in the name of John Quincy Adams. He believed that this was the divine reply, picked up the ballot and put it in the box. Adams was not completely happy about his election; he knew at least two-thirds of the nation was hostile to him. This presaged an uneasy administration.

At first Jackson took his defeat in good part and on the evening of the election, meeting Adams, he graciously congratulated him. The general's friends maintained that he had been beaten by fraud and that a disgraceful deal had been arranged between Adams and Clay. Jackson refused to believe it. But when Adams very tactlessly offered to make Clay Secretary of State, a unanimous outcry arose. Here was proof of "the bargain of corruption," said the Jacksonians. In reality there had been neither corruption nor a bargain. John Quincy Adams was "an honest man, in the worst sense of the word." Crawford's partisans, and even Jackson's, had offered Clay as much and more than those of Adams. But of these transactions no one spoke, and Adams was charged with all the guilt. Jackson broke with him on that very day and thenceforth pursued him with an inexorable hatred. The country came to dislike the President. John Randolph, the most malicious and the wittiest of the politicians, the man to whom Adams had applied Ovid's verse:

> His face is ashen, meagre his whole body,
> His breast is green with gall, suffused with poison his tongue. . . .

undertook a vigorous campaign against "The American House of Stuart," that is to say, the Adams dynasty. "I have borne," he said, "some humble part in putting down the dynasty of John the First and, by the grace of God, I hope to aid in putting down the dynasty of John the Second." And also: "This is the last four years of the Father resuscitated in the person of the Son." "John Quincy Adams is as mean a man for a Yankee as James Madison for a Virginian. . . ." Against Henry Clay, Randolph was still more violent: "This being, so brilliant yet so corrupt, which, like a rotten mackerel by moonlight, shines and stinks, and stinks and shines." It was Randolph who called the alliance of Adams and Clay "the coalition of Blifil and Black George." The era of ill will had begun.

To direct the policies of a country when one possesses neither a majority nor popularity and has against one a rival whom the masses adore is a hopeless task. It was rendered more difficult still by Adams's ineptitude at all measures of compromise. He disapproved of the spoils system, thought that the interest of the country demanded that government officials be continued in office, and refused to give posts to his supporters at the expense of his adversaries. Such was his stubbornness on this point—certainly honorable in itself—that it was impossible to get him to discharge even a bad employee. Consequences were easy to foresee; the President soon had Congress against him and all his measures were defeated. He wished to carry out a nationalist policy, give a liberal interpretation to the Constitution, have the federal government build the roads and canals desired by the West, establish a national university and observatories, encourage the exploitation of the continent, maintain a Bank of the United States, protect industry by import duties, and make America a closed system. This "American System" had hitherto been favored by the country, but

Adams's support was enough to make it unpopular, and moreover resurgent sectional antagonisms were undermining the national program. The Northeast, where a powerful industry was developing, would perhaps have supported Adams, but the South abandoned him and soon was opposing him. Clay thought he could bring him the support of the West; Jackson offered this support to the South and many former Jeffersonians—Calhoun, Crawford, and the New Yorker Van Buren—rallied to Jackson, for they saw very well that it was he and no longer Clay who could draw the western vote. Jackson addressed himself to the small farmers who controlled the West. He attacked the Bank of the United States, which in debtors' eyes seemed the very symbol of the creditor. He explained to the people that the "lords" of Virginia and Massachusetts had hitherto made government a family and caste affair, and that the time had come for a democracy to be governed by democrats. The party which he led, became known as the Democrat-Republican party, while the party of Adams and Clay called itself the National-Republican party. Thus was re-established under new names and with the new addition of the West the ancient division of the United States into Federalists and anti-Federalists. Hamilton and Jefferson were reborn in Clay and Jackson—because Hamilton and Jefferson are eternal.

Jackson's campaign for election in 1828 began the year after Adams's election. Admirably organized, it was promoted for three years throughout the whole country by committees, newspapers, and banquets. Everywhere Jackson found allies. In the Ohio Valley he had for him all those who were still animated by the spirit of the frontier, all those who were irritated by the aristocracy of the coast, all those who thought that "America begins on the other side of the Alleghenies." In the South, Georgia was furious at Adams because he had supported the Indians in their territorial claims, and the South in general accused the President of sacrificing states' rights. Even in the East the artisans and salaried workers supported Jackson's democratic movement because they thought themselves unjustly treated by local institutions. Finally, Van Buren, the master strategist, of whom John Quincy Adams had said that his principles were subordinated to his ambitions and that his policy would always be the one calculated to give him the best chance of getting ahead, decided beyond question that Jackson would win, for he joined him, bringing the support of a large part of the New York vote.

This powerful combination of enemies determined to keep Adams from winning a second term made his political life more difficult than that of any of his predecessors. Congress was debating an amendment to the Constitution providing for the direct election of the President by the nation, and in the course of the discussion the case of John Quincy Adams, President *against* the will of the American people, was cited many times in painful fashion. The South reproached him bitterly for having sent American delegates to the Pan-American Congress. This was a meeting of the recently liberated republics of South America. They had invited the participation of the government of the United States, which by the Monroe Doctrine had guaranteed their independence. But the South was aggrieved at these republics for having pronounced themselves opposed to slavery; the South feared the emancipation of the slaves in Cuba and Puerto Rico; worse still, it feared the recognition of Haiti, the Negro republic. If black diplomats should appear in Washington, what encouragement for an insurrection of the slaves! The Senate finally confirmed the sending of delegates to Panama, but by a small majority. The most innocent actions of the President became crimes in the eyes of his tormentors. Had he bought a billiard table for the White House? The purchase proved his futility—a curious epithet for an Adams. Did he speak French with Lafayette who, in 1825, was revisiting the country he so greatly loved? Immediately his European, un-American education was recalled. What would not have been said had it been known that he advised Lafayette to keep away from the revolutionary parties in France? Lafayette replied that he was sixty-eight years old, that he would leave revolutions to the young people, and that he was going to live quietly at La Grange. "But a fire smoldered beneath the ashes." On July 4, 1826, the fiftieth anniversary of the Declaration of Independence, John Adams, the father of the President, died, and on the same day Thomas Jefferson also. In his journal John Quincy Adams wrote: "The time, the manner, the coincidence with the decease of Jefferson are visible and palpable marks of divine favour for which I do humble myself in grateful and silent adoration before the Ruler of the Universe." It must be admitted that on this occasion the Ruler of the Universe set the scene with care, and that the almost simultaneous death on this day of the two noble and long since reconciled adversaries possessed unmistakable grandeur.

His loss earned the President no respite. The question of tariffs provoked new attacks. After the War of 1812, since England was exporting at a loss with the intention of ruining the infant American industries, it had seemed natural to protect American merchandise by import duties. At this time the factories were actually in the North, but the South hoped to build some of her own and gave her approval to the tariff. Later the attitude of the South changed. It was exporting cotton; it produced no finished goods and therefore had to buy them. And so it became hostile to tariffs. The West was in favor of them because it hoped that the revenues produced by import duties would be used in large public works in the West. These attitudes of the two sections which supported him created a difficult situation for Jackson as future candidate for the presidency. Not only the West, but Pennsylvania and New York, which had promised him their votes, were in favor of the tariff; the South, which Calhoun was to deliver to him, was against it. What could he do? What could he say? Van Buren, the master politician, advised Jackson to say nothing at all. But Jackson's friends in Congress did not know how to vote. Against the tariff? That meant losing New York. For the tariff? That meant losing the South. The astute Van Buren advised that they outbid the proposals of the administration and devise a tariff so high, so absurd, that the East itself would repudiate it, all the more readily as duties on raw materials would be mixed in with the others. New England wanted to sell its cloth for as much as possible, but to buy its wool as cheaply as possible. The ruse failed. New England, although it found the law absurd, voted for it nevertheless because it was emotionally committed to the tariff. Since at the same time the South and West voted for it out of malice and as a political maneuver, the measure passed. The South was exasperated. In Charleston flags were flown at half-mast. Calhoun protested against this "tariff of abominations" which forced the South to pay two-thirds of all the taxes of the nation. It was then that certain southerners again resorted to the doctrine of nullification, earlier expounded in the Kentucky and Virginia Resolves, which developed the "compact" or "states' rights" theory of the Constitution.

The fury of the South made it possible to foresee the results of the presidential election. Theoretically there was only one party: the Republican party. But the National-Republicans, with Adams and Henry Clay, were for the tariff, large public works, and a liberal interpretation of the Constitution; the Democratic-Republicans, with Calhoun and Jackson, supported states' rights and condemned the tariff. The campaign was violent. Jackson denounced the politicians and proved himself the most skillful of them. Adams complained of the cruel malice of the Jacksonians, but his friends treated Jackson with at least equal cruelty. They recalled his quarrels, his duels, and handed out little coffins bearing the names of his victims. They represented him as a drunkard, a gambler, an assassin, and a duelist. They even attacked his private life and brought up again what they called "his concubinage." Did the country want, asked the Adams press, to put an adulterous couple in the White House? Was one to see the President of the United States, pistol in hand, entering the Senate in order to shoot down his political adversaries? The intention of these respectable blackmailers was to provoke Jackson, the violence of whose character they well knew, to an outburst that would destroy him. But Jackson was too astute for them and controlled himself. As for the crowds, they shouted: "Hurrah for Jackson!" They had chosen their hero; they would listen to no arguments. And even in Kentucky, his own state, Clay felt that he was beaten. The result was crushing: Jackson had one hundred seventy-eight votes; Adams eighty-three. New England alone had remained true to the President. Calhoun, in return for his support, became Vice President. On the day following the election, the new President's wife died suddenly of a heart attack. Jackson said and believed that she had been assassinated by Adams's journalists, whose calumnies had crucified her. While the old warrior with chivalrous tenderness watched over the body of his companion, John Quincy Adams in the White House was sadly receiving the Indian chief, Red Jacket, who had come to say goodbye. "We both belong to the past," Red Jacket said, "and we shall both soon be called by the Great Spirit." Adams noted in his journal: "I answered him that was true, and I hoped it would be to a better world than this." Holding Adams responsible for the death of his wife, Jackson refused, when he came to Washington, to pay his predecessor the customary courtesy call. As a result John Quincy Adams, like his father, did not attend the inauguration of his successor.

CHAPTER XXIX

The Transformation

ANDREW JACKSON was not a cause but an effect. He did not, in his administration, transform American democracy; he became President because American democracy, between 1790 and 1830, had undergone a profound transformation. In those forty years the population of the United States had tripled, growing from almost four million to over twelve million, and its area had doubled. "We are large and we continue to grow rapidly. I had almost said *terribly*," wrote Calhoun in 1817. There was indeed something terrifying for any American government in the tide that submerged the West under successive waves of immigrants and in the continuous creation of new states which altered the political equilibrium of the country every ten years. In New England, pessimists, disturbed by this rush toward the West, feared that they would one day see their states deserted and grass growing in the ruined streets.

> It is generally imagined [said Tocqueville] that the American deserts are being settled by European emigrants who descend each year on the shores of the New World, while the American population thrives and multiplies on the ground already occupied by their fathers. This is a complete mistake. The European who lands in the United States arrives there without friends and often without resources; in order to live he is forced to sell his services and it is rare to see him go beyond the industrial zone that extends along the ocean. One cannot clear the wilderness without capital or credit; before venturing into the midst of the forest, the body must be habituated to the rigors of a new climate. And so it is the Americans who daily abandon the places of their birth and go to create vast domains for themselves in distant places.

This colonization of the Middle West by the inhabitants of the original states of the Union has a capital importance in the history of the United States. It was this that assured the unity of the country. Through it the virtues and defects of the New England Puritans were transplanted to Ohio and Illinois. Thanks to it the spirit of the West and its taste for adventure were grafted on the old American stock.

As soon as business in the East seemed to be slowing down, because of an economic or political crisis, thousands of adventurous families would set out for the Ohio Valley. As far as Pittsburgh they went on horseback or in covered wagons, carrying part of their food with them, buying the rest from farmers along the way. In Pittsburgh those who had a little money and thought they could handle a flatboat bought one for five shillings a ton and floated off with their families and their possessions. When the waters were high the current alone was enough to take them to their destination. Those who were too poor or who lacked confidence in their ability as mariners, rented places on the boats of others. Hundreds of rafts were to be seen bearing shacks made of branches, children, pigs, poultry, a hay rick, and a plow. Thus whole farms were transported from New England to the Mississippi Valley. "Honest Jonathan, surrounded with his scolding, grunting, squalling and neighing dependents, floats to the point proposed without leaving his own fireside; and on his arrival there may step on shore with his house."

The first weeks were hard, very hard. Almost always the lot sold the immigrant was in the forest. The family had to sleep on the boat while the men cut down the trees. All the arms and all the axes of the neighborhood seemed to be at the service of the newcomer. It was the custom to send one man from each family to help. The kindness and good will of the neighbors seemed to be the dominant characteristics of this society. No sooner had a plot of land been cleared than the wife started a kitchen garden. At the end of five weeks she was cooking her own vegetables. As for the house, made of rough-hewn logs, between which came light and wind and smoke, it went up even faster. A long thong of buffalo hide took the place of a closet, and on it were hung the clothes of the entire family. Beds, chairs, tables came from the forest. The dismantled raft was turned into planks. Household articles were rare. At first it required a long journey to find a store. The women spun and wove by hand in order to make themselves dresses, and those who possessed good taste showed it in the invention of designs. Materials and blankets of homespun were thick and durable. Later the first peddlers came, and, when the density of the population warranted it, some enterprising pioneer would open a general store. There everything would be sold: needles and anchors, sundials or clocks, thread and lace, whiskey and vinegar. "I have known a person to ask for a pair of shoes, and receive for answer that there were no shoes in the store, but some capital gin that could be recommended to him. . . . Another was directed by his wife to bring her a warming pan, smoothing irons and scrubbing brushes; but these were denied; and a wooden cuckoo-clock was sent home in their stead." The words "buy" and "sell" were rarely used. People said "trade." Money hardly entered the picture. Commerce was carried on by barter. The farmer would bring in flour, corn, apples, bacon, and take away cooking pans or glassware, which were sold to him at an advance of 300 per cent over the price in Baltimore or Philadelphia. Twice a year the trader would send the wares he had accumulated to New Orleans by water, or go there himself, make an enormous profit, come back with cash by way of Philadelphia to replenish his stock, and finally set out again toward the West. The circuit was immense, close to six thousand miles by boat and covered wagon, but great fortunes were made in this way.

The American frontier was not what Europeans call a frontier, the line of demarcation between two countries. The word "frontier," in America, meant "the fringe of foam that marked the extreme advance of the human waves," the zone where the population was more than two and less than six inhabitants per square mile. There the pioneer type established itself with its virtues and defects. The man of the West was rugged, optimistic, and independent. Daily life with its struggles against the Indians and the forest became an adventure novel. Equality in the West was not a principle; it was a fact. "The greater portion of these immigrants, besides their wives, a few benches and chairs, a Bible and a gun, commenced with little more than their hands." They saw their village grow, cities arise, states come to birth. They had acquired confidence in themselves and in their neighbors. "One became a Justice of Peace, another a County judge, and another a member of the legislative assembly." David Crockett dispensed justice before ever having studied law, but his honesty and common sense made him a good magistrate. Hence came the courageous faith in the human will and an immense hope for the future. "Others appeal to history, America to prophecy" is a sentence that expresses the spirit of the West. In the West every speculation was permissible, every ambition legitimate, every fairy tale probable. On lands that yesterday had been jungles civilization spread with the rapidity of a forest fire. It was a prodigious spectacle such as the world had never seen before. A French traveler who had been a witness of this soaring flight wrote mournfully: "America is rising, Europe sinking."

The other two sections also changed "terribly." For the East, the essential problems were: to develop its own industries and to attract to itself as large a part as possible of the commerce of the new states. England had been the first to have steam-driven machines for spinning and weaving. She had hoped to maintain a monopoly and for a long time forbade the emigration of technicians and workmen. But such secrets cannot be kept. Francis Cabot Lowell of Boston, after a long tour of inspection abroad, built a factory in Massachusetts where for the first time all the operations of spinning and weaving cloth were united under one roof. The War of 1812 gave an immense impetus to American industries: (a) by severing the connections with England; (b) by directing into the channels of industry funds that could no longer find a place in commerce. It was "the industrial war of independence." With his brother-in-law, Patrick Tracy Jackson, Lowell created a textile capital which bears his name. And a short time later in order to connect the city of Lowell with Boston, Jackson became largely responsible for one of the first railroads in America. In 1817 the Frenchmen Merle d'Aubigné was filled with admiration for a firm which manufactured beautiful blue and black cloth and which had been given by its founders the name of Nouveau-Louviers. In 1840 the textile industry employed more than one hundred thousand workmen. At this time the discovery of coal and iron in localities close to each other was leading to the development of the iron industry. This produced stoves and nails in great quantity. Canneries and shoe factories grew. In colonial times the South had been richer than the North; now the cities of the North prospered, those of the South declined. The southern planters had to seek capital from the northern bankers and blamed the protective tariff, instituted by the North, for their poverty.

The development of industry raised a labor problem. Hitherto the only labor problem had been to find workmen. In the small factories where the owner himself worked and in which the workmen had a chance of one day becoming owner, hours of work had been as ill defined as they are on a farm. They lasted from dawn to night, with barely a pause for lunch. At first manufacturers followed the same custom. In Lowell in 1839 laborers were still working twelve hours a day six full days a week, although many women and children were employed there. Since the cities were growing rapidly, lodgings were miserable. Lowell, which had only a few hundred inhabitants in 1820, had a population of twenty thousand in 1840. The hand weaver had been a countryman, half-farmer, who lived in a cottage and had a kitchen garden; the weaver who operated a mechanical loom lived in a hovel in the city and his means of subsistence had diminished. The manufacturers, absorbed by the rapid growth of their factories, gave little thought to their workmen; while the workmen, exhausted by their labors, gave little thought to uniting. Moreover the courts of justice were opposed to all collective activity among workmen. To reach an understanding for the purpose of asking a raise in wages was a "conspiracy." The only workmen's associations that were tolerated were the charitable societies. The English philanthropist, Richard Owen, tried to establish a co-operative community at New Harmony, Indiana, in 1825, but it was a failure. After 1825 labor unions, then called trade associations, multiplied. In 1828 for the first time the workmen's associations of a whole city, Philadelphia, joined a union. In 1834 there appeared a proposal for national federation. The political influence of the workmen's unions certainly contributed to Jackson's election. A movement to obtain a ten-hour day was started, and Jackson limited the working day in state-owned factories.

As to the South, its new problems were to dominate the history of America from 1830 to 1865. For a long time it had received its intellectual directives from Virginia. Since the prodigious development of cotton-growing, which had become the great source of wealth in the black belt, the generous, courtly, and humanitarian spirit of Virginia had been succeeded by the vigorous, harsh realism of the slaveowners of South Carolina. In ten years, slavery, which had been on the point of disappearing at the end of the eighteenth century, had become indispensable to the planters. And, as always happens, the latter had found reasons to justify in theory what was necessary to them in practice. Theoretically the thinkers of the South defended the ideal of Greek democracy, founded on slavery; practically they sought an alliance with the West to defend the peculiar institution to which they clung with all the greater ardor as they felt themselves criticized by the North. Nothing irritates men more than a moral judgment rendered by other men, who themselves are not above reproach. By what right did the employers of child labor condemn the employers of slave labor?

Clements Library

A typical American cabin, from up country Georgia, drawn by Captain Basil Hall and published in his *Forty Etchings*, London, 1829.

The American System was not simply an essay in economic autonomy; education and literature as well assumed, little by little, a purely American character. On the frontier schools were scarce; many children, like Andrew Jackson, educated themselves; a future President of the United States, Andrew Johnson, did not know how to read or write at the time of his marriage; from this resulted a certain contempt for the old culture and a wish for intellectual independence. The War of 1812 had stirred up resentment against England, while the Napoleonic wars had spoiled the friendship between the United States and France. The West was not, like Virginia or New England, sentimentally a son of the old continent. The sense of humor of the Mississippi Valley exercised itself at the expense of European tabus. America was becoming conscious of an intellectual emancipation. "I ask," said Everett in 1826, "whether more has not been done to extend the domain of civilization, in fifty years, since the Declaration of Independence, than would have been done in five centuries of continued colonial subjection?" Certain European visitors, Alexis de Tocqueville, for instance, accepted this judgment and came to America in search of lessons in government. Others protested. "During the thirty or forty years of their independence," said Sidney Smith, "they have done absolutely nothing for the sciences, for the arts, for literature. In the four quarters of the globe, who reads an American book, or goes to an American play, or looks at an American picture or statue?" But Sidney Smith, like all witty men, had a tendency to mistake an epigram for a statement of fact. Actually in "the four quarters of the globe" men were reading *The Last of the Mohicans*. James Fenimore Cooper appealed to the readers of the whole world because his work and his hero, Leatherstocking or Hawkeye, were of an epic and romantic character. He had begun by timidly writing a novel after the English pattern, *Precaution*. Then he had taken heart, and it could be said of his next novel, *The Spy*, that it was the literary declaration of independence of America. Washington Irving, another New Yorker, afforded Europe an example of a finished American writer, a perfect stylist in a class with the greatest English satirists. The place taken at that time in the intellectual life of the country by the aggressive financial city of New York was in itself an indication of the birth of a new America. "The bewilderment of old Rip, on his return from the hills, was the bewilderment of the colonial mind in the presence of a new order." America was becoming American.

CHAPTER XXX

Conclusion

DANIEL WEBSTER in the joint eulogy of John Adams and Thomas Jefferson which he delivered at Faneuil Hall said: "It cannot be denied, but by those who would dispute against the sun, that with America, and in America, a new era commences in human affairs. This era is distinguished by free representative governments, by entire religious liberty, by improved systems of national intercourse, by a newly awakened and unconquerable spirit of free enquiry, and by a diffusion of knowledge through the community such as has been before altogether unknown and unheard of." Was this proud claim justified? That, at the time of Jackson's election, the government of the United States had become representative of the entire nation was true. Before Jackson, the controls of government had been in the hands of a little aristocratic group, a liberal and benevolent aristocracy. But the people of the West did not want benevolence; they wanted power. The Federalists had formerly been alarmed by the acquisition of Louisiana. They had not been mistaken, for it was to bring about the ruin of their party and the end of the old ruling class. It is true that Henry Clay would attempt to enthrone a new governing class and to make it popular through the benefits bestowed by a paternal government. But by the election of Jackson the West had completely turned its back on Clay. From that day the valley of the Mississippi became "the Valley of Democracy." Already, in the larger part of the West, the property qualification for voting had been abolished. Nothing remained for the East but to follow this example. The West was rapidly drawing the entire country toward universal suffrage.

For a long time the congressional leaders had kept in their hands the right of choosing presidential candidates. The heads of each party met in caucus behind closed doors and discussed the merits of the candidates. From the time when larger and larger masses of citizens began to take part in elections, the custom arose of choosing the candidate by a popular convention of the party, made up of the active and influential men of each community. There is, therefore, a great difference between the type of candidate nominated before and after this change of method. At the time of the caucus, men of studious habits, like Adams and Madison, had their chance; under the convention system a candidate must be a popular hero who has imposed himself, or whom one can reasonably hope to impose, upon the attention of the country. In certain circumstances he may be a man without distinction upon whom the partisans of two great men, who are opposed to each other, can agree. In any event the election of Jackson put an end to the "parliamentary phase" of the presidency and began the plebiscitary phase. With the exception of Washington, who was a unique case, it is only since the time of Jackson that the Presidents of the United States have represented and incarnated the nation. This immense authority of the President, which was not provided for in the Constitution, had one advantage; it created an executive power that was strong and able to act. The danger was that the presidential election would become the one essential fact in the life of the nation, and that for almost two years out of four it would be the dominant concern of everyone.

What reason was there for the irresistible influence of the West over the rest of the country? The reason was that the future belonged to the West and that the two other sections knew this and sought its alliance. Between 1812 and 1821 five new western states had been admitted to the Union. That gave the section ten new senators, and it was evident that the number would increase. Beginning in 1828, for a period of twenty-four years with only brief interruptions, the agreement between the South and the West is going to keep the Democratic-Republican party in power. Then this alliance will be broken; slavery will isolate the South; the West, gradually becoming industrialized, will draw closer to the East. But as long as the partnership of the West and South endures, it will be dominated by the political philosophy of the West, a democratic agrarian philosophy, favorable to debtors and hostile to the privileged classes. An English historian suggests that, in order to understand what is going on in America, one might picture England lying on the Atlantic coast of the United States, with Canada and Australia situated on the other side of the Alleghenies, all together constituting a single country, on which the dominions have succeeded in imposing their policies. In Jackson's time the "dominion," which is the West, gains control of the "mother country," comprising the original colonies.

"Entire religious liberty" Webster had also said. Was this true? Great progress had been made in that direction. In New England, tolerance was accepted in institutions, if not as yet in custom. "Protestantism had made its fortune," Lowell said, "and it no longer protested." The Unitarians under the leadership of Dr. Channing were opposing their reasonable optimism to the pessimism of the Calvinists. In the South, the Episcopalian Church had been neutralized by the influx of Presbyterians and Methodists. In the West, founders of sects, wandering preachers, and camp meetings flourished. The multiplicity of beliefs was engendering a relative tolerance. The churches of the East vied with one another in their zeal to evangelize the West and found colleges there. In the whole country Christianity was incontestably dominant. Some professed it because they believed in it; "others because they feared to have the appearance of not believing in it." This at least apparent community of faith assured the unity of the nation, and the strength of tradition made daring political experimentation less hazardous.

"Let the people rule," was Jackson's motto. It had formerly been Jefferson's. But Jefferson's people, like the English people, governed through the medium of a small experienced minority; Jackson's people selected for themselves a leader after their own heart. Could the enterprise succeed? Alexis de Tocqueville pronounced a very favorable judgment on it. He found the country prosperous, free, and happy. What were the reasons for its success? In part natural conditions: the immensity of the virgin continent, the abundance of free, fertile lands. But in other countries the same conditions had not produced the same result. Tocqueville attributed the good fortune of the United States to the excellence of its law and the strictness of its morals. Montesquieu had already said that if the mainspring of monarchies is honor, the mainspring of democracies is virtue. When political power can be constantly shifted by vote of the people, it is vital that the nation should be protected against the rashness of its own decisions by the stability of its customs, and that the men in power, being unrestrained by any caste tradition, should be defended against the violence of their own impulses by the severity of public opinion. The American, living "in a land of prodigies," quite naturally became "enterprising, adventurous, experimental." The role of flywheel, necessary in every governmental mechanism, was played by family life, by women, and by religion. Puritanism produced strict consciences, men who were severe toward themselves and toward their neighbors. Women were treated with respect and exercised a profound and wholesome influence. The ministers of religion not only avoided all conflict with republican institutions but supported them with their whole authority.

As for the excellence of the laws that the Founding Fathers had given to the United States, time had served to prove it. The Constitution when put to work had revealed itself as a good instrument of government. While preserving the rights of popular control, it had created a strong and durable executive power. The federal formula allowed the Union to enjoy at the same time "the strength of a great republic and the security of a small one." Thanks to John Marshall, the judiciary power had understood its function, which was, not to oppose the wishes of a majority, but to regulate, direct, and moderate their activities. In a country where no landed aristocracy still remained (except in the South), where industry could never give rise to a governing class because popular suffrage never favors the rich, and where common law made legal interpretation difficult for the citizens, lawyers were sure to secure, and in fact did secure, an advantageous political situation. The results seemed far from bad. As a candidate, the lawyer flattered the voter, because that was to his interest; but once elected, the lawyer demanded respect for the law because that was his instinct. Those venerable arbiters, the justices of the Supreme Court, by placing the Constitution above the parties had put limits to partisan excesses.

Finally, Webster had been justified in saying that "the spirit of free enquiry" and a respect for free discussion were American traits. From their Anglo-Saxon ancestors Americans had inherited the forms of local government and of public parliamentary debate. In the smallest villages, in charitable societies, and in clubs use was made of the ancient rules that had assured the lasting internal security of England. The intellectual culture of the American masses was neither extensive nor deep; the humanities were neglected; the knowledge possessed by the average citizen about the history of Europe was negligible; but when it came to the administration of his own country, the average American showed amazing sense, willingness to work, and devotion. Like all men he had his weaknesses. Carried away, not so much by love of money, as by the great and magnificent game of continuous creation, he gave more thought to his plans and ambitions than to the suffering in which these sometimes resulted. The West remained insensible to the misfortunes of the Indians, who had been driven from their lands and deprived of their game; the South, to the hardships of slavery; the East, to the wretched working conditions in the factories. Taking everything into account, the work accomplished in fifty years was prodigious, and the eagerness of European immigrants proved that life on the new continent was happier than that on the old. Webster was right: With America and in America there began, about 1830, a new era in human affairs, that of political equality. Would it last? Would new hierarchies take the place of those hierarchies of Europe that the emigrants had left behind them? To this question experience, and experience alone, could give an answer; but at the time when Jackson, an old man with grey curls and a crown of glory, came riding from Tennessee to the White House, the beautiful dream of Americanism, woven of the happiness of deliverance, of great adventures hoped for, and of equal opportunities given to all on a gigantic continent whose fabulous resources were still untouched, obsessed and intoxicated men's minds.

ABRAHAM LINCOLN
Photograph by Alexander Gardner, November 8, 1863

CHAPTER XXXI

The Reign of Andrew Jackson

NOW for the first time a man who belonged neither to the Virginian dynasty nor to the Adams dynasty was entering the White House. And so the people put on a celebration for him. An army of admirers and followers fell upon the capitol on the eve of the inauguration. All the southern and western states supplied contingents. Some came to ask for positions in return for their campaign services; most came to see Jackson, to acclaim, to worship Jackson. The President's simple manners, his height, his handsome, stormy, veteran's face lent him great charm. When Chief Justice Marshall, who hated everything that Jackson stood for, administered the oath and held the Bible to his lips, a wave of joyful emotion traversed the ocean of spectators. Then there was a stampede toward the President. A group composed of "statesmen and stable boys, fine ladies and washerwomen, white people and blacks" followed him to the White House where the traditional reception was to take place. Then the saturnalia began. Tables of refreshments were taken by assault, waiters were thrown to the ground, chairs were trampled by muddy boots. So many hands wanted to shake those of Old Hickory that he had to beat a retreat and disappear. Terrified women leaped out of windows. To clear the apartments it was necessary to lure the crowd into the gardens by placing great bowls of orange punch on the lawn. When this orgy was over the White House resembled the palaces of Rome after the invasion. "Several thousand dollars worth of broken china and cut glass and many bleeding noses attested the fierceness of the struggle." Mrs. Harrison Smith, who was a spectator, compared it to the crowds pillaging the Tuileries at the time of the French Revolution. But the comparison was pointless: The visitors at the White House were friends, albeit a trifle high-spirited, not rioters, and Jackson, at the bottom of his heart, was not at all displeased.

Jackson loved the people, not as they are loved by rich liberals, from a

"The President of the United States." Of all the anti-Jackson caricatures, there are few more eloquent than this, which was intended as a serious illustration in Mrs. Frances Trollope's *Domestic Manners of the Americans*, London, 1832. It shows the President holding a subordinate's horse while the latter does an errand.

distance, but as they are loved by those who are of the people. The hardships of his family had taught him what humiliations and rancors the poor can feel. He was the natural representative not only of the small farmers of the West but of the eastern laborers as well. In the factories of the coast, since the War of 1812, a proletariat had been growing up composed in large measure of immigrants. In New York, Philadelphia, and Pittsburgh, all those among the laborers who had the right to vote were confirmed Jacksonians. Like them, Jackson hated monopolies, economic inequalities, and the profitable trickery of finance. As a pioneer, and then as a pioneers' lawyer, he had seen to what extent the East kept the West under its thumb. By manipulating the markets the businessmen of Boston and Philadelphia could buy at bottom prices the products of Tennessee and sell at top prices the products of Massachusetts and Pennsylvania. Jackson believed that one of his duties was to render such exploitation impossible.

The first problem the new President had to solve was the formation of a cabinet. About the post of Secretary of State there was no question. Jackson owed his election to Van Buren and Van Buren was born to rule. In him were combined elements of the philosopher, the statesman, the man of the world, and the electioneer. The elegance of his clothes and his language, his wit, his brilliant, well-told anecdotes, his mixture of benevolence and cynicism, had earned him the nickname of "the American Talleyrand." His friends called him "little Van" or "the little magician," and worshiped him. His enemies criticized him for being the friend of all the world and proved the charge untrue by their accusation. The masses did not love him instinctively as they did Jackson, but "Van" wished to be, and believed he was, "the second thought," the more considered thought, of the American people. He instantly accepted the proffered post, then regretted his acceptance when he learned who his colleagues were to be. Jackson's choices were less than mediocre, "the most unintellectual cabinet we ever had." Moreover, aside from Van Buren and perhaps Eaton, the official advisers of the President were not to be his real advisers. On all important questions Jackson consulted a group whom his adversaries called "the kitchen cabinet," and in which there figured newspapermen from Tennessee, like Amos Kendall, and personal friends, like Major William B. Lewis, who had been the manager of the presidential campaign. Lewis had that unreserved admiration for Jackson that is so precious to great men, and he knew how to translate into polished language his chief's vehement rough drafts. It was soon said in Washington that the kitchen cabinet controlled the President and through the President the country. This was a mistake: Jackson had a will of iron and never failed to have his own way.

His supporters were waiting for jobs. But, as another President had said, officeholders seldom die and never resign. Jackson decided "to clean the Augean stables"; that is, to dismiss a number of men hostile to his party. Of six hundred twelve appointments made by the preceding administration two hundred fifty were canceled. In addition, six hundred post offices were given new postmasters. Jackson had no scruples about it; he did not admit that a position can create a right or that experience was necessary for simple tasks such as postman or customs inspector. "It is rotation in office that will perpetuate our liberty." To him is often and mistakenly attributed the famous motto: "To the victors belong the spoils." It was actually said by Senator W. L. Marcy of New York. But Jackson himself saw no reason why government positions should not be made rewards for campaign services. How was one to impose a new policy if the officeholders remained loyal to the old tradition? Jackson, who was about to undertake a struggle against the money power, thought he ought to eliminate those men who had been put in office by that power. On the frontier he had seen more than one neighbor become, without preparation, a schoolmaster, a judge, an officer of the law; he believed in all sincerity that men are interchangeable and that a loyal follower of Jackson would make a better postman than a friend of Adams or Clay.

During the time of the campaign, the relations between the President and the Vice President had been good. Calhoun believed that he had been picked to succeed Jackson in 1832 and this hope appeased his troubled heart. He became worried when those near the President began to talk of a second term, and was beside himself when Van Buren was mentioned as a presidential possibility after that. The diabolical skill of the "little magician" haunted Calhoun's dreams from then on and the relations between the two men became strained. To embroil Calhoun with Jackson was the principal purpose of Van Buren's friends. The case of Peggy Eaton helped them. Eaton, who had been a senator and then Secretary of War, had married Peggy O'Neale, the daughter of an innkeeper at whose inn he had formerly lodged together with Jackson. The great ladies of Washington snubbed Peggy O'Neale and whispered that she had been Eaton's mistress during the lifetime of her former husband. The wives of the other cabinet ministers refused to receive her. Jackson defended her. He was chivalrous by nature; and moreover it seemed to him that the whole scandal was a social symbol. He demanded that the wives of his officials put an end to their vendetta. He was defeated; Mrs. Calhoun set the precedence of resistance, and thus drew upon her husband Jackson's hatred. The widower Van Buren, on the other hand, graciously received the Eatons and for that reason stood all the better at court. When the cabinet meetings became unbearable, Van Buren very skillfully proposed that they all resign. This gave the President a chance for a house cleaning. The secret of the little magician's maneuver was that he had his eye on the presidency and knew that Jackson was opposed to a cabinet member being a candidate. Jackson appointed him minister to Great Britain. The road to the White House was open.

A more serious political quarrel than the Peggy Eaton affair divided Jackson and Calhoun. Since the ratification of the Constitution one of the most controversial questions had been that of the respective rights of the states and the federal government. Could a state refuse to enforce a law passed by Congress? Could it, if it disapproved of the policy of the federal government, detach itself from the Union? The argument that secession was legitimate had been supported by the northern states at the time when they disapproved of "Mr. Madison's War"; it was supported by South Carolina, who protested against "the tariff of abominations." Calhoun himself, the Vice President of the United States, subscribed to a doctrine called "nullification": Since the Union was an agreement entered into by sovereign states, each of these states had the right to decide whether an act of Congress was constitutional. An infinitely dangerous doctrine. Jackson, patriot and nationalist, condemned it. Calhoun, "the living abstraction," was its passionate supporter. He said that he wished but a single inscription on his tombstone, the one word—*Nullification*. Many southern states approved it and hoped to gain the support of the West. The East had shown great reluctance in permitting the federal government to sell the available lands at a low price. Why? Because the migration toward the West was tending to depopulate the East and to deprive the manufacturers of labor. This conflict between the East and the West suggested to Calhoun's friends a fruitful agreement; the West should aid the South in its struggle against the tariff, and the South should aid the West against New England.

The oratorical peak of this controversy was the famous series of Hayne-Webster debates, in the course of which the two great orators expounded before the Senate two contradictory views of the Constitution. Daniel Webster, the easterner, the excellent lawyer, endowed by nature with a massive head, flashing eyes black as death, a voice that could be thunderous or moving according to need, had appeared at the beginning of his career, at a time when the East seemed to favor separation, as a champion of states' rights; then, at just the same time as his fellow New Englanders, he had become a nationalist. His ambition was as great as his talent: "I have done nothing," he said to a friend. "At thirty Alexander had conquered the world and I am forty. . . ." Although this pride sometimes rendered his eloquence bombastic and pretentious, he knew how to evoke strong emotions in his hearers and at his best moments attained greatness. Robert Y. Hayne, his adversary, had less genius but more distinction of mind. The two men delivered a series of orations. The attendance was large and long queues would form each time in front of the Senate doors. Hayne had accused New England of "sectionalism." Webster defended it superbly: "Mr. President, I shall enter on no encomium upon Massachusetts; she needs none. There she is. Behold her, and judge for yourselves. There is her history; the world knows it by heart. . . . There is Boston, and Concord, and Lexington, and Bunker Hill; and there they will remain forever." His essential theme was the defense of the Union. The Constitution, he said, had been at pains to specify the division of powers between the federal government and the states. If there were any doubt, it was the duty of the Supreme Court, and the Supreme Court alone, to decide. No state had the right to annul a federal law, for if a single state on a single occasion were to arrogate to itself this right there would be no more Union.

His peroration remains a classic text:

When my eyes shall be turned to behold for the last time the sun in heaven, may I not see him shining on the broken and dishonored fragments of a once glorious Union; on States dissevered, discordant, belligerent; on a land rent with civil feuds, or drenched, it may be, in fraternal blood! Let their last feeble and lingering glance rather behold the gorgeous ensign of the republic, now known and honored throughout the earth, still full high advanced, its arms and trophies streaming in their original lustre, not a stripe erased or polluted, nor a single star obscured, bearing for its motto, no such miserable interrogatory as "What is all this worth?" nor those other words of delusion and folly "Liberty first and Union afterward"; but everywhere, spread all over in characters of living light, blazing on all its ample folds, as they float over the sea and over the land, and in every wind under the whole heavens, that other sentiment, dear to every true American heart,—Liberty *and* Union, now and forever, one and inseparable!

An eloquent figure of speech does not solve an economic problem. The South had legitimate grievances against "the tariff of abominations." The increased production of cotton had led to a lowering of its price while the tariff, constantly raised by the demands of the northern manufacturers, raised the cost of manufactured goods. The planters felt strangled and threatened to revolt. If the Union was to become an instrument by which the North and the West exploited the South, all right: The South would annul the unjust laws and at need would withdraw from the Union. Calhoun said on one occasion that the President of the United States might be replaced by two consuls, after the Roman fashion, one chosen by the North and the other by the South. Jackson determined to break this tacit rebellion. In April, 1830, when the President and Vice President were both attending a banquet in celebration of Jefferson's birthday, Jackson, when the time for toasts came, arose and looking Calhoun straight in the eye cried: "Our Union! It must be preserved." Isaac Hiel, an eyewitness, has described the scene:

A proclamation of martial law in South Carolina and an order to arrest Calhoun where he sat could not have come with more blinding, staggering force. All hilarity ceased. The President, without adding one word in the way of speech, lifted up his glass as a notice that the toast was to be quaffed standing. Calhoun rose with the rest. His glass so trembled in his hand that a little of the amber fluid trickled down the side. Jackson stood silent and impassive. There was no response to the toast. Calhoun waited until all sat down. Then he slowly and with hesitating accent offered the second volunteer toast: "The Union! Next to our Liberty, most dear!" Then, after a minute's hesitation, he added: "May we all remember that it can only be preserved by respecting the rights of the States and by distributing equally the benefit and burden of the Union."

That Jackson had decided to suppress all attempts at secession none could doubt. He was willing that there should be discussion so long as it remained in the realm of theory. "But," he said, "if one drop of blood be shed there in defiance of the laws of the United States, I will hang the first man of them I can get my hands on to the first tree I can find." And a senator added: "When Jackson begins to talk about hanging, they can begin to look for the ropes." But Calhoun and his friends had taken up positions from which retreat was difficult. When in 1832 Jackson signed a new protective tariff, a South Carolina convention declared that the law was null and void and did not bind either the state, its officers, or its citizens. If the federal government attempted enforcement by violence, said the convention, then South Carolina would consider herself released from all ties to the Union and free to act as a sovereign state.

Jackson was not the man to leave such a threat unanswered. He issued orders to the navy to be in readiness to dispatch a squadron to Charleston. He armed the forts and declared "by the Eternal" he would defend the laws. A strong proclamation by the President answered the Statute of Nullification: "I consider, then, the power to annul a law of the United States, assumed by one State, incompatible with the existence of the Union, contradicted expressly by the letter of the Constitution . . . and destructive of the great object for which it was formed." From this time the country would have drifted toward civil war in spite of the astute

Van Buren, who feared that this controversy, by dividing the Democrats, would be damaging to his future political career. Henry Clay, who was not displeased at depriving Jackson of a brilliant and easy success, and who wanted to salvage as much as possible of his American System, Calhoun, who had no wish for an armed rebellion, and Webster worked together to achieve a compromise. Henry Clay, a master in this field, secured the passage of a new law that provided for the next ten years a progressively descending scale of tariffs. The South agreed. Both sides considered it a victory. That is always a proof of the excellence of an agreement. But Jackson, who did not have the same tender feelings for compromise measures as did Henry Clay, believed that the reckoning had only been postponed. He wrote to a friend that the tariff had been no more than a pretext; the real objective was a Confederacy of the South. "The next pretext will be the question of slavery."

CHAPTER XXXII

The Grandeur and Decline of the Little Magician

IN 1832 Jackson was elected President for a second term and Van Buren became Vice President. Jackson's opponent, Henry Clay, who was the most skillful of negotiators and the most inept of candidates, had in effect made him a present of the election by choosing the Bank of the United States as the campaign issue. Jackson hated the bank. Under the direction of Nicholas Biddle, it had rendered undeniable service to the country, but in the eyes of the constituents and friends of Jackson with heavily mortgaged farms, the bank represented the creditors, the capitalists, the enemy. Its shares were almost all owned by eastern industrialists or foreign bankers. Through its branches (there were twenty-five of them) it competed with local banks and even tried to supplant them. It was harsh toward debtors, which displeased the farmers, and opposed to inflation, which displeased the land speculators. On the whole it conducted its business strictly and prudently, laudable behavior for a private enterprise but behavior that entails serious difficulties in a public institution. Worst of all, it was guilty of what, in the eyes of Jackson and his followers, was the crime of crimes; it had given aid and support to their opponents. Bankers are seldom able to resist the temptation of becoming involved in politics; and this is their ruin. In a country that is jealous of its liberties, money destroys the causes it desires to support. When Congress, "instructed" by the bank, voted to prolong its monopoly, Jackson vetoed the measure. His constituents acclaimed this first blow by St. George against the Dragon. The Democratic party declared, without being contradicted, that Daniel Webster had received an advance of $32,000 from the bank; it is true that he was its counsel, but other members of Congress, without that claim, had received close to half a million dollars. A part of the press had been discreetly bought by advantageous loans. These revelations had contributed to Clay's defeat; and Jackson, considering his victory a mandate to complete the destruction of the monster, decided to withdraw the federal funds from the bank and entrust them to certain banks which were called Pet Banks because they were arbitrarily selected by the administration. Congress protested, but Jackson's old friend, Senator Thomas Benton, led the congressional fight for him and triumphed. In 1836 the license of the bank expired and no one dared to propose its renewal.

Jackson's second administration was marked by extraordinary prosperity. Land, houses, cotton, slaves all increased in value. There were healthy elements in this boom. The constant increase in population, the clearing of new lands, and the development of cities accounted for it in part. But there were other and alarming aspects. The state banks, inadequately supervised, were all authorized to issue banknotes and made use of this unsecured currency to grant dangerously large loans to land speculators, who counted on the rise in value of their holdings to repay what they had borrowed. These unproductive investments did not provide for even the payment of interest on the debt. The income from the sale of land by the government increased in 1836 to over twenty million dollars. Many foreign investors, attracted by the continuous rise in value and poorly informed about the American market, bought shares in railroads and canals at too high a price. Thus little by little were established the conditions that make great financial crises inevitable. But at the time the mechanism of these crises was little understood; the country basked, with peaceful mind, in its artificial prosperity; the national debt had been entirely repaid and there was even a surplus for distribution to the states. Jackson completed his second term in the false glow of the inflation. Nevertheless at the very end of his administration in 1836, on the advice of his financial counselors, he published a *Specie Circular* which enjoined all government agents from further sales of land except for hard cash. It was the first breath of the tempest. In the excitement of an election year this harbinger passed almost unnoticed.

In the election of 1836 the country was once more divided into two parties: the Jacksonian Democrats, who had Van Buren as their candidate; and the Whigs, made up of the National-Republicans plus various other opposition groups. They were called Whigs because they claimed, like the English Whigs of 1688, to be fighting against a "usurpation of the executive power." But whereas the English Whigs had struggled against an unpopular monarchy, the American Whigs were attacking an executive who was more popular than they themselves. The Jacksonian era had made the presidency a power at least equal to that of Congress and like "a third House of which he was the single member." Relying upon the people, Jackson had defied Congress and made full use of the veto. It is only since Jackson's time that the President of the United States has had the reputation of representing the nation better than Congress. This was not the intention of the founders. But through the prestige, first of Washington, then of Jefferson, then of Jackson, the presidency assumed, little by little, the function of a "plebiscitary monarchy" limited in duration and under the control of Congress. By his personal initiative Jackson had been able to modify completely the policy of the country, to put an end temporarily to the American System of Henry Clay, and to kill the Bank of the United States. He was also able to dictate the choice of his successor. The Whig leaders, Webster and Clay, were more brilliant and better known to the public than Van Buren, but Van Buren was Jackson's choice. That was enough; he was elected. On inauguration day the President that the crowd cheered was not the little man with the carefully curled red hair but the old soldier with his mane of white.

It had been expected that Van Buren's administration would be that of the Little Magician; instead it was that of the Sorcerer's Apprentice. Jackson had bequeathed to his friend a country pregnant with crisis. Banknotes without security, lands without purchasers, cities without inhabitants, canals without traffic, mortgages without value, artificially inflated prices, and the exorbitant cost of necessities had raised a fragile house of cards which must collapse at the first breath. A bad harvest, a deficit in the foreign trade balance, Jackson's *Specie Circular,* and bankruptcies in England finally brought on, in 1837, a panic of the first magnitude. For several months meetings which bordered on riots had been held in protest against the rise in prices. The public rushed to the banks to withdraw their deposits. At the doors women, pushed and jostled, cried: "Pay! Pay!" Troops had to be called out in New York to maintain order. Public opinion held the government responsible. It was said that the triumvirate of Jackson-Van Buren-Benton had been as harmful to the prosperity of the country as the triumvirate of Caesar-Pompey-Crassus to the liberties of Rome. The bad management of the banks added to the disaster. Almost all had issued too much paper money; their managers were incompetent; many of the banks failed. There was a lack of currency. Commercial houses had to supplement it by printing certificates. "This ticket will hold good," one of them read, "for a beef's tongue and two crackers."

Businessmen criticized the President for doing nothing to mitigate the crisis. His political enemies delightedly joined in the chorus. Van Buren maintained his calm and insisted that all the suggested measures would only increase the trouble. The government, he said, did not have the right to sustain the paper money and keep up the illusion that values can be created without work. He believed that the crisis would be more quickly over if each individual was allowed to work out his own salvation. This intentional inertia infuriated the business world. As for the state funds, Van Buren suggested that instead of depositing them in the banks and thus contributing to the inflation, they should be entrusted to an independent Treasury and that all payments by the federal government be made in gold or silver. This plan was not unreasonable, but reason is not what controls popularity; and Van Buren, who had never been loved by the crowds, was now hated. The panic was to cost him his second term.

It is always the ruin of a party to be in power during a depression. The President's policy of temporizing may have been wise, but the Whigs had succeeded in making it appear foolish. Moreover, while they were out of power they had given thought to the art of winning presidential elections. Since caucuses had been replaced by popular choice, a good candidate was no longer an old fox of the capitol but someone whose name could be associated with a resounding slogan, a man known to the masses, preferably for some extraordinary action or originality of character rather than for opinions that might divide the voters. It was better that he should not be an "aristocrat." Jackson's picturesque popular appeal had been the reason for his success. They must find another Jackson. Since old soldiers were at a premium, the Whigs went looking for an old soldier: They discovered General William Henry Harrison. He was not a great general, far from it; but he had once defeated the Indians at Tippecanoe . . . *Tippecanoe* . . . The word was sonorous and bizarre. Why not *Tippecanoe?* And so

Harrison was selected as candidate by the Whigs to the great disappointment of Henry Clay, a man infinitely more remarkable and, for that very reason, disturbing to his party. To gain the southern vote, the Whigs nominated as Vice President the Virginian John Tyler, an old states'-rights Democrat, a Jeffersonian at a time when the Whig party was Hamiltonian, the paradoxical champion of a cause that was not his own, but a useful chessman, so thought the campaign managers on

The log cabin and hard cider campaign of 1836. A flag showing two of the reasons for voting for William Henry Harrison. Such use of the flag is today forbidden by law. From original flag at the William L. Clements Library, University of Michigan.

the political board. "Tippecanoe and Tyler too"—the alliteration made a perfect campaign slogan. It was soon ringing throughout America.

The campaign was more comic opera than drama. The purpose of the Whigs was to make Harrison appear to be a man of the people with simple tastes and Van Buren appear as a voluptuous plutocrat who had made the White House a place of luxury and sinful delights. When the President went out he dressed with some elegance; he was pictured as perfuming himself with Queen Victoria's Double Extract and the Oil of Corinth. He was accused of the abominable crime of having brought a billiard table into the White House, of drinking from cups of massive silver, and of sitting on upholstered chairs. As a matter of fact, Van Buren had been born poor, and Harrison was the owner of an estate of two thousand acres. But what mattered the facts? A newspaper, friendly to Van Buren, had committed the blunder of saying about Harrison: "Give him a keg of hard cider and two thousand dollars a year; he will spend the rest of his days in his log cabin." Harrison's managers were smart enough to realize that their adversaries had given them a beautiful opening. They based their whole campaign on hard cider and the log cabin. "Teach the palace to show respect to the log cabin!" cried their newspapers. The whole country was crossed by floats that bore a trapper's cabin and a keg of hard cider which volunteers dispensed to the voters. The latter swelled their lungs in praise of William Henry Harrison and vituperation of Martin Van Buren. Accompanying the parade were crowds singing:

> Tippecanoe and Tyler too.
> Van, Van is a used-up man!
> With Tip and Tyler
> We'll bust Van's biler!

Or again:

> Farewell, dear Van,
> You're not our man.
> To steer the ship,
> We'll try old Tip.

"Never more enthusiasm and less thought." The people had suffered and the people wanted a change. "The breeze itself murmurs 'change!' Everyone's cry is 'Let's change!'" In the Boston parade a float representing Van Buren and his friends bore the inscription: "We have tried them in office; now we mean to try them out." Everywhere there were banners: "Welcome Whigs!" The Whigs' campaign speeches were easy to make. The orator would cry "Tippecanoe!" The crowd would reply: "And Tyler too!" It was clearly a good method, for Tippecanoe was elected—and Tyler too. John Quincy Adams sarcastically noted in his journal that this election showed that the direct and infallible road to the presidency was military service, combined with demagogic propaganda. For a half a century after this experience every candidate for the presidency was to attempt to prove that he was "a son of the people." Daniel Webster on one occasion apologized publicly for not having been born in a log cabin, but swore that his brother and sisters had been born in one; and added that if he ever showed any shame at this circumstance he hoped his name and that of his posterity would be forever effaced from the memory of mankind.

President Harrison was inaugurated on March 4, 1841. "He was not a great man but he had lived a long time and he had been associated with great undertakings." Clay and Webster, the leaders of the Whig party, believed they would have no trouble handling this old soldier, who seemed less crusty than Jackson. Webster, in superior and patronizing fashion, offered to write the inaugural address for the President, who would no doubt be very busy. "Oh! It's all ready," said Tippecanoe. He had indeed composed it, drawing heavily on classical allusions, and it was so incoherent a piece, so studded with consuls, triumphs, and lictors, that his friends besought him to let Webster adapt it to his style. The story is told that one evening Webster arrived late for dinner, and his hostess said: "I do hope nothing has happened?" He replied: "Madame, you wouldn't say that if you knew what I have just done: I have just killed seventeen Roman Proconsuls. . . ." A month later it was the President himself who was as dead as the proconsuls. He had caught pneumonia, thus playing a wretched trick on the Whigs. In the shadow of Tippecanoe, Clay had planned to become Mayor of the Palace and to reverse Jackson's policy completely by re-establishing a federal bank, a program of public works, and tariffs. His discomfiture and that of the party were great when Harrison's death brought to power Tyler, a Democrat who was hostile to the whole Whig program.

Was Tyler legally President of the United States? This was open to question. The Constitution simply said that in the event of the President's death the powers and duties of that office should pass to the Vice President. It was possible to understand this as a temporary measure pending a new election, and this interpretation would have been reasonable since the Vice President is not always chosen for those qualities that make a good President. For certain politicians the vice presidency had been a consolation prize; to others it had been offered as part of a sectional compromise. A strange way of choosing the supreme leader of the country. But Tyler demanded complete succession and his tenacity won out. John Quincy Adams, who went to see him, noted in his journal that Tyler was calling himself President of the United States and not Vice President acting as President, "which would have been the correct formula." Hence this paradoxical situation: a President without party; a Democrat who was at dagger's point with all the Democrats; an electee of the Whigs who was opposed to all their measures. At once there was a rain of vetoes—a veto on the bank, a veto on the public works program—resulting in the resignation of the whole cabinet, with the exception of Daniel Webster, who stayed on to complete his negotiations with Lord Ashburton, the representative of the British government.

There were a number of subjects of dispute between the United States and England. Several of them, and in particular the question of the Maine frontier, were settled by the Webster-Ashburton Treaty of 1842. But the question of Oregon remained undecided. This part of the Northwest had been coveted by America, England, and Russia. In 1824 the frontier of Russian Alaska had been fixed at 54°40′N.L. Below this line an Anglo-American condominium had been provisionally established. Since the time of Lewis and Clark many hunters and trappers had gone there, some from Canada, others by sea from the United States, finally others by land across the continent. In 1811 a ship belonging to John Jacob Astor, the son of a German butcher from Waldorf, who had become a great fur trader in New York, had doubled Cape Horn and anchored at the mouth of the Columbia River. There the city of Astoria was founded. The following year an expedition by land from the East reached the same river. Astor founded a whole series of posts along its banks connected by fast canoes. A real fur war broke out between Astor and the Canadians. As in the eighteenth century, the *coureurs des bois* vied for new territories and the friendship of the Indian tribes.

Several trails now led toward the Pacific. The Oregon Trail in the Northwest started from the Missouri at Independence, crossed the Rocky Mountains and the Blue Mountains, and ended at Astoria. After 1841 regular processions of pioneers crossed the continent in covered wagons accompanied by their livestock. It was a hard journey. They had to contend with mountains, Indians, wild animals and famine. Some died of hunger in the mountains; there were even instances of cannibalism. In 1843 the Americans of the Northwest held a meeting and, after the fashion of their ancestors, drew up a covenant: "We, the people of Oregon territory, for the purposes of mutual protection and to secure peace among ourselves, agree to adopt the following laws and regulations, until such time as the United States of America extend their jurisdiction over us." But the Webster-Ashburton Treaty had been signed the year before in 1842, prolonging the Anglo-American condominium. It was necessary to wait. Webster, once the treaty was signed, left the government, and with him disappeared the last vestige of the Whig victory.

CHAPTER XXXIII

The South's Peculiar Institution

THAT the human wave which had in a few decades peopled the immense valley of the Mississippi would gradually overrun the whole continent seemed likely. Neither Mexico nor Spain was strong enough to dam this tide. But within the United States itself it encountered opposition, for the question of annexation was bound up with that of slavery, the abscess that was poisoning the country. The Missouri Compromise, which prohibited slavery forever north of 36°30′ in the Louisiana Territory, except for Missouri, had been a temporary remedy. The deep-seated malady was still there. Why was it more acute in the nineteenth century than in the eighteenth? Because in the eighteenth many of the most prominent southerners, although provisionally willing to tolerate the institution, had themselves condemned it in principle. Washington and Jefferson, both slaveowners, were opposed to slavery; John Randolph freed his slaves. But theories are often, and sometimes unconsciously, warped by personal interest. At the end of the eighteenth century there occurred an event that transformed both the interests and the ideas of the South—the patenting of the cotton gin by Eli Whitney.

The gin made cotton the principal product of the South. It made possible and necessary the employment of an immense amount of slave labor. The economic weakness of slavery hitherto had been the necessity of supervision, the ineptness of the slave, and his lack of adaptability. But cotton-growing was easy, mechanical work, and it extended over the entire year; supervision was simple because of the low height of the cotton plants. The slave whose support cost, on an average, about twenty dollars a year was much cheaper than the free worker. Moreover, since 1800 the number of slaves had nearly doubled every twenty years; in 1850 it was to reach over three million two hundred thousand. The price of human flesh had risen as well. In 1780 a young male Negro sold for as much as $200; in 1818, as much as $1000; in 1860, from $1200 to $1800. These figures, however, are the peak prices paid for "prime field hands"; the average value of slaves was lower. The total value of the slaves in 1850 was estimated at around two and a half billion dollars. It was the South's greatest asset, for the land, impoverished by one-crop farming, was rapidly decreasing in value. Since the importation of slaves had been prohibited after 1808, they had become all the more valuable. Thus little by little the inhabitants of the South had rallied in perfect good faith to the defense of an institution that seemed to them one of the conditions of their existence.

Men have always found it only too easy to discover moral justification for profitable conduct. Sooner or later there were bound to appear apologists and doctrinaires of slavery. A certain Thomas R. Dew, a professor at William and Mary who had gone to study in Germany, learned there that inequality is the basis of societies: "It is the order of nature and of God that the being of superior faculties and knowledge, and therefore of superior power, should control and dispose of those who are inferior. It is as much in the order of nature that men should enslave each other as that other animals should prey upon each other." William Harper of South Carolina, another apologist, published a *Memoir on Slavery*. He maintained that no wrong is done a slave by those who keep him in that condition. "A slave has no hope that by a course of integrity, he can materially elevate his condition in society, nor can his offense against honesty materially depress it, or affect his means of support. . . . In Northern communities the unmarried woman who becomes a mother is an outcast from society. It is not so with the female slave. Her offspring is not a burden but an acquisition to her owner. The want of chastity among slaves hardly deserves a harsher name than weakness." Naturally Harper did not have the same ideas as Jefferson. He declared that men are born neither free nor equal, that laws are made to maintain and not to efface the differences, and that if there are servile tasks to be performed, there must necessarily be servile beings to perform them. Calhoun himself, Vice President of the United States, issued a reminder that Greek democracy, founded on slavery, had been the model for the whole Western world. "I hold slavery to be a good. . . . Moreover, there never has yet existed a wealthy and civilized society in which one portion of the community did not in fact live on the labor of the other." In Jefferson's time slavery had been tolerated; in Calhoun's it was extolled.

These reassuring paradoxes were favorably received by the planters. The South had read the works of Walter Scott and was passing through a period of chivalrous exaltation. This was the time when an image took shape of a romantic and feudal South that had to protect itself against the barbarism of the Yankees. At the apex of the social pyramid were enthroned those who owned more than one hundred slaves each. These (about eighteen hundred in number) constituted a society characterized by its lavish hospitality, its sense of honor, its courtesy and its respect for women. Below them came about six thousand proprietors who owned fifty or more slaves; eighty-four thousand who had ten or more; around two hundred and fifty-five thousand who had from one to nine. In the same way that in England the prestige of the aristocracy was dear to the middle classes, so the "cotton snobs" in their thoughts and dreams participated in the splendor of the finest plantations, rejoiced in the charm of that life, loved their section, and detested the Yankees. The Negroes themselves spoke with respect and affection of the great houses, of "Massa" and of his family. In that indulgent society the churches closed their eyes to the bleaker aspects of slavery, and the worldly moralists laughed when an occasional planter took a pretty mulatto girl to be his mistress. Had not Noah, according to Genesis, condemned all the swarthy sons of Ham to perpetual slavery? Had not the will of the Creator thus been expressed by the patriarch? The belt of land favorable for cotton-growing extended from South Carolina to the Mississippi across Georgia and Alabama. There cotton was king; there a plutocracy arose that tried to imitate the graces of the old aristocracy of the original provinces. Beautiful houses were built on the banks of the Father of Waters amid the magnolias and the oak trees. Virginia itself was not part of the cotton belt, but it found a market there for its tobacco, whiskey, and slaves and its interests were identical. Moreover, in all the southern states skillful politicians were successfully molding public opinion in favor of slavery.

Custom blunts sensibilities. The planters no longer saw the odious aspects of slavery any more than the northern manufacturers were moved by the ills resulting from child labor. Aware of the condemnation which their "peculiar institution" earned them under other skies, the planters were touchy and irritable on this subject. How were they to consider as other than natural the world in which they had been born? Charitable planters, and there were many of them, felt affection for their Negroes and made efforts to educate them. Thomas Dabney allowed his Negroes Saturday afternoon off and said "that more work was done in five and one-half days than six." Every year he distributed prizes to the best of them. Other planters drew up instructions for their managers which they considered models of kindliness and wisdom: "Punishments must never be cruel or abusive, for it is low and inhuman to beat a negro simply from anger or spite. . . . I wish the Gospel to be preached to the negroes. . . . This is to be done on Sunday. . . . It is my duty to assure the souls of those dependent on me. . . ." Another proprietor wrote: "I support at my expense a good flute player and I have him play for the negroes every Saturday night until midnight. . . . I also employ a good preacher. . . ."

Still another: "Sick negroes are to be the object of particular attention.
. . . If a negro dies an hour is to be selected for his burial. At this time
all work must cease and the plantation negroes will attend the funeral."
But visitors from foreign countries were not enthusiastic about the peculiar
institution. The use of the leather lash was a fact and the Negro had no
way of escaping unjust punishment, for the testimony of a black against
a white was not accepted. "All the negroes we have seen," wrote one
Englishman, "seemed inadequately nourished, miserably clad and lodged.
. . . The criminals in their prisons are better treated than these men whose
only crime is that they are of a darker color than their masters."

As a matter of fact, there were classes among the Negroes as among the
whites. Personal servants, born in their master's house and raised with
his children, were civilized and well treated. Slaves in the cities also had a
certain liberty and sometimes were authorized to work for themselves away
from their masters' houses. Field slaves were the most unfortunate, and the
two other classes of blacks looked down on them as inferiors. Perhaps the
standard of living of these agricultural slaves was often superior to that of
the northern worker. But the North, despite all that was said on the
subject, was not convinced.

In the North slavery was becoming more and more unpopular. There
self-interest and morality were in the same camp. On the little New
England farm with its diversified tasks, slave labor could not be used.
The representation accorded to the South on the basis of a slave population which was disfranchised appeared a monstrous and shocking injustice.
It was absurd and offensive. The Irish, Scotch, and German immigrants,
newly arrived from Europe, considered slavery an archaic and barbarous
institution. The North was determined not to let a majority of slave
states dominate the country. Each time a new state was admitted, the
North and South clashed. If Missouri asked to be admitted to the Union
as a slave state, the North demanded first the admission of Maine as a
free state to maintain the balance of power. Little by little the tone of the
controversy became more strident. Until 1820 it had been possible for one
to admit opposition to slavery in the South. There were even southern
societies that collected money to buy slaves and send them back to Africa.
After 1820 the pressure exercised by the cotton growers, economic
necessity, and above all the exasperation caused by northern criticism made
it dangerous to voice anti-slavery sentiments in the South.

Among the northern opponents of slavery two groups must be distinguished—the anti-slavery men and the abolitionists. The anti-slavery
people were only opposed in principle to the extension of slavery; the
abolitionists went farther and demanded the liberation of all slaves. In

the 1820's a New Jersey Quaker named Benjamin Lundy began an ardent campaign in favor of gradual emancipation. He traveled on foot through a large number of states. Almost everywhere he went women joined him in founding anti-slavery societies which were prudently called "reading circles, women's clubs or lecture societies." In 1828 Benjamin Lundy met William Lloyd Garrison, a young printer from Boston, and converted him so thoroughly that the disciple became more radical than the master. Garrison, with the aid of his partner Isaac Knapp, wrote, set-up, printed, and published *The Liberator,* a journal which demanded the immediate emancipation of all slaves. He wrote in an abrupt, violent, and fiery style: "On this subject I want neither to think, nor talk, nor write with moderation. No! No! Tell the man whose house is burning to cry 'Fire!' with moderation. . . . I shall be as brutal as the truth and as intransigent as justice. . . . The apathy of the people would suffice to make statues leap from their pedestals and to hasten the resurrection of the dead. . . ."

Unhappily for Garrison, the opening of his campaign coincided with the hideous massacre of sixty white men by Negroes in Virginia. Now Nat Turner, the slave who had directed this rebellion, knew how to read: It was charged that abolitionist literature, and *The Liberator* in particular, had incited him. Very severe laws were passed which aggravated the condition of the Negroes both slave and free. Even in Massachusetts "right-thinking people" did not approve the violence of Garrison's language. He said himself that he had encountered more violent opposition in the North than in the South. He was maltreated in the streets of Boston, and Charles Sumner, the well-known opponent of slavery, said that "a cart load of Boston abolitionists had done more harm to the anti-slavery cause than all its enemies." Intolerance kills the most just of causes. Men like Daniel Webster, opposed to slavery but reasonable in their opposition, recognized that the South had an economic and political problem which could not be solved by a few brutal phrases. It was certainly unfortunate that some millions of blacks had been introduced into the midst of a white society, but now they were there. Regrets and accusations are not solutions. The cotton crop had to be planted and picked. Webster considered that slavery, so far as the South was concerned, was "a calamity not a crime." He thought that if the Negroes were to be emancipated, some means would have to be found to indemnify the planters. This prudence exasperated the virtuous abolitionists. When it was urged that at least respect should be shown for the Constitution, which guarantees the free enjoyment of all forms of property, Garrison retorted that the Constitution was nothing but a pact with the demon and an agreement with hell; and he publicly burned a copy of the diabolical document. It may have been an excellent dramatic gesture; it was certainly not an intelligent policy. On one occasion Boston crowds almost hanged Garrison on the great elm on the Commons and he was saved only by the intervention of the mayor.

Many men in the North who disapproved the violence of the abolitionists nevertheless defended their rights as American citizens. In 1836, when the representatives from the South prevailed upon the House of Representatives to pass a measure refusing to consider any proposals whatever in regard to slavery (this was called "the gag rule"), old John Quincy Adams, the former President who had become a member of Congress and was still vigorous and courageous, fought for liberty of petition with all the resources at his command: "I hold this resolution," he said, "to be in direct violation of the Constitution of the United States, of the rules of this House, and of the rights of my constituents." He raised such an uproar that his opponents went to the extent of threatening him with expulsion. This unbelievable furor shows how violent sentiment had become. On both sides there was the atmosphere of civil war. The slavery question poisoned others that, without it, would have been simple. To add to the territory of the United States might have been and should have been everybody's wish. But would the new domains be slave or free? Would their acquisition alter the majority in the Senate? Partisan spirit for a time triumphed over national spirit.

CHAPTER XXXIV.

"Manifest Destiny"

ONE of the characteristics of the American pioneer was his apparent need to press on constantly toward virgin territories. In Europe a similar need was felt by certain individuals and it resulted in the conquest of colonies and the founding of empires. In America the words "conquest" and "empire" were unpopular. It was considered preferable to say that the "manifest destiny" of the people of the United States was to occupy and civilize the entire continent. "But it is a rather arbitrary virtue," wrote the English historian Pollard, "to confine an island people within their island, however small it may be, and to allow others to conquer a whole continent, however vast it may be." This was not the way the Americans felt. The western expansionists had an easy conscience because they were determined to admit into the Union, on a footing of equality, the inhabitants of the territories they annexed, and also because those territories were hardly inhabited at all. Could one make America a "hunting preserve maintained for the benefit of a few miserable savages"? The southern expansionists wanted new slave territories because they were determined to retain their position in Congress. For a long time they had hoped that the West would join them in favoring slavery, but the West was devoting itself more and more to the growing of wheat and corn; it remained expansionist but it was not pro-slavery. And if certain citizens of the North and East were anti-expansionists on their own account, it was not through virtue but through fear of the creation of new states that would upset the balance of power in the Senate.

The western farmers wanted lands; King Cotton demanded lands; where were they to be had? There was nothing to be done about Canada, for experience had shown that it was useless and dangerous to attack England. To the South and West, on the other hand, stretched the ancient Spanish empire whose weakness seemed to invite invasion. Texas, Mexico's vast and fertile province, was a fine prey, coveted by the pioneers of Tennessee, Mississippi, and Louisiana. The country was almost uninhabited. At the beginning of the century a few Americans settled there without asking permission from the Spanish authorities. Then in 1821 Moses Austin asked for authorization to settle three hundred American families there. Shortly thereafter he died, and his son Stephen inherited the enterprise. After the revolution which freed Mexico, Stephen Austin obtained a confirmation of his concession from the Mexicans. The only conditions named were that the property owners should be Catholics, should obey the Mexican laws and behave themselves. As a matter of fact, few of the Anglo-American pioneers were Catholics, but a colonist who was not troubled by too scrupulous a conscience could become a Catholic for ten minutes, the time required to obtain the necessary certificate. Thereafter for years at a time he would not see a single Spanish official. A farm in Texas was surely worth a mass, especially since these Texas farms were beauties. For each immigrant one hundred seventy-seven acres of pasture, no taxes, abundant game, and as much corn as he cared to raise. By 1830, according to one estimate, more than twenty thousand Americans were living in Texas, and some of them had transported their slaves there. The Mexicans, who had abolished slavery in their own country, were sorry to see it re-established in one of their provinces. The Americans, on the other hand, complained of the Mexican authorities, who, they said, tried to force them to speak Spanish, forbade immigration, and imposed duties on American products. In 1827 John Quincy Adams had offered to buy Texas for one million dollars, but his offer had been refused. Later Jackson made a similar offer, which was also rejected.

In 1834 a soldier named Antonio Lopez de Santa Anna gained control of the Mexican government. He was shocked at the condition of Texas, where the Mexican laws on Catholicism and slavery were being violated with impunity. He wished to make Texas a military province and enforce respect for the Mexican authorities. The Texans decided that Santa Anna was going too far. That they were on Mexican territory they could not deny, but in a hundred years Spain had sent into that immense country no more than three thousand colonists and the Americans there already constituted a considerable population. They decided to proclaim themselves an independent state within the framework of Mexico. Both Mexicans and Texans knew that complete secession was bound to follow sooner or later. It came in 1836. Santa Anna at the head of a small army marched on San Antonio. He very cruelly massacred a detachment of Texans. In San Antonio the inhabitants and soldiers had fortified the Alamo, a mission consisting of a chapel, a cloister, and a convent, the whole surrounded by thick walls. There about a hundred and eighty Texans defended themselves heroically against some four thousand Mexicans. The position was taken after the death of almost all its defenders, and at the moment of capture the five last survivors were massacred by order of Santa Anna. "Remember the Alamo" became the rallying cry of the Texans. One of them, General Sam Houston, raised an army and scored a complete victory over Santa Anna at San Jacinto (1836). Santa Anna, taken prisoner, granted Texas its independence. The Mexican government refused to honor a signature obtained by force. But the Texans, henceforth independent in fact if not by law, organized a republic and elected Sam Houston president. An excellent choice. Houston was an old friend of Andrew Jackson and he had a fine presence which awakened spontaneous and enthusiastic loyalty.

The Texans' flag bore a single star. It was their way of proclaiming their desire of taking a place in the American constellation. They called themselves Americans and hoped to be annexed by the United States. Many statesmen in Washington looked with favor on this desire. But to annex a territory by force was action of a kind from which the United States had hitherto refrained. Moreover, the opponents of slavery saw grave danger in the acquisition of an immense territory which, by its climate and its soil, was favorable for the employment of slaves. In the annexationists' camp were the western expan'onists who believed in the "manifest

destiny" of the United States, the slaveowners of the South who regarded
the Texans as probable allies, the land speculators, and also the owners of
Texas bonds, which would be funded immediately on annexation. During
the whole of Van Buren's administration (1836-40) there was no question
of admitting Texas. Van Buren was an easterner and an anti-slavery man;
moreover, he had other problems to deal with. But when Tyler, a southerner, suddenly found himself in power after Harrison's sudden death and
especially after Webster, the opponent of slavery, had resigned as Secretary
of State, it became obvious that the annexation of Texas was to play a
capital role in American politics.

English policy, on the other hand, was to try to prevent this annexation.
The English, inconvenienced by American tariffs, saw the possibility of
making Texas a vassal state and there buying cotton as well as gaining a
market independent of the United States. Moreover, the English public
had brought a great many Mexican bonds and England had no desire to
see one of her debtors go to war. And so she advised peace. To Mexico she
said that there was no chance of reconquering Texas and the best thing to
do was to maintain a buffer state between Mexico and the United States;
to Texas, that independence was better than annexation and England
would lend support to an independent Texas. Houston, the president of
Texas, gave ear to the sirens of the Foreign Office. He had already made
an offer to the United States without success. John Quincy Adams had
threatened to unleash a civil war if Texas were annexed. Why not turn
to England, who would finance the cultivation of cotton in Texas?
Houston sent word to his old friend Andrew Jackson that Texas loved
the United States tenderly and approached it like a bride arrayed for
the wedding night; but that if the bridegroom showed too little enterprise
there were other lovers on the list.

Following the death of Upshur, Webster's successor, Calhoun became
Secretary of State. He was of course an arch-southerner, an arch-supporter
of slavery, and an arch-expansionist. He immediately asked the Mexican
Minister whether a peaceful annexation or purchase would be acceptable
to his country. The reply was once more that annexation would mean
war. Despite this Calhoun, who did not fear the risks and saw in the
acquisition of Texas a means of strengthening the South, concluded a
treaty of annexation in April, 1844. The Senate refused to confirm it.
It was the year of a presidential election. Annexation became a campaign
weapon. It was possible to use it as a bait both for the South and for the
West by demanding simultaneously the reoccupation of Oregon and "the
reannexation of Texas." This was intended to imply that Texas and
Oregon already belonged by right to the United States. The candidate of

the Whig party was the perennial and charming Henry Clay, the compromise expert. Clay's taste for friendly arrangements did not spring from weakness of character but from a feeling of intellectual humility. He said that he sought an honorable compromise whenever he could. Life itself was only a long compromise with death. All legislation, all government, all societies rested on principles of mutual concession, politeness, and courtesy. Let the man who considered himself superhuman say, if he liked, that he would accept no compromise, but let him who believed himself subject to human frailties not despise compromise. Unfortunately, at moments of great tension, courtesy and politeness lose their virtue. Clay tried not to raise either the question of annexation or that of slavery; he succeeded brilliantly in alienating both sides.

At the Democratic convention, Van Buren, an anti-annexationist, could not obtain the two-thirds majority demanded by the rules of the Democratic party for the nomination, and Polk was chosen as candidate. James K. Polk of Tennessee was a much less famous statesman but an ardent expansionist. The Whigs asked: "Who is James K. Polk?" He had been governor of Tennessee; to many this did not seem enough. "Polk," said one of them. "Great God! What a choice!" But when Clay's young son said: "Guess whom they have selected, father?" "Cass?" "No." "Anderson?" "No." "But who the devil then?" "James K. Polk." ";By God! Then I'm beaten again," said Henry Clay. For he knew that Polk was both prudent in what he said and daring in what he did. Polk despised the vanities of the world. His wife, an energetic Presbyterian, forbade dancing at the White House; he had no sense of humor. But perhaps, from time to time, there has to be a President who is more solid than brilliant. As a candidate, Polk said to George Bancroft, a member of the Massachusetts delegation: "Four great measures will occupy my administration: reduction of tariffs; an independent treasury; settlement of the Oregon question; and the acquisition of California." It was a sufficient program to fill four years. Meanwhile candidate Henry Clay was declaring: "The question of slavery has nothing to do with the annexations," which he knew to be false. Thanks to the creation of a third party (an abolitionist party called "the Liberty party") which deprived Clay of votes, the country elected Polk. Henry Clay and his wife shed tears. "Husband," she said, "these ingrates will never appreciate you as long as you are alive!" While he complained of his supporters: "If there had been two Henry Clays, one would have made the other President." Tyler, the retiring President, accepted the verdict of the election and obtained from Congress a vote of annexation in February, 1845. The news was received in Texas with unprecedented enthusiasm, and toward the end of the year that country became one of the grandest states in the Union.

After he became President, Polk, in order to fulfill his program, had to annex Oregon. Up to what point? The most enthusiastic wanted to go all the way to the frontier of Russian Alaska (54° 40′); those who were more reasonable realized that Canada had to have a port on the Pacific and suggested 49°. Polk defied England: "The only way to treat John Bull is to look him straight in the eye." He thought that firmness was the surest means of maintaining peace. "Fifty-four forty or fight!" had been the cry of his party. But America could not wage war at the same time against England and Mexico. After long negotiations a treaty with Great Britain was signed. The forty-ninth parallel was agreed upon as the frontier. It was an equitable solution. There remained the question of the Mexican provinces. If no American wanted a war with England, many entertained without dismay the idea of a war with Mexico. The latter did not recognize the annexation of Texas, at least in theory, for in practice Mexico had never attempted to reconquer the province since it had claimed its independence. Polk sent John Slidell as minister extraordinary to Mexico, charged with the duty of proposing not only a settlement of the Texas question but the purchase by the United States of New Mexico and if possible of California. As a point of honor the Mexican government refused to receive Slidell, and General Taylor received orders to take up a position on the Rio Grande. Polk desired at once to send a message of war to Congress, but his Secretary of State, Buchanan, wanted to wait until the Mexicans had first committed some act of war. In April, 1846, a force of Mexicans crossed the river; there was a cavalry skirmish, men were killed, and Polk sent the following message to Congress: "The cup of forbearance has been exhausted. . . . Mexico . . . has invaded our territory, and shed American blood upon the American soil." Congress declared "that by the act of the Republic of Mexico a state of war existed" (May 12, 1846).

The real object of this war was the conquest of California. President Polk made no mystery of it, and his cynicism was pardonable. Only six to seven thousand inhabitants, more Spaniards than Mexicans, lived in this immense territory. Attracted by the mildness of the climate and the richness of the soil, Americans in small numbers had settled there. That California would one day belong to the United States seemed inevitable, but the Whigs thought that the fruit would fall of itself. This was not Polk's opinion. As early as 1845 the American fleet in the Pacific had received orders to seize the ports as soon as war in Mexico should be declared. In August, 1846, General Kearny and eighteen hundred men, of whom five hundred were Mormons, arrived at Santa Fe and took New Mexico without resistance. Pushing on to California with one hundred men. Kearny found the conquest completed. The navy had landed at Monterey. An American officer and explorer, John C. Frémont, happened at that time to be in the Rocky Mountains. Frémont, son of a French immigrant, had at first journeyed with Nicollet between the Mississippi and the Missouri. The ambitious and daring Frémont had then himself led other exploring expeditions to the Rockies. A romantic marriage had brought him into the highest circles of the Republic. He had secretly married the daughter of Thomas Hart Benton, the Democratic leader. The senator had wanted to have the marriage annulled; the daughter had replied in the words of Ruth in the Bible: "Whither thou goest I will go." Before such devotion the senator had to give way. And he became fond of his son-in-law Frémont. The latter had the support of his illustrious father-in-law, and with the aid of a handful of men succeeded in having himself recognized as the leader of the provisional government in California. A few comic-opera battles, without dead or wounded, had given him the whole country. General Kearny, arriving on the scene, came into conflict with the Mexicans and with Frémont. The latter, a spoiled child, who had thus far always had his own way, tried to resist. Kearny had him court-martialed for mutiny. Frémont was found guilty, refused the pardon Polk offered him, and resigned his commission. This little adventure had political consequences: It made enemies of the old friends Benton and Polk and made Frémont a victim, a senator from California, and, later on in 1856, a candidate for the presidency.

Meanwhile General Zachary Taylor was invading Mexico so successfully that he alarmed the Democrats. Not that the victories were unwelcome to them, but Taylor, carelessly dressed, ill shaven, adored by his men, nicknamed Old Rough and Ready, belonged to the same class of picturesque and impetuous generals as Jackson. It was a breed of which the Whigs all too easily made Presidents. Polk prudently ordered another general to land at Vera Cruz, this time Winfield Scott, a Whig like Taylor, but haughty and elegant and thus with small popular appeal. Scott was to take possession of Mexico City before Taylor won any dangerous successes. As bad luck would have it, they were both victorious, Taylor at Buena Vista, Scott at the gates of Mexico City. Among the officers who distinguished themselves in these campaigns were Taylor's son-in-law, Colonel Jefferson Davis, Captain Robert E. Lee, Captain McClellan, and Lieutenant Ulysses S. Grant. On September 17, 1847, American troops paraded in front of Scott and took possession of "the halls of Montezuma." By the Treaty of Guadalupe-Hidalgo (1848), Mexico recognized the Rio

Grande as its boundary and ceded New Mexico and Upper California in exchange for fifteen million dollars. This was not annexation; at very most it was a forced sale. Certain rabid expansionists wanted to absorb the whole of Mexico, but the President refused and the Senate, after the customary bitter speeches, ratified the treaty. Polk had given his country a million square miles and the Whig party two candidates. The problem was now to assimilate these conquests without destroying the balance of power between the two sections of the country.

CHAPTER XXXV

The Last Compromise

THE immense territories the United States had just acquired supported a very few white settlers, either American or Spanish. Difficulty of access explains this fact. Not only were the distances enormous and the journey by wagon very difficult, not only was it necessary to cross high mountains and vast deserts, but in the plains of the Middle West the emigrant, unless he was traveling in a well-defended convoy, was at the mercy of the Indian tribes which, after being driven from the East and deprived of their ancestral lands, had found a refuge there. Brave, cruel, half savage, these Indians lived by hunting buffalo. They had horses, the offspring of those formerly turned loose by the Spaniards. Their courage, their skill, their legitimate resentment, their knowledge of the land made them redoubtable enemies. Nevertheless, more and more numerous caravans adventurously set out on the different trails leading toward the Pacific. One of the strangest episodes was the founding by a religious sect called the Mormons of a prosperous commonwealth in the midst of the desert—Utah.

The founder and prophet of the group was a young man named Joseph Smith, who had been born in Vermont and at the age of about fifteen, while he was at his prayers, had seen, so he said, the apparition of an angel who had revealed to him the existence of sacred books engraved on tablets of gold which constituted the revelation of Christ to the ancient inhabitants of America. Guided by the angel, Smith had found the gold tablets and with the aid of magic spectacles had deciphered them. The book, called the Book of Mormon after the name of the prophet who had written it, was published and became the holy book of the Mormon Church, or the Church of the Latter-day Saints. Disciples gathered around Smith and about 1830 the church numbered more than three thousand loyal members, Smith from time to time had revelations. One of them commanded him to found the New Jerusalem. At first he thought he had found the land of the saints in Ohio. But that was not the opinion of the local inhabitants, who considered the Mormons infidels and made their life so difficult that they emigrated to Missouri, then into Illinois where they founded the city of Nauvoo. In 1843 a revelation commanded Joseph Smith to re-establish the polygamy of the Patriarchs among his people. These multiple marriages filled the Mormons' neighbors with indignation, and a violent campaign against them ended in the assassination of Joseph Smith.

Brigham Young, who succeeded him, and who was a bold and energetic organizer, led his persecuted people into the desert. Fifteen thousand Mormons set out in three thousand covered wagons. Their sufferings were great. Finally in a circle of high snow-capped mountains Brigham Young discovered a white lake which shone in the sun, a lake of salt. He felt that here was the place to build the New Jerusalem. To the river that flowed into this dead sea he gave the name Jordan, and he drew up his wagons and founded Salt Lake City. The beginnings were hard. The apparently sterile soil was entirely dependent on irrigation. But the Mormons had great qualities. Their Twelve Apostles organized the state with the same thoroughness as the church. Soon the tide of emigration toward the Pacific brought them prosperity. For travelers, Salt Lake City was a place to find repose and provisions. In 1850 Utah was organized as a territory, but for a long time remained a theocracy recognizing no laws but its own. It became a state of the Union in 1896, abandoned polygamy, and today stands as an example of perfect tolerance.

Oregon, California, New Mexico, Utah—it was inevitable that the acquisition of this great domain which once more vastly increased the area of the country should give rise to new controversies between the advocates and the opponents of slavery. Actually they were struggling for control of the federal government. The pro-slavery men were already hopelessly outnumbered in the House of Representatives, election to which was proportional to population. They were in a minority even when the slaves were counted in at three-fifths of their number as had been decided in the compromise of 1787. But in the Senate, to which each state sent two representatives whatever its population, they could hold their position provided the parity between the two groups of states was maintained.

In 1846, on the very day when news came of the peace with Mexico, David Wilmot, a northern Republican, proposed that slavery be forever banished from all territories acquired by conquest or purchase from Mexico. The House voted for the Wilmot resolution, but it was defeated in the Senate. The South retorted by demanding that slavery should not be forbidden in

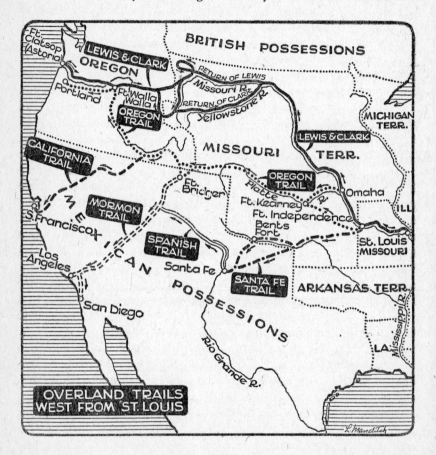

Oregon; this resolution was defeated in its turn; it was, moreover, unreasonable, for the rigorous climate of Oregon made the employment of slave labor impracticable. In the lands conquered from Mexico, on the other hand, the question of slavery arose naturally and had to be settled. A whole gamut of solutions could be conceived, ranging from total prohibition (Wilmot) to complete unrestriction (Calhoun and his disciples), and including the extension of the Missouri Compromise line (slavery south of 36° 30', liberty to the north), and the doctrine of squatter's sovereignty, which left the inhabitants in every territory free to decide by vote whether their state should be permanently free or slave.

It quickly became evident that this question was to dominate the presidential election of 1848. Polk wished to retire to his estate in Nashville and declined to be a candidate. "I shall soon cease to be a servant and become a sovereign," he said. The Democrats, who were sure of the southern vote, nominated a northerner, Lewis Cass of Michigan; the Whigs, who were sure of the Western vote, nominated a southerner, General Zachary Taylor, hero of the Mexican War. With old Zach they hoped to repeat the campaign of Tippecanoe. Taylor was the owner of slaves in Louisiana, but he had common sense and moderation and did not consider slavery a holy doctrine. Nevertheless he frightened certain anti-slavery Whigs in the North who, with the old Liberty party men and others, formed a new party, the Free-Soilers, whose motto was "Free soil, free speech, free labor, and free men." The Free-Soilers were not abolitionists like the former Liberty party, because they feared that the South would secede and they wished above all things to maintain the Union; they simply wanted to limit, localize, and discourage slavery. Their candidate was Van Buren, whose retirement had restored his presidential virginity. He was not elected, but in New York, which was his electoral bailiwick, he diverted a great many votes from the Democrat Cass, thus leading to Taylor's election.

Meanwhile, in the course of the year 1848, a new event had modified the California problem. When the Americans had occupied California it was a Spanish country, tranquil, majestic, voluptuous, where beautiful women in mantillas flirted with Kearny's officers in the haciendas, where the chanting of the Roman mass answered the guitars in the patio, and it seemed at first that this secular charm was never to be broken. One day an American named Marshall, employed by Captain Sutter, a Swiss colonist who had a small concession in the valley of the Sacramento, discovered gold in the spillway of Sutter's mill. He sent nuggets to San Francisco to be assayed. There was no question, it was gold. Quickly the news spread that the valley of the Sacramento was the richest gold region in the world. A true rumor, since in fifty years two billion dollars was to come from the mines of California. When the East heard this news the gold rush was on. In the single year of 1849 the population of California rose from six thousand to nearly one hundred thousand inhabitants. In a few years San Francisco, formerly a small fishing village, became a city of fifty thousand, then of two hundred thousand. Nevertheless the journey remained difficult. Some went by sea, making the voyage around Cape Horn; others by land and sea by crossing the Isthmus of Panama; many by the trails through Oregon and Utah. Thousands of human beings died on the way, victims of fatigue, hunger, the mountains, and the Indians. But by this grave-sown route others got through. These poor fellows thought all they had to do was sift the sands to make huge fortunes in a few weeks' time. This was not the case: For one miner who became wealthy, a hundred eked out a laborious livelihood. But around the mines other enterprises flourished. This new country lacked everything. Laundrymen, masons, prostitutes were at a premium. Taverns and gambling houses were more profitable than gold mines. The men who had run the risks of crossing a continent were tough through and through, fearing neither God nor devil. Stabbings were so common that no one paid any attention to them.

Lacking an established system of justice, the better citizens decided to take the police power into their own hands. Vigilance committees were organized in San Francisco; their methods were harsh but effective. In September, 1849, a group of colonists and gold hunters met at Monterey; they were of all nationalities—American, French, English, Mexican, Chinese—but they were in agreement on one point: They needed a government. The United States after the conquest had not organized the territory; the military forces administered it as best they could with the aid of the Spanish *alcades*. The convention at Monterey adopted a constitution. This excluded slavery because, in point of fact, there were no slaves in California. Thereupon California elected a legislature and a governor. It had not yet been recognized but it was behaving like a state of the Union.

When Congress met in 1849, the recognition of California as a free state immediately aroused fierce controversy. In the case of California the proponents of slavery were about to suffer a serious defeat. They had thought that by virtue of the Compromise of 1820 California would be divided into two states, one of which, south of 36° 30′, would have slaves. They realized with horror that if California was admitted the free states would have a majority in the Senate. What was to be done? Some thought of annexing Cuba, others of organizing slave states in the territories of Utah and New Mexico. But as a matter of fact no palliative could satisfy the aroused protagonists of slavery. It was one of those frequent instances in history when the partisan spirit becomes an obsession. The South's honor had been wounded by the denunciations of the abolitionists. Calhoun wrote to his daughter: "We have submitted for too long to the insults of the North." A senator from Georgia announced that if the North sought to drive the slaveowners from those territories that had been conquered at the cost of the blood of all the citizens, the

South would not hesitate to quit the Union. President Taylor replied, as Jackson had done formerly, that he would not hesitate to maintain the Union by force even if he had to lead the army himself. Henry Clay was now an old man, but in the defense of one last compromise he summoned up all the persuasive eloquence of his youth. With sunken face and feeble voice he nobly and passionately pleaded for civil peace. He besought the North not to insist upon the vain and offensive proclamations of abstract principles; he besought the South not to think that secession would be accepted without a struggle either by the North or by the Middle West. The people of the Mississippi Valley had struggled to prevent Spain, then France, then England from closing their river highway; they would never acquiesce in its being suddenly transformed into a route through foreign lands separated from them by a frontier.

This is the compromise that Henry Clay proposed: (a) California should be admitted as a free state; (b) the rest of the land gained from Mexico should be organized into territorial governments, with the inhabitants free to decide the question of slavery for themselves; (c) Texas should receive ten million dollars as compensation for a reduction in her western boundary; (d) a more effective law regarding fugitive slaves should be passed, making it easier for the South to recover them; and (e) the slave trade, but not slavery, should be prohibited in the District of Columbia. This compromise was proposed by Clay with his customary courtliness. It was inspired by the sentiments he had always had: pity for the infirmity of human nature and a desire to find an equitable and honorable solution. Another veteran, an old friend of Clay's, Calhoun, wanted to answer him. Emaciated but still possessed of his flashing eyes, Calhoun was a dying man. Tuberculosis of the larynx prevented him from speaking and his speech was read for him. With cavernous eyes, white hair thrown back, wrapped in a long black cape, he had the air of a phantom. The South, he said, had been attacked, slandered, despoiled. The North must restore her rights; equality in territories, the arrest of all fugitive slaves, the end of all campaigns against slavery—these were the minimal conditions for an understanding. Otherwise the cords that bound the states together would be severed one after another. On March 7 Webster, the last of the old guard, rose to speak. He too was terribly aged, but his manner was vigorous: "I speak today for the preservation of the Union . . . 'Hear me for my cause.' . . ." Many expected a tirade against slavery; they were disappointed. Webster sided with Clay in his search for a compromise. The abolitionists said that the desire to be President inspired Webster, who had formerly been their idol and who from this date on became their *bête noire*. But partisans are always willing to attribute low motives to those who spoil their plans. As a matter of fact Webster's attitude was a courageous one. The extreme abolitionist stand was taken by Senator William H. Seward of New York. He had great influence over President Taylor, and the latter would probably have vetoed the compromise. But when Taylor suddenly died and was succeeded by Vice President Fillmore, agreement became certain, and Clay's compromise was adopted. Neither its author, nor Calhoun, nor Webster was to survive for long. The first generation of great forebears came to an end in 1826; by 1852 the second had disappeared.

CHAPTER XXXVI

The Failure of the Compromise

THE wise men of both parties hoped that the Great Compromise of 1850 would reconcile the fraternal enemies. Actually, after three years' respite, it was destined to cause the break. The most dangerous element in it was the Fugitive Slave Law, the enforcement of which was to show the northerners the wrongs of slavery in their worst aspects and to transform a political agitation into an emotional revolt. The law charged federal officers with the apprehension of runaway slaves. It required everyone to assist in tracking down these unfortunates. It provided punishments for citizens who aided escaped slaves even though they might be ignorant that those in question were fleeing slaves. No proof was demanded for arrest; the testimony of Negroes was not admitted; the right of trial by jury was refused them. Such stark injustice could not but arouse the indignation of even the most moderate. Who could help feeling pity? One day a Negro arrived in Galesburg, Illinois, exhausted, almost naked, and dying of hunger. He related that he had escaped with five others from a plantation in Missouri. Two had been killed; three recaptured. Respectable men of the little city immediately hid the fugitive and made arrangements to send him to Canada, which was a haven of refuge for slaves. Thus from city to city organized assistance spontaneously grew up. A Negro had been hidden in a house; he told others about it; the house became a station on the mysterious underground railroad. It is said that the origin of this phrase was an exclamation by a planter who was pursuing his prey and had suddenly lost the trail. He cried: "He must have been swallowed up in some underground passage!" Railroads were new at that time and their vocabulary was the style. In the underground, "station masters" and "conductors" guided the "travelers," who were, of course, the fugitives. It had no central organization and each station knew only those next to it, which made police search more difficult.

The number of runaway slaves was not great and consequently the loss to the South was unimportant, but the law aroused the North. In New England, white citizens took Negroes away by force from those who were pursuing them, refused the use of local jails, and held protest meetings. When a Negro named Burns was arrested in Boston, despite the crowd, a subscription was taken up to buy his liberty. His master asked thirteen hundred dollars. This was raised. Whereupon the attorney general of Massachusetts forbade the purchase on the strange but legal grounds that the sale of slaves was not permitted in that state. Later, after Burns had been returned to Virginia, friends in the North purchased his freedom. *Uncle Tom's Cabin,* a novel which contained an emotional description of the fate of fugitive slaves, increased the indignation of the North. Its author, Harriet Beecher Stowe, the daughter of Lyman Beecher, a Congregational minister, had lived in Cincinnati, which only the Ohio separated from the slave states. She had seen human beings placed naked on a block and examined by the purchasers like beasts of burden; her father had been one of the "conductors" on the underground railroad; the Fugitive Slave Law had excited her indignation. Deeply religious, her book showed how anti-Christian it was to buy and sell beings endowed with immortal souls. Although she had tried to be fair, the South considered the picture false and incomplete. But the world at large accepted it as true, and the novel was translated into twenty-two languages. It contributed, perhaps more than the author would have wished, to the formation of public opinion. Later on when Lincoln met Harriet Beecher Stowe he saluted her as "the little woman who started a great war."

In 1852 the Democrats had elected, by an immense majority, their candidate Franklin Pierce, a man totally lacking in distinction but one who represented a coalition of the southern planters and the eastern businessmen. The Whigs had once more sent into the fray a military hero, General Winfield Scott; he failed to repeat Harrison's success. Pierce's election showed that the nation, despite all anti-slavery propaganda, remained faithful to the Compromise of 1850. It was a time of economic prosperity, and the voters, who were making money, were desirous of domestic peace. The discovery of gold and silver mines was producing a rise in prices; the lands of the Middle West were astonishing everyone by their fertility, and in the South cotton-growing was prospering. America was receiving many immigrants which the Revolution of 1848 in Germany and the famine in Ireland had driven from their homes. The flourishing country absorbed this new influx effortlessly. But the slaveholders had not laid down their arms. They now demanded the annexation of Cuba. The business had been dragging on for some time. President Polk had offered to buy the island from Spain and had received the reply that Spain would prefer to see Cuba sunk to the bottom of the ocean than transferred to another power. Then an adventurer named Lopez, with some young men from New Orleans, had tried to seize the island by force. He had been captured and shot; but Pierce sent as ambassador to Madrid an annexationist from Louisiana named Soulé, who compared Lopez to Lafayette! Soulé held a meeting in Belgium with the United States ambassadors to France and England, and these three diplomats drew up together a highly undiplomatic document called the Ostend Manifesto, which declared that Cuba naturally belonged to the great family of states of which the American Union was the providential nursery. Spain naturally protested. The Secretary of State disavowed the Ostend Manifesto, but the pro-slavery papers insisted: "If Spain won't sell Cuba to us, we must steal it!" The temperature of the country was rising.

The sentimentality of *Uncle Tom's Cabin* and the moral condemnation which resulted from it exasperated the South and led it to adopt a defiant attitude: "We cherish slavery as the apple of our eye and we are resolved to maintain it peacefully if we can, by war if we must!" The alliance of the South and the West, however, was the one possible policy for the Democratic party. The future belonged to that statesman who should succeed again, as Jefferson and Jackson had formerly done, in finding a common ground between these two sections. This is what Stephen A. Douglas, the Democratic senator from Illinois, attempted. "The little Giant" as the people called this massive, thickset, courageous, and brilliant man, was said to be "a Northerner with Southern principles." As a matter of fact, Douglas had few principles. He was an adroit politician, ambitious but generous. Unabashedly cynical, he used to say frankly that in every dispute between whites and blacks he was for the whites, and in every dispute between Negroes and crocodiles, he was for the Negroes. Douglas knew that the West desired the opening up of the fertile lands of Kansas and Nebraska. If he could assure the West of this, and at the same time contrive by some artifice to satisfy the South, he would stand a good chance of becoming President. But how could he attain this triple objective? By annulling the Compromise of 1820, by giving the South the hope of seeing new slave states born, and by offering the West a railroad to the Pacific and new lands to colonize. Stephen Douglas, who lived in Chicago and had large interests there, was determined that the railroad should terminate in that city. This led to the Kansas-Nebraska Act of 1854, which provided for the organization of two new territories and allowed the inhabitants themselves to decide whether they would permit slavery. This act repealed the Missouri Compromise, since Kansas and Nebraska lay north of 36° 30′. The opening up of Nebraska was to win the votes of the people of Missouri and assure Chicago of the transcontinental railroad, while the opening up of Kansas would give the South the chance of gaining a new slave state.

Legislators almost always lack imagination. They do not foresee the actual consequences of an abstract law. An act which entrusted the status of Kansas to the future decisions of its inhabitants quite naturally inspired in each of the parties the desire to colonize Kansas with its own partisans. In the North a group of men opposed to slavery adopted the name Anti-Nebraska Democrats and organized a company to encourage the migration to Kansas of colonists who shared their beliefs. Even in Chicago, Douglas was so violently attacked that after one stormy meeting he concluded by saying, since it was after midnight: "Now it is Sunday. I am going to church; you may go to the devil!" Many slaveholders from Missouri changed their residence to Kansas in order to have the right to vote there. An Alabama planter sold part of his slaves and devoted the proceeds to equipping three hundred southerners whom he armed and sent to Kansas, while in the churches in Connecticut members were taking up subscriptions for the purpose of sending arms to northerners in Kansas. Henry Ward Beecher, a Brooklyn minister, said from the pulpit that in the case of slaveowners the rifle was a stronger argument than the Bible. The phrase "Beecher's Bibles" became synonymous with firearms. In Kansas, farmers plowed with rifles slung across their backs. Soon two rival governments had been formed in this territory and there was open warfare. The city of Lawrence (the site today of the University of Kansas) was burned and pillaged by those favoring slavery, while John Brown, an abolitionist, with his five sons and their partisans, shot down slaveowners in cold blood. This John Brown was a zealot who had engaged in a number of professions before becoming, at the age of fifty, a fanatical abolitionist. He believed his mission was to deliver the slaves by force. Although he was pious, murder inspired no remorse in him, for he regarded himself as an instrument of divine vengeance.

Thus violence answered violence. On both sides mendacity was unrestrained. If one believed the abolitionist newspapers, southern planters took a sadistic joy in beating their Negroes, which was false. If one believed the slaveowners, Kansas could not live without slaves, which was absurd. Like many human quarrels, this was susceptible of settlement the moment the adversaries calmly examined the facts. In all Kansas there were not more than three slaves and the actual problem was without importance. But who bothered about facts? The "wounds of Kansas" and "bleeding Kansas" had become mere electioneering slogans.

In the presidential election of 1856 both parties had urgent need of campaign issues. Confusion was increasing in men's minds. The Whigs, bereft of their leaders Clay and Webster, had been divided into northern Whigs and southern Whigs by the abolitionists' campaign. The Democratic party supported slavery, but liberal Democrats (and there were many of them in the West and North) did not approve this stand. To unite the malcontents, small new groups were formed. Some of them, like the Native American or Know-Nothing party (so called because the organization was secret and if the members were subjected to questioning they were told to reply: "I know nothing about it") were opposed to the influence of foreign immigrants. The influx of Irish and Germans had alarmed the Puritans of New England, who saw a danger in this Catholic and proletarian invasion. The Free-Soilers, hostile to the extension of slavery but not themselves abolitionists, consisted of relatively moderate persons. In order to raise the temperature of all those antislavery elements recruited from the Whigs, the Free-Soilers, and even from the Democratic party to the fusing point the breath of some burning moral indignation was required. "Bleeding Kansas" and the accounts of the atrocities of the slaveowners acted as catalysts. Thus, in 1854, from heterogeneous elements was born a united party called Republican. It had taken the ancient name of Jefferson's supporters and as platform had adopted the resolution that, suspending all differences on the subject of political economy, its members would act in cordial union against the extension of slavery until the end of the conflict.

The Republicans chose as their candidate John C. Frémont, the soldier who had explored the Rocky Mountains and aided in the conquest of California. The Democrats skillfully avoided Douglas, who was too clearly marked by the part he had taken in the Kansas affair, and nominated a candidate from the North, James Buchanan, a colorless old man who brought them the votes of Pennsylvania. The violent tone of the Republican campaign alarmed the more conservative Whigs. Pierce, the retiring Democratic President, knowing that the victory of his party depended on peace in Kansas, carried on a policy of appeasement there and accused the Republicans of the contrary attempt to keep the wounds open until after election. This apparent moderation assured the victory of the Democrats in 1856. Buchanan was elected, but the Republicans, aided by several fine orators (one of them an Illinois lawyer named Abraham Lincoln), had a large number of votes. All they needed was a few mistakes by the South in order to win in 1860. The first mistake came from the Supreme Court; it was the decision in the famous Dred Scott case. Dred Scott was a Negro from Missouri who had been taken by his master into free territory in the North, then taken back to Missouri. Some years later the master died and Dred Scott instituted a law suit against the widow to gain his liberty, on the grounds that he had been emancipated *de facto* by his residence in free territory. Actually Dred Scott was illiterate, altogether incapable of starting such a suit, and the whole affair had been set in motion by the opponents of slavery for the purpose of securing a decision. The Missouri court had refused Dred Scott the right to sue on the grounds that he was not an American citizen. Appeal was taken to the Supreme Court, which confirmed the judgment against Dred Scott, and the Chief Justice, Roger B. Taney of Maryland, voiced the opinion that since the Constitution had been made for white men alone, Negroes had no rights at all and, since they were a form of property, the federal government had no power over them. Moreover, Taney declared the Compromise of 1820 to be unconstitutional, holding that Congress had no power to prohibit slavery in the territories.

That the Constitution guaranteed the rights of white men alone was a surprising thesis, for among those who had signed the Constitution many belonged to states of which Negroes were citizens; but the decision constituted a triumph for the southern extremists. They could now maintain that the Constitution allowed them to extend slavery to all territories without consulting either Congress or the local assemblies. Since the territories were the common property of the Union, each section had the right to introduce into them its customs and manners. This was a refutation of the doctrine of Douglas, who had supported local sovereignty, and theoretically it was also the death sentence of the Republican party, which was opposed to the extension of slavery. But practically the decision of the Supreme Court in the Dred Scott case gave the Republican party great strength because it was unenforceable. How was one to impose slavery in a territory where the majority was hostile to it? The extreme pro-slavery doctrine could lead only to civil war. Two more reasonable points of view were embodied in striking fashion in the course of a senatorial campaign in Illinois by the rival candidates, Stephen

Douglas and Abraham Lincoln. The two men were far from equal in point of prestige. Douglas had been a senator, a leader of his party, and a presidential possibility. Lincoln, although he was already forty-nine years old, had been nothing more than a congressman, but in Illinois where he practiced law he was famous for his honesty, common sense, humor, for the vigor of his logic and also for his physical strength. His large body with its awkward movements exhibited surprising vigor; his long arms, which had swung an axe to split fence rails, could still at need put down a village bully. But the victor would immediately make friends with the vanquished. Lincoln loved men of good will. He was one of them.

Abraham Lincoln had had a hard life. The son of a poor pioneer, he had lost his mother at an early age and received only the rudiments of an education. He said that when he reached his majority he knew very little—how to read, write, and use the rule of three—and that he had not gone to school since. But when his father remarried, his stepmother brought with her five books—the Bible, *Aesop's Fables, Robinson Crusoe, Pilgrim's Progress*, and *Sinbad the Sailor*. Lincoln read them so often that he knew them by heart. Later he added the *Life of Washington* by Parson Weems, and *Scott's Lessons*, a collection of speeches by Cicero, Demosthenes, and the heroes of Shakespeare. From this reading there was formed one of the finest English prose styles. But this combination of strength and poetry did not appear until later on when success had freed the true Lincoln. At the beginning of his career he was simply a lucid and precise orator. In place of Webster's rhetoric he preferred humor, and his stories are reminiscent of the fables of his beloved Aesop. Another favorite book was Euclid's *Geometry*; to it he owed the clarity, brevity, and precision of his arguments. Poor, unhappy in his family life, he sought refuge in revery. He had moments of strange humor and alternated between hypochondriacal depression and eloquent exaltation. About 1850 he had given up politics for the bar. After 1854 the controversy about slavery brought him back into the fray.

Lincoln's prudent realism kept him from being a fanatical abolitionist. He did not preach hatred toward the slaveowners; he recognized the difficulty of their position. But in the speech delivered in Springfield in July, 1858, in which he agreed to be a candidate for the Senate against Douglas, he courageously indicated the conclusions to which his long solitary meditations had led him. For five years the attempt had been made to treat the question in a spirit of compromise; the agitation, far from ceasing, had grown worse: "In my opinion it will not cease until a crisis will have been reached and passed. . . . 'A house divided against itself cannot stand.' I believe this government cannot endure permanently half slave and half free. I do not expect the Union to be dissolved—I do not expect the house to fall—but I do expect it will cease to be divided. It will become all one thing, or all the other."

Lincoln issued a challenge to Douglas. Would the latter agree to discuss the question of slavery in a series of debates in various cities of Illinois? Douglas agreed. These seven debates were the occasion of strange scenes. In Galesburg all the farmers of the neighborhood had come to town and had staged a parade. There was a series of floats, one with music, another with thirty-two pretty girls representing the thirty-two states of the Union, and behind them a sorry creature dressed in black and labeled *Kansas*; another with young men splitting fence rails, which was intended as homage to "Honest Abe." Douglas's friends raised banners with the inscription "Hurrah for the Little Giant!" The platform had been erected on the campus of Knox College. It was quickly surrounded by farmers in shirt sleeves accompanied by their families. When the two heroes arrived, all the spectators were at once struck by the contrast. Douglas, squat, pugnacious, beautifully dressed by an excellent tailor, gave an impression of prosperity and strength. Lincoln, with his worn face, his badly cut long coat, his overlong arms, his enormous feet, his pathetic awkwardness, his absent-minded and distressed manner, had the appearance of a statue of despair. "But when he spoke," wrote one of his auditors, "he ceased to appear awkward and became gracious and proud." The ideological positions of the two men were simple: In the matter of slavery, Douglas pronounced himself in favor of popular sovereignty for the states and territories; Lincoln, for the authority of Congress. Lincoln's whole strategy was to force Douglas to express himself on the subject of the Dred Scott decision. This was clever, for if Douglas did not accept the decision of the Supreme Court, he would alienate the southern extremists; if he did accept it, he would offend the moderate Democrats of Illinois and take a stand contradictory to his own doctrine. But Douglas was a wily adversary and his defense was able: "Slavery," he said, "cannot exist for one day or even for one hour in any state if it is not supported by the police of that state. . . ." And so local autonomy would necessarily obtain. Lincoln, for his part, was unwilling to accept either the moral justification of slavery or its extension to new territories; but he wanted to save the Union at all costs.

The voters of Illinois elected Douglas by a small majority, but the position that Lincoln had forced him to take later cost him the presidency; the southern Democrats would not forgive him for it. What the pro-slavery zealots demanded was not local autonomy but the protection of slavery by federal law. To this Douglas replied, reasonably enough, that neither the Democrats of the North nor even those of the Middle West would ever agree to it. Conciliation appeared impossible and a new raid by John Brown soon showed that the conflict could henceforth easily slip from the political sphere into that of military action. John Brown, since his exploits in Kansas, had grown more and more violent. In 1859 he conceived the idea of beginning a private war of liberation. Armed bands were to make raids in the South and bring back slaves and protect them against all who tried to pursue them. He began by an attack on the little Virginia town of Harper's Ferry, where he seized the United States arsenal. Marines, under the command of Robert E. Lee, recaptured the arsenal after a courageous defense by John Brown and his company. Taken prisoner, he was condemned to death by a jury in Virginia and hanged. "I can trust God," so he wrote to his children, "with both the time and the manner of my death, believing, as I now do, that for me at this time to seal my testimony (for God and humanity) with my blood, will do vastly more toward advancing the Cause I have earnestly endeavored to promote than all I have done in my life before." To the court that condemned him he said: "This Court acknowledges, as I suppose, the validity of the Law of God. . . . That teaches me that all things 'whatsoever I would that men should do unto me, I should do even so unto them.' . . . I endeavored to act up to that instruction. . . . Now, if it is deemed necessary that I should forfeit my life for the furtherance of the ends of justice, and mingle my blood further with the blood of my children, and with the blood of millions in this slave country whose rights are disregarded by wicked, cruel, and unjust enactments, I submit: . . . so let it be done!" That his death was heroic seems incontestable; that his actions were blameworthy seems no less so. Emerson called him later a great idealist of undeviating kindness. This was not the opinion of his victims. In the eyes of the abolitionists John Brown became a holy martyr. It was at this time that that famous song was written:

> *John Brown's body lies a-mouldering in the grave*
> *His soul goes marching on.*

In the South this exaltation of violence awakened the dread of an uprising of the Negroes and a massacre of the whites. The presidential election of 1860 was to take place in an atmosphere of terror.

It is important to understand just what this election meant to the South. The latter now felt itself completely different from the North. Not only was it defending a civilization founded on different principles, but it resented tariffs whereas the North wanted them; it remained rural and agricultural, whereas the North was becoming urban and industrial; it was hostile to bankers, whereas the North favored them. Most of the new railroads were built in the North and for the North. The immigrants, attracted by the factories and repelled by slavery, went to the North. Thus the population of the North was growing faster than that of the South and the difference in strength was increasing. Now what legal means did the South possess of defending its customs and its way of life? Congress? But it was inevitable that the North would, before long, be able to outvote the South in both Houses. The Supreme Court?

Clements Library

Lincoln defeats Douglas and Breckinridge in the election of 1860. By Currier and Ives (1860).

But the President named the justices, and a series of Presidents hostile to the South could, in time, make a Supreme Court completely favorable to the North. And so the presidency remained the last protection of the southerners. It is easy to understand their anxiety.

The Democrats could not decide upon a candidate. The northern faction nominated Douglas; the southern wing chose John C. Breckinridge of Kentucky. This division of the Democratic vote made the election of a Republican a certainty. The Republican convention was held in Chicago. The most celebrated and experienced statesman in the party was Senator Seward. He believed he had every chance of being nominated. But the western delegates were violent in their support of Lincoln, a man from their own country; they raised the Comanche war whoop. "If all the pigs killed in Ohio had squealed together," said one auditor, "they could not have made more noise." The party strategists realized that the choice of Abraham Lincoln would assure victory in Indiana and Illinois, which were doubtful states. In the North it was thought that his democratic simplicity and homely eloquence would attract the voters who had formerly contributed to Jackson's success. In the end he was nominated. "Never has an equal tumult been heard on earth." Seward, although profoundly disappointed, instantly assured Lincoln of his support. Meanwhile the Constitutional Unionists (conservative Whigs and former Know-Nothings) had nominated John Bell of Tennessee. There were now in the Union eighteen free states and fifteen slave states. Lincoln carried all the free states and was elected President; he had a minority of the popular vote but a majority in the electoral college. In the South he received only twenty-four thousand votes. Nine southern states had voted against him unanimously without a single dissenting voice. The nation was literally split in two by the axe of Abraham Lincoln. Every mail brought death threats to the President.

CHAPTER XXXVII

Toward Civil War

IN PLACE of the three traditional sections, East, South, and West, there were now two blocs, the North and the South—blocs of opposed passions and loyalties far more than of opposed interests. On each side there was implicit faith in the worth of the ideas that had been espoused. The people of the South sought to maintain an ancient and honorable society. They considered the emancipation of the slaves impossible and the condemnation of slavery base hypocrisy. Not that they harbored ill will toward their Negroes, quite the contrary; but they thought that since a whole nation of blacks had been thrust into the midst of a nation of whites, the only way for them to live was in slavery. The problem was not the same, they said, in Massachusetts, where a Negro was almost a curiosity, as in some southern community where there were more blacks than whites. Nevertheless, in the eyes of many northerners, nurtured on newspaper stories of atrocities, the baronial slaveowners appeared as tyrants, and it seemed obligatory to rescue their black victims. The workmen of New England had been impressed by the economic argument of the Republican orators: that the low price of slave labor threatened to reduce the salaries of white workmen. Sumner, the abolitionist, talked of the alliance between the lords of the whip and the lords of the machine. Fair-minded men were shocked by the monstrous injustice of the curse that rested on colored people. Actually, even in the North partisans of immediate emancipation were rare. To bring it about would require an amendment to the Constitution and a majority of three-fourths of the states, which was far from obtainable in the country at large. If the South had possessed detachment, it would have faced the future calmly. But reason has no control over hatred. Sectional hostility had supplanted the fraternal union. The election of 1860 had finally crystallized resentment. To the people of the South, Lincoln, that strange man with the great awkward body, the long arms, the provincial frock coat with sleeves that were too short, seemed a grotesque and unacceptable leader. The planters of the Carolinas dreamed of restoring a republic of gentlemen, such as their fathers had known in the first days of independence. "Resistance to Lincoln is obedience to God," they said. Henceforth an attempt at secession seemed certain. From moment to moment frightening events impended. What could be done to parry them?

At the very least the government should have taken measures of defense, arming its forts and protecting the federal administration in the South. But Lincoln was not to be inaugurated until March 4 and Buchanan, the retiring President, seemed paralyzed with terror. "He divided his time between prayer and tears," said one contemporary. "Such an imbecile has never been seen at the head of a country." Poor Buchanan was not an imbecile, but an honest and weak old man at a time when the country needed an energetic leader. He was overcome and crushed by his responsibility. Seward wrote to his wife that Buchanan proved irrefutably that a President's duty is to enforce the law— provided no one opposes it—and that no state has the right to leave the Union—provided it does not want to. Major Anderson, in command of the forts belonging to the federal government at the entrance to Charleston Harbor, asked for reinforcements, and when he did not receive them decided to assemble all his troops in Fort Sumter, which was the easier one to defend. South Carolina protested. Buchanan promised the South that he would give Anderson orders to evacuate the fort, and next day promised the North to keep Anderson where he was and to reinforce him. A steamer with men and provisions was sent to Charleston; Southern troops opened fire on it. It was the first cannon fire. Southern troops were already erecting batteries on the coast to bombard Fort Sumter. John A. Dix, Secretary of the Treasury, telegraphed to one of his subordinates that if anyone attempted to strike the colors of the United States he was to be killed instantly. This firmness pleased the North.

Had compromise become impossible? Just what were the new facts? The election of a President who had pledged himself to prevent the extension of slavery. Nothing more. But would he go farther? To those who asked him this question Lincoln replied that his ideas had been expressed publicly and they had only to read his speeches: "For the brave people of the South I shall willingly repeat them seventy times seven. . . . But I have bad men to deal with, both North and South; men eager for something new upon which to base new misrepresentations. . . ." The southerners believed that their political position was hopeless if they remained in the Union. The admission of three free states (California, Minnesota, Oregon) had destroyed the balance of power. Southern extremists maintained that secession would bring them great advantages. They would be free to arrange the life of the commonwealth to suit themselves; they would be free from tariffs designed and enacted to serve interests which were not theirs; their trade with Europe would therefore be facilitated; they could import more slaves from Africa, which would put an end to the rise in the cost of labor. To the southern moderates who feared a war, the extremists said that this war would never occur; that secession could be arranged on a friendly basis; that since the North needed the cotton and the markets of the South, it would accept the *fait accompli*; and finally that England for identical reasons would support the South. Even in the North there were those who had resigned themselves to the inevitable. They agreed that the Union was simply a confederation which the states had voted to join and which they could likewise vote to leave. The New England capitalists, to whom the South owed two hundred million dollars, were in favor of peace. In Boston "the aristocrats of Beacon Street" protested against a meeting in memory of John Brown. When South Carolina, the first and at that time the only state, declared that the Union was dissolved, Oliver Wendell Holmes composed *Brother Jonathan's Lament for Sister Carolina* which contained no threatening note:

She has gone,—she has left us in passion and pride,—
Our stormy-browed sister, so long at our side!

He promised to embrace the prodigal sister if ever she returned to the fold. Buchanan wept and prayed even harder. Senator Crittenden of Kentucky proposed a new compromise after the manner of Henry Clay. But the time for compromises was past. A northern congressman revealed the futility of these efforts *in extremis* by humorously proposing an amendment to the Constitution: "Whenever a party shall be beaten in any election for President, such party may rebel and take up arms." Such in effect was the essence of the secessionist doctrine.

This was far from acceptable to the whole South. Even ardent supporters of slavery like Jefferson Davis wished to give Lincoln a chance, but the village politicians were frenzied. "We can make better terms out of the Union than inside it," they said. At the beginning of 1861 Mississippi, Florida, Alabama, Georgia, and Louisiana had rallied to the support of South Carolina. Texas followed them, despite the pleas of the aged Sam Houston. Virginia, North Carolina, Arkansas, and Tennessee hesitated. For Virginia the choice was a sad one. She had, in some measure, founded the Union. She had given it its first Presidents. But she was loyal to the South and she lived in part from the slave trade. In February a convention of six of the seven states met in Alabama and founded the Confederate States of America. The South needed a president. Jefferson Davis was chosen. He was a graduate of West Point, a planter, a retired colonel who had served in the Mexican War, and for a long time he had been one of the most ardent defenders of states' rights. He was by no means a southern aristocrat, but the son of a farmer, born in a log cabin in Kentucky. His elder brother, Joseph Davis, who had become rich as a planter, had borne the cost of his education. Jefferson and Joseph both had a taste for reading, and they used to carry on long political discussions in one or the other of their handsome houses which stood near each other on the banks of the Mississippi. Through his second marriage Jefferson had been introduced to the local aristocracy. He liked and admired the social system to which he had thus gained entrance. His handsome face, dignity, grave voice, and intelligence assured his success. He had great qualities of courage and honesty, but at the time he became President of the Confederacy he was a prematurely worn-out man. Facial neuralgia and an affliction of the eyes had made him irritable. Since he had been a soldier and Secretary of War in Pierce's cabinet, he insisted on meddling in military operations with a persistence dangerous in a civilian. He was gathering roses in his garden when a messenger brought him news of his election. He was surprised. He had expected to be chosen as a general rather than as president. In Montgomery he delivered a grave and measured speech: "Placing our confidence in God, in the purity of our hearts and in the strength of our rights, we shall defend the Right to our utmost."

Meanwhile Lincoln was traveling toward Washington and, along the way, making optimistic speeches which irritated his followers. There is no crisis, he said, except an artificial one. He did not disguise the fact that he hoped to avoid war: "Blood will not flow unless the government's hand is forced." The inauguration took place on March 4. The occasion was lacking in brilliance. A plot to assassinate Lincoln had been discovered by the police and the President was strictly guarded. He seemed ill at ease and so embarrassed by his cane and high hat that his rival Douglas, who was near him on the platform, relieved him of them at the moment when he stood up to speak.

> That there are persons in one section or another who seek to destroy the Union at all events, and are glad of any pretext to do it, I will neither affirm nor deny; but if there be such, I need address no word to them. To those, however, who really love the Union may I not speak? . . . My countrymen, one and all, think calmly and well upon this whole subject. Nothing valuable can be lost by taking time. . . . In your hands, my dissatisfied fellow countrymen, and not in mine, is the momentous issue of civil war. The government will not assail you. You can have no conflict without being yourselves the aggressors. *You* have no oath registered in heaven to destroy the government, while *I* shall have the most solemn one to "preserve, protect, and defend it." . . . We are not enemies, but friends. We must not be enemies. Though passion may have strained, it must not break our bonds of affection. The mystic cords of memory, stretching from every battlefield, and patriot grave, to every living heart and hearthstone, all over this broad land, will yet swell the chorus of the Union, when again touched, as surely they will be, by the better angels of our nature.

Around him many watched with anxiety for the expected attack on his life. Hundreds of letters had predicted that Lincoln would never enter the White House alive. But no pistol was raised.

The crowd stared at the great, bony, heavily muscled body, at the roughly sculptured face with its look of a "benevolent satyr," at the Herculean, awkward arms, at the sad, deep-set eyes. The man produced a strange impression of strength and simplicity. He astonished people by his country manners, but he reassured them by his evident sincerity. Why had he been chosen? Was he a brilliant politician? In the cabinet he had just appointed at least three men—Seward, Secretary of State, Chase, Secretary of the Treasury, Cameron, Secretary of War— who believed themselves his superiors at this game and considered him a bumpkin whom they could do with as they liked. Nevertheless, there was discernible in his style a vigor and nobility not possessed by members of his cabinet. Did he really have profound learning? No, but what was better, he was a man of a few great books whose substance had been assimilated into his flesh and blood. Those who talked with him were surprised to find him amusing, full of jokes, almost frivolous. He loved to tell anecdotes which were often risqué. He introduced, Walt Whitman said, an element of comedy, almost of farce, into the tragedy of his country. It is true, but he also expressed better than anyone else the gravest of thoughts. He has been called an opportunist, and he was one whenever he considered intransigence useless. "What, Mr. President, you have changed your mind?" "Yes, and I have little regard for a man who is not wiser today than yesterday." He did not like to say no except when he felt moral indignation. He admitted once that he trembled at the thought of what would have happened to him if he had been a woman, but he was reassured by the realization that his ugliness would have been a safeguard to his amiability. "My policy," he said, "is to have no policy."

What then was the secret of his strength? Motley said he was the great American demos, honest, skillful, rustic, wise, gay, brave, sometimes making mistakes but progressing through those mistakes toward what he believed to be right. He was proud of being a man of the people: "As I would not be a slave, so I would not be a master. This expresses my idea of democracy." He loved common men and common things. He said that God, too, must have loved the common people because he made so many of them. Incarnating the best qualities of the American nation, he possessed a native wealth of charity and tender compassion. Unlike many Yankees, he felt no hatred for the people of the South. He called them "our late friends and adversaries." He understood the difficulty of their position and sympathized with them. His policy toward them was at once firm and moderate. He wished to limit the extension of slavery, perhaps progressively to liberate the slaves with an indemnity to their owners, but above all to save the Union. On this last point he was adamant and, when necessary, sharp: "If I could save the Union without freeing any slave, I would do it; and if I could save it by freeing all the slaves, I would do it; and if I could save it by freeing some and leaving others alone, I would also do that." In this, as in all Lincoln's pronouncements, one perceived the vigorous simplicity of his thought and the unique combination of conciliation and tenacity that made him a great man.

In order to save the Union it was first of all necessary to prevent the secession of more states. Those that formed the frontier between slave and free territories had not yet declared themselves. Lincoln took into his cabinet natives of Missouri and Maryland with a view to binding those states more closely to the Union. His hesitation about Fort Sumter also is to be explained by his fear of offending the wavering states. "Lincoln," sneered the southerners, "would like to have God on his side, but he needs Kentucky as well." However he had to make a decision. Major Anderson could not hold out without reinforcements. What was to be done? Evacuate Fort Sumter and cover up this retreat by blaming the preceding administration for its negligence? That was to accept defeat. Wait? That meant endangering Anderson. Lincoln, against the advice of his cabinet, decided to send supplies; but on April 12 the Confederate authorities took the initiative and bombarded the fort. Next day the fort was in flames and Anderson had to surrender. The flag of the Confederacy, the Stars and Bars, replaced the Stars and Stripes above the fort. On the fourteenth Anderson marched out proudly with colors flying and his band playing *Yankee Doodle*. On the fifteenth Lincoln issued a proclamation summoning seventy-five thousand militiamen for three months' service. In Washington the atmosphere around him grew stormy; the city was Virginian, southern at heart, and the offices were full of his enemies. But the bombardment of Fort Sumter rallied the whole North behind the President. The Confederates had fired on the flag of the Union. This offense united the parties. Pierce and Buchanan, the Democratic ex-Presidents, announced their support of Lincoln. "There cannot be any neutrals in this war," said Douglas, "only patriots or traitors." The South used the same language after the capture of Fort Sumter. A southern girl said: "God is on our side." Someone asked: "Why?" "Of course he hates the Yankees. You'll think that well of him!" Virginia, Tennessee, Arkansas, and North Carolina joined in secession, and the city of Richmond, Virginia, became the capital of the Confederate States. The Negroes expected great things, but in the beginning nothing in their attitude revealed this. They remained respectful and assumed an indifferent manner. Four slave states—Delaware, Maryland, Kentucky, and Missouri—stayed in the Union after sharp internal struggles.

Although the geographical division was a division into North and South, there were many northerners in the southern army and southerners in the northern army. Many families were divided. Three brothers of Mrs. Lincoln were to die in the South. The general on whom Lincoln was counting to command the Union armies, Robert E. Lee, became instead the best of the southern leaders. Lee was a noble character, and he was so little in favor of slavery that he had freed most of his own slaves; he did not believe in the right of secession, but he was a Virginian: "I have been unable to make up my mind to raise my hand against my native state, my relatives, my children and my home." George Washington was his model and his ideal, and Washington had been a great Virginian. Lee hoped that he would not have to fight against the Union; when the command of the Army of Virginia was offered to him he believed it his duty to accept. No one was more worthy of the post. By his military genius, his patience, courtesy, and constant generosity, his character recalls that of Turenne. His only fault was a fear of wounding subordinates that amounted sometimes to a weakness. But it was a weakness that sprang from excess of virtue. In the North during the early days popular enthusiasm ran high. Volunteers rushed to the colors shouting, "On to Richmond!" The government in Washington, on the other hand, was worried. Since the secession of Virginia the Stars and Bars had been floating on the other side of the Potomac and Lincoln expected to see Confederate gunboats on the river. Many inhabitants of Washington fled from the city. The President, striding up and down his office, called with anguish for the northern troops. "Why don't they come?" he repeated. "Why don't they come?" Finally they did come. A Massachusetts regiment was attacked while passing through Baltimore, a city that was southern in sympathy, and a bloody skirmish ensued. But other regiments from Massachusetts and New York arrived by sea and on April 25 a small army marched up Pennsylvania Avenue singing "John Brown's Body." The capital had been saved.

CHAPTER XXXVIII

The Civil War—Part One

HOW did the opposing sides compare with each other? The North had about twenty-two or -three million inhabitants; the South, five and a half million whites and close to four million slaves. Historians disagree about the total number of soldiers engaged in combat. Those from the South say the Confederacy put 600,000 men in the field as against 2,500,000 for the Union; but Colonel Thomas L. Livermore, in his *Numbers and Losses During the American Civil War,* estimates 1,556,678 services on the Union side as against 1,082,119 in the Confederate army. Short enlistments which were subsequently renewed complicate the problem, since the same soldier might be counted several times. In the matter of supplies, railroads, and bank deposits, the North had an advantage of three to one. Its industry was greatly superior to that of the South. The local production of arms and munitions at the beginning of the war was inadequate on both sides. In fourteen months the Union government bought 30,000 rifles in America and 726,000 in Europe. North and South had agents and scouts in the principal arms-producing countries. But purchase was nothing without transportation. There once more the North had a great advantage in the large number of ships and trained sailors at its command. Thus all material factors favored the Union.

On the other hand, the southern soldiers had more experience in sports than the northern ones, and this is good training for military life. The planters were good riders and good shots. Some of the best officers that had been graduated from West Point (Lee, Johnston, Jackson) came from the South and were destined to become the talented leaders of the Confederate armies. The militiamen of the North, who formed the nucleus of the army, had had no training. Most of their officers were civilians, elected to the lower ranks, nominated by state governors for the higher commissions. Some of them were to become brilliant soldiers but it took time to distinguish them. Some infantry regiments of Zouaves and Turcos were remarkable more for the brilliance of their uniforms than for the precision of their maneuvers. The commander of the Union armies was Winfield Scott, an able general but worn out by age and illness. He had been excellent at the time of the War of 1812 and the Mexican War; he could not direct from his bed the war of 1862. Nevertheless, during the first weeks of the war in 1861, when many thought that the campaign would be over in a few days and when Lincoln himself had only called out seventy-five thousand volunteers for a three-months' period, he had the wisdom to say that if a good general with three hundred thousand men won this war in three years, it would be a remarkable feat. The South could remain on the defensive. "We ask nothing from you," said the Confederate government to the Union government, "except to let us live in peace." The North was forced to act. Thus in the beginning the South had certain temporary advantages, but the North possessed a superior war potential. The question to be decided was "how long the resources of the South would last, how long the North would take to utilize its own."

What were the strategic objectives of the North? To conquer the whole South? That was an impossible enterprise. To occupy those territories huge armies would have been required which could not have been either recruited, or trained, or armed. To capture Richmond, the capital? The operation seemed easy enough since Richmond was not far from the frontier, but this was even more true of Washington. Moreover the capture of Richmond, only recently become a capital, while important, would not result in the surrender of the South. The really vulnerable points of the Confederacy were those controlling its line of communication. The southern states, a region of a few staple crops, imported much of their food from the states north of the Ohio, and counted on exchanging their money crops abroad for war supplies, munitions, medicines, and other manufactured goods. Now there were only three railroads which provided communication with the West. They crossed the Mississippi at Memphis, Vicksburg, and New Orleans respectively. The capture of these three cities, an expedition through the valley of the Ohio and the Mississippi, would cut the new nation in two and, supplemented by a blockade, the operation would assure victory. But this was not understood by the North till later on. In 1861 the Union plan was to enlist and train an army; to defend Washington and to take Richmond; to keep Kentucky and Missouri, both of which contained strong bodies of southerners, in the Union; and above all, to blockade the southern ports. As at the time of the War of Independence, the movement of armies was easier by sea than by land because of the distances involved and the problem of supply.

There were already thirty thousand volunteers fidgeting in Washington and shouting, "On to Richmond!" It was hard to restrain their eagerness. The military leaders asked for a respite to train the army. The government, egged on by public opinion, replied: "We are green, it is true, but they are green too." Scott finally yielded and preparation was made for an invasion of Virginia. To the West, General Patterson was sent into the Shenandoah Valley. In the East General Irvin MacDowell with a "grand army" of thirty thousand men crossed the Potomac to attack the Confederates who were about thirty-five miles southwest of Washington along the little river of Bull Run and were defending the railroad junction at Manassas. The army set out for battle as though for a picnic. No one doubted victory. Senators and congressmen followed the troops in the expectation of "seeing the Lord deliver the Philistines into their hands." The rebels were about to be crushed. One lady armed with opera glasses said gaily: "Tomorrow we'll be in Richmond!" Many farmers had come in spring wagons bringing their wives and hampers of provisions to see the battle. But of two poorly trained armies the one that is on the defensive has the advantage. When the reinforcements from the Shenandoah Valley came to the support of the Confederates, the northern army gave way and its retreat quickly became a rout. A stream of wagons and horsemen sent the spectators flying. The cavalry waving their sabers cried: "Turn back! We're whipped!" Disorganized regiments filled the streets of Washington; bars were crowded with dusty and bloody uniforms. If the Confederates had pursued the fugitives they would have taken Washington, for Scott and even Lincoln did not know what to do, but the southerners were as disorganized by victory as the northerners by defeat, and nothing decisive resulted from the battle of Bull Run.

At the time of the declaration of war the unity of the North was admirable, but defeat breeds discord. After Bull Run Congress blamed the President. Lincoln summoned General George B. McClellan, a young man of thirty-four who had been very successful in Virginia and in the West, and gave him command of the Army of the Potomac. Five months later he appointed him to the chief command of the military forces of the United States. The choice seemed bold and promising. McClellan, an officer of genius, had gone through West Point, had been nourished on the classic works of strategy, had served with distinction in the Mexican War, and had then been sent to Europe to follow the course of the Crimean War. And so he had had some experience of modern warfare. Resigning from the army he had become vice president of a railroad company, and in this civil post had shown remarkable qualities as an administrator and organizer. He was technically competent, methodical, and hard working. "He not only knew what was to be done, but he had the art of persuading everybody that he was the only man who could do it." Little Mac had, in common with Bonaparte, youth, a taste for literature, short stature, the habit of putting one hand in the bosom of his coat. One quality was lacking, the most important of all—character. He was vain, talked about "my army" and treated the President of the United States with disdain, almost with contempt, going so far as to keep him waiting for an hour in his ante-room. McClellan carried prudence to the point of indecision. Energetic in preparation, he was to show hmself impotent in action. "Don't let them hurry me," he kept begging the President. Lincoln admired him, let him have his own way, and did his best to prepare himself for the role of commander-in-chief by reading books on the art of war.

The general in command in the West was Frémont, the former presidential candidate, the hero of the Californian adventure, and the son-in-law of the powerful Senator Benton—and for all three reasons an unruly fellow. In St. Louis, where he established his headquarters, he created a scandal by his princely suite, the foreign officers he had around him, and most of all by the violence of his proclamations. He proclaimed martial law in the state of Missouri; announced that every armed rebel who was found would be shot, that the property of rebels would be confiscated and their slaves freed. Thus in his territory the general did what the President of the United States had not yet dared to do; he abolished slavery. When Lincoln read Frémont's proclamation he was indignant: "Should you shoot a man according to the proclamation, the Confederates would very certainly shoot our best men in their hands in retaliation; and so, man for man, indefinitely." As for the freedom of the slaves in Missouri, it threatened to throw all the slaveowners of Kentucky into the rebel camp. Between Lincoln and Frémont a serious difference arose. Lincoln exhibited calmness and dignity; Frémont maintained that his proclamation was as good as a victory and refused to withdraw it. To Lincoln he sent his wife, Jessie Frémont, an imperious and violent woman, who put the White House in an uproar by staging an incredible scene, then tried to turn public opinion against the President. A whole group of extremists strove to increase the bitterness of the war. Lincoln, on the other hand, tried to limit animosity and prevent the irrepressible conflict from degenerating into revolutionary strife carried on viciously and without quarter.

Cameron, the Secretary of War, showed himself less than mediocre and closed his eyes to incredible corruption. Lincoln replaced him with Edwin M. Stanton, a reliable man but one who was difficult to get along with. "Did Stanton tell you that I was an imbecile?" the President asked on one occasion. "Then I must be one, for he is always right." When complaints were brought to him about the Secretary of War, and it was suggested that he should find men who had his virtues without his faults, he said: "All that I can reply is that I have never met them. I do not know any. I should like to know them." Lincoln himself appeared in a better light than at the beginning of his presidency. In danger he exhibited calmness and common sense. One day when he seemed harassed, someone asked him: "Is the news bad, Mr. President?" "Oh, no," he replied, "it's the post office in Balderville. . . ."

After Bull Run all was quiet on the Potomac. Both sides were raising large armies. Volunteers came in crowds. To equip them both sides turned to Europe. The North made its purchases in England through the agency of Baring Brothers, and since the federal government lacked enterprise in giving orders, states like Ohio, Connecticut, and Massachusetts placed orders on their own account. All the factories in Belgium were working for the South. To receive shipments it was necessary to keep certain ports open. In this respect the North, the traditional home of shipowners, was in a better position and possessed a fleet superior to that of the South in the ratio of ten to one. But the South showed more daring and ingenuity. At the beginning of the war it had occupied the navy yard at Norfolk and there found the hull of the frigate *Merrimac*. In imitation of what Napoleon III had done in the Crimea, the southerners covered this hull with iron plate and armed it with cannon. Fortunately, the North had an answer in the *Monitor*, a strange craft covered with armor plate and bearing a movable turret, "like a cheese box on a raft." It was the work of a remarkable Swedish engineer named John Ericsson.

Each side was counting on the diplomatic support of England. The North expected the Protestant churches there to take a stand against slavery. The South hoped that the factory owners and workmen of Lancashire, who were starved for cotton, would unite to force the government's hand. At the start it seemed that England was southern in sympathy. Class feeling made the English aristocrats sympathize with the planters. As far as the liberal adversaries of slavery were concerned, the North's position seemed ambiguous to them. Why was Lincoln fighting? He declared that he was not an abolitionist. On what principle did he presume to impose union on those states which had repudiated it? Even Gladstone, the liberal Gladstone, said that Jefferson Davis and the other southern leaders had created an army, were by way of creating a navy, and more important still had created a nation. Lord John Russell reminded his country that the South was a client of England, the North a rival. The blockade of the Confederate ports by the northern navy led to incidents. The most serious of these was the *Trent* affair. This English ship was stopped on the high seas by a Union vessel which seized two Confederate commissioners on their way to Europe and made them prisoner. This action was in violation of international law and aroused such a furor in England that Russell drafted an ultimatum. It was thanks to Queen

Victoria, and especially to Prince Albert who (in the queen's name) modified the terms of the note, that an Anglo-American war was avoided at that time. The commissioners were released and allowed to continue on their way. But it was not until much later, when Lincoln had adopted a strong stand on the subject of slavery, that English public opinion veered about in favor of the Yankees.

General McClellan was a strange man. He had a large army, the largest that had ever been assembled on this continent. The government gave him all the arms, uniforms, and means of transport he could wish. But he made no move. He always believed that the enemy was stronger and better armed. Lincoln grew uneasy. It is impossible to maintain discipline and enthusiasm in an army that never fights. The President said that if nothing were done the whole cause would be endangered. And also: "If McClellan does not need the army, I would like to borrow it from him." The country's anger at McClellan burst out when the Confederate General Joseph E. Johnston suddenly, without any interference at all, abandoned the position at Bull Run which McClellan had been preparing for months to attack, and withdrew southward. There was a violent change in public opinion and the demand was made that the enemy should at least be pursued. But McClellan declared he could not take Richmond by frontal attack, and that he would proceed up the peninsula lying between the York and James rivers, sending his army there by sea. And he actually did transport, by means of a huge fleet, an army of about one hundred thousand men. Some frigates were sunk by the *Merrimac,* and for a time it was feared that this strange iron tent might become mistress of the seas. But the little *Monitor* attacked it bravely. It was a curious "duel between a dwarf and a giant, both of them deformed." Five times during the engagement the two boats touched and fired point-blank. The sailors' faces were black with powder. The battle ended in a draw; but it had shown that armored plate was, in large measure, the answer to gunfire. All the navies of the world weighed the consequences of this lesson; the era of wooden ships had come to an end.

The campaign in the peninsula is a classic example of a battle lost through lack of character in a general. When McClellan arrived before the entrenchments at Yorktown, they were held by a force hardly a third the size of his own. Did he finally attack? Not at all. He entrenched himself and wrote to Lincoln that he wished no misunderstandings on the subject of his apparent inaction, that not a day, not an hour was being lost, and that earthworks had been constructed that might fairly be called gigantic. The southern generals laughed at him: "No one but McClellan would have hesitated to attack." But he squandered the time of his greatest opportunity in writing to his wife beautiful letters destined for posterity, in which he lauded his own courage and his decisive character. General Lee, who was at this time military adviser to Jefferson Davis, with great audacity detached his best lieutenant, Thomas J. Jackson (nicknamed Stonewall Jackson) and sent him into the Shenandoah Valley to immobolize the federal troops by this feint. Jackson swept everything before him, captured three thousand prisoners and twenty-five thousand dollars' worth of provisions, then in June joined Lee at Richmond. From this raid McClellan deduced that Lee had at least two hundred thousand men. Otherwise, McClellan argued, he would never have dared to dispense with Jackson. What he forgot was that Lee now knew him with great accuracy and took his hesitations into account when making plans. Finally, a series of bloody engagements took place before Richmond called the Seven Days' battle, in which Lee lost over twenty thousand men killed, wounded and missing; McClellan, about sixteen thousand. Again at that time McClellan could have taken Richmond. He gave the order to retreat and withdrew toward his base, losing a great number of arms and wagons which were seized by the Confederates. When this temporizing Napoleon brought his Grand Army back to the Potomac, he was relieved of his command. Then, as his successors fared no better and indeed met defeat in a second battle of Bull Run which opened the way for an invasion of Maryland, he was recalled and finally stopped Lee at Antietam. On the evening of the victory Lincoln telegraphed: "God bless you and all those who are with you. Destroy the rebel army if it is possible." But McClellan was not in the habit of acting with such decisiveness. Once again he allowed Lee to withdraw while he wrote to his wife: "I have sent the President a vigorous and strong letter. . . . If he follows my advice the country will be saved." This time Lincoln got rid of him for good, in spite of the general's indignant followers, who maintained that he had been on the point of winning the decisive battle of the war.

By stopping the invasion, the Battle of Antietam put an end to a period that had been disastrous to the North. It was time, for Lincoln's position was becoming difficult. Many of those around him thought the South could not be beaten. This was also the opinion of the English and French governments, both of which would have recognized the South if Lee had taken Baltimore. In France, Napoleon III, who was hoping at that time to install his protégé the Emperor Maximilian in Mexico, thought that he would need the friendship of the South and he gave Slidell assurances of his sympathy. He even secretly authorized Lucien Arman of Bordeaux, a shipbuilder who was a friend of his, to build two cruisers and four corvettes for the Confederates. But later on when a northern victory seemed likely Napoleon III forbade the delivery of these vessels, which, together with certain other events, ruined the French shipbuilder. In England the emancipation of the slaves was the only thing that could reverse public opinion. But Lincoln took a long time in making that decision. Firmly resolved to end this war by a peace of reconciliation, he did not wish to arouse the slaveowners by premature action. Actually, in all the territories occupied by the Union armies the slaves were liberated and organized into labor battalions. But Lincoln had always said that the question of slavery interested him only to the degree in which it was

Clements Library

"Writing the Emancipation Proclamation." Cartoon by A. J. Volck, a German artist who visited the United States during the Civil War period and sympathized with the South.

bound up with saving the Union, and he had to give thought to the slave states that had stayed in the Union. In addition, Seward had convinced him of the necessity of waiting for a victory. After Antietam, in September, 1862, Lincoln called together the members of his cabinet and said that he was going to act without consulting them. He had vowed to free the slaves as soon as Maryland was saved. God had done his part; he would do his. He did not intend to ask Congress or to apply the measure to those states that had remained in the Union, but rather to act in virtue of his powers as commander-in-chief, which was his right in enemy country.

A preliminary proclamation declared that after January 1, 1863, all slaves in the rebellious states should be free forever and that the federal government recognized their liberty.

On January 1 Lincoln signed the definitive proclamation. "I have never been more certain," he said, "of doing right than I am in signing this document." His cabinet members were delighted. They playfully dubbed each other abolitionists. A few days later Jefferson Davis replied in a message to the Confederate Congress: "Our hatred of those who have signed the most execrable act in the history of mankind is tempered by a profound contempt for the impotent rage that it reveals. . . ." The results of the proclamation were surprising. That the South, threatened by the loss of its possessions and its form of society, should be more determined than ever to fight to the death is natural enough. But one might have supposed that the North would acquire renewed fervor through this act. This was not the case. The abolitionists saw in the gesture a belated adherence to their doctrines. The northern Democrats denounced it as a political maneuver. Only the slaves felt the stirring of the first breath of freedom, and Julia Ward Howe, poetess and reformer, wrote "The Battle Hymn of the Republic":

> Mine eyes have seen the glory of the coming of the Lord;
> He is trampling out the vintage where the grapes of wrath are stored.
> He hath loosed the fateful lightning of His terrible, swift sword.
> His truth is marching on. . . .

CHAPTER XXXIX

The Civil War—Part Two: The West

THE objective of the war in the East was Richmond; the objective of the war in the West was the conquest of the Mississippi. It was there that the great northern generals, Grant, Sheridan, and Sherman, proved their worth. Ulysses S. Grant was one of those eccentric military figures whom armies discard in time of peace and whose value is suddenly realized by war. He had gone through West Point where he had left a reputation for untidiness. After a campaign in Mexico, he had been asked to resign his commission because of his drinking. His family considered him a failure but a nice young man. He became a farmer, a storekeeper, a leather salesman, all without success. When the Civil War began he volunteered, and as a retired officer was made colonel of an Illinois regiment. A few successful engagements brought him the rank of brigadier general. "Look out, Ulysses," his father said to him. "Here you are a general; it's a good job; don't lose it." In February, 1862, he captured Fort Donelson on the Cumberland River, thus assuring the Union the possession of Kentucky; and when the enemy asked for terms, he replied: "Unconditional and immediate surrender!" The uncompromising answer caught the attention of the country, which thereafter knew him by the name of "Unconditional Surrender" Grant. The officers of Grant's general staff could not very well understand why he was successful; he passed through long periods of lethargy, but when he emerged from them it was to make decisions and execute them with extraordinary energy. Lincoln had paid especial attention to Grant's proclamation in Kentucky, which was so different from Frémont's in Missouri: "I have come among you, not as an enemy but as your friend and fellow citizen. . . . I have nothing to do with opinions. I shall deal only with armed rebellion and its aiders and abettors." The jealousy of certain generals toward this intruder who won battles by disregarding the rules hampered him for a long time. When, with a few gunboats and an army of boys from the Middle West, he won the battle of Shiloh, but at the cost of frightful losses, his enemies demanded that the President remove him. Lincoln said: "I can't spare this man: he fights." When the familiar accounts of his drinking were revived, the President replied: "If Grant drinks I'd like to know the brand to give the other generals whiskey of the same keg. . . ." In the fall of 1863 he entrusted the Army of the Mississippi to Major General Grant.

Of the three crossing points on the Mississippi that had assured the transport of reinforcements and supplies between the Southeast and the Southwest, two, Memphis and New Orleans, were in the hands of the northerners by the middle of 1862. Late in April, New Orleans had been very courageously captured by the gunboats of Captain David G. Farragut, who commanded the little flotilla of the Mississippi. After this the Union troops had ascended the river burning and destroying everything on their way. The South justifiably complained of the brutality of the Yankees. Many soldiers pillaged the homes of the Confederates, slashed the paintings, burned the documents, and ended by setting fire to the house. Civil wars always excite fierce emotions and the northern officers refused to feel sympathy for "those damn Secesh women." After the loss of New Orleans there remained only one artery through which the South could obtain nourishment and recruits from the West—Vicksburg. If Grant took Vicksburg the southern government would find itself cut off from its western states. The strategic problem was thus a simple one, but the tactical execution was difficult. Vicksburg, a fortress perched on a plateau, was the Gibraltar of the Mississippi. It could not be attacked from the front, or from the North or East. The river which regularly overflowed its banks had formed around the city an immense swamp which no army could cross. The only ground from which an attack could be launched was that south of Vicksburg. Sherman joined Grant there with almost thirty-two thousand men. The Union forces and those of the Confederacy in that region were approximately equal but the Confederate forces were scattered. Taking advantage of interior lines, Grant with great skill first defeated the Confederates at Jackson, Mississippi, then with his rear secure undertook the siege of Vicksburg. What could the Confederates do? Nothing, for their means of transportation did not allow them to send a new army to attack Grant from the rear. Thereupon a siege in the classic manner was begun, with mines, counter-mines, breaches, and forays, and ended on July 4 with the surrender of the city. Grant captured thirty-one thousand prisoners, one hundred seventy cannon, and fifty thousand small arms. He generously gave orders to his men not to make any slighting remarks to the vanquished. Soldiers in blue and gray fraternized. The besieged welcomed the victors to their trenches; the besiegers studied the effects of their gunfire. On both sides courtesy and magnanimity gave rise to friendly conversation. Grant paroled and sent home all the prisoners who came from the Southwest. The capture of Vicksburg was an important victory inasmuch as it gave the North control of the Mississippi.

On the preceding day, July 3, 1863, the southern armies had suffered another grave defeat. General Robert E. Lee, hero of the campaign in Virginia, had invaded Pennsylvania with the intention of reducing the pressure on Vicksburg and securing provisions for his army. He believed that if he got possession of Baltimore, Philadelphia, or Washington he would accomplish two things: In America, he would lift the siege of Vicksburg, and in Europe he would gain recognition for the Confederacy. It was a daring move, for it left Richmond unguarded. Someone said to Lee: "What if the Union armies take Richmond in your absence?" He replied: "We should swap queens." He marched up the valley of the Shenandoah, and at first everything went well. The southern army rounded up all the horses in Pennsylvania and subsisted on its cattle, pigs, and poultry, but it respected the Yankees' homes. Lincoln sent General George Gordon Meade against Lee, and the two armies met near Gettysburg. Lee had about 75,000 men; Meade, 88,289. Lee was in a position to accept or decline battle. He accepted. "And this time," he said to his officers, "we are going to show Yankees how we can fight." His army had been victorious so often that he thought it could do anything, and as a matter of fact men have never attacked more bravely than did Pickett's Virginians on the third day of the battle, advancing behind their blue flag. But before they reached the crest of the hill the northern fire decimated them. The losses were so great that Lee was compelled to order a retreat toward the Potomac. Meade could have pursued and destroyed him. But he was a hesitant and prudent general of the same type as McClellan. Despite Lincoln's insistence he let the enemy escape. Lincoln said: "Our army held the war in the hollow of their hand, and they would not close it. . . . We had gone all through the labor of tilling and planting an enormous crop, and when it was ripe we did not harvest it! . . ." Lee's lieutenants, Ewell and Longstreet, had been guilty of many mistakes. With his customary generosity Lee assumed responsibility: "Never mind, General," he said to Willcox, who was almost in tears as he described the condition of his brigade, "never mind, all this has been my fault. It is I that have lost the fight; now help me to do what I can to save what is left."

It was on the battlefield of Gettysburg where the many dead had been buried that Lincoln delivered the famous speech that remains a classic of English prose worthy of a Pericles or a Demosthenes:

Four-score and seven years ago our fathers brought forth on this continent a new nation, conceived in liberty, and dedicated to the proposition that all men are created equal. Now we are engaged in a great civil war, testing whether that nation, or any nation so conceived and so dedicated, can long endure. We are met on a great battlefield of that war. We have come to dedicate a portion of that field, as a final resting place for those who here gave their lives that that nation might live. It is altogether fitting and proper that we should do this. But, in a larger sense, we cannot dedicate—we cannot consecrate—we cannot hallow—this ground. The brave men, living and dead, who struggled here, have consecrated it, far above our poor power to add or detract. The world will little note, nor long remember, what we say here, but it can never forget what they did here. It is for us the living, rather, to be dedicated here to the unfinished work which they who fought here have thus far so nobly advanced. It is rather for us to be here dedicated to the great task remaining before us,—that from these honored dead we take increased devotion to that cause for which they gave the last full measure of devotion—that we here highly resolve that these dead shall not have died in vain—that this nation, under God, shall have a new birth of freedom—and that government of the people, by the people, for the people, shall not perish from the earth.

Although Lee had saved his army after Gettysburg, the position of the South was becoming critical. The capture of Vicksburg had completely separated the eastern states of the Confederacy from the western states—Arkansas, Louisiana, and Texas; the blockade isolated the Confederacy from Europe; it was henceforth a besieged city around which the ring of assailants grew daily tighter. The federal navy was blockading the ports and the South lacked everything: food, clothing, munitions, wagons. The army suffered as well as the civilians. The only hope that remained to the South was weariness on the part of the North. There was some reason to anticipate it. Lincoln and the war seemed unpopular. In the beginning volunteers in the North had rushed to the colors. But toward 1863 they had become so few in numbers that many states had to offer bounties to attract them. But a soldier who is attracted by a bounty is not a very good soldier. Conscription proved more successful. With certain exceptions, all able-bodied men from twenty to forty-five were registered. A man chosen by lot had the right to buy himself off for three hundred dollars or to hire a substitute. These anti-democratic methods enraged the masses: "A rich man's war fought by the poor," they said. Especially in New York Irish Democrats rebelled against a system that permitted a banker to continue with his business while a shopkeeper had to go and fight in Virginia. During the summer of 1863 there were riots and men shouted: "The Hell with draft and the war!" The crowd broke into army offices and set fire to them, crying: "Down with the rich!" Houses and churches were burned. There were barricades in the streets, officers were stopped and beaten up, telegraph wires were cut. There was an atmosphere of riot and rebellion. The crowds killed thirty Negroes, holding them responsible for a war that was being fought to free them. Two thousand men had to be summoned from the Army of the Potomac and West Point and even had to open fire on the crowd. In the South hopes ran high.

During the autumn of 1863 Grant's successes continued. Congress revived the rank of lieutenant general for him and he was made commander-in-chief of the Union armies. On March 8, 1864, Grant went to Washington for the first time in his life. His position was difficult. Secretary of War Stanton claimed the right of commanding the armies himself. Now Stanton was pusillanimous and thought only of protecting Washington. Grant, on the contrary, wished to provide defense by attacking and to march on Richmond. Lincoln wanted him to take the city, which hitherto had resisted all assaults. Grant thought the operation possible. The northern armies were now armies of veterans; the service of supply was well organized; Generals Sherman, Sheridan, and Thomas were animated by the same offensive spirit as Grant himself. The method of frontal attack would be costly. But the North had a vast reservoir of men and could make good its losses. In the Spring of 1864, Grant's campaign to destroy the army of northern Virginia and take Richmond got under way.

At the same time General Sherman was to make his way across Georgia and sever Richmond's communications with the South. If Sherman and Grant could close this vise on Lee the war would be over. Sherman's career had been no less unconventional than Grant's. A retired officer, he had managed the branch of a bank, then a military school in Louisiana. During the war he had shown himself an energetic leader with clear ideas and a firm will. In September, 1864, after a hard four months' campaign, he captured the city of Atlanta. Treating the inhabitants with extreme severity because he did not wish to spare troops for an occupation, he burned everything that might be useful to the enemy and drove out the population. "If the people raise a howl," he said, "against my cruelty, I shall reply that war is war. . . . If they want peace, they and their relatives must stop the war." In his march to the sea Sherman laid waste everything he found on his way, destroying railroads, enveloping cities in the smoke of the fires he had set, and leaving behind him dreadful memories that took years to efface. More than one southern woman said at that time that she would love to hang the Yankees with her own hands. This march through the midst of enemy country might have appeared dangerous, but Sherman knew that the population was demoralized and unarmed. As a matter of fact his march was not interfered with. The weather was magnificent. The military bands played "John Brown's Body." The soldiers enthusiastically responded: "Glory, glory, Halleluiah." The air of victory quickened the men's steps. The Negroes gathered to watch them pass and rejoiced at the arrival of the Angel of the Lord.

Lincoln was a candidate for re-election in 1864. He had changed a great deal in four years and his character had further developed. The masses had become fond of him, of his humor, of his strangeness, of his love for the people. Honest people realized that he had done his duty without hesitation in dreadfully difficult circumstances. Hawthorne wrote that he would rather see Uncle Abe at the head of the country than any other man. John Hay, his secretary, made this notation: "The Tycoon is in fine whack. I have rarely seen him more serene and busy. He is managing this war, the draft, foreign relations, and planning a reconstruction of the Union, all at once. I never knew with what a tyrannous authority he rules the Cabinet till now. The most important things he decides, and there is no cavil. I am growing more convinced that the good of the country absolutely demands that he should be kept where he is till this thing is over. There is no man in the country so wise, so gentle and so firm. . . ." But a peace party was opposed to Lincoln. He was accused of having misused his powers as commander-in-chief, of having suspended *habeas corpus* without an act of Congress, of having authorized illegal judgments by military tribunals. Vallandigham, a Democrat from Ohio, stopped calling him Lincoln and referred to him as Caesar. Some wished to force the President to release political prisoners who had staged peace rallies. "Must I," he asked, "shoot a simple-minded soldier boy who deserts, while I must not touch a hair of a wily agitator who induces him to desert?" Within his own party he was assailed by the radicals who demanded the immediate abolition of slavery in all states. The Democratic convention of 1864 met in Chicago, called to order by August Belmont, agent of the House of Rothschild in New York. It was hard to agree upon a platform because the party was divided half and half between pacifists and supporters of the war. The Democrats finally declared in favor of the cessation of hostilities and chose a general for their candidate, the renowned McClellan. He accepted the nomination, but wrote a letter to the national committee saying he could not endorse the platform. The confusion resulting from this misunderstanding, combined with the victories of the summer, gave the election to Lincoln by an electoral vote of two hundred and twelve to twenty-one. Andrew Johnson, a Democrat and a supporter of the war, became Vice President. Lincoln's election did as much good as a victory. Only the North could make the North lose the war. Since the North had decided to fight, it was sure to win.

Sherman marched through the Carolinas, wreaking even more havoc than in Georgia. His soldiers had become experts in pillaging. They emptied closets, sent their wives the linen belonging to the women of the South, smashed pianos, and burned books. It was a strange orgy of hatred, owing perhaps to the length of the war. From a military point of view, the objective was to join forces with Grant, but the latter did not wait for Sherman. After the battles of the Wilderness, Spottsylvania, and Cold Harbor in the spring of 1864, Grant had crossed the James River and in June had begun the siege of Petersburg. After a summer and winter of steady campaigning, in March, 1865, he pressed home his attack against Petersburg. Lee, greatly outnumbered, on April 2 abandoned the capital and advised Jefferson Davis to leave Richmond. The Confederate government fled. On April 5, 1865, Lincoln came to Richmond, the conquered capital, said a few kindly words, and was received by the Negroes who greeted him as the Messiah come to deliver them; they awaited some miracle, though they did not know what. Lee beat a retreat, followed and enveloped by Sheridan's cavalry. On April 7 Grant sent a note to Lee: "General, the result of last week should convince you of the vanity of

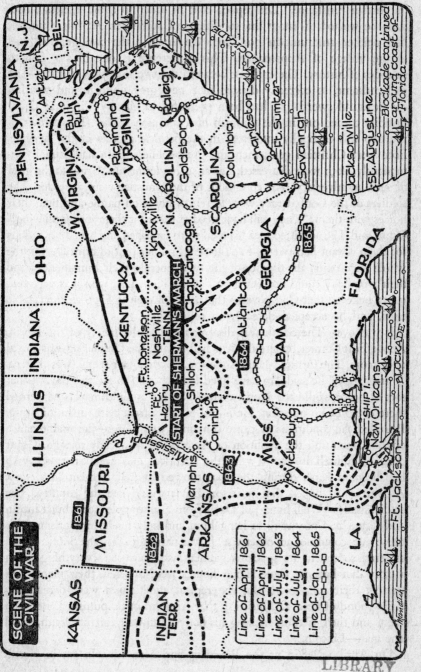

SCENE OF THE CIVIL WAR

KANSAS

MISSOURI

1861

ILLINOIS

INDIANA

OHIO

KENTUCKY

W. VIRGINIA

PENNSYLVANIA

N.J.

DEL.

Antietam

Bull Run

Richmond

VIRGINIA

N. CAROLINA

Raleigh

Goldsboro

Knoxville

Chattanooga

TENN.

Ft. Donelson

Nashville

Ft. Henry

Shiloh

START OF SHERMAN'S MARCH

Corinth

Memphis

Mississippi R.

1862

1863

ARKANSAS

INDIAN TERR.

MISS.

Vicksburg

ALABAMA

GEORGIA

1864 Atlanta

1865

S. CAROLINA

Columbia

Charleston

Ft. Sumter

Savannah

Jacksonville

St. Augustine

BLOCKADE

Blockade continued
around coast of
Florida

FLORIDA

SHIP I.

New Orleans

BLOCKADE

Ft. Jackson

LA.

Line of April 1861
Line of April 1862
Line of July 1863
Line of July 1864
Line of Jan. 1865

all further resistance." Lee replied that in order to avoid useless blood-shed he wished to know the conditions of surrender. At this time Lee had neither ammunition nor food. On April 9 the two generals met at the village of Appomattox. This conference is one of the famous episodes of history. The contrast between the two men was striking—Lee so handsome, so correctly dressed in a new gray uniform and wearing the beautiful sword that had been presented to him by Virginia; Grant untidily turned out in the uniform of a common soldier. But neither of the two was especially interested in the political aspects of the struggle. Both were Christian gentlemen and great soldiers. Both had fought cou-rageously. Both were distressed, Lee at surrendering and Grant at the grief of such an adversary. The conditions of the armistice were generous. The soldiers of the Confederacy were to return home on parole and take their horses with them. "They will have need of them for their spring plowing," Grant said. Lee admitted that his men were famished and asked for rations for them. Grant had twenty-five thousand rations sent to him. During the whole negotiation the dignity of the two generals, their humaneness, and their simplicity could not but arouse admiration. Lee, who was very reli-gious, believed that God governs the affairs of men to his own inscrutable ends, and he accepted defeat with resignation.

It was over. The South was disarmed and at the mercy of the North. Above Fort Sumter, where the war had begun, the Union flag was raised once more. The former Major Anderson, now major general, was present. "I am happy," he said, "to have lived long enough to see this day." What sort of peace would the North dictate? So far as Lincoln was concerned there could be no question. He hoped to reconstruct without humiliating. Provided the conditions of peace contained two things—the maintenance of the Union and the abolition of slavery—he was ready to sign. Grant declared himself in accord with the President and even Sherman, who had been so harsh during the war, showed himself clement in victory. All three had hoped that Jefferson Davis would flee the country. The soldiers sang: "We'll hang Jeff Davis from a sour apple tree"; but Lincoln and Grant had no desire to hang him, and only made him prisoner be-cause they could not act otherwise. It was natural to pity the South. It had suffered so much. Its gracious women had sacrificed everything for a victory that had not come. Their houses were in ashes, their plantations ruined, their sons dead. But the radical abolitionists were demanding their pound of flesh and insisting that crime must be punished. Between them and their victims, making his body a bulwark for the South, stood one man—Lincoln.

On April 14, 1865, as the President and Mrs. Lincoln sat in Ford's

Theatre, the bullet of an assassin put an end to Lincoln's life. John Wilkes Booth, a half-mad actor and fanatical secessionist, had killed the President. It was Good Friday. That morning Lincoln had said to the members of his cabinet: "I had a strange dream. . . . I seemed to be in a singular and indescribable vessel, that was moving with great rapidity toward a dark and indefinite shore. I have had this extraordinary dream before great events, before victories. I had it preceding Antietam, Stone River, Gettysburg, Vicksburg. . . ." A victory? No, Lincoln's death was not a victory; for all Americans it was a dreadful defeat. "It would be impossible for me," said Grant, "to describe the feeling that overcame me at the news. I knew his goodness of heart, and above all his desire to see all the people of the United States enter again upon the full privileges of citizenship with equality among all. I felt that reconstruction had been set back, no telling how far."

CHAPTER XL

Conclusion

"LIBERTY and Union, one and inseparable" had been a famous toast. Both Liberty and Union were henceforth free from danger. The question of national unity would not be raised again. That was a great gain; but it had been achieved only at the cost of a bloody war. Would it have been possible to reach the same result by a series of compromises in the style of Henry Clay? Could the Civil War have been avoided? An American has written that if the worst of the agitators in both camps had been put in a coach and the coach had been pushed into a river, it would then have been easy to get the innumerable good citizens of the North and South to adopt a middle-of-the-road solution; for example, progressive emancipation of the slaves with compensation to their owners. But reasonable solutions presuppose reasonable people, and at certain epochs common sense plays only a subsidiary role in human affairs. Nations, like individuals, have their crises of passion and folly. Before the trial by fire neither North or South would have accepted the verdict of reason.

The victory of the Union entailed far-reaching consequences. From the Rio Grande to the Canadian frontier, from Mexico to Oregon, the United States possessed a prodigious continental domain, the exploitation of which had been delayed by the latent conflict between the North and South. This domain was as yet settled only by rare and widely separated communities. Henceforth these lands were to be free of all ideological mortgages. There was no further conflict to fear. It is true that the South remained deeply wounded at heart and very quick to resent the Yankees, while in the North zealous radicals were loudly demanding reprisals. But if a military struggle is not resumed passions must subside with time, and because of the disparity in strength this struggle *could* not recommence. Moreover, colonization was facilitated from this time on by the Homestead Act which Congress had passed in 1862. Every head of a family or citizen over twenty-one had a right to one hundred sixty acres of the public domain, on the one condition that he cultivate these lands for at least five years. The old dream of the West was thus realized; emigrants would pour in. There was every indication that the post-war period would be a time of development for the entire continent.

The Civil War put an end to the feudal period in American history. The United States had not witnessed, as Europe had in its time, a struggle of the great barons amongst themselves and then their common revolt against a centralized monarchy, but the rivalry of the states had played an analogous part. The victory of the Union disposed of Calhoun's theories about the rights of secession and nullification. Lincoln, like Richelieu, had assured the victory of the central power. The South recognized that the question of secession had been settled once and for all, and agreed not to begin that agitation anew. This did not prevent the supporters of states' rights from continuing to protest, as they had a right to do, against all excessive centralization. For a long time the Democratic party adopted the role of champion of the states against the federal government. But this attitude was made possible by the fact that the Democrats were not in power. When they were, and when they had to supervise the conduct of great wars, they succumbed just as much as the Republicans had done to the temptation of reinforcing the central government. Necessity is a great molder of doctrines.

The period from 1830 to 1860 had been a romantic one; that is, a period of intellectual and sentimental escape. Like the French Republicans of 1848, the American liberals believed (and still believe) in the perfectibility of man and in social progress. In New England an important intellectual movement called transcendentalism was born from the contact of German philosophy with French idealism. For two hundred years in New England all mysticism had been smothered, first by seventeenth-century Calvinism, then by the rationalism of the eighteenth century. Toward the middle of the nineteenth century Emerson, Thoreau, Alcott, and Hawthorne appealed to men's hearts by a moral and secular mysticism. A number of their group went to live in the charming village of Concord near Boston. They paid scant attention to public affairs. Emerson was a strong critic of the materialism of his times, but a critic is not necessarily a reformer. At first Emerson showed great reluctance to take part in the slavery controversy. "I have quite other slaves to free than those Negroes, to wit, imprisoned spirits, imprisoned thoughts." Later, after the Kansas-Nebraska campaign, he was drawn in. When the Fugitive Slave Law was passed he said: "This filthy enactment was made in the nineteenth century by people who could read and write. I will not obey it, by God!"

Thoreau sought true riches in nature. He freed himself to a large extent from "the shackles of society." "Enjoy the earth," he said, "but do not possess it"; and also, "We should be men first and subjects afterwards." Less individualistic, the Reverend George Ripley, Nathaniel Hawthorne, Margaret Fuller, an ardent feminist, born a half-century too soon, and Bronson Alcott, "the fastidious archangel," attempted for several years to live in a phalanstery at Brook Farm. The experiment at first seemed successful, then in 1846 a fire destroyed the buildings and incidentally the institution. It was during this period that the young Henry Adams was discovering with regret "that the universe was just as real as Mr. Emerson"; Walt Whitman was learning that America is a great poem; and Edgar Allan Poe, that morbid and inhuman genius, was producing by chemical combination poems and stories of a mathematical and glacial beauty. Meanwhile about the year 1853 Mark Twain was learning the profession of river pilot on the Mississippi. More than any other, at the close of the Civil War, he represented the true hope of a genuinely American literature.

Mark Twain no longer sought models among European writers. On the contrary, he got his best effects by satirizing the Old World. It is significant that this satire was received with so much enthusiasm by American readers. After 1860 the umbilical cord between Europe and America seemed cut. The young nation was turning toward the great plains, toward the vast prairies, rather than toward the oceans. For several years it remained obsessed by the war. It put generals in the White House and veterans on the pension list. On election days it waved "the bloody shirt" of Lincoln, of the soldiers of Grant and Sherman. Engaged in developing its new territories, America for decades paid scant attention to Europe. Until 1815 it had been passionately interested in European quarrels; from 1815 to 1860 it had profited by these quarrels to acquire a continent. If England, France, and Spain had not been profoundly divided, they would never have permitted a new nation to achieve such power. Their jealousy had been their weakness. After the War of Secession, which showed the military resources of the United States, the Monroe Doctrine was no longer just a wish, it was a barrier. But thirty years more were to pass before the new power pitted itself in war against the powers of Europe. About 1870, like an adolescent, it was completely absorbed with itself. It was growing. As long as it had a frontier where adventurous spirits could find opportunity for combat and creation, it did not concern itself with the outside world. On the day when the last frontier disappeared, it began to look about it and then it was that it entered into the life of nations.

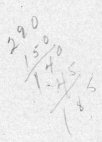

GROVER CLEVELAND
in his study at Princeton

Book Five

THE GILDED AGE

CHAPTER XLI

Reconstruction

THE death of a President of the United States during his term of office always creates a surprising situation by placing at the head of the nation a man not selected for that post. Sometimes the surprise is a happy one and the adventitious President proves better than his predecessor; sometimes it is painful. "Then God help us!" said one of the Confederate leaders upon learning of Lincoln's assassination. "If that is true it is the worst blow that has yet struck the South." Certainly Andrew Johnson was not Lincoln's equal, and he seemed much less capable of liquidating the war without useless suffering. Nevertheless he was far from being an unworthy executive. He was a picturesque person. Born in North Carolina of a very poor family, and having lost his father in childhood, he was apprenticed at the age of ten to a tailor, ran away to Tennessee where he became a tailor himself, and married at nineteen. His wife taught him to read and write. His desire for an education was so great that he hired people to read aloud to him while he sewed. He prospered in his trade and at thirty-four possessed a fortune and some slaves. Since the books he had read were principally collections of speeches, he had acquired through them a kind of vigorous eloquence. Then he entered political life and slowly climbed the ladder of honors rung by rung. Dickens, who met him, observed that he had a remarkable face and that one could unmistakably recognize in him a man of character.

His political position was complicated. Offspring of poor whites, he hated the rich planters who constituted the slavocracy. One of his adversaries said that if Johnson had been a serpent he would hide in the grass in order to bite the heels of the children of the rich. He had made his career in the southern Democratic party and had been violently opposed to slavery. The convention that chose him as Vice President called itself Unionist and not Republican. It had associated him with Lincoln in order to place in the administration a man from the South who believed in the Union.

In secondary position, he had been an influential figure. In the highest place, his lack of tact and the violence of his rages were to augment the difficulties of a troublous period. Johnson was a much better man than appearances indicated. He was sincere, law-abiding, and devoted to his country; he had few ideas but was faithful to them. He could not be, as his enemies claimed, a traitor to the Republican party, for he had never belonged to that party. Nor was it any truer that he was an inveterate drunkard as the hostile newspapers maintained. Quite the contrary. If he appeared ill the day he had to take the oath as Vice President, it was because he had, by exception, drunk a glass of brandy to fortify himself, and because his stomach was not used to strong drink. The ill will of his adversaries, supplemented by his own lack of tact, made his administration a tragedy.

The situation that Lincoln had bequeathed to him was dangerous, in spite of the victory. Two questions seemed settled: The Negroes were no longer slaves and the Union was no longer threatened. But these negative solutions were clearly not enough. What was to be done with the emancipated slaves? And what should be the nature of the Union between the victors and the vanquished? In most of the southern states there was no more legal government. Only the presence of the federal army kept the inhabitants from anarchy. The veterans who returned home in their tattered gray uniforms found nothing but ruins, burned houses and farms, ravaged cities, and plantations turned to wasteland. Of many a beautiful home nothing remained but a chimney. Women who had formerly been rich went begging for their children. Planters sold molasses and flowers to their former slaves. The simplest objects were lacking. Corncobs served as shuttles. Grass grew in the streets. The Negroes had no clear understanding of what had happened to them and thought that the government was going to give each of them a farm and livestock. They wandered about on the plantations, slipped into the camps, and expected a miracle from every bluecoat. Among the planters, resentment was strong against the Yankees, and even more so among the women. The violence of these hatreds made all collaboration difficult. In 1865 Carl Schurz observed: "At this time one still observes among the people of the South a complete absence of national feeling." Even among themselves the southerners were not united. A Virginian who had fought in the northern ranks was boycotted; a Confederate soldier whose home was in Tennessee dared not return there.

In the North hysterical radicals, maddened by hatred, were demanding punishment for the rebels, confiscation of their property, and the death penalty for their leaders. The worst was Thaddeus Stevens, a pale, cruel old man of sixty-three who had himself carried to the capitol in a litter by young Negroes, and who lived, it is said, with a mulatto girl, Lydia Smith, and was reputed to be the natural son of Talleyrand, whose wit and cynicism he possessed, but not his skepticism and tolerance. A fanatic by nature and profession, he had been successively an anti-Jacksonian, an anti-Freemason and an anti-southerner. His only consistent characteristic was ferocity. To those who felt scruples of conscience at certain extreme measures, he shouted: "Conscience! Tell your conscience to go to the devil and follow the party line!" He detested Johnson. "You must remember he is a self-made man," someone said to him. "I am happy to hear it," Stevens replied. "That relieves the Creator of a terrible responsibility." For him the principal meaning of victory was the joy of abusing the vanquished. This was a far cry from Lincoln's beautiful serenity and his "charity for all." Ministers who called themselves Christians and believed they were Christians calmly consigned all Confederates to hell. William Brownlow, a renegade southerner who had become governor of Tennessee, said: "I should prefer to be buried in a Negro cemetery rather than in a rebel cemetery; and after my death I should prefer to go to a black Paradise rather than to a Hell of rebellious whites." The desire of the radicals was not to bind up the wounds of the country and restore its unity but to humiliate that proud oligarchy and to see that it was governed by the blacks it had oppressed.

This had certainly not been Lincoln's post-war plan. His ideas were well known; they had been applied even during the war in Tennessee, Arkansas, and Louisiana. This was his plan: Whenever in any state 10 per cent of the number who voted in 1860 should recognize emancipation, take an oath of allegiance to the Union, and set up a government, that government would be recognized and the state relieved of military rule. However, Congress was to decide whether it would receive the newly elected senators and representatives from those states. All those who had taken part in the rebellion should be given amnesty except the leaders of the movement, and even for these latter Lincoln planned neither death nor imprisonment. He would have forced them either to leave the country or to sign an appeal for mercy, and these appeals would have been granted. The citizens of the South would thus have regained possession of their civil rights. The loyalty of tomorrow interested Lincoln more than the errors of yesterday. This wise and generous attitude had irritated the radicals in Congress, who spoke with contempt of "a policy of tenderness toward the rebels." If Lincoln had survived he would have encountered fierce opposition among these fanatics. Johnson's elevation to the presidency had at first reassured them. Had he not always denounced the "odious and dangerous aristocracy"? Had he not said that their great plantations should be seized, divided into small farms, and sold to honest workmen? But as soon as he was in power Johnson felt the danger of a policy of revenge. In May, 1865, he granted an amnesty to the rebels. The fury excited by Lincoln's assassination kept this from being as complete as Lincoln would have desired. But at least those who were excluded by its terms had the right to ask for pardon, and most of them received it. Johnson interviewed the suppliants all day long in the White House, where a pile of pardons lay on a table guarded by a young officer. Jefferson Davis was at first imprisoned in Fortress Monroe. Then his wife interceded in his behalf with Horace Greeley, an influential Republican and great journalist, who agreed to go surety for the former president of the Confederacy, his opponent; this generosity cost him some of his popularity. Davis was thereupon set at liberty, went to Canada and to Europe, and ended his life in the United States writing the history of those great events in which he had had a part. Lee, who had intended to seek refuge in some home in the woods, became president of Washington College (now Washington and Lee) and taught young Virginians their duty as good Americans, to the great annoyance of Thaddeus Stevens. "It is, I am convinced," Lee wrote, "the duty of all to unite in the restoration of the country and the re-establishment of peace and harmony."

The Negro problem was far from being settled by emancipation. In 1860 there were about 4,000,000 blacks in the South. Of this number about 260,000 were free Negroes. Around 186,000 had served in the federal armies and 300,000 had been progressively liberated in the reconquered states. In all, a considerable number of colored men had served some apprenticeship in liberty. However, there remained more than 3,000,000 human beings who had always lived on the plantations and who suddenly found themselves forced to shift for themselves. They no longer had masters, but they did not have homes either or social position or trades. At first many stayed on the plantations. The master would call them together in front of his house and tell them that they were free. They would reply: "Massa, we stay here with you." Left to themselves, the planters and the freedmen would probably have reached a compromise. Most of the Negroes were kindly and easygoing by nature. But agitators circulated among these unhappy masses, telling them that they must prove their independence by leaving their masters, refusing to work, maltreating the whites, and taking over their churches. The planters could not deny the equality of all men before God. Nevertheless the first time a black man in Richmond knelt among the whites for

communion, those near him drew back. On this occasion it was General
Lee, with his customary dignity, who took his place beside the Negro,
thus setting an example which was followed. Immediately the Negroes,
eager for learning, filled the few inadequate schools that were open to
them. For the rest they waited for the federal government to become a
Santa Claus and give each of them "forty acres and a mule." As a matter
of fact, the agitators from the North were making use of the Negroes
for their own purposes; what they wanted was the black vote, and they
were trying to make sure of it in advance.

During the summer of 1865, taking advantage of the fact that Congress
was not in session, Johnson tried to put Lincoln's plan into operation. In
a number of states he appointed reconstruction governors under whose
protection conventions met to set up new state governments and elect
legislatures which would abolish the ordinances of secession, ratify the
Thirteenth Amendment ("Neither slavery nor involuntary servitude,
except as a punishment for crime whereof the party shall have been duly
convicted, shall exist within the United States, or any place subject to
their jurisdiction . . .") and cancel all war debts. But when, in December,
1865, the senators and representatives of the states of this reformed Confederacy presented themselves in Washington, Congress refused to
recognize "Johnson governments," which was its right since each House
has the privilege of passing upon the credentials of its members. These
"Johnson governments" had tried, in their southern fashion, to solve
the Negro problem. The South accepted its defeat and the emancipation.
It did not believe in the immediate equality of two races, one of which
had been more anciently civilized and had acquired its privileges by
slow degrees. Most of the southern states agreed to recognize equal
rights for the Negroes with respect to the protection of property, life,
and liberty, but it maintained the social barriers. The "black codes"
forbade mixed marriages and maintained the principle of the segregation
of races in the schools. Laws concerning vagrants imposed a fine upon
Negroes without employment and condemned them to pay the fine in
the form of forced labor. If equality was possible, thought the people of
the South, it was so only by a slow process of growth. But the radicals
in Congress were enraged and maintained that the South was trying
to re-establish slavery under another name.

The temporary solution adopted by Congress was to pass a Civil Rights
Bill, giving Negroes equal civil rights with whites, and to continue the
Freedmen's Bureau, an administration made up of military and civilian
personnel, charged with the duty of settling all questions of aid for the
Negroes, regulation of their work, their schools, and tribunals, as well as

the operation of those properties confiscated from the rebels. The Freedmen's Bureau became the Negroes' guardian, and the latter were thought of as wards of the nation. This attitude was hardly more liberal than that of the black codes. Nevertheless the institution might have given good results if it had been in competent hands; it was entrusted to a venal personnel. "There may have been," the people of the South said sadly, "*one* honest man in the bureau." On one point alone the bureau and the planters worked together: on the question of working agreements. It was certainly necessary that between a white employer and a black worker there should be some legal relationship. But the Negroes were afraid of all contracts; that was not their idea of liberty. Little by little a system arose of dividing the plantations into lots, the tenant of each lot being called a cropper, and the plantation continuing as a single organization under the authority of the owner or manager.

The radicals in Congress who had put all their hopes in Johnson were now exasperated by his mildness. Thaddeus Stevens with his bitter eloquence proposed to treat the southern states as conquered territories which by their secession had lost all civil rights. This thesis was absurd since the reason for the war had been the proposition that a state could not separate itself from the Union. Stevens and his friends wanted to proscribe the Confederates and strip them of their goods to the profit of the Negroes. They spoke of the Constitution of the United States as "a scrap of worthless paper." Charles Sumner, the leader of the radicals in the Senate, talked about idealism but was really trying to secure the vote of the Negoes for the purpose of keeping his party in power indefinitely. Lincoln had been in favor of giving the vote to those Negroes who knew how to read and write and to those who had fought in the federal armies, which was a just and reasonable proposal. The zealots demanded a vote even for the illiterates. In June, 1866, they submitted to the states a Fourteenth Amendment which (a) guaranteed citizenship and civil rights to Negroes; (b) provided that if any state denied male suffrage to Negroes, the basis of its representation in Congress should be proportionately reduced; (c) disqualified all those who had participated in any insurrection or rebellion against the government from holding any public office; and (d) declared the war debt of the confederacy void. Johnson opposed the measures initiated by the radicals in Congress and vetoed one after another. On their side they persecuted him throughout the country, treating him with no respect, interrupting his speeches and acting toward him in most unseemly fashion. They had formed a kind of committee of public safety, (the Joint Committee on Reconstruction) consisting of fifteen members, and tried to usurp the place of the administration. The reconstruction had become a revolution in which Stevens and his friends were the Jacobins.

The Fourteenth Amendment was not ratified in 1866 by three-fourths of the states. Of all the former Confederate States, only Tennessee voted for it. Delaware, Maryland, and Kentucky, former slave states which had not seceded, also voted against it. The radicals, angered by this resistance and armed with a majority in the North, secured the passage over the President's veto of a law that divided the ten unreconstructed states into five military districts under the orders of five major generals, after the manner of Cromwell. Conventions elected in each state by white loyalists and by the Negroes were to promulgate constitutions giving the vote to the blacks and denying it to the rebels. The constitutions were then to be submitted to this new electorate and to Congress, and the new state legislatures were required to ratify the Fourteenth Amendment. There could be no doubt of the result. The only representatives of the South with a right to a place in Congress would be the representatives of this reconstructed South. "The future condition of the vanquished will depend," said Stevens, "upon the will of the conquerors. They can only enter the Union as new States or as conquered provinces." One cannot imagine a more illogical doctrine. The whole object of the war had been to prove that the Union was an immutable fact and secession impossible. But the attitude of the radicals could not be explained except by accepting secession as a fact and return to the Union as a favor.

All tyrants are abominable, but military tyranny is sometimes less abominable than political tyranny. Although the South complained of the "satraps sent by the North," it considered them less dangerous than the radical politicians. The moderation of certain generals irritated Congress. No other government existed since the generals made appointments to all offices. The southern whites preferred these arbitrary choices to those of the Negroes and their advisers. An army of adventurers had descended on the reconquered states and were looking forward to large profits from the exploitation of the simple Negroes who had suddenly become voters. From the North and East traveling salesmen and electioneers, greedy and poor, rushed in with no other luggage than a carpetbag (thus earning the name of *carpetbaggers*) and organized the conventions to suit themselves; other adventurers recruited from the southern underworld (*scalawags*) joined them in the undertaking. All preached hatred for the ex-rebels, and the Negroes, not through malice but through ignorance, collaborated with these destroyers. Their first move was to revise the electoral lists, the revision consisting in depriving everyone who was not a Negro or a radical of the right to vote. In October, 1867, after the first revision of the list, there were in the former states of the Confederacy 703,000 black voters, 627,000 white. In all the states except North Carolina, Texas, and Virginia, constitutional conventions were formed with a majority of Negroes and scalawags. In Alabama only two of the Negro deputies knew how to write. Surprising laws were passed. The major generals had done their best to mitigate the stupidity of the carpet-baggers; when the new legislators took office, they disappeared. The Supreme Court itself was in one case reduced to impotence by the radicals who jeered at the Constitution.

The only obstacle to their vengeance was still Andrew Johnson, the President. "Impeach him! Remove him!" cried the radicals. "Otherwise the boys in blue will do it." Some fanatics talked of beheading him. "They can cut off my head," Johnson said, "but when it is cut I want the American people to be my witness. Doesn't one martyr suffice them?" Congress bullied him in every way it could. The Tenure of Office Act was passed to deprive him of the right to change even the members of his own cabinet without the consent of the Senate. In spite of the Constitution, he was relieved of the supreme command of the army. The reasons for Congress's hatred of the President were in part the authority assumed by the executive during the war and in part Johnson's opposition to radical measures. Although he had not been untrue to any of his principles, he was treated as a renegade. Stanton, the Secretary of War, was in sympathy with the radicals, and the Tenure of Office Act had been voted in the hope that the President would disobey it, remove Stanton, and that then it would be possible to impeach him by virtue of Article I, Section 3, Paragraph 6 of the Constitution. On February 21 Johnson dismissed Stanton and three days later the House by a vote of one hundred twenty-six to forty-seven voted for impeachment. It was the first time that this provision had been applied. The Senate transformed itself into a high court and before it were laid eleven principal accusations of which the only serious one was the violation of the Tenure of Office Act. The trial was carried on with such evident prejudice that public opinion began to veer in favor of Johnson. All Washington was tremendously excited. Johnson remained very calm. The dying Stevens was borne to the capitol by his Negroes and himself delivered one of the speeches for the prosecution before the Senate. The case was very feeble. Incredible efforts were made to obtain a condemnation. In the speeches of Stevens and his friends, Johnson was represented as Satan incarnate. An audience of carpetbaggers in the galleries made noisy demonstrations against the President. But Chief Justice Salmon P. Chase, who presided, conducted himself as a magistrate and not as a partisan. The Democratic senators would naturally vote for acquittal. Seven Republican senators joined them, some because they were honest men (Ross was one of these), others because they did not want Wade, who was president of the Senate, to become President of the United States. With these Republican votes the acquittal was assured. As his Negroes bore him out, Thaddeus Stevens cried: "The country is going to the devil!" The vote of the Senate was an important event, not because of Johnson, who was coming to the end of his term and had lost all chance of re-election, but for the safety of the Constitution and the independence of the executive.

CHAPTER XLII

The New South

THE northern voter liked to think that it was enough to give slaves the vote in order to instill in them instantly the political instincts that had been developed by centuries of civilization. Unfortunately this was not true. Life on the plantations had of course improved the manners of the African Negroes. A great number of them were affectionate and simple in disposition; some were later to prove their intelligence and their talent in the most diverse professions. But the majority remained credulous, saturated with the bizarre superstitions of voodoo, ready to believe in ghosts, in witchcraft, and to follow any skillful demagogue. Since the northern victory the Negroes had worshiped the Yankee, the Union soldier, the bluecoat, the Freedman's Bureau. What did they expect of these new gods? They had no very clear idea: that the bell summoning them to work on the plantations would not ring any more; that overseers would be eliminated; that every Negro would be provided with a mule, one day a week, to take him into town. Some planters, hoping to appease the blacks, hired former Yankee soldiers as managers; but the latter knew nothing about cotton-growing and the results were disastrous. One planter said to Carl Schurz during his travels through the South: "It is impossible to make the Negroes work without physical constraint." The liberal senator was profoundly shocked. He said that the current opinion in the South seemed to be that the Negro had been brought into this world for the sole purpose of growing cotton, rice, and sugar for the whites, and that it was altogether inadmissible for him to seek his happiness in his own way like other men.

The votes of the Negroes were controlled by a small number of carpet-baggers and scalawags. The radicals in the North had united in 1862 in Union Leagues of America, whose members pledged themselves to defend the Union. After the war this league undertook to organize the black vote and admitted Negroes with mysterious initiation ceremonies. The league insured the political fidelity of these members by means of oaths administered in darkness to the sound of rattling chains. The members of the league agreed never to attend a Democratic meeting. All were to vote for the candidates of the league. This became an electoral instrument of great power for the Republican party. In the southern states it elected governments composed of carpetbaggers and Negroes. When the time to vote came, all the Negroes were searched to make sure they had only one ballot with them and that it was the right one. They were told that if the Democrats returned to power they would re-establish slavery. The results were amazing. Men who did not know how to read were elected as representatives, governors, and even judges. The debates of the assemblies became burlesques. At the same time it is only fair to realize that the worst elements of the reconstruction were represented not by the Negroes but by the white adventurers. A colored historian, W. E. B. Du Bois, has said that in this difficult period criticism and condemnation were justified, but that to address these criticisms to the Negro voters alone is an incredible distortion of truth. Yet, whoever was responsible, the South could not continue to live under such a regime.

The financial management of the unhappy "reconstructed states" was disastrous. The lawmakers voted themselves whisky, gold cuspidors, and sumptuous restaurants where everything was free. During this period Louisiana contracted a debt of over fifty-four million dollars; North Carolina's debt grew from sixteen to forty-two millions; Alabama had a debt of thirty-two millions. It is fair to say that at this same time the North had its share of scandals. It was a period of public dishonesty and the reconstruction governments were not the only culprits. An effort was made to give colored men an education. The desire for learning among the Negroes was sincere and touching. Unfortunately too many of the schools organized by northern radicals became new hotbeds of racial hatred. In 1865 Lincoln could hope that the wounds would be quickly healed and that the best of the Negroes would be, little by little, with the consent of the whites, admitted to all rights of citizens. In 1868 the effects of "The Reconstruction" had been such that the southern whites were firmly determined to prevent, as long as they could, all Negroes from voting. As often happens, the Negroes had been the victims of too zealous friends. The attitude of the Republican party in this matter resulted in the suspension for a long time of all political life in the South and in making fidelity to the Democratic party there an article of faith.

Between 1868 and 1870 the "reconstructed" states of the South ratified the Fifteenth Amendment, which forbade the United States or any state to refuse suffrage to a man because of race, color, or previous condition of servitude. By 1870, all the seceded states had returned to the Union but were working to destroy in secret the conditions they had accepted publicly. When a people or a group sees itself deprived of all legal means of defense, it loses confidence in law and starts to fend for itself. Throughout the South secret societies were formed. The two best known were the Ku Klux Klan and the Knights of the White Camellia. The Ku Klux Klan was born in Pulaski, a small town in Tennessee. There some young Confederates for purposes of entertainment had founded a *kyklos* (the Greek word for circle). At night they would disguise themselves as ghosts by wrapping themselves in shrouds and seek amusement by frightening the Negroes. The effect was so great that other towns thought this might be a means of effective action. Little by little the Invisible Empire extended all over the South. The supreme chief was the Grand Wizard; each state constituted a realm governed by a Grand Dragon. The members were Ghouls or Specters. They rode at night in long, white winding sheets on horses caparisoned in white. They rattled bones beneath their robes, dangled skeletons at the end of long poles, seated themselves on tombs in cemeteries—simple antics which terrified the blacks. When a phantom knocked at a Negro's door, asked for a drink, swallowed three pails of water (which he did by pouring them into a leather sack hidden under his clothes), murmured: "It's so hot in hell," and then ordered the Negro to swear that he would never return to the Union League, he was obeyed. For a long time violence was unnecessary; terror sufficed to keep a large number of blacks away from the polls. The White Camellia, which had its headquarters in New Orleans, also claimed that its object was the maintenance of white supremacy "while at the same time respecting all the legitimate rights of the blacks."

Then the extremists killed the Klan by their excesses, as the extremists in the North had killed radicalism. The movement became violent and the federal government intervened. An investigation proved that all the members of the Klan had been given the order to provide themselves with pistols. "This," said the indictment, "endangers all our fellow citizens of African origin." The Klan was prosecuted and the Grand Wizard (General N. B. Forrest) ordered its dissolution. A Ku Klux Act of 1871 authorized the federal government to make use of the army to suppress the activities of the Klan. But in the South the whites had already won the game and the radical majority was rapidly diminishing. In 1872 an amnesty act restored political rights to most of the former rebels. The Negroes were prevented from voting, not by violence which would have been denounced, but by secret threats. Little by little the Democrats reconquered all the southern states. In 1875 only South Carolina, Louisiana, and Florida remained under radical control. In the North the Republican party was still winning elections by waving "the bloody shirt," that is, by evoking memories of the war, but little by little the electors were growing tired of the intervention of federal troops in the South and were complaining of the fantastic behavior of the reconstruction governments. In 1877 the withdrawal of the last troops assured the final overthrow of the carpetbaggers and the re-establishment of white domination.

Congress's great mistake had been to devote its energies to the hasty and premature solution of a political problem when the most urgent problem was an economic one. The planters were ruined; as completely or more completely than the French nobility after the Revolution. Between planters and slaves the ancient bond had been broken. How were the plantations to be cultivated, and how were the freedmen to live? The method generally adopted was that of sharing the crops. The great plantations were broken up into small lots on each of which lived a family. The proprietor had to advance the farmer everything he needed, build him a house, give him tools, fertilizers, and seed. In return the proprietor had a right to two-thirds of the crop. Unfortunately most of the proprietors had to borrow the necessary capital from the banks. Heavy mortgages weighed upon agriculture. The leaders, needing a security that could easily be liquidated, insisted upon a single crop, tobacco or cotton— farther to the south, rice or sugar cane. It was not until 1880 that corn and wheat secured an important place in the production of the South. At the time of the reconstruction, instead of small farms or tenant properties developing as had happened in France, where a variety of things were grown and there was cattle breeding to boot, an agricultural proletariat was formed in the South in which the whites were no better off than the blacks. Bankers and real-estate dealers for a long time were the only ones to profit by this agrarian revolution. A whole new army of ruined planters came to swell the ranks of the "poor whites." In the sandy hills of Alabama and the sterile pine forests of Georgia lived people who had been reduced to the miserable verge of existence. They were called "crackers" or "hillbillies." They still exist, and Erskine Caldwell has described them in *Tobacco Road* and in *God's Little Acre*.

Defeat had not destroyed in the hearts of the men and women of the South their love of their civilization or their firm intention of maintaining it. Quite the contrary. Persecution had strengthened local patriotism. It had also enlarged it. Before the Civil War many would have called themselves citizens of Virginia, South Carolina, Tennessee. It was the Civil War that gave a precise meaning to the adjective southern. After Appomattox many people prided themselves on being "men of the South," unreconstructed and unreconstructible, and they maintained a united and jealously guarded society. A man who came from the North, if he wanted to be on good terms with his southern neighbors, had to take care to refrain from expressing northern sentiments. One result of this state of mind was unfortunately to accentuate race feeling. The Negroes were less well treated between 1880 and 1900 than they had been between 1840 and 1880. Frightful lynchings resulted from the obstinate determination to keep the Negro in the place that had formerly been his. Little by little, nevertheless, in the twentieth century the violence of these feelings began to abate. Lynchings became rare. But life remained distressing for educated Negroes who were graduates of the Negro universities. Even today the Negro or mulatto, no matter how cultivated he may be or how perfect his manners, cannot enter the same railroad car in the South as the whites or live at the same hotel. The result was that, aside from a few apostles, the best of the Negroes emigrated to the North, leaving behind them a black proletariat without leaders. This has made the problem more difficult still. It is not susceptible of an immediate solution but demands patient forbearance on both sides.

Another result of post-war southern patriotism was the birth of industry in the South. To struggle against the North even peacefully there was need to make use of northern arms. To save the "poor whites" from destitution, which was turning them into agricultural workers in competition with Negroes, it was necessary to open factories. The existence in the South of great deposits of coal, iron, and copper attracted metal workers. Cotton-growing suggested a textile industry. At Durham the tobacco industry became extremely important. It is true that the industrial life of the South was handicapped by the climate, by the habits of an old agrarian civilization, and by the railroad rates and customs duties which even today are the tariffs of northerners made by northerners for northerners. On the other hand, the southern factories benefited by the low cost of labor and by the strange paternalism which was a survival of the plantation system. It is to this active industrial South that American historians have often given the name of the New South. In reality the New South was conceived and created for the sole purpose of preserving the essence of the Old South. It was one way of expressing the passionate feelings which for a period of thirty years turned the South into an army of loyal veterans drawn up behind its leaders, and which even today struggles to safeguard what it has loved so well.

CHAPTER XLIII

The Opening of the Continent

AFTER the war the North was "reconstructed"—or transformed— just as completely as the South. The America of Johnson still resembled in many ways that of Jackson. The sources of great fortunes still were, as they had been in the eighteenth century, commerce and navigation. The new aristocracy of the North—the Astors, the Goelets, the Beekmans, the Rhinelanders—still invested their capital in land and owned vast estates like those of the Van Rensselaers and the Schuylers of another day. Industry remained at the stage of a family enterprise created by an individual who ran it in a paternal fashion and bequeathed it to his son. Corporations had existed since 1860 but they played no great role. One of the most important was the Western Union Telegraph Company, which had combined fifty small enterprises. A part of industry had remained in the handicraft stage; contractors distributed piecework to country women who did the sewing in their own homes. Most of the deposits of minerals remained untouched. In 1859 petroleum had been found in Pennsylvania but its exploitation had hardly been begun: Horse-drawn carriages were still the sole means of transportation in the big cities. In 1860 Americans had admired as a remarkable novelty the organization of the Pony Express, a system for carrying the mails by fast riders from St. Joseph, Missouri, to Sacramento, California. The regular time was ten days. The riders leaped from one horse to the next at the relay stations. It was a fine sporting spectacle. But this enterprise, which had always operated at a loss, soon gave place to the railroad and the telegraph. The world had changed more between 1865 and 1900 than from the time of Caesar to that of Washington.

The war had upset and stimulated the economy of the North. To arm, clothe, and shoe the soldiers it had been necessary to increase production and expand factories. Bankers and manufacturers had learned to make better use of credit. Adequate food supplies for the army had been procured only through the use of farm machinery and by the creation of the meat-packing industry. When peace came machinery made possible the exploitation of the immense regions that were still available in Missouri, Iowa, Nebraska, and Kansas. The demobilization of the armies provided daring and hardened emigrants to clear this new frontier. But first of all, it had to be made accessible. This was the task of another type of pioneer—the railroad builder. His beginnings in the United States had been modest. At first animals had supplied the motive power. The only reason for building a track had been to reduce friction and permit horses to haul heavier loads. The first locomotives had had small success. They covered the travelers with soot; they frightened the animals along the way; they irritated the farmers, who accused them of setting fire to their hayricks. For a while the canal seemed to have won an easy victory over the railroad. The public praised the comfort of the barges. Nevertheless, small companies built lines between neighboring cities: Hartford and New Haven; Baltimore and Washington. Because of the absence of any organized system it was necessary to change trains several times even for short trips and often to cover part of the distance on foot, on horseback, by carriage, or by boat. About 1860 there existed in the United States approximately thirty thousand miles of railroads divided among a number of companies. The great arterial river, the Father of Waters, retained its pre-eminence. It was by way of the Mississippi that the whole commerce of the West moved.

The Civil War closed the river. Suddenly the importance of all the railroads that connected the West with the East was augmented. Chicago and St. Louis became commercial centers of the first magnitude. The branch lines were united into systems. After the war five important lines vied for the east-west traffic—the New York Central, the Pennsylvania, the Erie, the Baltimore and Ohio, and the Grand Trunk Line. In 1867 Pullman conceived the idea of the sleeping car which bears his name. The diner made it possible to eliminate long stops at station restaurants. Steel rails replaced iron rails. The development was so rapid that in 1880 there were 93,000 miles of tracks; in 1890, 167,000 miles. Philip Guedalla has said that the true history of the United States between 1865 and 1890 is the history of transportation, in which the names of rail-road presidents are more important than those of the Presidents of the United States. It is the time of homeric struggles between Commodore Vanderbilt, Jay Gould, Daniel Drew, Hill, and the bankers Morgan and Belmont for the control of the great "systems"; the time of the tariff wars; the time of the battle between Philadelphia and New York for trade with Chicago. Cornelius Vanderbilt was the first of these pirates of genius who unified the railroads of the United States with great profit to themselves and indisputable advantage to the country. Vanderbilt was born poor and made his first fortune by transporting passengers from Staten Island to New York. Because he owned boats he was called "the Commodore." Later he became interested in railroads. It was he and his son who made a unified system of the New York Central, not without financial maneuvers that shocked many decent people. The Erie Railroad became the favorite battlefield of the freebooters of finance. Thanks to the complicity of certain legislators in Albany, Daniel Drew secured the unexpected passage of laws which upset the market. One of them, for example, authorized him to link together the subsidiary companies and convert their stock into shares of the Erie. This allowed him to carry out with complete safety a prodigious stock-exchange deal. Time and again the directors of the Erie were threatened with imprisonment and had to seek refuge in New Jersey. On each occasion when the battle was over Drew, Vanderbilt, Gould, and Fisk ended by making peace at the public expense.

The most remunerative enterprises of this time were the transcontinental railroads. In 1862 Congress had authorized the construction of the Union Pacific, running west from Omaha, Nebraska, and of the Central Pacific, running east from San Francisco. In 1869 the two lines met near Ogden, Utah. It was amazing that they had succeeded in crossing the wilderness in spite of the Indians, the nature of the terrain, and the labor problems. It had been necessary to arm the workmen and to have them escorted by soldiers. Gangs of bridgebuilders worked miles in advance of the rail layers. The Union Pacific employed a large number of Irish; the Central Pacific large numbers of Chinese; when the working forces drew close to each other there were violent fights. Finally the two lines met; each engineer broke a bottle of champagne on the other's locomotive; ministers offered prayers; gold and silver spikes were driven into the last tie. Space had been conquered. The exploit had been an expensive one for the federal government. Not only had it loaned the companies sixteen thousand dollars in government bonds for every mile of track constructed, but in addition it had given the railroads right of way and made them liberal land grants. The Union Pacific, for instance, received in all about twenty million acres. What difference did it make? Opening the continent was a magnificent game that was to pay off a hundredfold.

At the time of Lincoln's death the immense territory extending from the Rocky Mountains on the west to Minnesota, Iowa, Missouri, Arkansas on the east—roughly to the meridian of 100°—was still in the nature of a "frontier." Scattered cities—Salt Lake City, Denver, and beyond the Rockies Sacramento, San Francisco, Portland, and Seattle—were, like the early English and French forts, hardly more than advance outposts. As soon as you left them, you found the open prairie where the buffaloes roamed. In 1865 millions of these enormous beasts lived in huge herds. Hunters undertook the methodical destruction of these animals and in a few years annihilated them almost completely. It was here the Captain William F. Cody, called Buffalo Bill, won fame. He had been one of the Pony Express riders. During the construction of the Union Pacific he became the great purveyor for the gangs of workmen, supplying them with buffalo meat. Later he organized the first Wild West Show and toured the whole of Europe with his wild horses and his Indians in feather head-dresses. The destruction of the buffaloes spelled the ruin of the Indian tribes to whom these animals had supplied food, tents, and clothing. Deprived of their prey, despoiled of their lands by the white cattle raisers and farmers, the Indians fought back, but it was a losing fight.

This problem of the Indians was a difficult one. At the end of the Civil War there remained about two hundred ninety-four thousand aborigines in the United States. Many of the tribes were civilized. In all good faith they signed treaties with the United States which granted them ownership of certain lands. Then the whites requested right of passage. They agreed. After that came the cattlemen and the farmers, who undertook to force the Indians to sell their lands. If they refused, the pale faces massacred them. In Oregon in 1871 the whites, with the aid of dogs, hunted down certain Indians, cornered them in a cave and slaughtered them all, men, women, and children. Naturally the Indians sought revenge. They were helped by a permanent conflict between the War Department and the Bureau of Indian Affairs in the Department of the Interior. The Department of the Interior, attributing the Indians' troubles to lack of game, distributed guns to them to help them hunt buffalo. The following spring the Indians made use of the guns to attack stagecoaches, convoys, and forts. When the Indians became too dangerous the Department of the Interior appealed to the War Department. The War Department protested against the sentimentalism of the Department of the Interior. The government was forced to maintain a permanent force of twenty-five thousand men in the Indian territories. The army would have liked to make a real war and be done with it. "The only good Indian is a dead Indian," said Sheridan. And Sherman: "We must act with vindictive earnestness against the Sioux, even to their extermination, men, women and children." But the Department of the Interior continued to recommend clemency.

From 1868 to 1876 two hostile chiefs, Sitting Bull and Crazy Horse, victoriously resisted the armies of the United States and the troops had to abandon Fort Kearney and Fort Reno. On June 26, 1876, the Sioux surprised Custer's regiment and killed him and his men to the last one. After that, Sitting Bull fled to Canada. It was the dragon's last convulsion. Before the terrifying strength of the whites, the Indians finally resigned themselves. By 1887 the Dawes Act, dividing the reservation lands among the Indians, had pretty well settled the administration of Indian affairs. In 1901 the members of five civilized tribes acquired American citizenship. Finally in 1924 an act of Congress decreed that henceforth every Indian born on American soil should be a citizen. Many of them still live in tribes and own their lands in common. A considerable number of whites have married Indian women in order to become members of wealthy tribes such as the Osages, who are the owners of rich oil lands in Oklahoma. Today, thanks to better hygienic conditions, the number of Indians is tending to rise once more, and there will soon be a half-million in the United States and Canada. But most of them are of mixed blood and the ancient masters of the continent will one day end by melting into the white population.

Before the Civil War, few pioneers had thought about the economic consequences of the similarity between the buffalo and the bull. They were obvious nevertheless; on the prairie grass that had so amply nourished the wild herds, domestic cattle were to prosper as well. The settling of the prairies was at first the work of the cowboys who came from the South, bringing their cattle. From the time of the Spaniards, Texas and Mexico had bred stock for their local needs, but because there was no market the beasts had little value. They remained half-wild. Whoever needed meat or leather killed a steer. Mexicans and Texans, who were all good riders, knew how to throw a lasso, rope cattle, and brand calves. Once a herd was marked the owner turned it loose for the whole winter and knew just about where to find the cattle again in the spring. When the great territories to the north were opened, the ranchers discovered that the grass there was better than at home, and moreover there was a market. Their goal became the railroad, which enabled them to sell their cattle to the meat-packing houses in Chicago, St. Louis, Kansas City, and Omaha. The long trails which ran from Texas to Kansas and Nebraska were soon trodden into deep furrows by the hoofs of cattle. The whole Middle West soon came to recognize the cowboy by his high boots, his large hat that served both as umbrella and raincoat, the red scarf around his neck, his pistol, and his rope. Large cities grew up along the railroad. About 1880 cattle raising was transformed by the invention of barbed wire, which at that time became so cheap it was possible to enclose land at small cost. Rich cattlemen seized lands that had formerly been public property. Queen Grass became as powerful in the West as King Cotton had once been in the South. At the same time farmers, encouraged by the Homestead Act, many of them emigrants from overpopulated Europe, spread out in waves beyond the Mississippi. There they found land quite different from that which they had been used to working. On the prairie there were no trees and thus there was no possibility, until barbed wire was invented, of building fences cheaply. On the prairie it did not rain, hence it was necessary to devise the new technique of dry farming. When the farmers completed the conquest of the great plains it was the end of the "frontier." With it disappeared one of the great forces that had molded America. Until then the existence of free lands had been enough to insure the protection of the poor against the rich; generations of pioneers had believed that the best government is the one that governs least. After 1890 the new American proletariat no longer found free lands and was forced to settle in the cities. And so the problem of safeguarding labor became a difficult and important one.

The miners had been among the first to settle the new West. They were the ones who had caused the meteoric development of California. In Colorado, Arizona, Idaho, Montana, Nevada, and Wyoming small communities grew up around copper mines, silver mines, lead mines, or gold mines. In Nevada the Comstock lode produced in twenty years three hundred million dollars' worth of silver. The desert was peopled with millionaires. As soon as a new deposit began to be exploited, a camp consisting of hundreds of tents immediately sprang up. Saloons, bars, and gambling houses were opened. Streetwalkers flocked there. A mushroom city arose. Around it farmers cleared the ground, thinking that they would find an easy market by selling their produce to the miners. Then the deposit would peter out, the city would die, the miners depart, and the farmers would remain alone. Near Denver one can see a ghost town, Central City, which had its time of prosperity and which today is completly deserted. During the time of the mining fever new states were born: Nevada was admitted in 1864; Nebraska in 1867; Colorado in 1876. The territories of Idaho, Dakota, and Washington were growing with the construction of the railroads and were asking for admission. North and South Dakota, Washington, and Montana were admitted in 1889, and Wyoming and Idaho in 1890. Thus the West's power in the Senate was assured. This was not without danger, for it gave a minority the power to control the foreign policy of the country.

The Americans had reached their last frontier, but the spirit of the frontier was not dead. By a counter-shock it had returned to the East and there animated pioneers of a new kind. Great bankers and industrialists were showing the impatience and the aggressive individualism of the frontier. That generation "opened the continent" and in the intoxication of its achievement it gave little evidence of scruples. The men of Jackson's era, like the Europeans of 1848, had been obsessed by the romanticism of progress; they had dreamed of an America always more free, more democratic, more generous. The men of 1870 were still romantics, but their romanticism was that of business. They dreamed of a world in which everything—factories, businesses, cities—would grow larger and richer day by day. To realize this dream, they did not hesitate to draw upon the riches of the nation. The cattle kings, like the railroad kings, carved out principalities for themselves from the national domain. It was a time when beneath their high silk hats and behind their carefully trimmed beards, businessmen and legislators concealed the implacable and brutal souls of pirates. Mark Twain named this epoch the Gilded Age. It was not the Golden Age of Jefferson. Gone was the time of good taste, of culture, and of the beautiful mansions of Virginia. The interiors of 1880 were overweighted with moldings, the walls were covered with bad paintings. The first millionaire to be worth one hundred million dollars, Commodore Vanderbilt, "had read a single book, *Pilgrim's Progress* and that only after having reached the age of seventy."

In politics the Machiavellis of the Gilded Age seemed primarily interested in one question: How can one make use of the Constitution, Congress, state, and city governments to further private interests? The epoch was immoral because the temptations were great and the controls inadequate. Since the fortunes created were immense, it was easy for businessmen to turn part of them over to politicians who were in a position to do everything to help them. In a city like New York two-thirds of the voters were recently naturalized citizens who understood nothing about the finances of the city. From this arose the power of the Tweed Ring which pillaged the municipal government and divided millions of dollars among its members. The legislators of certain states were no better. Congress itself was filled with politicians of a new type, chosen by the great interests as their representatives. The worst danger to the country at this time was cynicism. Henry Adams noted with horror that "the grossest satires on American Senators and politicians never failed to excite the laughter and applause of every audience. Rich and poor joined in throwing contempt on their own representatives. Society laughed in vacant and meaningless derision over its own failure." Failure? No, American democracy was not a failure. It had unexpectedly undergone so rapid a growth that neither its laws nor its traditions could adjust themselves quickly enough. The historical sequel will show that it was capable of regaining self-control and of reacting to the new circumstances. But first it had to pass through a number of painful years.

CHAPTER XLIV

Grant's Administration

THE presidential election of 1868 was an event of capital importance to all the citizens of the United States. For the Republicans it meant a chance of securing their party's hold on the national government by confirming the Negroes' right to vote; for the bankers and manufacturers, of making the most of a handsomely subsidized program to "open the continent"; for the Democrats, of winning the peace after having lost the war, of restoring to the states a part of their rights, of depriving the Negroes of the vote and of combating the tariffs. The Republicans' chances were much greater than those of their adversaries; they had the prestige of victory and of money, and the halo of their martyred President Abraham Lincoln. It is seldom that money and virtue are on the same side. For once they seemed to meet, or so at least the party and the country thought. Lincoln's blood sanctified men whose personal sanctity might appear debatable. The Republican platform insisted first of all upon the retention of the principles of the reconstruction. But another and almost equally serious question was occupying people's minds at that time; the payment of the debt contracted during the war. Should it be discharged in gold or in greenbacks? The Republican bankers who held the bonds favored payment in gold; the Democratic farmers considered reimbursement in paper more equitable. The candidate of the Democrats was Horatio Seymour, a former governor of New York and a man unhampered by prestige or talent. The Republican convention chose by acclamation Ulysses S. Grant, the famous general who possessed a glorious military past but so little political experience that he was not even sure he was a Republican. As a matter of fact, when the general had voted (a rare event), he had voted the Democratic ticket.

"A great soldier may be an infant in politics." Grant possessed charming simplicity, kindness, and a naïve confidence in his friends. His military victories had made him conscious of his country's debt to him. He considered the presidency not as a responsibility but as a reward. Of the Constitution and the duties of the President he was completely ignorant, and he made no effort to inform himself. Moreover, the war had worn him out. He still showed flashes of will power during which his natural honesty became evident, but he quickly relapsed into a torpor that rendered his decisions as disconcerting, said Henry Adams, as though they had sprung from the complex mind of a Talleyrand. "It was impossible to follow the General's process of thought. One was not even altogether sure that he did think." That evolution should have produced Grant after Washington, remarked the same Adams, was enough to refute Darwin. Since his triumph the general had become so accustomed to being the spoiled child of the nation that he accepted, as legitimate tokens of homage, very costly presents which in the eyes of those who gave them were intended to pave the way for secret and profitable projects. A group of businessmen gave him a library worth sixty-five thousand dollars; another, a pair of very fine trotting horses; others still gave him houses, cashmere shawls for his wife, and overly elaborate toys for his son. Grant had been poor all his life and he loved the glamour of riches. When a speculator took him out on his yacht and presented him with large cigars, the ease of that life seemed to inspire him with a dangerous sense of well-being. That the United States should make him the gift of the presidency seemed quite natural to him. The northern voters felt about it as he did. They voted in 1868, not for a program but, as Allen Nevins has said, "for an indestructible legend, for a national hero. . . . You pronounced that monosyllabic name Grant and the prosaic workman, farmer, employee for once in his life had a vision. It was the vision of four years of terror and glory." They voted for Vicksburg, for Appomattox. Nevertheless Grant's popular majority was very small, barely three hundred thousand votes. Since the Negro vote had been seven hundred thousand, the Republican party noted with alarm that, despite the military triumph, its domination was precarious. This had the result of making it more determined than ever to retain the reconstruction laws.

Since the President was incompetent, the selection of a Secretary of State assumed special importance. In Johnson's time Seward had

occupied that difficult post with distinction; he had succeeded in liquidating Napoleon III's Mexican enterprise without a war, and in persuading the Russians to sell him Alaska (1867). As Seward's successor
the name of Motley, the great historian, was suggested to Grant. "No,"
the President said with distaste, "he parts his hair in the middle and
wears a monocle." Hamilton Fish was given the post and acquitted
himself well, even though the President caused him anguish. Without
consulting his cabinet, Grant negotiated a treaty annexing the Republic
of Santo Domingo. Colonel Babcock, the President's secretary, had
arranged the affair for a million and a half dollars with a revolutionary
government of doubtful authority. When Grant proudly announced
this news to his stupefied cabinet, Hamilton Fish tendered his resignation. Grant begged him, in his disarming fashion, to remain: "I need
you and Mrs. Grant needs your wife." For Mrs. Hamilton Fish, an
experienced woman of the world, acted as Mrs. Grant's adviser in
diplomatic etiquette. The treaty was rejected by the Senate; but the
episode showed that under the influence of skillful and selfish men
Grant was capable of making dangerous moves. On the other hand,
he was reasonable enough in the *Alabama* affair. In this old controversy
between America and England, the United States demanded compensation for the damage caused by a Confederate cruiser which the British
had illegally allowed to be built in British ship yards and to leave their
territorial waters. By the Treaty of Washington (1871) the two countries
agreed to submit the case to the arbitration of a tribunal that was to
meet in Geneva. The following year this tribunal awarded the United
States fifteen and one-half million dollars, which England promptly
paid. It was a fine example of international good sense.

Thieves swarmed in the charnal house. In the time following the
Civil War monetary disorder, uncertainty about the value of greenbacks, and the follies of the reconstruction, gave rise in the United
States to bandits of heroic proportions. For some of them brigandage
was the road to respectability; for others, to prison. The President's
entourage was not above reproach. His own secretary, Babcock, was
compromised in a whisky scandal. Corbin, his brother-in-law, played
a guilty part in the celebrated gold speculation of Gould and Fisk. Jay
Gould was a stock-market speculator and the president of various railroads. With his friend, James Fisk, he conceived the idea of buying up
all the gold on the market and then of making new contracts that
would call for more than the available amount of that metal; then he
would demand delivery; the value of gold would mount vertically;
the rise in gold would lead to a fall in prices; the terrified farmers

would sell their wheat and Gould, who would transport the wheat on his railroads, would profit on both sides of the ledger. It was simple and brilliant, but the operation presented one danger. The Treasury of the United States owned six hundred million dollars' worth of gold; it could thwart the whole maneuver if it chose to throw this gold on the market. Gould and Fisk believed they had found a guarantee against such a counterattack by giving the President's brother-in-law Corbin a part in the affair. Set a thief to catch a thief: Corbin told his accomplices that his sister, Mrs. Grant, was speculating with him and that this assured the President's protection. But neither the President nor Mrs. Grant knew anything about it. When they found out, their honesty was outraged. The President ordered the Treasury to bring about a reduction in the price of gold and on a certain "Black Friday" (September 24, 1869) prices collapsed. Jay Gould had scented danger, withdrawn his investment, and played the market short. But his associate Fisk was temporarily ruined. The whole country was indignant at the weakness of the President in tolerating such shady adventurers in the White House.

Within the Republican party many good citizens were growing uneasy both at the latent corruption and at the brutal turn the policy of reconstruction was taking. A group of reformers grew up inside the party. At its head were Senator Carl Schurz, a German refugee, a liberal, a soldier, journalist, and historian; Charles Francis Adams of the royal house of Massachusetts; and G. W. Curtis, editor-in-chief of *Harper's Weekly*. The reformers wished to withdraw federal troops from the support of the carpetbag governments, reduce the tariffs "which enriched the rich and impoverished the poor," and to make appointment to public offices the result of competitive examinations rather than the reward of campaign services.

A large part of the country approved the reformers and they would have had a chance in 1872 to keep Grant from winning a second term if they had chosen a strong candidate. After prolonged quarrels, they nominated Horace Greeley, editor of the *Tribune,* a New York newspaper. He was an honest and talented man. All the reformers of the country, "men with long hair and women with short hair," considered him their savior. Greeley had been a passionate opponent of slavery, and we have already noted that at the time when Mrs. Jefferson Davis needed a sponsor for her husband so that he might be liberated, she had appealed to Horace Greeley as the most generous of his enemies, and he had given his signature. But fanatics confuse greatness of soul with treason. The radical reconstructionists had accused Greeley of betraying the cause. At the time of the presidential election, when the Democrats were supporting Greeley against Grant, his former Republican friends treated him very badly. "I have been assailed so bitterly that I hardly knew whether I was running for the Presidency or the Penitentiary." Grant was re-elected by an immense majority. Greeley died a month after the election. Justice is not of this world.

Grant's second term, like his first, was tarnished by scandals. The most serious of them, the Crédit Mobilier, extended as far as the Vice President of the United States, Schuyler Colfax. The founders of the Union Pacific had obtained from the federal government a loan of twenty-seven million dollars, secured by a second mortgage on the railroad under construction. After this, they had given a first mortgage on the same property to a small company, the Crédit Mobiler, in which they owned all the stock and which was to build a portion of the road. Experts later discovered that the price paid to the Crédit Mobilier was two or three times as high as the real cost of the work. In short, the operation consisted in robbing (a) the government, (b) the Union Pacific, to the profit of the Crédit Mobilier, which handed out 800 per cent in dividends to a small group of favored persons. This transaction, which was more ingenious than honest, might easily precipitate a violent reaction in public opinion. And so the beneficiaries attempted, as was their wont, to protect themselves by associating important personages in their game. Mr. Oakes Ames, a congressman from Massachusetts, agreed to indicate secretly to members of Congress that the shares of the Crédit Mobilier were "diamond mines." Vice President Colfax was one of those who took advantage of this advice, perhaps in all innocence. But when in 1872 Mr. Ames was called upon to testify and opened his notebook filled with names, this innocence was challenged. At once the President wrote Colfax a letter assuring him of his sympathy. Grant was like that, incapable of imagining that his friends could be dishonest, or if they were, that they were so intentionally.

This scandal was just starting to subside when a financial tornado swept the country. Economic crises were becoming periodical. It seemed impossible to adjust buying power and production. As a matter of fact, no one tried to do it. When business was going well enterprises multiplied; prices and salaries rose; credits expanded. A moment came when the credits exceeded real values and when the market, in unstable equilibrium, was at the mercy of the slightest jar. That was what happened in 1873. Europe ceased to buy American securities. Jay Cooke's bank, famous for having financed the Civil War in the North, suspended payments. The event turned the business world upside down. The public believed Jay Cooke was as solid as the Bank of England. On the day following this bankruptcy the market went to pieces within a few hours. Soon factories were closing. In the great cities there were hundreds of thousands of unemployed walking the streets. In 1874 there were six thousand bankruptcies; in 1875, eight thousand; in 1876, nine thousand. The number of suicides increased. Distrust became a collective neurosis. It was no longer possible to borrow a hundred dollars on a farm of a hundred acres. The crisis was still in progress at the time of the presidential election of 1876. Thus the latter took place in an atmosphere of protest. The whole country, not without cause, was demanding reform. It was the end of easy elections scored against the South by waving "the bloody shirt."

CHAPTER XLV

Abuses and Disorders

AMONG those who had suffered from the panic of 1873, the bitterest were the farmers. It must be admitted that they had serious causes for complaint. The government was distributing the nation's patrimony to speculators. How could it fail to shock the farmers to see poor settlers paying, however little it might be, for their meager acres, while railroad magnates received vast domains without disbursing a cent? These immense gifts were exhausting the available lands. The new farmers in the regions of the great plains had to cultivate for export. But then they entered into competition with the European markets where salaries were low and they were handicapped by high tariffs, shipping costs, and duties. Their interests were quite different from those of the industrialist or the banker. What the agriculturists demanded was cheap money, low freight rates, economy in government services, and the elimination of middlemen. In the beginning the railroads had seemed to be the farmers' friend; they brought him closer to the urban centers; they enabled him to send his products long distances. Later the financial scandals, the manipulation of freight rates, and the ruin of bondholders had, on the contrary, created a lively antagonism between the farm and the rail.

In 1867 one man reached the conclusion that it was necessary for the farmers to unite in their own defense. This was a federal employee named Oliver H. Kelley, who had been in charge of an investigation in the South and had observed the distress of the farmers and their intellectual isolation. He founded an organization called the Patrons of Husbandry, an outgrowth of freemasonry, with local chapters called granges. Theoretically, there were to have been granges in all the states, but Kelley had so little money to launch his project that he could hardly afford to buy stamps. If an organization was ever founded on "the rock of poverty," it was this one. Nevertheless by 1873 it had over eight hundred thousand members, and taking on a political character, it succeeded in getting a number of its candidates elected to local legislatures in several states. It carried on a struggle against the railroads, successfully in many respects, and imposed more reasonable rates upon the companies. After the panic of 1873, this movement gave way in part to the Greenbackers, who demanded the retention of paper money. It was a natural reaction of the debt-ridden farmers against their creditors. When the purchasing power of the dollar falls the price of wheat rises and mortgages are lightened. In the presidential election of 1876 the Greenbackers organized an independent party and succeeded in alarming the old parties in several states. An Indiana Republican wrote: "A Bloody Shirt campaign and electoral funds, and Indiana is ours. . . . A campaign on monetary questions and no subsidies, we are beaten."

This election of 1876 was one of the strangest in the history of the country. It seemed likely that the Republican candidate would be James G. Blaine of Maine, a politician celebrated for his graciousness, magnetism, and irrestistible charm of manner. Blaine arrived at the convention with so many delegates pledged to him that he believed he was certain of the nomination. But his adversaries stirred up old scandals: Blaine was not completely above reproach. Not that he had been actually dishonest, but he treated money matters with a superb negligence. Like Panurge, he knew a thousand ways of spending it and some ways of earning it that were not altogether orthodox. Moreover, he had the bad luck to suffer from sunstroke on the eve of the convention; a report was circulated that he was dead; this rumor spoiled his chances and the party nominated Rutherford B. Hayes, governor of Ohio, a respectable retired general with a long square beard, who would have liked all citizens to be disciplined soldiers and was saddened when he found them unreasonable. The Democrats had found another man of fine character, Governor Samuel J. Tilden of New York. It was a year when honesty was at a premium, but the devil still held the strings. Although Blaine had not been nominated, it was he who imposed on the party its campaign issue, "Emancipation of the Negroes," and its slogan, "Vote as you shot." Blaine still believed in the virtues of "the bloody shirt." In the South the election was carried on amid great disorders; there was violence, fraud, and confusion. One hundred eighty-five votes were required for election. When it became known that Tilden, the Democrat, had one hundred eighty-four votes to his credit, it was thought he had been elected. But the returns from three states, Florida, Louisiana, South Carolina, and one vote from Oregon, were contested. A long debate began in Congress.

The election officials in Louisiana and Florida were Republicans. They received tempting promises and, under pretexts as ingenious as they were fallacious, threw out a sufficient number of ballots to give these two states to Hayes. The Democrats protested violently. Law and common sense would have proclaimed Tilden President. But the Republicans had had long acquaintance with the machinery of government. They exhibited an energy and an absence of scruple which, added to the confusion, turned their defeat into victory. As the Constitution had not provided for this situation, Congress passed a law creating an electoral commission composed of ten members of Congress, five representatives, five senators, and five members of the Supreme Court, four of whom were to be designated by Congress. The four judges were to name the fifth. At first they selected an independent, but he was elected senator from Illinois and refused to preside. Judge Bradley, a Republican, replaced him, and the Republicans having thenceforth a majority on the commission gave themselves a majority in the election, with a cynicism which was rewarded by success. This solution was adopted on March 2. It was time. The President was to be inaugurated two days later. Hayes accepted his artificial victory, not without scruples of conscience. He wondered whether he had really been elected.

It is a great proof of Americans' respect for their government and of their love of order that the Democrats acquiesced in the strange procedure that made Hayes President. No doubt there would have been less complaint if Hayes had not given assurances to the southern politicians. In return for their support he promised them not to employ federal troops to maintain the carpetbaggers, which amounted to saying that white domination would be immediately re-established. And so the Civil War was finally over and the Republican Hayes had done for the South "what no Democratic President could have done." From the day when the federal troops were withdrawn, the Negroes in the South in effect lost the right of suffrage. In some cases the southern states imposed conditions compatible with the Fifteenth Amendment, but which deprived the Negroes of their vote (a voter had to know how to read and write, or have had a grandfather who voted, which was not the case with any Negro); in some cases they were restrained by violence from entering the polls; finally, in some cases they were intimidated by threats. Many Republicans still talked of the necessity of exacting respect for the Constitution. But a white Democratic bloc had formed in the South and it was all-powerful. It was what has been called the Solid South, composed of ten states of the former Confederacy. Henceforth it was to be improper and almost inconceivable for a white man in the South not to vote the Democratic ticket. Since the Civil War the party had found itself barred from the Presidency; its members seemed compelled to renounce all political places and influence in the nation. But the tabu remained inflexible. A white man in the South who voted for the Republicans was a traitor.

President Hayes was an excellent executive and as impartial as possible, but nevertheless he had a difficult administration. The Republicans themselves were not fond of the President they had elected with so much difficulty. They found him too fair-minded, too moderate, and they referred to him as "Granny Hayes." They accused him of making former Confederates postmasters, a heinous crime. "He has no idea," members of the party said, "of what is popular." However, he had a very clear idea of what was wise. He found excellent solutions for several thorny questions. The importation of Chinese labor at low wages was irritating the workmen of California. Hayes reached an agreement with the Chinese government to limit this immigration. Strikes of great violence, accompanied by incendiarism and bloodshed, broke out in Pittsburgh and Chicago in 1877; the President summoned the militia of several states and re-established order. But he noted in his journal: "The strikes have been put down by force; but now for the real remedy. Can't something be done by education of the strikers, by judicious control of the capitalists, by wise general policy to end or diminish the evil?" And in fact these were the problems that America now had to solve.

Hayes was also at odds with the owners of the silver mines. In the seventies, many European countries went on a gold basis, and in addition enormous deposits of silver had been discovered in Nevada and the production of silver had increased more than tenfold. Up until this time silversmiths had absorbed all the available silver so that Congress in 1873 had been able to suspend the minting of silver money without irritating anyone. When the silversmiths became incapable of using the enormous output of metal, the silver states began to demand the free coinage of silver at the old ratio of sixteen to one. A law, the Bland-

Allison Bill, required the government to buy each month between two and four million dollars' worth of silver. But as the value of silver in relation to gold had fallen, by 1880, the market value of the silver dollar had declined to eighty-eight and a half cents. It was absurd to try to impose upon the public and upon foreign nations a currency in whose value no reasonable person could believe. But absurdity has never stopped fanaticism or selfish interests.

Hayes, an honest man and a good executive, should have had a second term. His honesty brought him into conflict with his party "machine," a powerful combination of politicians, great and small, whose purpose was to influence the voters. The elementary cogs in the machine were the local organizations. Each city had its boss who distributed offices and favors and harvested the votes. In New York Tammany Hall remained the headquarters of the Democratic machine. In a metropolis where each year thousands of immigrants arrived who did not know the language or the laws of the country, Tammany could render innumerable services. From the moment of the immigrant's arrival the machine guided him in his undertakings, helped him to become naturalized, and asked nothing in return except his vote. The system had its advantages, for the aid thus given to these unfortunates was useful and genuine. The small services of the machine resembled those that a French deputy used to render his constituents. But there were abuses. In cities that were growing constantly and rapidly, electric light, transportation, and police services had to be developed. Too often this was an occasion for the friends of the machine to enrich themselves. Politics became for many adventurers a high road to wealth. In the name of one or the other of the two great parties one man would seek a well-paid position; another a streetcar concession; a third, a contract for paving or for the construction of some municipal building. Too often the electoral machine was made the agent of private interests.

These manipulations were rendered easier by the two great parties' lack of principles. In theory, the Republican party was supposed to be nationalist and favorable to industry, while the Democratic party was the defender of states' rights and of agriculture. But the Civil War had altered loyalties. The farmers of the West voted the Republican ticket in memory of Lincoln. Because of its struggle against slavery, the Republican party had also enlisted a certain number of intellectuals. It so completely dominated a large section of the country that to many Americans "not to be a Republican seemed a curious infirmity." The Democrats got almost as many votes at election time as their adversaries, but the nature of these votes accounted for their relative weakness. Their party was hardly more than an aggregate of minorities: the South, because of the memory of the war; Irish Catholics because of their opposition to the Protestant majority; Germans because they were afraid that the Anglo-Saxon Puritans would favor prohibition and thus deprive them of their beer. In the absence of great political discussions on questions of principle, the interests dictated the platforms. In New York state two senators, the stately Roscoe Conkling and the cynical Thomas C. Platt, nicknamed "Me Too" Platt because he followed Conkling in everything, ran things to suit themselves with the aid of the Collector of the Port, Chester Arthur. The latter, at great expense to the government, multiplied useless offices in order to give them to his friends. Hayes dismissed him, an act which aroused the hatred of the machine which, having got him elected President, thought it could count on his gratitude and support.

In 1880 the Republican party was cut in two. The *Stalwarts*, or, in other words, "The Toughs," were for the spoils system, for compulsory contributions by officeholders to the party funds, for high tariffs, for votes for Negroes, for the machine. The *Half Breeds* were "The Softies," the reformists who had the effrontery to think that all was not for the best in the best of all possible parties. "The Toughs" had had the idea of advocating another term for Grant, who had just returned from a triumphal world tour and was still playing to a good house. "The Softies" were thinking of Blaine or John Sherman, Secretary of the Treasury. But the convention had one of those sudden impulses to which assemblies are subject and, crying, "Anything to beat Grant!" it nominated the obscure General James A. Garfield of Ohio. To appease the great tumult of "The Stalwarts," one of their own men, Chester Arthur, the customs collector who had been dismissed by Hayes, was chosen as Vice President. The election of Garfield exasperated the masters of the machine, Roscoe Conkling and "Me Too" Platt, who went to the length of handing in their resignations as senators. Four months after the inauguration, a half-demented fanatic and disappointed office-seeker, Charles Guiteau, fired on the President, saying: "I am a Stalwart of Stalwarts. Arthur is President now!" Garfield languished for several months, then died, which did indeed put Chester Arthur into the White House. Once more events showed to what extent the law which makes the Vice President heir presumptive of the President exposed the country to surprises. In this case, however, the surprise was a happy one, for Chester Arthur, whom everyone thought completely partisan, proved reasonable and moderate.

CHAPTER XLVI

Grover Cleveland and His Time

FOR almost twenty-five years the Republican party had been master of the country, and no one could say that the use it had made of its power had been either happy or adroit. By its policy of reprisal it had earned the hatred of the South. Because of the corruption of some of those whom it had put in office it had lost the confidence of the public. It retained the favor of the business world and of the veterans of the Civil War, but its majority was narrow and precarious. Within the party itself many respectable citizens were hoping for reform. These were surprised and irritated when in 1884 the magnetic James G. Blaine was chosen as candidate by the Republican convention. Blaine was the most loved and the most hated man of his time. His wife, who adored him, wrote during his absence: "I miss his constant attention and his no less constant neglect." He was the avowed and willing champion of government of the politicians, by the politicians, for the politicians. It was at least a clearly defined attitude. Blaine had been speaker of the House of Representatives, senator and Secretary of State under Garfield. He belonged to that school of politicians who make friendship a remunerative profession. He was marvelously proficient in putting his arm around the shoulders of an adversary in the most engaging fashion. He had a reputation, rightly or wrongly, for tolerating corruption and even participating in it himself. There was talk of a certain compromising letter which ended with the postscript: "Burn this letter." Roscoe Conkling himself, who was neither a saint nor squeamish, had refused to campaign for Blaine, saying: "I do not engage in criminal practice." This was unfair, but a certain number of party leaders decided in disgust to vote for the Democratic candidate provided only that he was an honest man. These eminent turncoats were ironically called Mugwumps, an Indian name meaning great chieftains. The nomination by the Democrats of Grover Cleveland satisfied the Mugwumps.

Grover Cleveland, a brave and energetic man, had little genius, but he did have solid intelligence, common sense, and character. He had first been employed as a clerk in a grocery store, then went by chance at the age of eighteen to see an uncle in Buffalo and remained there in a lawyer's offices. Entering public life, he became sheriff of the county. His brutal honesty and his courage attracted attention, and in 1881 he was elected mayor of Buffalo and later governor of New York. "I never sought an office of any kind," he said, and it was true. In these two posts he proved that he had the stature to resist the most cynical businessmen and the most cunning politicians. "He had a real gift of silence" and deserved the nickname of "the veto mayor." He won friends by his frankness. "They talk about the importance of playing politics," he said. "Look at the men who played it. Have they got as far, after all, as I have?" He was not cultured, but from time to time he coined an excellent phrase: "A public office is a public trust. . . . It is a condition that confronts us, not a theory." When the tide of revolt against the Republican party mounted it carried Grover Cleveland to the head of the reformers. His enemies tried to make capital of his private life: he had had an illegitimate child in Buffalo. His friends asked him what they should say in reply. "Whatever you say, tell the truth," he answered. The Republicans chanted: "Ma! Ma! where is my Pa? Gone to the White House. Ha! Ha! Ha!" to which the Democrats replied: "Burn this letter, James G. Blaine. Burn this letter, James G. Blaine." The contest was close and the result depended on New York state. There Irish Catholics were powerful. A Republican supporter, the Reverend Dr. Burchard, committed the incredible blunder of describing the Democratic party as standing for: "Rum, romanism and rebellion," that is as being anti-prohibitionist, Catholic, and southern. It has been claimed that this unfortunate and offensive phrase, sedulously exploited by the Democrats, gave New York to Grover Cleveland, who was elected President, breaking his party's jinx and defeating the magnetic Blaine. "It is all horror to me," wrote the charming Mrs. Blaine. "I was certain of the election." As for Cleveland, he learned of his election while working at the governor's desk in Albany. "Well, anyhow," he said, "we'll finish up the work." He demonstrated his courage, on inauguration day, by delivering a grave speech without aid of notes at the Capitol, and a little later, by marrying a girl who had just graduated from college. It was a happy marriage. Success seemed to come as the reward of courage. "Sometimes I wake at night in the White House," said the President, "and rub my eyes and wonder if it is not all a dream."

Nevertheless Cleveland's position was difficult. He wanted to reform the civil service and safeguard most offices against the spoils system; the Mugwumps adjured him not to dismiss any officeholders; his own famished party demanded posts. "Never allow yourself," one of the old foxes said to him, "to lose sight of the fact that politics, not poker, is our great American game. Nobody ever dreamt of starting a reform movement in poker." When he talked about keeping Republicans in office, his friends murmured ironically: "To the vanquished belong the spoils." He had to surrender in a large number of cases, but he did succeed in adding twelve thousand positions to the list of offices given for merit alone. Cleveland thought that pensions were another abuse. The veterans of the Civil War had organized themselves as the G.A.R. (Grand Army of the Republic) and were exercising a political influence that made them powerful. Agents, in return for this political support, undertook to secure pensions that were sometimes entirely unmerited. In 1879 a law concerning arrears in pensions had been passed which allowed those whose applications were approved to receive their pensions from the day when they had left the army. In 1885 there were three hundred twenty-five thousand pensioners. For those whose requests were rejected by the Pension Bureau, Congress went so far as to pass individual acts and, in 1887, decided to pension every disabled soldier who had served as much as three months, not necessarily at the front, and was dependent upon his own exertions or on the support of others. Cleveland vetoed this law and also a good number of the individual acts. The G.A.R. was especially enraged because Cleveland had not fought in the war and because he was proposing to return their flags to the former Confederate states. He did not succeed in putting an end to the scandal of Civil War pensions and in 1890, after he had left office, a general pension law was voted which doubled the number of pensioners. In 1912 there were, counting dependents, over eight hundred thousand on the pension list. The farther one got from the war, the more warriors there were to be found.

After Cleveland's inauguration, Carl Schurz, "number one Mugwump," had gone to see him at the White House, and the President had asked him: "What is the most important question of the day?" "The tariff," Schurz replied. "I am ashamed," Cleveland said, "but I know nothing about the tariff." He studied the question. The high tariffs that had been enforced during the Civil War no longer seemed necessary. It was no longer possible to justify them as protection for the growing industries since the "war babies" had grown up and were fending quite well for themselves. On the other hand, the financial state of the country was so fine that the budget showed a surplus and it was easily possible to get along without customs duties. Cleveland adopted the principle: "Duties for revenue only." To put it another way: no protective tariffs. This aroused the anger of the manufacturers and the resentment of

Congress, which looked upon the surplus as a reservoir upon which to draw for local favors and pensions. All these resentments resulted in Cleveland's defeat in 1888 by the obscure Republican, Benjamin Harrison, a man of culture, whose chief qualifications were the fact that his father had been a congressman, his grandfather President (Tippecanoe), and his great-grandfather a signer of the Declaration of Independence. The second General Harrison had been a good soldier in the Civil War, during which he had commanded a brigade. When he learned of his election he cried: "Providence has given us the victory!" This exclamation shocked John Wanamaker of Philadelphia, treasurer of the Republican party, who had collected the funds for the campaign. Harrison, as President, was reserved, modest, cold, and therefore unpopular. He sincerely intended to refuse all compromises. But he was forced to give in, like so many others, and to expend the surplus in favors and pensions. John Wanamaker, whom he made Postmaster General, did not reform the civil service but distributed post offices to his political friends as he had been expected to do. As for pensions, the cabinet believed that "you cannot weigh the rights of veterans on apothecary's scales."

The most important law of this period was the Sherman Anti-Trust Act of 1890. Its object was to impose regulations upon manufacturers and bankers whose unchecked individualism was becoming dangerous. American industry in the course of thirty or forty years had developed in prodigious fashion. At the beginning of the century, Jefferson had thought that America would be a rural and agricultural country; it became an industrial and urban one. In 1890 one could foresee that it would outstrip all the old European nations combined. Why this triumph? The reason was that America had every advantage: She possessed the finest deposits of coal, iron, and petroleum and of ten other secondary metals; she had immense reserves of water power; she received each year from Europe new floods of labor; she offered industry a vast market without trade barriers; she produced talented inventors— Fulton of the steamboat; Morse of the telegraph; Bell of the telephone; Edison of the electric light; Sholes and Glidden of the typewriter; McCormick of agricultural machines; later Ford of the automobile; Orville and Wilbur Wright of the airplane—finally she produced daring business leaders who were not handicapped by the weight of tradition and who showed themselves ready to run great risks because they were playing for huge stakes. In a few decades America had become dotted with factories.

In the metals industries in particular concentration had been rapid. Andrew Carnegie, who had started as a workman, showed such intelligence and ability that at thirty he had made a great fortune. In 1865 he decided to devote himself exclusively to iron: rails, bridges, locomotives. When Kelly in America and Bessemer in England discovered that a blast of air could be used to convert iron into steel, Carnegie perceived the possibilities in this discovery. With the financial support of the Pennsylvania Railroad he became the great master of the steel mills of the country. Associated with Frick, the coke king, he acquired great fleets of steamers on the Great Lakes, mines, ports, and railroad companies. Thanks to him, by 1890 the production of iron and steel in the United States had passed that of Great Britain. Nevertheless, Carnegie did not have a monopoly. His rivals were numerous and powerful, and in his old age he found himself menaced by a price war. Tired out and ready to retire, he decided to mobilize his fortune for the foundations that were to survive him. In 1901 he agreed to sell all his business interests to a company, organized by the banker J. P. Morgan, which brought together most of the steel mills of the country: United States Steel, with a capital of one billion four hundred million dollars.

Thus the steel trust came into being. At first the word "trust" was used for a group of companies whose stock was placed in the hands of trustees, charged with the duty of running them; then for any combination of interests brought together to reduce competition. Many such combinations had been formed before United States Steel. John D. Rockefeller had organized Standard Oil and little by little eliminated all competitors. The great packing interests (Swift, Armour) had come to an understanding. Guggenheim had created the copper trust. There had been a sugar trust, a whisky trust, a nickel trust.

Was this concentration of businesses advantageous to the consumer? The trusts maintained that it was. Mass production in great factories, they said, reduced the cost of production and consequently the sales price. But this was not necessarily so. What would prevent the trusts in the absence of all competition from reducing the cost price without reducing the sales price, and thus augmenting their profit? Moreover, was it not unwise to permit the creation of monstrous and arbitrary fortunes which were no longer due to the work of a lifetime, as those of the former manufacturers had been, but to the stroke of a pen? Public opinion was very suspicious of the trusts. How could they be controlled? A corporation could be organized in any state whatever; although it might carry on business in the whole country, it need obey only the laws of the chosen state. Naturally corporations were organized in the states which imposed no restrictions upon them, and thus left them free to act as they pleased. They made use of their strength to strangle all possible competition, for example, by obtaining from the railroad companies rebates on the shipment of their products. If some state decided to treat them severely, the trust could take refuge behind the Fourteenth Amendment, which protected a citizen from being deprived of his property rights without due process of law. This amendment, which had been originally enacted to emancipate the Negroes, had never given them any advantage whatever, but it had been carefully drafted by subtle and farsighted lawyers to protect private property and, thanks to the support of the Supreme Court, it had performed this supplementary function marvelously well.

In 1887 Congress had voted a law governing interstate commerce, and an Interstate Commerce Commission had been created to control the commerce of the nation, but a long time was to elapse before these measures became effective. The Sherman Anti-Trust Act of 1890 ruled: (a) that every contract, combination, or conspiracy in restraint of trade between the states or with foreign nations was illegal; (b) that any person who attempted to monopolize any part of this commerce was guilty of a crime. The obvious intent of the law was to allow federal courts to intervene, for by virtue of the Constitution Congress had the right to legislate on commerce between the states. But the Sherman Act did not clearly define what constituted a violation, and it was hard to enforce. Nevertheless some measure was necessary. The active and greedy individualism that had dominated industry since the Civil War had served its purpose. To its aggressiveness was due the commercial development of the country. But if all businesses ended by being concentrated in a few hands, if all competition became an illusion, if a single trust dominated each industry, what would become of the spirit of initiative and daring that had made the new America? What recourse would the public have? And was it not to be feared that political liberties themselves might one day be menaced by an economic oligarchy? In both of the great parties groups of reformers were beginning to ask these questions.

CHAPTER XLVII

Upon a Cross of Gold

THE America of 1890 was a rich but unsatisfied country. Among the masses a wave of discontent was mounting. Why? Because the last frontier had been reached, because good lands were becoming rare, because the farmer and the workmen were not receiving a large enough share in the wealth of the country, because the tariffs were increasing the cost of manufactured goods while the price of agricultural products was falling, because the new type of immigrants seemed less easily assimilable than the old. As late as 1880 the majority of immigrants were Anglo-Saxon, Irish, German and Scandinavian. After 1880, and especially from 1890 to 1910, the south and southwest of Europe, and Poland as well, poured millions of families into the United States. These late arrivals, finding no free land, settled in the cities, forming foreign quarters where for a long time they remained loyal to their native languages and customs. The foreign workmen's ignorance and their immediate needs forced them to accept low wages. American workmen suffered from this continuously replenished source of competition. They had to organize to maintain their wages.

But if, of all the working classes in the world, that in the United States was at that time the one most in need of protection by a powerful trade union, it was also the one in which such an organization seemed hardest to promote. The obstacles were, on the one hand, a constant influx of immigrants who did not speak English, whom no propaganda could reach, and who had an urgent need of work; and on the other hand, the federal character of the country. If one state demanded conditions for labor which the manufacturers thought too favorable, the latter had the option of transporting their factories to a less liberal state. Moreover, public opinion and the courts of law were generally hostile to organized labor. For a long time the only use made of the Sherman Anti-Trust Act was as a weapon against what the judge's called "workmen's conspiracies." Nevertheless labor unions slowly developed. The order of the Knights of Labor, open to all workmen, proposed to assure them of a share in the profits. In 1881 Samuel Gompers, a Dutch tobacco worker, who had studied European trade unionism, organized the American Federation of Labor. His policy was like that of the British trade unions. It was cautious, adroit, non-violent, and little by little it gained the confidence of a public that had at first been hostile. As for the syndicalist and revolutionary groups, they remained sporadic and unimportant until 1905, at which date the Independent Workers of the World became organized.

More discontented even than the workmen were the farmers. "The Grange" had disappeared, but not the spirit of the Grange. The farmers were suffering from a deflation of agricultural prices which made it impossible for them to pay the interest on their borrowings. Mary Lease, the "Pythoness of Kansas" advised them "to raise less corn and more hell." Many lands of the Middle West were mortgaged. The situation was the same as in the time of Jackson. The new states had been fitted out on borrowed money. Speculators had pushed land prices to too high a level. The debt-ridden West accused its creditor, the East, of being responsible for its ills and demanded a more abundant currency to increase the price of its products. The grievances of the western pioneers were comprehensible. They had crossed prairies and deserts; they had wrung harvests from a hitherto sterile land. And what was their reward? Poverty. Toward 1890 they tried to join up with some labor groups to form a new party— the People's Party or the Populists. In 1891 they held a convention in Cincinnati and wrote a platform which included free coinage of silver, abolition of national banks, an income tax, nationalization of the railroads, and election of United States senators by popular suffrage. As presidential candidate in the election of 1892 they nominated James B. Weaver, who received a million votes and carried several states. This unusual success of a third party showed the extent of discontent among the people. The two old parties had nominated proved candidates: Cleveland and Harrison. Cleveland was elected.

A commercial crisis of the first order was in preparation. All the premonitory signs could be detected. The building of railroads and of cities had stopped. Goods no longer found a ready market. Unemployment was increasing. The Democratic Party was split on the question of silver money. For a long time eastern Democrats had favored hard money, southern and western Democrats easy money. It was the old debate between industrial and agrarian democracy, between debtor and creditor, between inflation and deflation. But in the nineties the advocates of inflation were no longer in favor of Greenbackism. They preached bimetallism. Why? Because they thought it dangerous to make prices dependent on the supply of ore metal—gold; because they had an impression that Great Britain was attempting to force upon the world a single gold standard; because some of the western states were large producers of silver. Impoverished miners, farmers, and workmen looked to silver as their salvation. To many, it became an international controversy. "Why must we accept for our money the metal England selects?" To others it was a class question. Silver was the money of the people, gold the money of the millionaire. Monometallists objected that if the government of the United States undertook to exchange gold for silver at a fixed ratio of 16 to 1, and other countries did not agree, there would be a run on the Treasury's gold.

Cleveland took a position for hard money. "He was an eastern Democrat with little to distinguish him from a Republican but his views on tariffs and on the crimes of Jeff Davis," comments D. W. Brogan. He had to decide whether he would please Main Street or Wall Street. Against the agrarian wing of his party, he chose Wall Street, or at least orthodox economy, and asked Congress to repeal the Sherman Silver Purchase Act, which made it obligatory for the government to purchase silver at the expense of the gold reserve. Despite the senators from the seven silver states, the President had his way. Then, since gold continued to flee the country, Cleveland decided to sell government bonds. Finding no buyers, he turned to Wall Street. J. P. Morgan agreed to supply the Treasury with sixty-two million dollars in gold in exchange for 4 per-cent bonds. Part of this gold came from abroad, and this improved the situation. Cleveland's enemies said that the conditions he had made were much too advantageous to the banker. He maintained, on the contrary, that he had been very fortunate in finding Mr. Morgan. From this time on, Cleveland was hated by the breadwinning multitude as no President since Johnson had been. Bimetallists called him "Shylock," "vampire," "the tool of Wall Street." Beneath the storm of insults he remained stoic and immovable.

His difficulties became even greater when labor troubles broke out. At the end of 1893 the crisis was in full swing with the usual accompaniments of reduced salaries, bankruptcies, and discharged workmen. An army of unemployed, led by Jacob Coxey, a businessman from Ohio, marched on Washington. Coxey demanded that Congress issue five hundred million dollars in bonds for road construction designed to give work to the unemployed. This "Army of the Commonwealth of Ohio" was due to bring the protests of the people to Congress on May 1. Its strength was small but the newspapers gave it a great deal of publicity. Coxey was arrested by the police for "walking on the grass" at the Capitol. His army encamped in Washington and finally was disbanded and given free tickets to return home. In the summer of 1894 a strike broke out in the Chicago Pullman works. Because of the crisis, Pullman had discharged four thousand workmen and employees and reduced the wages of others. The personnel, knowing the immense reserves of the company, thought the company might have held off and proposed to submit the question to arbitration. When the company refused, the railroad union, of which Eugene V. Debs, a Socialist, was president, refused to handle Pullman cars. Soon stations and tracks were blocked. John P. Altgeld, the Democratic and Populist governor of Illinois, sympathized with the strikers and refused to intervene. When Cleveland saw that the strike was producing riots, he sent federal troops to Chicago on the pretext that the strikers were holding up the United States mail. The governor protested: The President's action was, said Altgeld, contrary to states' rights, the fetish of the Democratic party. Debs called for a general strike of all labor organizations, but a conference of labor unions refused to follow him. He was arrested and imprisoned on a charge of conspiracy to kill. He was acquitted on that count but later sentenced to six months' imprisonment for contempt of court. Cleveland had broken the strike but his unpopularity soon became greater than ever. In the Democratic party a revolt took shape against a leader who, it was said, was following Republican policies and "prostituting the government in the service of capitalists."

Cleveland was assailed also for having offered to return the Hawaiian Islands to the native queen who was their legitimate ruler. The latter had been deposed in the time of President Harrison by a provisional white government which had had the support of the United States. Cleveland proposed to restore her to the throne if she would abandon her plans for vengeance against the Americans. She proved unreasonable and the islands were later annexed (July, 1898). But Cleveland had energetically maintained the United States traditional doctrine: respect for small nations and the supremacy of right over might. This earned him new insults. On the other hand, he was acclaimed for the first time in his administration when he refused to give in to England on the question of the frontier between Venezuela and British Guiana. Venezuela had appealed to the United States. The State Department had protested in the name of the Monroe Doctrine and Lord Salisbury had replied, in effect, that it had better mind its own business. Cleveland sent a message to Congress in which he asked for an appropriation to send an American commission, charged with the duty of adjusting the question of Venezuela's frontier, while taking into full account the responsibilities involved and the possible consequences. This meant that he was not afraid of war with England. But English public opinion was opposed at all costs to war. The protests of members of Parliament led Lord Salisbury, who had common sense and who, moreover, knew his case was good, to accept arbitration which in part upheld the English claims.

When his term ended in 1896, Cleveland had earned lasting hatreds.

But public hatreds are phenomena and not judgments. Cleveland had been a statesman, an energetic leader, a rock in the midst of the tempest. He was to die saying: "I have tried so hard to act well. . . ." and he had the right to say it. His enemies had nicknamed him "His Obstinacy." His Democratic friends, to replace him, looked about for a man more responsive to the will of the people. They found William Jennings Bryan. Cleveland had said: "The citizen must serve the nation; not the nation the citizen." Bryan would have liked to put the government at the disposal of the public. A little Nebraska lawyer, a native of Illinois, naturally eloquent and handsome of face, he had won election to Congress in 1890 by a majority of seven thousand in a district that had been Republican two years before. In Congress he made speeches on the tariff and the silver question that attracted wide attention. In 1894 he began to travel through the Middle West preaching the gospel of the free coinage of silver, and begging his party to be on the side of the people and not on the side of "the idle holders of idle capital." His fine presence, his "moral seriousness," and his sincerity gave him a tremendous hold on the crowds. When he came to the Democratic convention of 1896 as a delegate from Nebraska, and cried in his ringing voice: "I am come to speak in defense of a cause as holy as the cause of liberty—the cause of humanity," he moved all the delegates. He was (perhaps unconsciously) an excellent actor and a brilliant rhetorician; he aroused frantic enthusiasm. "His speech contained everything that might appeal to popular prejudices: praise of the pioneers, defiance of England, acceptance of martyrdom." He concluded: "Having behind us the producing masses of this nation and the world, supported by the commercial interests, the laboring interests, and the toilers everywhere, we will answer their demand for a gold standard by saying to them: 'You shall not press down upon the brow of labor this crown of thorns, you shall not crucify mankind upon a cross of gold.'" The applause lasted for an hour and all the delegations filed by and dipped their flags before the flag of Nebraska. As a result of this speech, Bryan was nominated as the Democratic candidate. The Populist party also agreed to support him. They had no alternative, as he had run away with their platform. Silver Republicans also came to him, while many gold Democrats flocked to the opposite party. "I am a Democrat still, very still," said Senator David Hill of New York, when asked if he was going to bolt Bryan. His remark represented the feeling of a good many other Democrats. Bryan, the "boy orator," was only thirty-six, but his followers made him "the new Lincoln," "the lion of Nebraska." The Republican "gold-bugs" nominated Major William McKinley of Ohio, a retired officer and a professional politician, well educated and well dressed.

"Wall Street's new guardian." Homer Davenport's caricature of Mark Hanna in the dollar mark suit, displacing the statue of George Washington in front of the subtreasury building in New York City. Campaign of 1896, in which the wealth of the Republican party as mobilized by Hanna elected McKinley.

The "Majah" had "the face of an Italian ecclesiastic of the fifteenth century." "What a priest he would have made!" said Monseigneur Ireland. In his state, of which he was governor, he was beloved as "a skillful conciliator, an agreeable neighbor and everybody's friend." He was especially admired by Mr. Marcus A. Hanna, "Uncle Mark," a rich businessman of Ohio, the owner of mines, oil wells, and street railways, who was ready to spend a great deal of money in politics. Mark Hanna had decided to pilot McKinley into the White House. First he got the Republican nomination for him, then he set to work to launch him throughout the country. The election slogan was "McKinley and the Full Dinner Pail." Hanna secured contributions from manufacturers and insurance companies and went so far as to exact a fixed percentage of the capital of the big banks. Thus he amassed four, some say six or ten, million dollars for the election campaign. He employed eighteen hundred speakers. Many a big firm ordered its employees to vote for McKinley. The Democratic party received contributions from the owners of silver mines, but they did not show themselves very generous and the party fund did not amount to one-tenth of the Republican fund. Bryan traveled feverishly from one ocean to the other, making six hundred speeches in fourteen weeks. This "Battle of the Standards" was the hardest presidential campaign since Lincoln's in 1860. Bryan's crusade made an overwhelming impression on the people of America. Right or wrong, he was a splendid speaker and had a noble presence. One of his principal subjects was, of course, silver money. Suppose the international bankers were opposed to it; why should America accept the ukase of the international bankers? Why give the metal gold, amassed in the East, preference over the metal silver, which the West produced in abundance? He had said in his convention speech: "You tell us that the great cities are in favor of the gold standard; we reply that the great cities rest upon our broad and fertile prairies. Burn down your cities and leave our farms and your cities will spring up again as if by magic; but destroy your farms and the grass will grow in the streets of every city in the country." McKinley was elected by a large majority. Gold and industry had won over silver and agriculture. But Bryan had received six and a half million votes. Incidentally, this election tolled the knell of Populism. As to the Democrats, having chosen a western leader they now stood very low in the eyes of the eastern businessmen, but they had a chance of becoming one day the party of the masses.

CHAPTER XLVIII

America Enters the World

PRESIDENT McKINLEY was a perfect man, almost too perfect. He was honest, scrupulous, kindly, indulgent, responsive to popular desires. "He was the incarnation of the ballot box in its noblest mood." "He had the art of throwing a moral gloss over policies which were dubious, and this he did with a sort of self-deceiving sincerity." Six different senators would recommend six different protégés to him for the same office and he would send each of them away convinced that his man would be nominated, whereas he himself had long since settled on a seventh candidate. At his side watched the Warwick who had made this king, Marcus Hanna of Ohio, ambassador to Washington "of a triumphant plutocracy." Neither Senator Hanna nor President McKinley had any desire to become involved in discussions of international policy. What interested them was the business world, its prosperity, the maintenance of the tariff, and the victory of the gold standard. But these questions which had stirred up such violent emotions quickly fell into second place. In 1896 thousands of Americans had been ready to fight for silver money. Then came the discovery of gold mines in the Klondike and in South Africa; this had led to a drop in the value of gold and a rise in prices; in the Middle West an abundant harvest had been sold at a good price; and the searchlight of public opinion had swung in another direction.

For a long time the citizens of the United States had entertained great contempt for the imperialism of European powers. No doubt their own "manifest destiny" had led them, also, to conquer territories, but sooner or later these territories had been admitted as states of the Union. In every instance "the Constitution had followed the flag." About 1890, since the last frontier had officially disappeared, certain Americans began to think that manifest destiny might not stop at the shores of the ocean. A great historian and strategist, Captain Mahan, elucidated in his works the role played in the life of nations by navies and naval bases. Senator Henry Cabot Lodge of Massachusetts wrote: "From the Rio Grande to the Arctic Ocean there must be only one flag, one country." It was necessary, said the senator, to dig a canal between the two oceans; for the protection of this canal and that of American commerce in the Pacific, it would be useful to control the Hawaiian Islands and to have at least one base in the

West Indies. "And," continued this Yankee Picrochole, "when the Nicaraguan Canal has been constructed the Island of Cuba will become a necessity for us." In McKinley's time these ideas had been disseminated by a nationalistic press. They were no longer simply the ideas of a few imperialists, they found favor with the masses as well as with the Daughters of the American Revolution. A minority of intellectual liberals and pacifists opposed this doctrine, but one can imagine cases in which the passions of the liberals and those of imperialists would coincide—for example, if it were a question of coming to the aid of a small nation oppressed by a great power. Americans were warmhearted; the character of Don Quixote appealed to them; they asked nothing better than to play that role on the international stage; it was ironical that they should have had to play it for the first time against the country of Cervantes.

The question of Cuba had concerned more than one administration. The island lay close to the continent; Americans had large commercial interests there; they bought its sugar and tobacco; Spanish domination there had been accepted reluctantly. But the United States had not officially intervened in any of the numerous Cuban revolutions. As long as the controversy between the North and the South continued, the Cuban affair had been judged, not on its own merits, but for its possible repercussions on the politics of the United States. Later the Cuban Revolution of 1868 had aroused warm sympathy in North America; the Cuban flag had been flown in New York. But the North, which had just defended a government's right to stamp out rebellion, could hardly refuse this same right to the Spanish government. In 1895 a new Cuban Revolution, due in large measure to American tariffs, which were ruining the Cuban planters and forcing down salaries on the island, was suppressed with extreme severity by the Spanish General Weyler. He organized concentration camps (*reconcendrado*); it was reported that women and children died in them by the thousands. Certain newspapers exaggerated the Spanish atrocities and launched a campaign for war as one might launch a campaign for a new cigarette. One of them gambled three million dollars that war would come. The Cubans' desire for independence pleased the many American liberals who were hostile in principle to every authoritarian monarchy. The Cleveland administration made an attempt to persuade the Spaniards to grant the island autonomy, but firmly resisted the newspaper campaign for military intervention.

By 1897 the anarchy in Cuba had begun to disturb Americans who had plantations there. Spain refused to assume responsibility for the havoc caused by the insurrection. American citizens were arrested and maltreated. McKinley began negotiations and hoped that he could reach a solution that would give the island independence in fact while maintaining, in order to satisfy Spanish honor, a bond with Spain analogous to that which unites Canada to England. When the liberal, Sagasta, came to power in Spain and General Weyler was recalled, it seemed likely that patience was to be rewarded. But in February, 1898, a new incident occurred. The Spanish ambassador in Washington, Señor Dupuy de Lome, wrote a letter to one of his friends in which he described McKinley as a hesitant and opportunistic politician. The letter fell into the hands of Hearst's New York *Journal*, which published it. Dupuy de Lome was forced to resign. The cruiser *Maine* was sent to Havana to protect American citizens. Senator Hanna, who was opposed to war, did not approve this measure. He said it was like amusing oneself by throwing a lighted match into an oil well. Events quickly proved him right. On February 15, 1898, the *Maine* blew up and a large part of the crew were killed. What caused the explosion? Several hypotheses seemed tenable: an accident, a premeditated crime by the Spanish government, a crime committed by individuals, a crime planned by the insurgents to provoke war. The truth was not known and never will be known, but American public opinion held the Spanish government responsible. As years before the cry had been: "Remember the Alamo!" the cry now was "Remember the Maine!" The Spanish government, which did not want war, tried to negotiate. It offered to accept an inquiry and arbitration; it asked the pope to intervene; it even offered autonomy to the Cubans. But McKinley sent his war message to Congress, fearing that if he did not go the whole way he would cut his party in two. On the nineteenth of April Congress declared that a state of war existed between the United States and Spain. Senator Hanna was not happy.

"It has been a splendid little war," wrote, later on, John Hay, the learned, ironical, and charming Secretary of State, one of the best diplomats of his time and a man who tried to follow both the golden rule and the Monroe Doctrine. It was indeed a war without anguish, in which victory never changed sides, for which the enthusiasm of the country was unanimous, and in which Democrats and Republicans, northerners and southerners were united once more in the service of a single common cause. A former southern general wrote a patriotic song of reconciliation:

> He laid away his suit of grey—
> To wear the Union blue. . . .

In the eyes of a minority it was an imperialist's war, but necessary; in those of the majority it was an idealist's war. It was a question of freeing their unhappy and oppressed neighbors. No one doubted that there would be a quick victory, and yet on examination of the facts such a doubt would have been reasonable. The American navy seemed to be in good shape and it proved its excellence in action. On the other hand, the army had been sadly neglected: It numbered barely eighty thousand men, and for the one hundred twenty-five thousand volunteers who were summoned there was great difficulty in supplying arms and uniforms. The Spanish army, though more numerous, was ill equipped and badly commanded. A small American expeditionary force of seventeen thousand men was able to capture Cuba, thanks to the support of the fleet, which destroyed a Spanish squadron in the Bay of Santiago. There, an Assistant Secretary of the Navy, who had resigned his office to take command of a regiment of Rough Riders, won distinction. His name was Theodore Roosevelt. In the Pacific, Commodore Dewey with a small squadron appeared in Manila Bay and destroyed the Spanish fleet without losing a ship or a man, beneath the jealous eye of a German admiral and the friendly eye of an English admiral. However, it was not until August 13, after peace had been signed, that the city of Manila was taken with the aid of Philippine insurgents commanded by Emilio Aguinaldo. As for the Spanish island of Puerto Rico, resistance there was so brief that one humorist spoke of the campaign as a large-scale picnic or a moonlight excursion.

Spain signed a treaty in Paris, though the conditions were bitter. She gave up Cuba and ceded Puerto Rico, Guam, and the Philippines to the United States, the latter in return for twenty million dollars. It was the end of the Spanish empire, and it was galling for this proud nation to lose its last possessions in the very location where she had been the first to introduce Western civilization. For the United States this victory raised serious questions of principle. It was a time when Kipling in England was justifying imperialistic policies and praising the white man for accepting the burden of power. Many liberal Americans believed that "the white man's burden" threatened rather to be a burden for the red, black, and yellow man. In November, 1898, an anti-imperialist league had been organized in Boston by Charles Francis Adams and Carl Schurz; its program was to oppose the acquisition of colonies. So far as Cuba was concerned this doctrine triumphed. General Leonard Wood stayed there only long enough to allow a convention to prepare a constitution. But Cuba had to undertake never to enter into agreements involving her sovereignty without the consent of the United States; to lease or sell to the United States necessary naval bases; to accept the intervention of the Washington government in the event of an attack upon the island by a foreign country approved his foreign policy. The voters did in fact remain loyal to him and gave him a second term. Bryan once again was his rival, and since the bi-metallist furor had waned, he made an anti-imperialist campaign. He maintained that "every government that is not founded on the consent of the governed is a tyranny," that "an empire can no longer be a republic," and that the ideas expressed in the Declaration of Independence were not compatible with the government of enslaved populations: "We must abandon our fine contempt for other nations which govern by force. . . . We must either abandon this protectorate or renounce those principles for which our fathers fought in the Revolution. . . ." The anti-imperialists Adams and Schurz supported Bryan, though they thought him mad. The country showed more prudence. McKinley won easily. He had a popular plurality of more than eight hundred thousand over Bryan, and to mark all the more clearly the national character of the election, Theodore Roosevelt, the colonel of Rough Riders who had become governor of New York, was made Vice President, contrary to his wishes and those of McKinley. As a matter of fact, the machine in New York state had made Roosevelt Vice President to get him away from Albany, where the politicians found him independent and hard to handle. But machines themselves can miscalculate, and this one, in trying to disembarrass itself of a governor, turned him into a President. For on September 6, 1901, in the first year of his second term McKinley was assassinated by an anarchist and died as he had lived, saying exactly the right thing. He had been, said John Hay, "one of the sweetest and quietest natures I have ever known among public men." The dynamic and fiery Colonel Roosevelt became President.

CHAPTER XLIX

Conclusion

FROM the Civil War to the end of the century the history of the United States is an extraordinary blend of satire and epic. The illustrious names of this period, the names that people remember, are not those of the Presidents, nor of the thinkers, but those of the captains of industry. The work accomplished verges on the miraculous. In less than half a century a continent was crisscrossed with railroads, settled, power; and finally not to contract debts the interest on which could not be met by the normal budget of the island. In Puerto Rico a compromise solution was adopted. In 1900 the citizens of the island received the right to elect a house of representatives. A council and a governor were appointed by the President of the United States. Later, in 1917, the Puerto Ricans became American citizens. The council was replaced by an elected senate, the governor alone being appointed by the United States. Today some of the Puerto Ricans hope their island will become a state of the Union; others desire independence.

The Philippine question was more complex. If America retained these distant possessions she would become a colonial power. Many Americans disliked this idea. Others felt that their consciences would be satisfied if a payment were made to Spain, which was provided for in the treaty. John Hay, Secretary of State, wrote: "The only question in my mind is to know how far it is *possible* for us to evacuate the Philippines." On the other hand, the Filipinos had formed a government with Aguinaldo at its head. With an army of between thirty and forty thousand men Aguinaldo encircled Manila, which the American General Otis had occupied with about fifteen thousand men. How strong was Aguinaldo's army? Events were to show that the natives were divided. By means of a stratagem, Aguinaldo was captured. Thereafter it seemed certain that the United States would keep the islands and also Guam, between Hawaii and the Philippines, which an expedition had conquered in passing. For governing such conquered but not yet assimilated territories, the Constitution of the United States provided no machinery. The President, in his capacity of commander-in-chief, alone had authority. He appointed a commission to help him and later he sent a civil governor, Judge William Howard Taft, an amiable giant whose good sense and moderation accomplished wonders. The Americans succeeded in making the Filipinos like them, and at the time when war broke out in 1941, they had the honorable and generous intention of giving the Philippines complete independence in 1946.

But in 1900 the controversies on the subject of imperialism were violent. Many professors, philosophers, and writers thought that America would lose her soul if, like the old and corrupt nations of Europe, she began to play the colonial game. Mark Twain wrote to the President and suggested that in future the white stripes in the American flag should be replaced by black stripes and the stars by a death's head. But McKinley knew his people. Lord Salisbury had said formerly of Queen Victoria that if one wanted to know what the English masses were thinking about, all one had to do was to consult the queen. McKinley's thought was in spontaneous accord with that of the majority of Americans. He knew that at this time the cleared, exploited. But the conquistadors of the nineteenth century showed few scruples, accumulated superhuman fortunes by inhuman methods, and treated the masses who served them as fodder for their machines. Man in their eyes was a means not an end. The idealism of the past no longer possessed any power over their minds; they went to church, but they were no longer religious; they talked of liberty on election day, but they gave thought to the Constitution only to circumvent it, and to politics only to protect their own interests; they had little taste, fewer manners; and no aesthetic morality replaced their lost religious morality. It was a period of great individuals, monstrously egoistic, marvelously efficient.

Perhaps their implacable force was necessary to forge the instrument. But by the end of the century a time came when the excess of individualism made the average man's life difficult. Would plutocracy succeed in dominating democracy? That was the great question of those thirty-five years. By 1880 public opinion was demanding that businessmen be subjected to supervision and that political life be made more honest. Henry Adams said that the art of governing at that time consisted in controlling men who were socially as remote as pagan divinities, who were unknown to the voter but indispensable for him to know, and who, even if they had been flayed alive, could have found nothing to say about political values. Soon the reformers were winning out at election time over the businessmen. Occasionally the businessman, in his latter days, became a reformer. Carnegie and Rockefeller gave their fortunes to foundations which thenceforth played a role in the intellectual development of the country. In both parties the progressive wing became powerful. Laws to restrain trusts were popular. Although this period was disturbing because of its immorality, by 1890 there were numerous reassuring indications that the country had remained sound at the core. There were scandals and corruption, but both were denounced. If the evil was great, the correction was sure to follow. No one can demand perfection in human affairs. All a reasonable citizen requires is that the institutions of his country shall permit it to right itself and to oscillate about a mean point. This is the case in the United States.

This period in America was the time of historic centenaries: 1876, the anniversary of the Declaration of Independence; 1881, the anniversary of Yorktown; 1887, the anniversary of the Constitution. These milestones made it possible to measure the course that had been run. What in 1776 had been but a frail hope, the daring idea of a few men, had become in 1876 a gigantic and prosperous country, one of the most powerful in the world. The Constitution, which was so painfully elaborated in Philadelphia, had stood the test of a century and showed an amazing youthfulness. Nevertheless the America of Washington and of Jefferson was no more. The America of Hamilton had been born, a posthumous child of genius and very different from what Hamilton had imagined. A great part of the population was henceforth to live in cities. Riches and luxury took on offensive aspects. Class feeling increased. In New York the Four Hundred and the Four Million confronted each other. "The America of Fisk and of Gould, of Boss Tweed and the Crédit Mobilier," said an American writer, "fell far short of satisfying the demands of a rational civilization. After four hundred years to have produced such heroes as these, to be thus far sunk in the mud, was not the outcome of a great experiment that one could contemplate with pride." This judgment is too severe. The great experiment had produced other heroes besides Fisk and Gould, other institutions than the Crédit Mobilier. But it was true that a realistic criticism had become necessary. This had not yet found either its spokesmen or its means of expression in American letters.

The institutions adopted at the end of the eighteenth century were still functioning in fairly satisfactory fashion at the end of the nineteenth. This was due in part to the liberal traditions that America inherited from Great Britain, and in part to the Constitution itself. The middle-western pioneers were Anglo-Saxon by tradition. They cherished their liberties. They believed in free discussion, trial by jury, and the principle of "no taxation without representation." They had carried with them from New England the town meeting and the custom of orderly public discussion. And so the political experience of the United States had been long and sound. The executive power and the right of amendment made it possible to achieve all necessary reforms except in the case of slavery. Johnson's acquittal had preserved Congress from the temptation of putting itself above the law. Nevertheless, certain changes seemed necessary. In particular the liberals wished to have United States senators elected by popular vote. The Constitution of 1787 had given the right of electing senators to the legislatures of the different states. This indirect method of election would permit, so the Founders thought, the selection of eminent men and would free them from the necessity of campaigning for office. This was by no means unreasonable, and at the close of the century a good many senators belonged to a class of consular quality, true elders of the Republic and ambassadors from their states to Washington. But indirect election also made it easier, so said its opponents, for businessmen to get their representatives into the Senate. The Senate had become "a rich man's club" over which public opinion had almost no control. It is hard to say who was right in this controversy; however that may be, the partisans of direct election gained ground, and in 1913 an amendment to the Constitution was to change the method of election to the Senate. In some states the voters also demanded direct primaries; that is, the right of the voters in each party to choose the candidates instead of voting for candidates placed on the ticket by the "machine."

The cities grew monstrously. New York's population increased from 1,174,779 in 1860 to 3,437,202 in 1900; that of Chicago from 109,260 in 1860 to 1,698,575 in 1900. Minneapolis, St. Paul, Detroit, Cleveland, Milwaukee doubled and tripled the number of their inhabitants. The builders of this New World showed more daring than taste. The pretentious brownstone palaces built at this time along Fifth Avenue and on Riverside Drive were adorned with useless turrets; they were copies of Renaissance chateaux, Italian villas, Flemish town halls. They were filled with too heavily carved furniture, too elaborate marquetry, too heavy curtains, hideous *bibelots,* and French and English paintings of the worst periods. Godkin, founder of the weekly magazine *The Nation,* called this epoch "The Age of the Chromo" and indeed the rigors of business life awakened, through need of compensation, a bathetic sentimentalism. Crocheting was a popular pastime with the women of this period. Furniture, objects, and minds were swathed in useless covers. Dogs and Cynics wore crocheted muzzles. In 1870 the first apartment house was built on East 18th Street in New York. It was a great success, and this type of building was destined to multiply.

Fortunes were more ostentatious than formerly. A million dollars was no longer great wealth. Certain financial magnates had fifty or a hundred millions. In their homes butlers, imported from England, reigned over liveried valets and attempted to impose British traditions on their masters. Leonard Jerome gave a banquet at Delmonico's for seventy-two friends at a cost of ten thousand dollars. The centerpiece of the table was a lake on which were swans, and golden railings fenced them off from the guests. Amusements, too, in this period were lacking in taste. The principal requirement was to amaze. The first American circuses had been simple and charming, with a single ring like all European circuses. P. T. Barnum conceived the idea of showing the public two rings at the same time, then three. He had begun his career almost half a century earlier by exhibiting an old Negro woman who, he said, had been George Washington's nurse. Then he had traveled throughout the country presenting "General" Tom Thumb and the "Swedish nightingale," Jenny Lind. Now he was transporting by railroad "The Greatest

Show on Earth." Sarah Bernhardt, too, had been launched in the United States as "the greatest actress in the world." A taste for the theater was increasing. Between 1880 and 1900 the number of actors grew from five thousand to fifteen thousand. *Uncle Tom's Cabin* and *The Orphans of the Storm* made fortunes for traveling companies. It was the time when America was beginning to be a paradise for European virtuosos. Symphony orchestras were organized, in New York (1878), in Boston (1881), in Chicago (1891). In New York friends of music endowed the Metropolitan Opera (1883); every great family made it a point of honor to have its family box there, just as it had its carriage, its victoria, brougham, barouche. The automobile, at the end of the century, was no more than an experiment. But Henry Adams at the age of fifty solemnly and painfully learned to ride a bicycle.

The poverty in certain sections of the big cities was distressing. Charitable organizations made an effort, not only to bring aid to the unfortunates, but to find remedies. Settlements were founded (Henry Street in New York, Hull House in Chicago). Jane Addams at Hull House made an effort to meet the families and solve their difficulties, and to gain the friendship of the children. Charitable workers joined together in organizations. A campaign against saloons, where alcohol and prostitution held sway, was led by courageous and pious young women who knelt on the sidewalk at the doors of the saloons to pray for their closing, despite the jeers of the drunkards. The Women's Christian Temperance Union soon added action to prayer. Temperance was taught in the schools. Opposition was encountered from the "wet interests" and the immigrants from all countries who were unwilling to abandon their native customs. The Germans especially clung to their beer. In 1895 the Anti-Saloon League of America was organized and was destined to play an important part in politics. A Prohibition party even nominated candidates but without much success. Nevertheless, there were some who declared themselves in favor of the total prohibition of alcoholic beverages: certain Puritans, manufacturers who considered drink harmful to work, and part of the medical profession which held alcohol responsible for many ills.

America at the end of the century remained—and on the whole desired to remain—a Protestant country. But immigration had considerably increased the Catholic elements. In 1900 between nine and ten million Catholics (Irish, French, Italian, German, Polish) lived in the United States. In Baltimore, Cardinal Gibbons extended his protection to the workmen and their trade unions. Archbishop Ireland of St. Paul intervened in the great strikes. The Protestant churches retained their members and their church buildings on Sunday were filled, but many troubled minds were studying the conflicts between science and religion. Darwinism and Biblical criticism disturbed the sons of the Puritans. Certain liberal Protestants saw in the Bible only a beautiful book of great poetic and moral value. In more than one college professors were dismissed for teaching the new doctrines. Colonel Robert Ingersoll, an agnostic, publicly attacked the Scriptures; his position was "I don't know. I do not deny. But I do not believe." New sects—Theosophy and Christian Science—gained a numerous following. In 1895 a Christian Science church was built in Boston. Secret societies directed against the Catholics and the Jews were reborn in the South and the West. The number of Jews on the rolls in the synagogues amounted, at the close of the century, to almost a million. The levers of control in most of the professions, especially in education, remained in the hands of the Protestants.

Between 1870 and 1900 the number of pupils in the public schools increased from seven million to fifteen and a half million; in the high schools, from eighty thousand in 1875 to five hundred thousand in 1900. The states, as soon as they had the financial means, founded universities. Among the rich it became the style to make princely gifts to the old private colleges. Harvard, Yale, Princeton saw their endowments mounting. In elementary education there was still much ground to be covered. Teachers were very badly paid. Their average monthly salary at the close of the century was forty-five dollars for a man, thirty-eight dollars for a woman. Their social and moral position left much to be desired. The traditions that made education in Europe a routine sanctioned by centuries of experience were lacking here and too often curricula were turned upside down by the enthusiasts of some new fad. As for adult education, it was making real progress. Public libraries were opening everywhere. The early ones, such as the Athenaeum in Boston, were clubs and it was necessary to buy a membership in order to belong. But Andrew Carnegie gave forty-five million dollars to libraries, and others imitated him. Cities paid them tribute. About the middle of the century serious periodicals—*Harper's, The Atlantic Monthly, Scribner's*—began to make their appearance and to form the minds and taste of the public. Lecture courses were arranged by lecture societies. On the shore of Lake Chautauqua, near New York, a liberal open-air university met every summer at which adults refreshed, completed, or at need began their education. Curiosity and a taste for learning became more and more American virtues.

The names of Walt Whitman and Mark Twain were still dominant at the end of this period. After them there had been few great names in literature. Whitman himself, a professional enthusiast, admitted discouragement. He said that, although the democracy of the New World might be considered a success with respect to material progress, productivity, and a certain superficial popular culture, it was illusory and had hitherto been a complete failure in its social aspects and in every religious, moral literary, and aesthetic result. There were, however, thinkers in the Gilded Age. In philosophy, the mysticism of the transcendentalists gave place to the realism of the pragmatists. William James, Charles Peirce, and John Dewey made truth "a receipt" which is to be accepted if it works. The determinism of the savants produced a pessimism very different from the romantic hopes of the first part of the century. Among the novelists, Bret Harte and Jack London gave expression to the adventurous aspect of the West; Hamlin Garland wrote the epic of the pioneer. William Dean Howells expressed the eastern tradition, that of the sober and well-built novel. Henry James, though seduced by European culture, retained his originality in his deliberate and scrupulous style, and remained more American than he himself suspected. The exotic tree, dug up and replanted beneath other skies, if it flourishes at all, continues to put forth flowers of its own kind.

The writers and lecturers of the Gilded Age had more women than men as readers and auditors. The American man of the nineteenth century "made" money; his wife, who had more leisure, spent it in cultivating herself. American women were respected and spoiled in their own country and highly esteemed by French and English aristocrats. In 1895 Boni de Castellane married Anna Gould; and the Duke of Marlborough, Consuelo Vanderbilt. Toward the end of the century the birth rate was falling: four children per family in 1890; only three in 1900. Divorce was difficult; it remained comparatively rare. In 1887 there were twenty-seven divorces per hundred thousand citizens in the United States; in 1897, sixty-two. In 1880 two and a half million women worked; in 1890, over four million. Many professions—selling, secretarial work, journalism, medicine—were open to them; but the women who took advantage of these opportunities were still a cause of astonishment. By the end of the nineteenth century the problem of domestic help had become acute in the United States, perhaps because of the campaigns against slavery and no doubt also because the free citizens of America had no love for that sort of work. As a result, mothers of families who had a profession of their own acquired the habit of serving warmed-up canned goods in their homes. Women's clubs multiplied: book clubs, art clubs, music clubs, athletic clubs. Harriet Beecher Stowe and Julia

Ward Howe had campaigned for women's suffrage. At the end of the century the American woman was much more independent than the English or French woman. Women's colleges—Vassar, Barnard, Smith, Wellesley, Mount Holyoke, Bryn Mawr—were already flourishing.

It is the custom to speak very harshly of this Age of the Chromo. It is easy and moreover proper to condemn the immorality of its businessmen, the venality of its politicians, the inadequacy of its social laws, and the ugliness of its styles. With the Civil War a world died in America and any survivor of that world, any descendant of the Puritan fathers, found himself less at ease in the new America than an immigrant freshly arrived from Kiev or Naples. This resulted in regrets and criticisms. These must not make us forget that another world had been born. During these thirty years of feverish work, the industrial plant of the country had been created. It was to make possible the correction of many inequalities. Thanks to the powerful industries, a uniform standard of living had become possible. Mass production of clothes would soon permit men and women of modest means to dress approximately as well as the rich and to follow the annual styles. The big stores were to put at the disposal of the masses almost all those objects formerly reserved for the privileged classes. Toward the end of the century America had a great sculptor, St. Gaudens, as well as talented architects. In 1893 an exposition opened in Chicago to celebrate the four hundredth anniversary of the discovery of America and revived the classic style and inspired the average American with a desire for better-planned cities, parks, and gardens. There the middle western farmer had a taste of the new comforts which he would soon be able to afford, for, from 1894 to 1900, there was a series of good harvests sold at high prices. The population on the whole participated in the country's increased wealth. What the reformers maintained from there on, and justly, was that in the distribution of this wealth capital's part was too large. In his *New Viewpoints in American History*, A. M. Schlesinger writes:

> With the increasing complexities of modern life the feeling has grown that the liberties and opportunities of the individual can be properly safeguarded only by the protective oversight of the government. Conditions in the United States have not reached the degree of wretchedness which would give Socialism or Communism a strong popular appeal; and the dominant thought of America is agreed that intelligent social control furnishes the best preventive of ruthless individualism, on the one hand, and of government paternalism on the other.

Book Six

WORLD POWER

CHAPTER L

Theodore Roosevelt

W HAT is possible is always close to what is necessary." A reform in the political life of America had been demanded by most Americans. The reformer was sure to appear. Theodore Roosevelt had been born in 1858, of one of the oldest and most respectable New York families. In him Dutch blood was mixed with that of the French Huguenots, the Scots, the Welsh, and the Quakers of Pennsylvania. His ancestors had occupied various local administrative posts, but he, in his childhood, seemed too frail for public life. He had a narrow chest and suffered from asthma. On his father's advice he undertook to build up a strong body through will power and persistence. Daily gymnastics made him not only a normal man but an athlete with muscles of iron. In reaction against his own preferences, which were those of a historian and a man of letters, he acquired an enthusiastic taste for boxing, hunting, life in the open air, and all forms of energetic and violent action. Upon leaving Harvard, he decided to embark upon a political career. His friends said that a young man of good family, as he was, would find this a rough and disagreeable life and in general "dirty business." He replied that the true ruling classes were to be found in political committee meetings and not in fashionable drawing rooms. Then with energy and courage he plunged into the municipal life of New York.

Public life at that time was far from wholesome. A satirist summed it up as follows: "Government of the people, by the bosses, for the businessmen." Roosevelt and a group of young friends rolled up their sleeves and sailed into the prevaricators, the corrupt judges, and Senator "Me Too" Platt, grand master of the Republican machine in New York. As commissioner of civil service and president of the Police Commission of New York, he cleaned up the departments that were entrusted to his care and inspired his subordinates with a new and wholesome conception of their duties. To the dismay of the professional politicians,

WOODROW WILSON
Courtesy of the Woodrow Wilson Foundation

Davenport

"He's good enough for me." Homer Davenport's most popular cartoon in the presidential campaign of 1900. It appeared originally in the New York *Evening Mail*.

he chose his assistants without regard to party or opinions. His interest in the little people, the pains he took to discover their feelings and their needs earned him the name of Haroun al Roosevelt. In 1889 Kipling hearing him turn loose a torrent of projects and judgments on every subject in the world, got the impression that this young "Teddy" made the planet turn. But his impetuosity did not prevent him from acquiring a reputation as an efficient administrator, and at the time of the Spanish war McKinley appointed him Assistant Secretary of the Navy. His enthusiastic activity at first alarmed the members of the department. His superior, John Davis Long, said that this new assistant threatened to cause more dangerous explosions in the navy than that of the *Maine*. Happily Roosevelt himself resigned in order to go to Cuba as colonel of the Rough Riders. He believed that a man who loves his country and hopes one day to govern it should be willing to fight for it. "It was not a big war," he said almost regretfully, "but we didn't have any other." His courage made him popular, and on his return he was elected governor of New York. In this important post he so annoyed Senator Platt by his independence that in 1900 the latter, in order to get rid of him, had Roosevelt, to his disgust, nominated as candidate for the vice presidency. "Vice President?" said Roosevelt. "I don't see what I could do. I should be simply president of the Senate and that would bore me to death." Certain of the party elders did not wish any more than he did to see him nominated. Senator Marcus Hanna, the boss of bosses, asked McKinley if he had taken into consideration what would happen if by mischance "this damned cowboy" should become President of the United States. When McKinley was assassinated and the damned cowboy became President, Senator Hanna had to accept the situation. Very soon the President was calling the senator "old boy" and Senator Hanna was calling the President "Teddy." Although he was a vigorous reformer, Roosevelt knew how to make concessions to persons when superior interests demanded it. He planned to fight certain abuses; he knew that he could not do it without the support of the party and he was determined to retain that support.

When he left the White House in 1908, Theodore Roosevelt said that perhaps others had lived there longer than he had and liked it as much but certainly no one "has had as much fun there as we had." By *we* he meant his family as well as himself. The Roosevelt children, mounted on stilts or roller skates, dashed through the sacred corridors like whirlwinds; while the President, as young as his children, played tennis, rode horseback, and took lessons in boxing and jiujitsu from Mike Donovan. All this without loss to his work for, contrary to popular opinion, he attached little importance to his athletic prowess, while he did take pride in the seething activity of his mind and the extent of his knowledge. He had at once become popular. Not that he was a demagogue, but he was fair. He was determined to assure labor as well as capital of a "square deal." He was determined to make the Republican party the party of reason, of political sanity. Excessive radicalism, he thought, would result in throwing the party into the arms of the reactionaries. Firmly resolved to fight against the omnipotence of those whom he called "malefactors of great wealth," he did not think, and he did not say, that all men of great wealth were malefactors.

There are good and bad men of all nationalities, creeds and colors; and if this world of ours is ever to become what we hope some day it may become, it must be the general recognition that the man's heart and soul determine his standing. I should be sorry to lose the Presidency, but I should be a hundredfold more sorry to gain it by failing to try, in every way in my power, to put a stop to brutality and wrong of any kind; or by failing on the one hand, to make the very wealthiest and most powerful men in the country obey the law; or by failing on the other hand, to make the laboring men obey the law and realize that envy is as evil a thing as arrogance, and that crimes of violence and riot shall be as sternly punished as crimes of greed and cunning.

These are elementary ideas, but it always requires great courage to follow this middle course in which the politician is not sustained by any group of active partisans. Roosevelt, as he had expected, was denounced as a socialist by the industrialists and as a capitalist by the workers. He consoled himself by quoting Lincoln: "Labor is prior to, and independent of, capital. Capital is only the fruit of labor, and could never have existed if labor had not first existed. . . . Capital has its rights, which are as worthy of protection as any other rights." In principle Roosevelt allowed capital and labor to discuss their contracts by themselves. If their discussions endangered the state, he intervened. In 1902 he threatened to take over the striking coal mines and have them operated by the army unless the operators reached an agreement with the miners. He said that as long as he was President, he wished the workman to feel that he, as well as the capitalist, had access to him, and that the doors of the White House would open as easily to a wage earner as to the president of a great corporation—as easily but not *more* easily.

At the time when Roosevelt was elected, American public opinion had been observing with alarm the increasing power of the giant corporations. The Sherman Anti-Trust Law had not prevented the development of trusts. Roosevelt did not think that large size in a company was in itself reprehensible. He was willing to see big businessmen make big profits, provided they contributed largely to the enrichment of the country; but he demanded that they should be honest and that their business methods should be lawful. Could one, for example, let a trust hire men to wreck the machinery of an independent company? Could one allow a railroad to favor one oil refinery at the expense of another? Or permit the sugar trust to bribe the customs authorities? It was the government's business to enforce respect for the law and the President was determined that it should do so. Law suits were instituted against the most powerful of the wayward companies. The latter, much annoyed, threatened to stop their contributions to the campaign funds of the party. But Roosevelt administered the country justly, "without fear or favor." During his administration the Meat Inspection Act and the Pure Food and Drug Act were passed, thanks to which even today the food of the American people is the most carefully safeguarded in the world. Thereafter it was illegal to pass off a product as anything except what it actually was. This was a great and laudable novelty. But when the movement gave birth to a horde of writers who, after castigating the genuine misdeeds of the trusts, turned their attention to imaginary ones and invented crimes only for the purpose of exposing them, the President condemned this taste for scandalmongering and its practitioners, whom he called "muckrakers." To restore morality to its proper place in the business world was a pious idea (and this was Roosevelt's purpose); but to make morality a trade was diabolical, and Roosevelt never hesitated to say what he thought of the devil even when he found him in his own camp.

Because the President was an outdoor man and had an inquiring mind, he was well acquainted with the geology and geography of his country. He knew that one of the grave dangers that threatened the America of the future was the mad prodigality with which the America of the past had squandered her natural resources. Coal mines and oil wells had seemed so inexhaustible to the Americans of the nineteenth century that they had made no effort to conserve them. If a region became deforested, if the land was exhausted, what did it matter? There were other lands farther on. Little by little this optimism ceased to be justified. By the beginning of the twentieth century the forest trees felled each year were three times the number of the new trees. The disappearance of wooded areas altered the rainfall of the country, removed the protection against the wind and became the cause of disastrous erosion over immense areas. The public grazing lands were subjected to ruinous treatment by the great cattle raisers. Roosevelt undertook (a) to conserve the existing resources;

(b) to create new ones. To save the forests he annexed many of them to the national domain. To protect the grazing lands, he exacted payments from those who had hitherto used them free of charge. Naturally these measures aroused fierce opposition and lasting resentment. To create new resources, the President undertook to irrigate arid lands and constructed most successfully the Roosevelt dam in Arizona, which opened seven hundred fifty thousand acres to agriculture.

Theodore Roosevelt's foreign policy was a happy combination of firmness and moderation. He made frequent use of the familiar adage: "Walk softly but carry a big stick, and you will go far." If the American people spoke softly and at the same time kept the Navy at top efficiency, he maintained that the Monroe Doctrine would go far. Throughout his administration Roosevelt carried a big stick, but he carried it behind his back, and when he spoke firmly, he did it with such discretion that his interlocutor's honor was never in danger. When in 1902 Venezuela repudiated certain debts which she owed to citizens of Germany, England, and Italy, Roosevelt was able to persuade those countries to submit their claims to the arbitration of the Hague Tribunal. The state legislature of California had adopted resolutions demanding the exclusion of Japanese by Congress; the city of San Francisco, exasperated by the invasion of Japanese coolies, had taken measures against them which were not justified by the treaties then in force, and the Japanese were complaining bitterly. Roosevelt spoke softly to the Californians about possible action by federal troops, to the Japanese about eventual action by the American navy. He obtained from the former a withdrawal of the unfriendly segregation measures, and from the latter a limitation of Japanese immigration. "Nine-tenths of wisdom," Roosevelt said, "consists in being wise in time." He was so.

The Panama Canal is one of the monuments of the Roosevelt administration. In 1888 an attempt to pierce the Isthmus had been made by a French company under the direction of Ferdinand de Lesseps, the builder of the Suez Canal. It had failed for technical, political, and financial reasons. The canal remained uncompleted. This project was of great importance to the United States, not only from a commercial point of view but from a strategic one as well. The United States new interests in the Pacific made it desirable that the fleet should be able to move easily from one ocean to the other. During the Spanish War, the cruiser *Oregon* had been forced to make its way around Cape Horn, and the length of the voyage had emphasized the need for a canal. But the treaty of 1850 between England and the United States constituted a serious obstacle, for the two nations had agreed not to exercise exclusive control over any such canal. John Hay, formerly United States ambassador to the Court of St. James and then Secretary of State, determined to secure a friendly annulment of this treaty, and in the end he succeeded. In America itself there were two opposed schools of thought on the subject of the canal; one advocated buying the French concession in Panama, the other wanted to dig the canal through Nicaragua. The first proposal (Panama) was the easier to carry out, but the French company was asking one hundred ten million dollars, and the American government was willing to pay only forty million. Moreover, the country of Panama was theoretically a part of the Republic of Colombia, although it was separated from it by high mountains. Now Colombia was making very heavy demands on its own account. When in 1903 the French company agreed to accept forty million, the Nicaraguan proposal lost ground. It lost even more when William Nelson Cromwell, the sponsor of the New Panama Company, had the generous idea of donating sixty thousand dollars to the Republican campaign fund.

Philippe Bunau-Varilla, a French engineer who had worked with Lesseps, came to New York and proposed a simple means of dealing with growing demands of Colombia. If a revolution were to break out in Panama, if the Panamanian nation were to declare itself independent and grant the United States the land necessary to build the canal, there would be no further problem. The government of the United States had to admit that this solution would indeed be very fine, but it declared through the mouth of Secretary of State John Hay that it could not take part in negotiations as unorthodox as these. "Our policy must be in the eyes of the world, like Mrs. Caesar, above all suspicion." Nevertheless, the conspirators were discreetly informed that in the event of a revolution the American fleet would blockade the coast, which would prevent the Colombian troops from landing. The absence of opposition would assure the innocuousness of the struggle. In November, 1903, the Panamanians revolted; the revolution was carried out without loss of life; a new state was born; the American fleet gave it protection; Bunau-Varilla was named minister from Panama to the United States and signed a treaty leasing the Canal Zone to the government in Washington. Since a treaty with England (the Hay-Pauncefote Treaty of 1901) had prepared the way, there were no protests from abroad except those of Colombia, and she ended, about twenty years later, by settling for twenty-five million dollars. "I accepted the Canal which Bunau-Varilla brought me on a silver platter," Roosevelt said later. When certain people condemned this policy as being too bold for their taste and spoke of "the theft of Panama," he replied that if he had followed the usual procedure and consulted the Senate there would have been a great number of remarkable speeches, a half-century of discussion, and then perhaps the canal. "I deemed it better not to have half a century of debate prior to starting in on the canal; I thought that instead of debating for half a century before building the canal, it would be better to build the canal first and debate me for a half-century afterward."

His domestic policy of the square deal, his foreign policy of the big stick, the air of great adventure which he imparted to the life of the country, and the frank and naïve joy he took in driving the bandwagon, had clearly made "Teddy" very dear to the voters, for he was elected in 1904 for a second term by a large majority. In the course of this second term his prestige was further enhanced by the authority he was able to exert in world affairs. He belonged to that breed of Americans who, when they see an act of injustice to be performed, are impelled to rush to the aid of the underdog. It was through his good offices in 1905 that peace was concluded between Russia and Japan. At the Conference of Algeciras in 1906 he helped, by his forceful action, to prevent a European war. His policy was not always strictly constitutional, for he sometimes undertook commitments that threatened to lead his country into war without the consent of Congress, but he taught the European world to take account of the strength of the United States. And indeed, far from precipitating wars, he dissipated more than one menace. He could easily have obtained a third term in 1908, but he had always said he would not ask for it and worked to secure the election, against the perennial Bryan, of his Secretary of War, William Howard Taft.

Taft's most obvious claim to the White House was his friendship with Roosevelt. The latter made him President as Jackson had Van Buren. Taft was a good candidate possessing sterling personal qualities. He was a blond giant, amiable and easygoing, and his gentle voice issuing from that enormous body was a constant surprise. He had, thanks to his common sense and the contagious laughter which made him shake like a bowl of jelly, succeeded admirably in the Philippines. His friends called him Big Bill and loved him. They failed to see that he was first of all one of themselves, "a clubman and a gentleman," by no means suited to govern a democracy. After the inauguration of his successor, Roosevelt planned to leave on a long trip, so as not to embarrass Taft, to whom he thought he could entrust his work and his organization. Hardly had the retiring President left when Taft, not through disloyalty but by instinct, called back "the old guard." From the very beginning, the men Roosevelt had appointed were removed from key positions. When the ex-President returned after hunting big game in Africa, receiving the Nobel Prize and an Oxford Doctorate, and sojourning with the sovereigns of Europe, he was given a triumphal reception in New York and found his party boiling. All the liberal Republicans were up in arms against Taft. They blamed him for the weak attitude he had taken about the tariff, for his "dollar diplomacy," for what they charged was a relaxation of the conservation policy; they blamed him in short for being Taft and not Roosevelt.

The latter studied the situation. "Taft means well," he was to say later, "but he means well feebly." What was to be done? Roosevelt was only fifty-two years old; he felt as strong as a bull moose; he had an ardent desire to continue to serve his country; he thought his program of reforms was far from completed. When a group of governors suggested that he should be the candidate in 1912, he hesitated, then accepted. "My hat is in the ring," he said. Taft was deeply wounded. Why should his best friend try to deprive him of a second term? The Republican convention, which was dominated by the machine, nominated Taft, but Roosevelt withdrew in disgust and organized a new party, called the Progressives but named by the public the Bull Moose party (since the Republican party had an elephant for its mascot and the Democratic party a donkey). The Progressive party naturally nominated Roosevelt as its candidate. The rupture between Taft and Roosevelt was complete; it was unfortunate, for both were good men. It put an end to Teddy's public life and earned him the lasting hatred of the G.O.P. But the failure of the Progressive party should not obscure the importance of the work accomplished by Roosevelt from 1901 to 1908. He had helped Americans to recognize the necessity of aiding the poor, protecting the public, and maintaining peace in industry. He had made his country respected abroad; he had not involved it in any ill-fated enterprise; and he had established it in the position of a world arbiter. Seven well-filled years.

CHAPTER LI

Enter Woodrow Wilson

SINCE the Republicans were divided, the Democrats had an excellent chance of winning the presidential election of 1912. Whom should they choose as standard bearer? As orthodox and regular candidates the machine offered Champ Clark of Missouri and Oscar W. Underwood of Alabama. Bryan, who was tired of his many defeats, led the liberal elements in the party and secured the nomination of Woodrow Wilson, governor of New Jersey. Who was Wilson? A professor who had entered political life barely two years before, and who represented a type of candidate new in presidential contests. But the choice was less surprising than it seemed. Born in 1856, the son of a southern Presbyterian minister, Woodrow Wilson had taught social science and history at Bryn Mawr, Wesleyan University, and Princeton. Everywhere he had been an immediate success. The distinction of his manners, the beauty of his diction, the precision of his language, and the clarity of his expositions all contributed. He had written a number of works on history and jurisprudence, among them *Congressional Government* and *A History of the American People*. The very nature of the subjects he taught led him to express political ideas; his oratorical abilities attracted attention; in 1902 he was appointed president of Princeton.

In the United States the president of a large university is a politician *in partibus*. His speeches are quoted in the newspapers. If he has ability and tact he becomes a moral authority. Wilson increased his by making himself the champion of democracy in the University of Princeton against the old aristocratic hierarchy of the clubs. He wanted the undergraduates to live in common dormitories. The alumni and the trustees, loyal to Princeton traditions, rose in opposition. The liberal professors defended Wilson and the faculty was divided into two factions—pro-Wilson and anti-Wilson. The president's character made any debate difficult. Among his students he was famous for his charm; his colleagues learned to know, as well, his anger and his pride. Very sure of himself, and justly proud of the clarity of his mind, he would not tolerate contradiction. The violence of his character astounded those who had judged him on the basis of the austere and polished language of his speeches. Between him and the Board of Trustees there was soon open conflict, not only on the question of the clubs but on almost every other point as well. Meanwhile rumors of this battle for democracy waged by the president of the most aristocratic of the universities reached the general public and won Wilson great popularity. From 1906 on, certain influential members of the Democratic party had their eyes on him. In 1910 the bosses of New Jersey offered to make him their candidate for governor of the state. Perhaps they had been prompted by the trustees of Princeton, who eagerly wished to be disembarrassed of Wilson and some of whom (Grover Cleveland, for example) were not without influence in the party. Wilson needed some honorable means of escape from an impossible situation. He accepted.

As governor of New Jersey, Wilson astounded those who had put him into office. The bosses had thought that this professor, this babe in politics, would be at their mercy. Wilson proved himself a remarkable politician and a very poor servant of the machine. Supported by public opinion he defied the bosses. The latter, disgusted by his ingratitude, tried to reduce him to impotence. Without paying further attention to them, he appealed over their heads to the people and adopted a position that was more evangelical than political; he was to maintain it all his life. The liberals in the Democratic party began to think of him as a possible candidate in 1912. A gentleman from Texas, Colonel House, a small, mysterious, and affable man, who was tempted by the role of Grey Eminence, undertook to make Woodrow Wilson President of the United States. At the Baltimore convention, the conservative Champ Clark was the candidate of the machine, but Bryan declared himself in favor of Wilson. The Bryan boys cried: "We want Wilson!" And on the forty-sixth ballot he was nominated. In his campaign he was aided by his oratorical talent and the deep split that divided the Republicans. Wilson and Roosevelt stood for substantially the same ideas and demanded the same reforms, but Roosevelt did not have the solid framework of an old traditional party to support him. Both were eloquent: Roosevelt's eloquence was aggressive; Wilson's, persuasive. "Their methods of campaigning," wrote Morison and Commager, "had no more in common than their personalities. Roosevelt's tone was that of a fighting parson; Wilson already showed some glint of the spiritual quality of Lincoln. Roosevelt, with Biblical imagery and a voice like a shrilling fife, stirred men to wrath, to combat, and to antique virtue; Wilson, serene and confident, lifted men out of themselves by phrases that sang in their hearts, to a vision of a better world. It was the Old Testament against the New Testament, and the New won. . . ." Wilson had the support of the western farmers, brought to him by Bryan; the Solid South, happy to vote for a southerner;

and, in the East, the Irish and the liberals. Samuel Gompers, head of the American Federation of Labor, had advised the workmen to vote for Wilson. Taft and Roosevelt divided the Republican votes about equally, and Wilson was elected.

What would this professor do in the White House? The politicians anxiously asked this question. The reply was simple: He would teach. Wilson always retained the attitude of a man accustomed to speak *ex cathedra*. If he had an important question to settle, he studied the facts as one would prepare a lecture, listened attentively to opinions, made his decision, clothed it in general ideas, and thereafter resisted all opposition. He demanded from his collaborators complete obedience and submission at all times. On various occasions he did not hesitate to break old friendships because he no longer found the intellectual loyalty he demanded. When principles were at stake, he would have preferred to sacrifice his life and the world rather than recede one step. Although, among intimates, he had a light touch and even a sense of humor, his timidity and his academic manner never allowed him to get on friendly terms with the senators or the newspapermen in Washington. "He loved mankind but could not stand men." His strength lay, not in the conquest of individuals, at which he was inept, but in a sincere desire to seize the currents of opinion as they rose from the masses, and in his art of stating what everyone thought in perfect phrases which he would pronounce with an irresistible authority. It has been said that he had the temperament of a theologian; most of all he had the temperament of a moralist. In his eyes the only fundamental distinction was that between good and evil. Happier than most men, he seemed to know in all circumstances where the good was to be found. Some said that once he became Caesar he had a tendency to believe that he was God.

When on March 4 he delivered his inaugural address, Woodrow Wilson was acclaimed with enthusiasm by the crowds massed in front of the Capitol. In language that was perfect in form and devoid of demagogic or partisan coloring, he talked to them of their duties as well as of their rights. "This is not a day of triumph," he told them piously, "it is a day of consecration." He exalted the strength and the wealth of America, but he reminded his audience that evil was still everywhere mixed with the good and that it was the duty of all "to cleanse, to reconsider, to restore, to correct the evil without impairing the good, to purify and humanize every process of our common life. . . ." He described the sufferings of women and children in the factories: "The great Government we loved has too often been made use of for private and selfish purposes, and those who used it had forgotten the people." He enumerated the necessary reforms: in the tariff, in the banking system, in industry. It was the program of William Jennings Bryan. He did not have the literary genius of Lincoln but his sentiments were elevated, his tone serious, his voice precise and agreeable. The professor pleased the nation.

For the first time since Jefferson, who had given up the custom, the President addressed Congress in person. Wilson knew that eloquence was his forte and he exercised a constant pressure on the two Houses to obtain a quick vote for those measures which lay close to his heart. He won respect there. His capacity for work, his obstinacy, his appeals to public opinion compelled submission if not friendship. It was said that he treated Congress like a class and kept them at their desks for five hundred sixty-seven days at a stretch. And so the legislative accomplishments of the first two years were considerable. Despite the vehement protest of the industries affected, the tariff was reduced. The banking system of the country was completely reformed by the creation of twelve Federal Reserve Banks, each entrusted with a vast territory and authorized to issue bank-notes against a security of commercial paper. A Federal Reserve Board controlled their operations. All national banks of the country were required to affiliate themselves with the Federal Reserve System and to pass over their paper to it, and all other banks were urged but not compelled to do so. This solution was more complicated than those embodied in the bank of France and the Bank of England; but the Democratic party retained too bitter a memory of its battles against the Bank of the United States to resuscitate the monster. Moreover, the Federal Reserve System rendered all the services expected of it. An anti-trust law (the Clayton Act) was passed in an attempt to control the increasing and dangerous concentration of wealth and to prevent multiple interlocking directorates. A Federal Trade Commission was created to prevent unfair competition. The labor unions were protected and given more power; the farmers were given new credit facilities. Wilson studied all these questions, employing Colonel House as his liaison officer, and himself tapped out on his typewriter his plans and decisions. By 1914 he had become an undeniable moral force in America and even in Europe.

Bryan had campaigned for Wilson; he had brought him the western radicals; in return Wilson made him Secretary of State. Perhaps it was a happy choice from a political point of view, but it was certainly a bad diplomatic choice. Bryan, the lyrical demagogue, knew exactly how to sway crowds; he was completely ignorant of world affairs. He violently shocked the State Department by continuing to give paid lectures after he had become Secretary of State. Arrayed in simple honesty and a white alpaca coat, smiling, benign, and affable, Bryan believed in the possibility of maintaining international peace by distributing pacifist tracts to war-like peoples. Wilson's encyclopedic intelligence bewildered him. Actually it was the President who handled the larger issues of foreign policy, using Colonel House as *missus dominicus*. Wilson approached diplomacy, as he approached everything else, from the point of view of good and evil. He promised at once that never again would the United States seek to acquire by conquest a single foot of foreign territory. Sometimes his acts were not in complete conformity with his principles. American marines occupied Nicaragua, Haiti, and Santo Domingo. But it must be admitted that they did not remain there, and in the case of Mexico, Wilson gave evidence of genuine patience.

Until 1910, the dictator Porfirio Diaz had maintained order in that country in the interests of the big landowners and the foreign capitalists. When a popular revolution, inspired by Francisco Madero, overthrew Diaz, the rich raised up another dictator, Victoriano Huerta, who was a combination of bandit and military leader, with a preponderance of bandit. Most of the European states recognized Huerta in the hope of protecting their investments, and the American capitalists demanded that Wilson follow their example. He refused. "We hold that just government rests always upon the consent of the governed, and that there can be no freedom without order based upon law, and upon public conscience and approval. . . . We can have no sympathy with those who seize the power of government to advance their own political interest or ambition." This attitude produced a certain tension between England and the United States. Wilson wanted the two countries, both of which had interests in Mexico, to pursue the same policy. Now he found that he had a bargaining point. The Panama Canal was just being completed and Congress had decided, in 1912, that all American coastwise shipping should be exempt from tolls. Great Britain maintained that this decision was a violation of the Hay-Pauncefote Treaty. Congress replied that the phrase "open to all nations on terms of entire equality" meant "foreign nations" and did not apply to the United States, which had built the canal. Wilson sent Colonel House to carry on negotiations with Sir Edward Grey, then appeared himself before Congress to demand, with unusual vigor, the abrogation of this clause. In a speech surcharged with mystery, he hinted that he needed this concession to England in order to arrange a more delicate matter. Congress understood that this meant Mexico, and consented. The canal was opened, an event of great commercial and strategic importance. All the nations were treated on terms of equality and Great Britain's policy in Mexico from that day forward became strangely similar to that of the United States.

In 1914, when Huerta arrested American sailors without reason, the President demanded an apology. It was refused. The American marines, always prepared, took Vera Cruz. A war with Mexico seemed inevitable, but Wilson was firmly resolved not to make war. Perhaps he would have failed if "the ABC powers" (Argentina, Brazil, and Chile) had not offered to mediate. Wilson accepted, and the powers proposed the creation of a constitutional government in Mexico. This was not what Huerta wanted but, finding no support in Europe, he fled; and an elected president, Carranza, replaced him. Disorder continued in that country. The bandit Villa crossed the frontier on several occasions to raid American estates in Texas. Anyone but Wilson would doubtless have annexed Mexico at the cost of a short war. The campaign would have been easy and profitable but morally wrong, and, despite the pressure of public opinion, the President attempted instead to stabilize the Carranza government. Events have proved that Wilson's patience was wise. Relations between the two neighboring nations became, and are still growing, ever more friendly. By and large, Wilson's first term had been a success in the eyes of the masses and the liberals. The so-called "governing classes" blamed the President for his distrust of the business world and for a foreign policy that was more virtuous than heroic. Since 1914 Europe had been at war, and arguments about what attitude the United States should adopt now divided the country almost as completely as the struggles of France and England had at the beginning of the Republic.

CHAPTER LII

Neutrality

TODAY those who study the war of 1914, after a lapse of thirty years and in the context of subsequent events, can see it clearly as a first attempt on the part of Germany to dominate the world, and it is a little hard to understand why the Americans did not realize immediately that the very principles on which their civilization had been established were at stake. In the violation of Belgian neutrality, a doctrine of might arose to challenge the doctrine of right. There seemed little doubt what choice men of good will would make. But the political tradition of America was hostile to all foreign entanglement. Washington in his Farewell Address had warned the country against them. At the time of the French Revolution Americans had been divided into pro-French and pro-English, but these distinctions had disappeared after 1815. For a century the foreign policy of the United States had been dominated by two principles: not to meddle in European affairs and not to permit Europeans to meddle in American affairs.

This attitude was even more inflexible in the Middle West and the West than on the Atlantic coast. The eastern states had kept in constant contact with Europe. They saw more Europeans; they could travel there more easily. To an Iowa farmer "Europe" was a word that called up no precise picture. In certain states the population was partly of German origin. They were good citizens but some of them remained loyal to Germany and immediately accused France and England of hypocrisy. Although the business world of the East was favorable to Great Britain, in the mind of the common people, whose memory is tenacious, there persisted a distrust of the English that harked back to the time of Samuel Adams. The Irish, who were politically influential, were hostile to England. France, to be sure, still benefited from the prestige of Lafayette; but the affection bestowed on her was more sentimental than active, and her alliance with tsarist Russia had shocked the liberals. Americans observed the vendettas of Europe with a troubled surprise. Why all this turmoil? To be sure America herself had had her Civil War. But she failed to discern in Europe moral questions comparable to that of slavery; moreover in 1914 the Civil War had been pretty well forgotten. For a decade the United States had been enjoying remarkable prosperity. The people saw their numbers and their wealth increasing; they believed in progress because, with Roosevelt and Wilson, the reformers had been in office and had made good use of it. They could not understand why Europe should have recourse to methods that seemed to them outmoded, brutal, and stupid. Powerful pacifist groups reinforced these ideas by their propaganda. Few Americans in August, 1914, thought that their country would ever take part in the war, and fewer still that it was a duty for her to take part in it.

President Wilson was in favor of neutrality. He wished to be an example of the power of moral ideas: "We are champions of peace and concord," he said, "and we should be very jealous of this distinction which we have sought to earn." To which the friends of France and England replied that peace and concord were being defended by these two nations. But in 1914 Wilson did not believe it. Not only did he proclaim the neutrality of the United States, he demanded that his fellow citizens should be neutral in thought as well as in deed, and that they should reserve their judgment on this conflict until the end of the war. He declared that the United States should set an example of a strong nation that refused to make use of force; that war always demoralizes those who engage in it; and that moreover his program of domestic reform, to which he was passionately attached, could not be carried out except under conditions of peace. Later he admitted that he had been mistaken about the real meaning of this war, and in 1919 he went so far as to say: "We, at the distance of America, looked on at first without a full comprehension of what the plot was getting into." Nevertheless, Wilson himself was drawn, quickly enough though against his will, toward the Allies by the call of blood and culture. Whether he liked it or not he belonged to the British tradition and he understood the arguments of the English better than those of the Germans. Bryan, who was Secretary of State and a thoroughgoing pacifist, thought the President was prejudiced in favor of the Allies. This was not the opinon of the Allies.

Neutrality is a difficult condition. The United States had realized that clearly at the time of the Napoleonic wars. In 1914 once more British Orders in Council forbade all commerce with Germany whether directly or through a neutral port. England and France, taking advantage of their control of the sea, declared the Channel and the North Sea military zones. American merchants were hit by these measures and there were numerous protests. But these complaints were fated to remain without effect because neither the President nor the State Department had any intention of declaring war on the Allies and the Allies knew it. The Germans, for their part, had recourse to measures even farther outside international law than the British blockade. At least the blockade did not entail any loss of life for neutrals, whereas Americans were very soon killed by German submarines and mines. Wilson announced that the German government would be held responsible for all loss of life and property. In this he was upheld by public opinion, which was veering quite rapidly in a direction hostile to the Central Powers. The German ambassador himself confessed that German propaganda in the United States had been a complete failure.

Soon America became the great purveyor of supplies and ammunition to the Allies. France and England were the principal clients of American industry because they alone, thanks to their control of the seas, could take delivery of their orders. A period of unprecedented prosperity began in the United States. Germany complained of the favorable treatment of her enemies, but America replied that if the Allies were masters of the seas that was a fact for which the United States could not be held responsible. Moreover, it was certain that a part of the American exports found its way, via neutral countries, to the Central Powers. Meanwhile, after purchase and transportation, payment became necessary. At first France and England sold all the American securities they possessed and thus obtained credits; later, they had recourse to loans. Bryan opposed this, but private banks were authorized to make advances to the belligerents. Contrary to a popular legend that has had its hour, it seems absolutely untrue that these banks exercised pressure of any sort in favor of the entry of the United States into the war. In September, 1915, public subscriptions for a loan to the Allies were opened. A billion and a half dollars were subscribed before the country entered the war.

On May 7, 1915, the liner *Lusitania* was torpedoed without warning. Among the eleven hundred fifty-three victims were one hundred twenty-four Americans. A cry of horror went up from the whole world. The excuse given by the German government was that the *Lusitania* was transporting contraband of war, and that moreover a warning to the passengers had been published by the German ambassador in the American newspapers. But to announce a crime by sending a letter to the newspapers cannot be considered an extenuating circumstance. The anger that shook the country showed, for the first time, that sooner or later the United States would enter the war. When three days later the President said that one could quite easily conceive of a man who was "too proud to fight," the phrase was not well received. Roosevelt and his friends assailed Wilson for his pacifism, while Bryan and his friends criticized him for being too warlike. A number of notes were exchanged with the German government. Finally, as a result of the sinking of the *Sussex* in the Channel, the President secured a promise from Germany that in future she would not torpedo merchant ships without warning and that she would make an effort to save the lives of passengers. This was, for Wilson, a diplomatic victory.

Many Americans did not believe that Germany would keep her promise, and they demanded that the country should prepare for a war that they now judged to be inevitable. In 1914 a National Security League had been formed to advocate conscription. In 1915 General Leonard Wood established an officers' training camp for volunteers. Other measures were taken, but they were inadequate. The standing army was increased to one hundred sixty-five thousand men; the construction of numerous warships was authorized; fifty million dollars were allotted for the merchant marine. Although the President remained hostile to the idea of war, he commenced to think that there were certain essential ideas for which it was clearly necessary to fight. "America ought to keep out of this war, at the expense of anything, except this single thing upon which her character and history are founded: her sense of humanity and justice." And, a little later: "We are participants, whether we would or not, in the life of the world. The interests of all nations are our own also. We are partners with the rest. What affects mankind is inevitably our affair, as well as the nations of Europe and of Asia."

1916 was a presidential election year. Roosevelt, who represented the policy of intervention, might have stood a good chance against Wilson, but the Republicans could not pardon him for causing their defeat in 1912. A Progressive convention nominated him as candidate; he sent a telegram saying that he could not accept the nomination before he knew the attitude of the candidate of the G.O.P. (Grand Old Party) on the vital question of the day. This candidate was Charles Evans Hughes, justice of the Supreme Court, who had been governor of New York. He would have been elected if the Progressives and the Republicans had all voted for him; but many Progressives, upon Roosevelt's refusal of the nomination, turned to Wilson, who, like them, stood for reform in domestic politics. "He kept us out of war" became the campaign slogan, which pleased the West and the Middle West. Wilson said that he had two duties: to maintain the peace and to safeguard the honor of the United States; and that a time might come when it would be impossible to fulfill both duties simultaneously. Meanwhile Roosevelt was violently attacking Wilson and saying that his election would prove that America was ready to accept any insult, including the massacre of its women and children, in order "to make money." On the evening of election day it was thought that Hughes was President. The New York *Times* announced it. But some returns were not yet in; when all the votes were finally counted, Wilson had been elected by two hundred seventy-seven electoral votes to two hundred fifty-four.

At this time Germany seemed very strong; to be sure she had failed at Verdun, but she had been victorious in Roumania; she had stopped the Allied offensive in the West and the East, and it seemed to her a favorable moment to make peace. In the course of the month of December that followed his re-election, Wilson offered to call a conference of the belligerents. Since this move followed close upon a proposal from Germany, the Allies distrusted it. Moreover there was no common ground for an understanding. Germany was still demanding a victor's peace; the Allies did not feel beaten, and were not. In January, 1911, Wilson delivered a speech before the Senate in which he defined the conditions on which the United States would agree to co-operate in establishing world peace. He demanded a peace "without annexations or indemnities." A peace of humiliation, he said, would leave bitter memories and would be built on shifting sands: "Only a peace between equals can last." This peace should guarantee the security of small nations, the freedom of the seas, the limitation of armaments, and governments founded on the consent of the governed. Finally Wilson demanded an organized force, a league, to maintain the future peace. This appeal was not well received. The idea of peace without victory was displeasing to the Allies as well as to the Germans.

The decision to throw America into the war was made neither by Wilson nor by the American friends of the Allies, but by the German general staff. Hindenburg and Ludendorff demanded unlimited submarine warfare and the Emperor Wilhelm II wrote on the margin of their request: "Now once for all an *end* to negotiations with America! If Wilson wants war, let him make it." The German general staff knew very well that this decision would provoke the United States' entrance into the war, but they thought that submarine warfare would bring about the capitulation of the Allies before American aid could become effective, and moreover they failed to estimate that eventual aid at its true value. Wilson still tried to temporize. He proposed to arm merchant vessels. On March 4 there was published a note from the German foreign minister Zimmermann to the German ambassador at Washington, a note that had been handed over to the State Department by the British intelligence. In it Germany proposed to Mexico an alliance against the United States in the event of war, the reward for which was to be Texas, Arizona, and New Mexico. This time the measure overflowed. On April 2, 1917, Wilson appeared before Congress and read a message in which he asked the latter to proclaim the existence of a state of war, brought about by Germany:

> We have no quarrel with the German people. . . . The world must be made safe for democracy. . . . It is a fearful thing to lead this great peaceful people into war, into the most terrible and disastrous of all wars, civilization itself seeming to be in the balance. But the right is more precious than peace, and we shall fight for the things which we have always carried nearest our hearts,—for democracy, for the right of those who submit to authority to have a voice in their own Governments, for the rights and liberties of small nations, for a universal dominion of right by such a concert of free peoples as shall bring peace and safety to all nations and make the world itself at last free. To such a task we can dedicate our lives and our fortunes, everything that we are and everything that we have, with the pride of those who know that the day has come when America is privileged to spend her blood and her might for the principles that gave her birth and happiness and the peace which she has treasured. God helping her, she can do no other.

On April 6, 1917, the United States declared war on Germany. War was not declared against Austria-Hungary until December 7, and never against Turkey or Bulgaria. Moreover, because the war aims of America were different from those of the other powers, the latter were termed officially not the Allies, but the Associates of the United States.

CHAPTER LIII

The First World War

THE United States was not rushing to take part in a victory already won. In 1917 the Allies' prospects were not brilliant. Roumania had collapsed; Russia was turning tail; Italy had just met with a serious defeat; France had no more men upon whom to call; England lacked ships and her reserve supply of provisions was barely sufficient for six weeks. Shipping losses constituted the most immediate danger; they were so great (close to a million tons a month) that if they were to continue for long they would spell disaster for the Allies. It was for this reason that Germany had not hesitated to provoke the United States rather than limit her submarine warfare. The English Admiral Jellicoe said to Admiral Sims: "It is impossible for us to go on, if losses like this continue. . . . The Germans will win unless we can stop the losses, and stop them soon." In regard to land warfare, General Pershing was no more optimistic: "We must come to their relief in 1918. The year after may be too late." And so the Allies expected from their "associate," first of all ships, then participation in the war against submarines—food, arms, and reinforcements. This support had to be supplied with extreme speed; otherwise there was a chance that it would be useless.

At sea, America supplied everything the Allies had expected of her. The German ships that happened to be in American ports were seized. A merchant fleet totaling eleven million tons was built by the Emergency Fleet Corporation. More than two million American soldiers were transported to France, one million in English ships, nine hundred twenty-seven thousand in American ships, and the rest in French and Italian vessels. The American navy escorted a large part of these convoys without loss of life. At the same time American destroyers took part in the battle against the submarines, and American mine layers co-operated with the Allies in sowing an immense barrier across the whole of the North Sea. On land an army was improvised in a very short time by conscription (as Wilson wished) and not by voluntary enlistment (as Congress desired). At the end of the war the United States had about four million men under arms. Training camps were organized. The Allies sent instructors who were attached as officers to the regular American army. The commander of these armies was General Pershing, an experienced soldier, taciturn and energetic, who moved to France with his general staff in June, 1917. He was received with an enthusiasm that proved French morale was still good. The greeting, commonly but erroneously credited to him: "Lafayette, we are here!" is still famous. On July 4 the Americans marched down the Rue de Rivoli amid a crowd that threw flowers and shouted, *"Vive l'Amérique!"* By the end of 1917 only two hundred thousand American soldiers were in France and there was one division at the front. Although military aid was not immediate, the moral support and the great hope it aroused gave the Allies strength to hold on.

The army, the navy, and the air force had to be equipped. Hence it became necessary to organize the war industries. To carry out this gigantic task the President obtained from Congress unprecedented powers of requisition and control; he transferred these powers to men or to committees, of which the most important was the War Industries Board under the direction of Bernard Baruch. This czar of industry was a financier, in his forties, with a genius for organization. All peacetime industries that consumed raw materials necessary for armaments were suspended or regimented. From then on there was only one model of baby carriages, only two kinds of trunks. The number of stops an elevator could make and the number of passengers it could carry were fixed by decree. To all this the American public adapted itself with good grace. In March, 1918, all the railroads were taken in hand by the government and unified under the direction of William G. McAdoo, Secretary of the Treasury. The leaders of American industry put their time and experience at the service of the government at the salary of one dollar a year. It was this spirit of team play, of co-operation, and of patriotism that made the success of the War Industries Board. The failures—for of course there were failures, particularly in the manufacture of machine guns and airplanes—were due to shortness of time allowed and conflicts of jurisdiction. If Wilson's administration is open to criticism, it is for not having foreseen, while America was still at peace, the needs of war. Nevertheless, American production astonished the Allies and consummated the ruin of the Central Powers.

The food czar was Herbert Hoover, an engineer from California, who had already proved his extraordinary talents as an administrator by organizing American relief in the occupied territories, especially in Belgium. He was a brusque man, cold and ironical on the surface, but at heart capable of pity, sympathy, and, above all, courage. When he was appointed Food Administrator his task was to feed the Allies and, at home, to increase production while simultaneously reducing consumption. To encourage production he bought entire crops in advance by guaranteeing a minimum price to the growers. To reduce consumption, he imposed meatless days, sugarless candies, wheatless bread. His slogan was: "Food will win the war; don't waste it." "Hooverize" became a word in common use. No ration cards: Hoover appealed to the conscience of America. On every unoccupied scrap of ground victory gardens were planted. There was an increase in the area of ground under cultivation and in the number of cattle raised. Thanks to these wise measures, and despite the fact that it had been a bad year, the exports to starving Europe in 1918 exceeded all the promises America had made.

There are three ways of financing a war: by printing money, by borrowing, and by taxation. The first leads to inflation and a rise in prices; McAdoo had recourse to the other two and decided to raise one-third by taxation. Some people thought he could have gone farther. Bonds totaling eighteen and a half billion dollars were offered to the public. The people subscribed nearly twenty-two and a half billion. There was great enthusiasm. Banks helped to the best of their ability, even though they were not on the best of terms with President Wilson. Movie stars, heroes of war and of sport were transformed into salesmen. The country was plastered with signs announcing the Liberty Loan drives. Close to ten billion dollars was loaned by the United States to the Allied governments.

There can be no enthusiasm without faith. It was necessary to inspire this faith in the average American and make him understand the meaning of the war. This was the task of the Committee on Public Information whose chairman was George Creel. He made use of every means. Seventy-five thousand volunteer "four-minute speakers" addressed audiences in the theaters and movie houses of the country. Pamphlets, translated into every language spoken in America, broadcast hatred of the enemy. Abroad the most effective propagandist was the President. He exerted a real influence on the morale of the Germans and Austro-Hungarians by repeating that the United States was not making war for any material advantage but for justice, and that the peace would be a just peace. On January 8, 1918, he enumerated the Fourteen Points of his program. Those of the enemy who believed these Fourteen Points were acceptable resigned themselves, at the bottom of their hearts, to an Allied victory. The Fourteen Points were: (1) no secret treaties; (2) freedom of the seas; (3) commercial equality; (4) reduction of armaments; (5) readjustment of colonies in the interests of the Colonial peoples; (6) evacuation of Russia; (7) evacuation and restoration of Belgium; (8) evacuation of France and return to her of Alsace-Lorraine; (9) rectification of the Italian frontiers; (10) independence for the peoples of Austria-Hungary; (11) adjustments in the Balkans; (12) self-determination for the peoples of Turkey and free passage through the Dardanelles; (13) independence of Poland with access to the sea; (14) creation of a league of nations which would mutually guarantee territorial integrity. Almost all these ideas were just, but many of them were vague, and some of them were not acceptable to the Allies. For example, England's ideas about the freedom of the seas were not the same as those of the President of the United States. But at that time no one dared contradict Wilson. All through 1918 he kept saying in various ways that this war was a crusade of the democracies against the autocracies. The other governments listened to him respectfully, for he had a great many fresh troops.

There is no shadow of a doubt that it was these fresh troops that made it possible to win the war in November, 1918. Germany was still scoring great successes in March, in April, and in June. Once more her armies had advanced as far as the Marne and were threatening Paris. England and France had no more troops with which to oppose her. Up to then Pershing had insisted that the American soldiers should be used as a separate army under his command. When Foch, who had been made generalissimo, told him that the war might be lost through numerical inferiority, he generously gave up his project and put all the trained men he possessed at the disposal of the commander-in-chief. It was then that the First and Second American Divisions distinguished themselves and that the marines retook Belleau Wood. On July 14, American troops helped to throw back the last German offensive and on the eighteenth they took part in Foch's counterattack, which was the first clarion call of victory. Once the danger was past Pershing obtained, as he had desired, a regrouping of the American army so that he could have a sector of his own. This was the sector of Saint-Mihiel south of Verdun. The Americans mopped it up and advanced rapidly. Then General Foch entrusted to a million two hundred thousand Americans the battle that was destined to free the Meuse and the Argonne and that constituted a part of his general offensive. Many of these American divisions had never been in combat; they fought well but suffered heavy losses. As for Ludendorff, he was lost and knew it. Whereas the Allies could count upon the inexhaustible reserves of the American army, the Germans were growing weaker day by day. The disparity could only increase; for Germany there remained no hope of winning the war. On October 4, 1918, Prince Max of Baden, the new German chancellor, accepted President Wilson's Fourteen Points as a basis for negotiation.

The Germans have often said that they were tricked by Wilson and that, having laid down their arms because they had faith in a generous enemy, they were compelled to sign an armistice and a peace the conditions of which were much harsher than the Fourteen Points. This is not accurate. The Germans did not ask for an armistice in 1918 because they believed in the Fourteen Points but because they had been militarily defeated and were incapable of continuing the war. Moreover, most of the Allied military leaders were opposed to the idea of a premature armistice. They thought it desirable to invade Germany and make her feel the brunt of defeat. General Pershing belonged to this school. Marshal Foch did not wish to sacrifice human lives uselessly; he wished to cease firing as soon as victory had been won and the enemy was incapable of doing further damage; but he was not in favor of the Fourteen Points, which threatened to prevent France from insuring her future security through the terms of the peace treaty. The conditions of the armistice were what they had to be; by the very nature of an armistice they were provisional. It now remained to be seen whether the peace would be the peace of Wilson or that of Clemenceau.

CHAPTER LIV

The Peace Treaty

THE nations of Europe had fought a hard and bloody war. America had come to their aid at the moment when they were about to succumb. She had thrown herself into this battle in all good faith to defend right against might. As leader, she had a man of good will whose determination was to build a better world. This leader had the confidence of the European masses, who expected him to give them a just and durable peace. Never have circumstances been so favorable; never have results been so disillusioning. How, in a few years' time, victory was transformed into defeat is a subject that belongs to European history; but how Wood-

immediately acquire a domain to administer. The professor of history quite rightly recalled the role that had been played in the unification of the United States by the Northwest Ordinance. In three weeks' time, with a special committee of which General Smuts, Léon Bourgeois, Eleutherios Venizelos, and Lord Robert Cecil were members, Wilson drew up a plan. The League was to be administered by a council of nine members. Its decisions had to be unanimous. An assembly of all the members was to meet each year but it was not sustained by any executive power. The covenant also provided for a permanent secretariat at Geneva and a world court to arbitrate international disputes. Article X (which was to cause trouble) stated that: "The members of the League undertake to respect and preserve as against external aggression the territorial integrity, and existing political independence, of all members of the League." Article XVI gave the council the right to demand of the various governments the support of their military and naval forces to enforce respect for the pact. As soon as these provisions became known, more than one-third of the United States Senate signed a protest against commitments that might compel America to make war for foreign causes without the consent of Congress. Congress demanded that the peace treaty and the pact should be two separate documents so that it might be able to ratify one and reject the other. That was exactly what the President did not wish. For the League of Nations he had a father's love and the faith of an apostle. Through it he hoped to go down in posterity as one of the great benefactors of mankind. For it he was prepared to make the greatest sacrifices.

He had to make them. In order to get the pact incorporated in the treaty he surrendered several of the Fourteen Points. At the beginning of 1919 he made a quick trip to the United States. His reception there was not enthusiastic. To Congress he said: "When the Treaty comes back, gentlemen on this side will find the Covenant not only in it, but so many threads of the Treaty tied to the Covenant that you cannot detach it from the Treaty without destroying the whole vital structure," and the senators saw in this statement a threat that completely alienated them. Upon his return to France, Wilson perceived that his authority had been impaired and he was forced to accept a program of reparations and indemnities that were inflated to astronomical proportions. Thus was elaborated a treaty "too harsh to have any softness, too soft to have any strength" which gave the world a much shorter time of respite than had the Treaty of 1815. But on April 28, 1919, the Pact of the League of Nations was unanimously adopted, and this success was balm to Wilson's wounds. On June 20 the Germans accepted the peace terms in the Trianon Palace at Versailles and on June 28 they signed in the Hall of Mirrors. Next day President Wilson sailed to champion his work in the United States.

He was ill prepared for it. In the course of the long months of the conference his health had been shattered by overwork. His intellectual stubbornness, nourished by acclamations, had grown. Any comment seemed to him an offense, any reserve a lack of loyalty, any criticism a blasphemy. He had broken with Colonel House, the most devoted of his friends; he was to break with Joseph P. Tumulty, his loyal secretary. That men "with the minds of pygmies" should oppose the designs of this Demiurge of the Peace seemed to him a sacrilege. But when the pygmies were senators, they had the power to bind Gulliver. Actually they would have preferred to come to an understanding with him. Senator Lodge, chairman of the Senate Committee on Foreign Relations, had no love for Wilson. The two men differed in background, religion, and temperament. Moreover, both possessed a certain intellectual pedantry, and their arrogant minds came into opposition. But Lodge realized that a treaty was necessary; he only asked that the President write into it certain reservations for the purpose of maintaining Congress's right to declare war and to redefine the Monroe Doctrine. Wilson could have reached an understanding with him, with Borah, and with Johnson who led the opposition. Unfortunately the President made a personal issue of the ratification of the treaty just as it was, without the change of a comma. Rather than struggle with the pygmy minds he addressed himself, over the heads of the opposition, to the people of the United States. He decided to make a tour of the country and to speak in all the big cities of the Middle West and the Far West, the two most refractory regions.

This trip and the thirty speeches he delivered completed the destruction of Wilson's health. In Colorado he had a stroke and had to be brought back half-paralyzed to the White House. From that time on he was an invisible invalid, a mysterious phantom who no longer communicated with the outside world except through his doctor or through Mrs. Wilson. This isolation and illness increased the President's stubbornness. In the Senate the battle continued over Article X of the pact; it was the one on which Wilson was unwilling to accept any reservations. When a vote was taken the unmodified treaty failed to receive the necessary two-thirds vote. The treaty, with reservations, was likewise rejected. Congress tried to end the state of war by a simple resolution; the President vetoed it. It was a deplorable situation and the peace of the world was to be the cost of this stubborn rivalry. Without the United States, the League of Nations could impose respect neither for frontiers nor for the rights of man. With the United States any hope would have been permissible. The return to isolationism of the most powerful and the most disinterested country in the world was a dreadful misfortune for all the nations of the earth. Wilson had shown loftiness of conception, moral grandeur, and courage. He had been betrayed by his character and his physical strength.

The last months of his administration were marked by labor troubles. During the war a War Labor Board had successfully arbitrated labor disputes. External peace was the signal for the reopening of internal strife. This was natural. As a result of wartime inflation prices were rising; salaries should have followed. In 1919 John L. Lewis, president of the United Mine Workers, ended a strike by saying: "We are Americans, we cannot fight against the Government." But more revolutionary agitators, the Independent Workers of the World, waved the red flag. Bombs were thrown. Wilson said: "With the free expression of opinion and with the advocacy of orderly political change, however fundamental, there must be no interference; but towards passions and malevolence tending to incite criminal insurrections under the guise of political evolution, there should be no leniency." Over two hundred agitators were deported to Russia on a transport nicknamed the "Red Ark," and the American Federation of Labor disowned the violent methods of the Independent Workers of the World. Some people thought that the railroads, which had been taken over by the government during the war, should continue to be operated by the nation, but Wilson decided to return them to private ownership.

Two amendments to the Constitution were ratified in 1919 and 1920. The Eighteenth decreed the prohibition of intoxicating beverages; the Nineteenth gave women the suffrage. Each of them had been prepared for by a long campaign. The Nineteenth Amendment increased the number of possible voters in the election of 1920 by twenty million; it did not appreciably modify the relative strength of the parties. The Eighteenth Amendment exerted the worst possible influence upon the habits of the country. Young men and girls carried with them on their outings flasks filled with bad gin or whisky. A country that had always been law-abiding began to regard with indulgence those who violated the Eighteenth Amendment. The bootleggers became enormously powerful personages who won fortunes and exercised political power. Good citizens received in their homes the law-breakers who furnished them with liquor. Libraries were transformed into bars and cellars into restaurants. A part of the police forces in the big cities became corrupt. At the end of a few years the danger had grown so great that a campaign was started for the repeal of Prohibition. The country was divided into *wets* and *drys*. Finally in 1933 the Eighteenth Amendment was repealed by the Twenty-first Amendment.

The experiment had shown once again that "he who tries to play the Angel, plays the Beast."

Shakespeare conceived nothing more tragic than the end of Woodrow Wilson. For more than a year the specter of a President governed America. From time to time, from his impenetrable retreat in the White House, there emerged a recommendation for a law or a veto signed in a trembling hand. When stories were circulated that Wilson had lost his mind, he made an appearance at a cabinet meeting where he seemed sane enough but diminished, and only with difficulty able to concentrate. Little by little, life returned to his numbed limbs, and on March 4, 1921, he was able to accompany his successor, Warren G. Harding, to the Capitol. In the car Harding, not knowing what to say, began to tell Wilson an inoffensive anecdote about an elephant. The retiring President burst into tears. Upon returning to private life Wilson did not leave Washington, but lived there in strict seclusion. In 1922, and again in 1923 on Armistice Day, he appeared on his balcony and, in a voice still thickened by paralysis, said a few words to the crowd. He spoke of the shame for America of having remained outside the League of Nations. Finally, on February 3, 1924, he died after prolonged and cruel suffering. He had made great and noble plans; he had failed to carry them out; he died a defeated man after witnessing the complete ruin of his hopes. But it is possible that the fire which he lighted and which is still smoldering beneath the ashes of war will one day blaze afresh and the name of Woodrow Wilson will then shine with a new glory.

CHAPTER LV

Actions and Reactions

THE period from 1920 to 1928 has often been compared by American historians to that which followed the Civil War. In both cases, they point out, the Republican party was in office for a long period; in both cases it was necessary to liquidate a situation and return to normal. In both cases a nation, tired of public sacrifice, tried for a mad decade to concern itself exclusively with its private affairs; in both cases excessive individualism gave rise to political and financial scandals. One may question the validity of this comparison. The Republican party in 1865 found itself in office because it had won the war; the Republican party in 1920 came into office as a result of the reaction against the war. The corruption was more serious and more extensive after the Civil War than after the World War. What is true in both cases is that the war led to extraordinary technical progress. In 1865 America was building transcontinental railroads; in 1920 it developed new industries; moving pictures, radio, aviation. There resulted in both epochs a rise in prices, discontent among the farmers, and finally a financial panic followed by a new swing of the pendulum.

The election of 1920 had a double character. It was in part a vote against Wilson, against the treaty, against the League of Nations. Many Americans felt sorry that they had become involved in European affairs. An adroitly contrived campaign tended to disgust them with their victory, to make them believe they had fought for the bankers, and to supplant their friendship for their former Allies by pity for their former enemies. Wilson's illness and his seclusion had undermined the prestige of the Democratic party. The voters wanted most of all to return to their pre-war life, which had been, they believed, a happier one. They had the illusion that a change of leaders and of politics would restore business freedom and the good old times. Since Theodore Roosevelt had died in 1919, the Republican party lacked a hero but it could have its choice of several distinguished men: Governor Frank Lowden of Illinois, General Leonard Wood, and President Nicholas Murray Butler of Columbia University. After long debate the convention of 1920 nominated Warren G. Harding, a senator from Ohio, who had nothing to recommend him for the office of President except perhaps his very insignificance. The country was tired of great minds. The Senate was finding out that with brilliant and domineering Presidents like Roosevelt and Wilson, Congress was reduced to the role of rubber stamp. Nicholas Murray Butler tells of a senator who said ironically that in Harding they would have a man who would sign the acts sent to him by the Senate instead of sending acts to the Senate with an order to pass them. His name had been suggested at the start by Harry Daugherty, one of his Ohio friends and the representative of the oil interests at the convention. The candidate's fine presence, hatred of Wilson, fear of the Reds, and distrust of men of ideas won the day. It was a triumphal election. James M. Cox, the Democratic candidate, received nine million votes; Harding, sixteen million—one of the greatest majorities ever given to a President of the United States. Someone said: "It's not an avalanche, it's an earthquake." Eugene V. Debs, the Socialist, who was in prison at the time, received about one million votes. The Vice President was Calvin Coolidge, former governor of Massachusetts, famous for having suppressed a police strike in Boston and for having declared that the right to endanger the public safety by a strike did not belong to "anybody, anywhere, anytime." The Right turn made by the Ship of State in 1920 was abrupt and violent.

But the new pilot did not know his trade. Harding was not of presidential caliber. He tried to make up for his incompetence by putting in his cabinet certain able men, such as Hughes as Secretary of State and Hoover as Secretary of Commerce. The appointment to the Treasury of Andrew Mellon, one of the richest men in the country, pleased Mellon's millionaire confrères. Unfortunately, Harding had obligations to the men who had raised him to the presidency and whose honesty was open to question. Thus he gave the Interior Department to Albert B. Fall, a speculator who was even then in a highly ambiguous position and whose relations with the petroleum interests were well known. Mysterious negotiations began between Fall, Denby (who was Secretary of the Navy), and certain oil magnates such as Doheny and Sinclair. The United States government possessed rich oil reserves in California and in Wyoming. A law had put them at the disposal of the navy and had allowed the latter to lease them or to entrust their exploitation to private companies. Fall persuaded Denby to transfer this right to the Department of the Interior of which he, Fall, was Secretary, and thereupon in great secrecy leased Teapot Dome (the huge oil property in Wyoming, thus called because of a mountain in the shape of a teapot) and the Elk Hills reserves to his friend Harry F. Sinclair without having advertised for competitive bids. As a result stock in the Sinclair enterprises increased in value by fifty million dollars. When an investigation was opened by the Senate, Fall maintained that the deal was advantageous to the nation, but it was proved that he had accepted enormous commissions and he was forced to resign, sentenced to a year in prison and a fine of one hundred thousand dollars. Meanwhile, Attorney General Harry M. Daugherty was covering up certain extremely shady transactions and Colonel Forbes, Head of the Veterans' Bureau and a personal friend of Harding, was selling army supplies at less than 20 per cent of their real value to a business house in Boston, once more without advertising for bids or holding an auction. An investigation showed that in many instances Forbes was handing over for twenty cents what the bureau had to repurchase the same day for a dollar. Harding's friends seemed even more sordid than Grant's.

Harding, like Grant before him, was innocent of any fraudulent transactions, but he was a weak and pleasure-loving man who had put rogues into office and who therefore bore the responsibility. He realized it and toward 1923 his handsome face changed visibly. He had to make a trip to

Alaska. As he was leaving he said: "In this job I am not worried about my enemies. It is my friends that are keeping me awake nights." During the trip he repeatedly asked those around him: "What can a President do when his friends betray him?" For a time he thought of making a public confession. While aboard ship, returning from Alaska, he received a coded radio message which increased his despondency. An air of tragedy hung over the presidential party. At San Francisco he fell ill. It was said that he had been poisoned by canned crab meat, but there had been no canned crab meat on the ship, and rumors of a very different sort went the rounds. Whatever the case may be, on August 2, while Mrs. Harding was reading to him, he died. "Embolism," the doctors said. The public did not believe it. The startling news reached Vice President Coolidge on the night of August 2, 1923, at his father's farm in Vermont where he had gone to spend his vacation. His father was a county justice of the peace. By the light of an oil lamp held by Mrs. Coolidge, wearing a hastily donned dressing gown, the father administered the oath of office to the son on the old family Bible. The nation was delighted by this little scene, in the tradition of the Founding Fathers. It was reassuring to think that the President who had had the worst associates and who had been the least moral in the history of the United States had for a successor a Yankee and a Puritan.

Calvin Coolidge had reddish hair, blue eyes, and the most remarkable nasal accent New England ever produced. It was said that the word cow, as pronounced by him, had at least four syllables. But he had a right to linger over his words, for legend has it that he uttered very few of them. By nature, by education, and above all because he had nothing to say, he had always been taciturn. When he entered political life and discovered that his laconic sentences amused people and converted him into a picturesque figure in the eyes of the public, he made a practice of what had originally been a weakness and formed the habit of making brief replies that were at once obvious and droll. Coolidge had a sort of negative sense of humor and his solemn buffoonery entertained no one more than himself. Though modest in appearance, he was delighted with his own success. He knew that his silences had served him well. Of his friend Senator Murray Crane, he said: "He confirmed my opinion as to the value of a silence, which avoids creating a situation where one would not otherwise exist." To a general who accosted him by saying: "Hello, Chatterbox!" he replied: "Well, General, I notice what I don't say gets me in less trouble than what you do say." A classic example of a Coolidgism is his comment on the war debts: "They hired the money, didn't they?" To a reporter who asked him: "Why don't you have artists, musicians, actors, poets, around the White House, as Wilson and Roosevelt did?" he replied: "I knew a poet once, when I was at Amherst. Class poet. Name of Smith." He paused, ruminated for a moment, and then added: "Never heard of him since." These mannerisms became strangely dear to the American people and Coolidge was a popular President. He had entered the White House as a result of Harding's death; when he ran on his own account in 1924 against John W. Davis, a famous New York lawyer, and Robert M. La Follette, he received almost all Harding's votes, to the great disappointment of the Democrats, who thought the G. O. P. had been ruined by the scandals. But a happy nation does not change its politics, and the American people in 1924 were far from believing themselves unhappy.

Wall Street was bursting with riches. The graphs of securities reached vertiginous heights. It was the Coolidge boom and he was proud of it. Not that he speculated himself. Never was there a more prudent man. But he loved the spectacle of America "making money." "Work and economize, economize and work" was the text of one of his brief speeches, whereby one can see that he was not afraid of platitudes. On the contrary; he gloried in being banal. It was this that made him original. Mrs. Coolidge, a charming and simple woman, even after a long married life considered her husband an impenetrable enigma. As for the country, it was so prosperous that ways of reducing taxation became the principal concern of the Treasury. What was the source of all this money? Pyramided credits. The United States granted credits to Germany; Germany made use of them to pay reparations to France and England; France and England to repay the war debts to America. Thus the money moved in a circle, and the United States received back what the United States itself had poured in at the beginning of the circuit. In 1928 loans to stock brokers rose to four billion dollars, which disturbed the old-line market experts. They predicted a catastrophe. But the enthusiasts proclaimed: "The laws of classical economics do not apply to mass production. Mankind has entered a new era. Prosperity and rising prices will never stop!" Securities continued to mount; it was easy to get rich. All you had to do was to buy at random. The whole country was speculating. Under a silent and sober President America was living in a world of magic.

In Harding's administration a conference in Washington had fixed the relative strength of the capital ships of the world's principal navies. Great Britain had agreed to equality with the United States; Japan had accepted three-fifths of the tonnage granted to each of these nations. Upon France, the conference had imposed equality with Italy. England, Japan, France, and the United States had promised to respect one another's island possessions in the Pacific (including the Philippines) and to construct no new fortifications there. In 1927 Coolidge proposed to extend the naval agreement to cruisers, torpedo boats, and submarines. He met with refusals and was forced to make up his mind to an increase in the United States navy. However, in 1928 he signed, in company with thirteen other nations, a new pact called the Kellogg-Briand Pact, which outlawed war as a means of settling international disputes and agreed to the substitution of pacific methods. This pact was ratified by the Senate unanimously except for one vote, which proved that it could not contain much of anything. But Briand, who was more of a realist than his critics knew, hoped by this agreement to lead America into the path of international co-operation. With its South American neighbors the United States was on good terms; Coolidge went as far as Havana to open a Pan-American Congress and to reaffirm the United States' belief in the equality of nations. Senator Dwight W. Morrow, a member of the House of Morgan, smoothed out, by his tact and intelligence, many of the old quarrels with Mexico, whither Coolidge had sent him as ambassador. Nicaragua alone remained in a state of unrest, and certain senators accused the administration of making it "a protectorate of Wall Street."

Many thought Coolidge would be a candidate again in 1928, and his name was so linked with the idea of prosperity that he would have had an excellent chance of election. But when the moment drew near he issued a statement of ten words: "I do not choose to run for President in 1928." It was a perfect Coolidgism. The news surprised the whole world, including Mrs. Coolidge: "Isn't it like that man? He never gave me the slightest intimation of his intentions. I had no idea." Did Coolidge fear an economic crisis and wish to avoid being in office when it broke? Or did he hope that the Republican convention would force his hand? If the second supposition is true, he was much deceived, for the convention nominated almost unanimously the Secretary of Commerce, Herbert Hoover, who had been as successful in that office as he had been in the ones he had occupied during the war of 1917. Hoover was a liberal in the nineteenth-century sense of the word. "Absolute freedom of the press to discuss public questions," he said, "is a foundation stone of American liberty." Confronted with a choice between "the American system of rugged individualism and the European doctrine of paternalism and state socialism," he had chosen free enterprise. The Democratic convention nominated Alfred E. Smith, governor of New York state, who was a Catholic, a "wet," and a Tammany man. As a result, the Republican party scored one of its most brilliant victories. Hoover carried forty states, including a large part of the solid South, which was thought to be nothing short of a miracle.

The period following the election of Hoover has not yet emerged from the domain of polemics and entered that of history. Hoover said during his campaign that America was nearer the final triumph over poverty than any country had ever been before. In this he was probably right. The means of production were sufficient to provide a decent life for all Americans. But distribution and business organization were still faulty. The orgy of speculation that had marked the end of Coolidge's administration was to bring about an economic crisis of the first magnitude. Contrary to the belief of the optimists, no new era had opened in human affairs; the same causes still produced the same effects, and the excessive rise had paved the way for an excessive drop. At the beginning of the Hoover administration, the Coolidge boom continued. Stocks went on rising; the public went on borrowing; the farmers went on producing. But a market built on confidence was bound to crash at the first symptom of distrust. The crisis that began in October, 1929, was more serious and more prolonged than any that had preceded it. By 1933, the number of unemployed rose to thirteen or fourteen millions, a catastrophic figure. The national income declined from eighty-one billion dollars in 1929 to forty billion dollars in 1932. Hoover, like Van Buren before him, had found "the nation pregnant with a crisis" for which he was not responsible; but in the eyes of the voters he was to blame for their misfortunes and he was not re-elected in 1932. Hoover was not a Wall Street man. During the war of 1914 he had shown his disinterestedness and his philanthropy. But the depression ruined his political career. Poverty and unemployment inspired the American people with a bitter distrust of those who had controlled the country for the past ten years. The captains of industry were discredited. As in the time of Cleveland, the nation turned to the reformers.

Hoover's successor, Franklin Delano Roosevelt, a man of courage and of great personal charm, inherited a tragic situation. Not only were there thirteen million unemployed demanding help, but six million farmers were crushed under the weight of ten billion dollars in mortgages. A newspaper proposed the following definition: "FARM: a plot of arable ground surrounded on all sides by creditors and covered with mortgages, on which a family of seven tries in vain to supply the needs of a second-hand car whose gas tank is empty." Cotton had fallen to five cents; wheat to thirty-seven. Farmers were evicted from their homes by their creditors; because loans on real estate could not be repaid thousands of local banks closed. Depositors in the big banks became frightened and withdrew their funds. By the day of Roosevelt's inauguration payment had been suspended in twenty-three states. In his inaugural address at the Capitol the President said:

In such a spirit on my part and on yours we face our common difficulties. They concern, thank God, only material things. Values have shrunken to fantastic levels . . . a host of unemployed citizens face the grim problem of existence. . . . Only a foolish optimist can deny the dark realities of the moment. . . . The money changers have fled from their high seats in the temple of our civilization We may now restore that temple to the ancient truths. The measure of that restoration lies in the extent to which we apply social values more noble than mere monetary profit. . . . The nation asks for action, and action now. Our greatest primary task is to put people to work.

Never since Lincoln had a President been inaugurated in such dramatic circumstances. Millions of unemployed, their number growing day by day; farmers in revolt; banks closed; all the pillars of the social structure crumbling one after the other, with terrifying rapidity—such was the backdrop which one could discern in the shadows behind the long star-spangled banners.

There were three possible economic policies: the classical one of *laissez faire* which would have meant waiting for the play of individual actions to re-establish equilibrium; the Socialist and Communist solution (an end to the private ownership of the means of production); and finally, a directed or planned ecoonmy. It was this last that the new President favored. To raise the price level he depreciated the dollar by 40 per cent. To help the unemployed find work he had the nation undertake numerous public works which ran all the way from the construction of enormous dams to the adornment of monuments. To raise wages he encouraged collective contracts. To protect the public against fraudulent securities he instituted a stricter control over banks of issue, prohibiting them from being also banks of deposit, and had them watched over by the Securities and Exchange Commission. To relieve the farmers, he took over, in the name of the government, part of the mortgages and reduced the rate of interest. To check the fall in agricultural prices, he asked the farmers to limit the areas devoted to cotton and wheat growing. This policy, which has been given the name of the New Deal, had fanatic partisans and opponents. The former claimed it had saved the country; the latter, that it was ruining it. *Adhuc sub judice lis est.* But Republicans and Democrats approved almost unanimously Roosevelt's foreign policy and praised him for having understood, long before the voters, that isolationism in the new conflict that was brewing in Europe was a most dangerous attitude for the United States.

So far as foreign policy was concerned, President Roosevelt found himself in a difficult position. The campaign against the League of Nations and the question of the war debts had, since 1920, embittered the United States' relations with France and England. Since a one-year moratorium on all governmental debts and reparations payments had been declared by Hoover in 1931, the circulation of money had ceased, the European nations suspending their payments to the United States, which aroused much resentment because the people did not understand that the means of payment no longer existed. Certain writers, some of whom later regretted it, had led the public to think that America's participation in the preceding war had been neither just nor necessary. The conservative elements in the country were isolationists by tradition; the liberal elements were so from spite, and grew more so when they gained the impression that the Western democracies were abandoning Ethiopia, Spain and Czechoslovakia. Most Americans did not see that the totalitarians threatened their own country as much as Europe. They were under the illusion that in case of a new war they could keep themselves aloof, and their statesmen sought to eliminate all possible causes of American participation. Three neutrality acts were voted between 1935 and 1937. They were designed to strengthen the position of Congress by depriving the President of some of his prerogatives. To prevent the repetition of a tragedy like that of the *Lusitania*, Americans were forbidden to travel on ships belonging to the belligerents; loans to warring nations were prohibited; the export of arms and munitions to foreign belligerents was forbidden; and warring nations were required to pay cash for any purchases made in this country. The passage of these laws strengthened Germany in her determination to conquer Europe.

When war broke out in 1939 Congress, at the President's request, lifted the embargo on arms on condition that the countries buying them should pay cash and provide their own means of transportation (cash-and-carry). American ships were forbidden to sail in the territorial waters of the belligerent countries. It was the time of the "phony war," when military operations on the French front were practically at a standstill and when German propaganda was holding out chimerical hopes of an easy peace. The majority of Americans were definitely hostile to Hitler, but thought that France and England would be strong enough to stop him. The defeat of France was a terrible moral shock to America. But when Paul Reynaud asked President Roosevelt for help, the latter could promise him nothing since every decision involving war was the prerogative of Congress and it had always shown itself very jealous of its rights in this matter. In September, 1940, the President announced the transfer to Great Britain of fifty over-age American destroyers in exchange for air and naval bases on islands belonging to Great Britain. At the end of the year came the presidential election. The two candidates, Franklin D. Roosevelt and Wendell

L. Willkie, the Republican, both declared themselves in favor of aid to Great Britain but not in favor of a declaration of war: "All aid, short of war." President Roosevelt was re-elected, the first time in the history of the United States that a President had asked for and obtained a third term.

The country's endorsement gave the President full authority to carry out his policy of aid to England. At the beginning of 1941 he obtained from Congress the passage of the Lend-Lease Bill which allowed him to lend or lease to the English without payment the materials of war that were indispensable to them. It was a wise measure, for England's dollar balances were rapidly dwindling. At the same time the President was preparing the country, much more completely than Wilson in similar circumstances had done, for a war that was becoming, if not certain, at least probable. While the country was still at peace Congress instituted conscription and put eight hundred thousand soldiers in training. War plants were equipped. America was making no pretense of neutrality; she was openly hostile to Germany and took steps which, in any other circumstances, would have provoked a declaration of war from the Reich: the occupation of Greenland, the escorting of convoys, the arming of merchant vessels. In the United States isolationists and interventionists battled each other in pamphlets and on lecture platforms, but it was evident that the interventionists had the best of it in the opinion of the public. Nevertheless this masked war might have continued for a long time if Japan, Germany's ally and like her a totalitarian state, which had long awaited a chance to establish its hegemony in the Pacific, had not attacked without warning the American base at Pearl Harbor in the Hawaiian Islands. The declaration of war against Japan was quickly followed by declarations against Germany and Italy. These surprised no one and the whole country approved the decisions of Congress and the President.

CHAPTER LVI

The New America

ETWEEN 1900 and 1940 America had changed as rapidly as between 1860 and 1900. The cities continued to devour the countryside. Of the one hundred thirty-one million inhabitants in 1940, seventy-four million lived in cities. From 1905 to 1910, average annual immigration had been around a million a year. After 1929 it was reduced by law to a maximum of one hundred fifty thousand, each country having the right to a "quota" based on the proportion of its nationals in the population of the United States in 1920. In other words America undertook to stabilize the racial and linguistic composition of her population. Meanwhile the mixing of the diverse elements had been accelerated by the development of the means of transportation. In 1900 there had been four thousand automobiles in America; in 1941 there were thirty-two million. A great system of modern roads had been built. Air transport had outstripped the anticipations of H. G. Wells. From the first flights of the Wright brothers to the war of 1914, aviation had belonged to the domain of sport and of scientific research. Today the airways, marked out by aerial beacons, crisscross the country. Every large town has its airport. A network of invisible beams enables airplanes to find their way in the dark. The continent can be crossed in sixteen hours. To go from Pittsburgh to Philadelphia in 1812 required six days; in 1845, fourteen hours; in 1940, two hours. In 1941 four and one-half million passengers flew in the United States, the number of fatal acidents being only 2.2 per hundred million miles flown. In May, 1927, Charles Lindbergh startled the world by flying the Atlantic from New York to Paris. Today transoceanic clippers leave and return with the regularity of ocean liners. After this war, it is probable that aerial buses for Europe will be as numerous as Fifth Avenue buses.

The means of public information, like those of transportation, have unified the country. The station KDKA in Pittsburgh was the first to broadcast news when it transmitted press bulletins on the Harding-Cox election. Then the Columbia Broadcasting Company, the National Broadcasting Company, and numerous independent stations were born. In the United States today radio has as much influence on public opinion as the newspapers. At every hour of the day and night news bulletins are broadcast and commentators, some clamly, others excitedly, explain to the masses

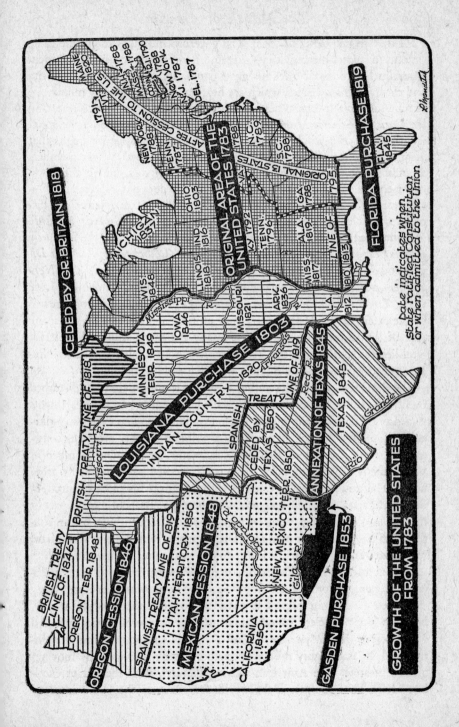

GROWTH OF THE UNITED STATES FROM 1783

what they should think of them. The government makes use of the radio systems to communicate with its citizens on important occasions. President Franklin D. Roosevelt owes his great popularity in part to the simplicity and clarity of his speeches, which are heard at their firesides by millions of families. Although certain newspapers (such as the New York *Times* and the *Christian Science Monitor*) are read by the élite throughout the country, the press as a whole remains local. There are newspaper chains that belong to groups (Scripps-Howard press, Hearst press) whose members all publish the same articles on the same day. The columnist is the newspaper equivalent of the radio commentator. He does not express an editorial policy but his own personal views. A number of magazines are distributed in all the forty-eight states. *Harper's* and the *Atlantic Monthly* play the role that belong in France to the *Revue de Paris* and the *Nouvelle Revue Française*. The *Saturday Evening Post, Collier's,* the *Reader's Digest* and *Liberty* have attained circulations of several million. The *New Yorker* and the group of magazines belonging to Henry Robinson Luce (*Life, Time, Fortune*), more satiric and sometimes cynical in tone, reveal by the extent of their popularity a new attitude and a reaction against the Age of the Chromo on the part of many American minds. The leftist weeklies, the *Nation* and the *New Republic,* exert a fairly extensive influence because they are read by men who shape public opinion.

The development of cities and of means of transportation has disturbed family life. In the big cities the high rents have reduced family apartments to a size that makes communal life uncomfortable. The increasing difficulty of finding household servants contributes to this problem, consequently, with the aid of the automobile and the growing number of hotels, many Americans have become accustomed to living away from home. The midday meal is eaten by everyone near his place of business, in either a restaurant or a cafeteria. Children are at school a good part of the day. In the evening young men and women frequently go out in couples with friends of their own age. The liberty permitted them would have scandalized their ancestors. It is due to the weakening of the sexual tabus, to birth control, to the diffusion of a pseudo-Freudianism, and to the influences of elements other than Anglo-Saxon. The movies offer a sanctuary to all these wandering couples. It was about 1903 that the first "plot movie" was shown as public entertainment; in 1913 the first serial stories appeared on the screen (*The Mysteries of New York*); in 1926 sound films were introduced. In 1940 eighty million spectators a week thronged the moving-picture theaters. The American moving pictures, with the aid of excellent actors, have conquered the world. On America they have imposed their optimistic and naïve view of life. Nevertheless, during the last few years a touch of bitterness and of realism has found its way into certain stories: *Grapes of Wrath, The Little Foxes, The Philadelphia Story*. In 1940 adultery was still practically banned from the screen, but it does not play the same role in America that it does in Europe as a mitigator of monogamy, which in this country is rendered bearable by successive marriages. Certain states, especially Nevada (Reno), have turned divorce into a profitable industry. The number of divorces per hundred thousand inhabitants doubled between 1914 and 1940—rising from one hundred to two hundred. (Two hundred sixty-four thousand divorces and fifteen hundred sixty-five thousand marriages in 1940.)

Mass production, which has become the dominant characteristic of American industry, has had two major effects: reduction of the cost of living and uniformity in the way of living. The standard of living of the average American is in many respects superior to that of the European and it is tending to rise. Thanks to government control of foodstuffs, the poorest can buy as pure produce as the richest; the American cuisine, after long neglect, has made remarkable progress, and household work has been rendered easier by ingenious machines (refrigerators, automatic washing machines, devices for fast cooking, dishwashing machines, etc). Ready-made clothes are well cut, and custom tailors have become rare. Automobiles, radios, bathrooms are available to a large portion of the population and, before the war, could be purchased on the installment plan. The weak point of American social life is housing. Many poor quarters should be torn down and replaced. One solution is to build auxiliary communities near enough to the big cities to permit daily commutation. If America succeeds in completely eliminating slums and unemployment, which seems by no means impossible, she will have created for her citizens national conditions of life superior to any that have been known by mankind up to this time. The other side of the picture is the excessive uniformity encouraged by mass production abetted by incessant advertising. In any given month millions of Americans drink the same beverage (in 1940 Coca-Cola), read the same books (Book-of-the-Month Club), see the same films, eat the same cereals, tell the same jokes, take the same medicines, and then, with amazing unanimity, pass on to next month's craze.

The status of the Negro remains a distressing problem. It presents two different aspects, depending on whether one views it in the North or in the South. At the time of the war in 1917 a very considerable black migration from the South to the North took place. It was caused by the necessity of replacing the soldiers in the factories and by the attraction exerted on colored people by those states that recognize their civil rights. In 1940 there were some two and a half million Negroes in the North, almost ten million in the South, and around one hundred and seventy thousand in the West. Those in the North could vote freely, which gave them a certain influence on local government and enabled them to obtain hospitals and schools, which are still inadequate but nevertheless mark a real advance. Colored lawyers and doctors practice their profession only among their own people. The two populations, white and black, for the most part live in separate districts. In the South the great majority of Negroes are not allowed to vote. They are debarred from the polls under various pretexts. Equality before the law, in the eyes of the Negro, can be nothing but a white man's myth. Nevertheless the American Negro has made great intellectual progress. Negro universities (for example, Spellman University in Atlanta) produce cultured men and women. Negro literature, music, and painting are of high quality. The Republican party stands for the abolition of those restrictions that keep Negroes from voting in the South, while President and Mrs. Roosevelt are making a personal effort to improve the Negro's social standing.

Religious life is less fervent than it was in the nineteenth century. About 50 per cent of Americans are not members of any church; however this figure does not represent the private sentiments of the country. America remains essentially Christian, but by this must be understood emotional reactions rather than doctrinal beliefs. The average American still feels the necessity of justifying his actions on ethical grounds. "Unethical" is a word that immediately rules out any proposal or transaction. Religious life and political life are closely associated. Subjects for sermons are borrowed from internal or foreign political controveries; they are announced in the newspapers among the paid advertisements. Famous clergymen are consulted on national problems just as are the presidents of universities. Nevertheless their influence is only effective within narrow limits. Prohibition was a failure and the Protestant churches do not dare attack birth control. Quite different is the attitude of the Catholic Church, which maintains its traditional disciplines and imposes rigid rules of conduct upon its members. Birth control is still prohibited, divorce is not recognized, annulments are rare. In the United States the Catholic Church numbers around twenty-two million members, almost all from Europe: Irish, German, Polish, Italian, and a small number of French. It possesses its own schools and universities, but it retains the characteristics and the attitude of a minority. To be a Catholic hitherto has been an insurmountable obstacle for any candidate for the presidency. American Jews have reached the number of almost five million. Many of them have a tendency to depart from rigid orthodoxy; reformed Jewish churches, with services in English, are numerous. Conferences of Jews and Christians make it their purpose to preach and to practice tolerance. This is a necessary undertaking for, from time to time, waves of intolerance can be seen gathering in the United States (renaissance of the Ku Klux Klan, against the Negroes and the Jews; the anti-Semitic campaign of Father Coughlin).

Education is one of the most formidable problems of the America of tomorrow. No country takes education more seriously: There are about twenty million boys and girls in the elementary schools, five million in the high schools, almost a million and a half in the colleges and universities. Everywhere the traveler can admire the fine campuses with their modern or neo-Gothic buildings, the gay crowds of college men and girls, the playing fields, the laboratories, and, in larger towns, schools that are palatial. But the intellectual results seem less brilliant than those obtained in the eighteenth century in the little red schools of New England. During this war conscription has shown that illiteracy in certain regions is dangerously high. College presidents, such as Robert Maynard Hutchins of Chicago, complain of the mediocre training of the students sent to them by the high schools. What are the reasons for this situation which, to a European, would seem to indicate relative failure? In part, the complete lack of unity in teaching programs. Every European child receives willy-nilly the same fundamentals of education. In the United States, the standards vary with the different states. Higher education is sometimes excellent but it cannot build a solid culture in minds that are without foundations. Certain poor states economize on their teaching staffs, and in such states teachers and professors are badly paid. They do not have the social position that should be theirs. Institutions of no intellectual worth have the right to bestow diplomas, licenses, and doctorates. The money of the rich universities is often spent for buildings rather than for chairs. Instructors (with some very honorable exceptions) make no attempt to mold critical minds; many of them demand a knowledge of facts rather than of methods and forget that "information is not culture." On the other hand American colleges are more successful than European ones in teaching the art of communal life. The universities produce good citizens; and they leave almost all their graduates, both men and women, with a memory of four enchanted years.

During the period from 1900 to 1940, American literature detached itself from English literature. The language, constantly renewed by brilliant inventions and figures of speech, recalls the fluidity of sixteenth-century English. The tone and the subjects became thoroughly American. Theodore Dreiser, Sinclair Lewis, and later Hemingway, Steinbeck, Faulkner, and Caldwell have painted American life with a realism and a harshness that are reminiscent of French naturalism. They represent a reaction against complacent optimism, against puritanism, and against sentimentalism. In *Main Street* and in *Babbitt*, Sinclair Lewis has drawn a cruel picture of the small towns of the Middle West. Is this indictment of the American middle classes fair? Vernon Parrington replies that Sinclair Lewis and the other novelists of the school of disillusion fail to see what is the essence of Americanism and what redeems its faults:

> A rich and abundant life, motivated by a fine sense of ethical responsibility and disciplined by a democratic public school, is, in sober fact, the distinguishing characteristic of America that sets our country apart from all other lands in western civilization. . . . Where else has the industrial revolution been brought so completely and happily under dominion to the democratic ideal, or been so ennobled by ethical values? Here it has scattered its wealth among the plain people with a bountiful hand, until the poorest family enjoys its nickel-plated plumbing, its flivver, its telephone, its radio, its movies, its funnies, and all the thousand aids to comfort and intelligence which a few generations ago were denied kings.

It is a fact that the industrial revolution in America enriched the nation: public libraries, museums, free hospitals and clinics, universities open to all. All these fine institutions of a rich and generous community go to make up a society worthy of men's love, capable of improvement, and able to inspire in its members a devotion whose strength the present war has shown. The American is not a nationalist in the European sense of the word; he cannot be, since for many citizens of the United States language, customs, and traditions are different from those of their neighbors. But Americans, even those of recent date, are united in their love for a certain kind of life which is theirs and which they are ready to defend.

One can measure some of the changes that have taken place in American society during the present century by rereading a book which won a merited success in 1899: Thorstein Veblen's *The Theory of the Leisure Class*. Veblen's thesis was that human beings, once they have raised themselves above the average and, with surplus wealth, have acquired the right to leisure, do not so much try to be happy as to make a parade of their possessions and emphasize their superiority to the rest of mankind. This is the reason, said Veblen, for codes of conduct, of dress, of language and manners whose sole value is that they are impossible for the laborer to follow. The high silk hat, patent-leather shoes, etiquette, contempt for manual work, knowledge of art and grammar are just so many diverse forms of the need to prove that one belongs to the leisure class for which the only honorable occupations are hunting, war, and government. This thesis may have been true in 1900 when businessmen, once they had made a fortune, and more still their descendants, tried to acquire the tastes of the ancient leisure classes. It has completely ceased to be true in 1943. The granddaughter of the millionaire of 1900 works in a factory and is proud of it. She laughs at the tabus of dress, manners, and language of the former governing classes. What has happened? Since war has become principally industrial, work shares in the prestige that formerly belonged to the warrior alone. The workshop now is seen as an extension of the army. The army itself is nothing but an immense workshop that sends out machines, services them, and repairs them. The officer as well as the soldier must be a resourceful mechanic. This has produced real equality.

CHAPTER LVII

Conclusion

IT IS no exaggeration to talk about an American miracle. The growth of the United States has been more rapid than that of any other human community. In a century and a half there has taken shape in North America a nation that is today one of the most powerful on earth and that has become an asylum for the oppressed and afflicted of the entire world. It has created means of production that enable it in time of war to arm not only its own soldiers but those of its allies as well and that will enable it in time of peace, if they are properly employed, to free most of its citizens from want. No doubt much misery and inequality still exist in America; no doubt American institutions remain imperfect; no doubt ambition and corruption play their role here as in every country. But an impartial judge must recognize that from 1787 to 1940 America has given its citizens more peace, stability, and happiness than have the great nations of Europe.

The population of America is made up of elements from the Old World. Why do these elements seem to have improved on being transplanted? We have seen how the abundance of land in America for a long time made the struggle for existence less bitter. The untouched resources of the continent permitted the development of production simultaneously with the increase in population. The ancient feuds of the Europeans were, if not obliterated, at least toned down, and after two or three generations they were forgotten. The country was constantly rejuvenated by the arrival of new contingents, who came not as conquerors or as captives but as equals and associates. The enormous field open to the pioneers, to the builders of cities and of railroads, to the enterprises of the captains of industry gave rise to an enthusiastic, confident, and daring activity that was not to be dismayed by the most gigantic undertakings. From their Anglo-Saxon ancestors the first Americans had inherited puritanism, which predisposed them to activity, and the whole priceless tradition of public discussion. America did not serve an apprenticeship in liberty, because England had served it for her. But she herself from the very beginning invented new forms of liberty well adapted to her needs, and her founders elaborated a Constitution which for one hundred fifty years has allowed her to remake herself without revolution and bloodshed. Finally, the separation, in space and in interests, from the other great powers has given the United States long periods of peace, thanks to which she has achieved the conquest and development of the continent.

Although America and England both call themselves democracies their institutions are founded on different systems. In England the responsibility of the cabinet to Parliament and the right of Parliament to dismiss the Prime Minister are the guarantees of the people's liberties. In America the cabinet depends on the President alone, and Congress cannot turn the latter out of office except through impeachment, a difficult and little-used procedure. Thus the executive power in the United States is at once stronger and more stable. Nevertheless liberties are safe. They are protected: (a) by the right of Congress to override the President's veto; (b) by the exclusive right of Congress to impose taxes; (c) by the courts; (d) by the Bill of Rights which forms a part of the Constitution; (e) by the immense power of public opinion. Actually the conflicts between President and Congress have never seriously hindered the administration of the country; no President has attempted to act as a dictator. Discipline and liberty in the United States live happily together. The institutions are accepted by all and revolutionary minorities themselves do not dare to declare themselves openly hostile to representative government. The two traditional American parties with their ill-defined programs seem, at first sight, less intelligible than the Conservative party and the Labour party in England. But in politics it is wise to make use of what exists so long as that functions fairly well. It is a fact that inside the Republican and Democratic parties American conservatives and reformers are able to express themselves and that they come into power alternately, approximately as in England, thus maintaining that oscillation of the pendulum which is the essence of government.

The equilibrium of America and its internal peace demand that the parties should be national and not sectional. The sections have played a capital role in the history of the United States. The East and the West were in opposition as early as the time of the Founding Fathers; the South and the North provide examples of two different types of society; the South and the West by their alliance governed the country for a long period; later the Far West acquired distinctive characteristics. But most of the conflicts of interest were peaceably settled in Congress. The custom arose of maintaining the equilibrium between the various regions by the division of offices. The only occasion on which a sectional conflict gave rise to war was the Civil War between the North and the South, because in that instance the Republican party was completely identified with the North. That Lincoln received only twenty-six thousand votes in the South explains the tragedy. There remains in the South a diffuse bitterness and a feeling that in the general economy of the country the South is not so well treated as the North or the West. In general, although intersectional differences are tending to diminish, there still exist regional groupings of economic and even political interests. In the present war the East is suffering more from the shortage of gasoline than the Middle West or the South. The Pacific coast attaches more importance than the Atlantic coast to the war against Japan. The South does not see the Negro problem in the same light as does the rest of the nation. Political life is still made up in fairly large measure of pressures exerted in Washington by local groups. But sectional rivalries remain within the framework of the Constitution and give no cause of apprehension for the future.

Class conflicts do not have the same bitterness as in Europe. Not through equality in income, but through equality in the standard of living, America is tending toward a classless society. The enormous taxes are slowly leveling fortunes. In the United States there is no labor party like the English one, and the Socialist party is without wide influence. Labor unions have been strengthened by the Roosevelt administration, which has imposed them upon employers as agents for negotiation, but they have been weakened by their internal dissensions. Two federations are trying to unite them; the old American Federation of Labor of Gompers (now under William Green), which has always been moderate, and the C. I. O. (Congress of Industrial Organizations) organized by John L. Lewis, president of the United Mine Workers. In 1936 the C. I. O. supported the election of the President and for some time the administration was favorable to Lewis. Then a war broke out between Mr. Roosevelt and John L.

Lewis, who abandoned the C. I. O. and stayed with his miners alone. Today labor unions retain political importance, but it is limited by the reactions of public opinion. This was to be seen in the case of strikes in wartime.

Although Americans are united in their affection for their institutions, they are divided on the subject of national economy. The example of Russia, the depression of 1929, and the extent of unemployment have inspired a number of intellectuals in the course of the last decade with a desire to substitute a planned economy for free competition. The war of 1941 (as formerly that of 1917) has favored this tendency and has led to the creation in Washington of central offices to control production and distribution. Following the depression, a part of the economy of the country had already been taken over by the different "agencies" of the New Deal. Washington had become, and is today more than ever, the capital of the country in a sense that was not true in the nineteenth century. This tendency toward centralization is opposed by those who think that the greatness of America was the work of individual enterprise and who fear the survival, after the war, of an all-powerful bureaucracy. These maintain: (a) that the astonishing war production of America which will be the decisive cause of the victory is the work of private industry; (b) that it would have been impossible without the experience and devotion of the leaders of private industry; (c) that liberties will be endangered if political and economic power is ever concentrated in the same hands. It would seem that here a compromise is necessary. The control exercised by political power must be great enough to prevent the recurrence of crises as serious as that of 1929; but it would be dangerous for the United States to abandon those creative virtues which have been its strength. Between individualism and planning it is not necessary (it is not even possible) to choose. Private enterprise and federal control are not contradictory ideas. American economy will one day find its Henry Clay.

It has been said that the creative virtues were the virtues of the pioneer and that the time of the pioneer is past. "Today it is no longer a question of clearing forests," Turner said, "but of conserving them." It is true that the pioneer no longer has new lands to discover, but "the frontier" has other forms. We have seen in the course of this war that a whole industry can be transformed in a few months by modern pioneers. As their ancestors cut down trees, they have ripped out machines, cleared the factory, and planted new material which a few weeks later was producing airplanes. This courage, this audacity are as vital as ever. Furthermore, has the frontier really disappeared? The traveler who journeys through America is impressed, as Tocqueville was long ago, by the uninhabited lands he sees, sometimes at the very edge of great cities. The North American continent remains a continental preserve which could support a larger population. Its resources in minerals, coal, oil, and natural gas are still immense. Much land that today is desert will be reclaimed sometime by irrigation or other means. The replacement of unhealthy slums in the big cities will be a gigantic task worthy of the talents of a new race of pioneers. The United States does not appear to a historian as a country that has reached the saturation point, that has arrived at a time of stagnation, but as a young country, romantic and vigorous, which has its maturity and classic period still before it. For many years there will still be "a frontier" in America for those who are worthy of it.

United States policy will have to take into consideration the new inventions and their effects on the life of the planet. "Isolationism" was a reasonable doctrine in Washington's time. It was becoming difficult in Wilson's. Today it would be absurd. America is only a few hours from Europe. The Monroe Doctrine cannot be maintained unless the United States defends the western hemisphere at a very great distance. It would seem necessary for her to have allies, for it is quite possible to imagine more than one combination of powers that might endanger America. After the war the United States may either conclude an alliance with the European powers (England, France, Russia) or use its influence toward the creation of a world organization analogous to Woodrow Wilson's League of Nations. The foreign policy of the country has often been hampered by the provision in the Constitution that demands a two-thirds majority of the Senate for the ratification of a treaty. It is a fact that in any assembly massive majorities are rarely attained. If one adds that in the United States there are a number of small states, each having two senators, it becomes clear that the most important and advantageous treaty might run the risk of rejection by a tiny minority of the citizens. (Three million constituents in the West have as many votes in the Senate as forty million in the East). John Hay, when he was Secretary of State, said: "A treaty entering the Senate is like a bull going into the arena: No one can say just how or when the final blow will fall, but one thing is certain—it will never leave the arena alive." Here again a compromise and an amendment will be necessary to enable the United States to play its role in world affairs.

If isolationism is losing ground in the United States, imperialism is not gaining. The country as a whole does not want colonial possessions or subject peoples. Certain businessmen would like to see a "dollar diplomacy," but the average American is much more interested in a diplomacy of sentiment. America has always been ready to fight for moral ideals, for the weak against the strong, for liberty against autocracy. Wilson was sincere in saying that the flag of the United States is the flag of humanity. The American's natural tendency is to rush to the aid of a victim. The danger is that some accomplished hypocrite may pass himself off as a victim. A government by public opinion, like that in the United States, cannot pursue a reasonable foreign policy unless public opinion is protected against those who have a selfish interest in perverting it. Freedom of speech is not freedom to lie. The rigid control that is exercised in time of war over the propaganda of foreign nations will be no less necessary in time of peace. Between 1920 and 1940 the American people were in error because they had been misled, and their errors were one of the causes of the present war. But this is an essentially honest nation. It strives to move forward, from error to error, toward what it believes to be right. Tomorrow it will be, if it is well informed, the world's greatest force in the service of justice.

Bibliography

ADAMS, JAMES TRUSLOW. *The Epic of America.* Boston: Little, Brown & Company, 1931

BEARD, CHARLES AND MARY. *The American Spirit. A Study of the Idea of Civilization in the United States.* New York: The Macmillan Company, 1942.

———. *History of the United States. A Study in American Civilization.* New York: The Macmillan Company, 1941.

———. *The Rise of American Civilization.* New York: The Macmillan Company, 1933.

BEMIS, SAMUEL FLAGG. *A Diplomatic History of the United States.* New York: Henry Holt & Company, 1936.

BOGART, ERNEST LUDLOW, AND THOMPSON, CHARLES MANFRED, EDS. *Readings in the Economic History of the United States.* New York: Longmans, Green & Company, 1916.

BROGAN, DENIS WILLIAM. *American Foreign Policy.* New York: Oxford University Press, 1941.

———. *Government of the People. A Study in the American Political System.* New York: Harper & Brothers, 1933.

BRYCE, JAMES (Viscount Bryce). *The American Commonwealth.* London: Macmillan & Company, 1893-1895 (3 volumes).

CHANNING, EDWARD. *A History of the United States.* New York: The Macmillan Company, 1921-1926 (6 volumes).

CHESTERTON, CECIL. *A History of the United States.* London: J. M. Dent & Sons, Ltd., 1940.

FARRAND, LIVINGSTON. *Basis of American History, 1500-1900.* New York: Harper & Brothers, 1904.

FAULKNER, HAROLD UNDERWOOD. *American Economic History.* New York: Harper & Brothers, 1924.

———. *American Political and Social History.* New York: F. S. Crofts & Company, 1937.

———, AND FLÜGEL, FELIX. *Readings in the Economic and Social History of the United States.* New York: Harper & Brothers, 1929.

FISKE, JOHN. *American Political Ideas Viewed from the Standpoint of Universal History.* Boston: Houghton Mifflin Company, 1911.

HART, ALBERT BUSHNELL. *The American Nation, a History from Original Sources.* New York: Harper & Brothers, 1904-1908.

———, AND CURTIS, J. G., EDS. *American History Told by Contemporaries.* New York: The Macmillan Company, 1901-1930 (5 volumes).

JOHNSON, ALLEN, ED. *The Chronicles of America Series.* New Haven: Yale University Press, 1919-1924 (26 volumes).

MAHAN, ALFRED THAYER. *The Influence of Sea Power upon History, 1660-1783.* Boston: Little, Brown & Company, 1897.

MORISON, SAMUEL ELIOT. *The Oxford History of the United States, 1783-1917.* New York: Oxford University Press. 1927.

——, AND COMMAGER, HENRY STEELE. *The Growth of the American Republic.* New York: Oxford University Press, 1930.

MORSE, EDWIN W. *Causes and Effects in American History.* New York: Charles Scribner's Sons, 1912.

MUZZEY, DAVID SAVILLE. *Histoire des Etats-Unis d'Amérique,* translated by A. de Lapradelle. Paris: Larousse, 1926.

——. *History of the American People,* rev. ed. Boston: Ginn & Company, 1933. Boston: Ginn & Company, 1933.

NEVINS, ALLEN AND COMMAGER, HENRY STEELE. *America, the Story of a Free People.* Boston: Little, Brown & Company, 1942.

——, EDS. *The Heritage of America.* Boston: Little, Brown & Company, 1939.

PARRINGTON, VERNON LOUIS. *Main Currents in American Thought.* New York: Harcourt, Brace & Company, 1927.

PAXSON, FREDERIC LOGAN. *History of the American Frontier, 1763-1893.* Boston: Houghton Mifflin Company, 1924.

PERRY, BLISS. *The American Mind and American Idealism.* Boston: Houghton Mifflin Company, 1913.

——. *The American Spirit in Literature.* New Haven: Yale University Press, 1918.

POLLARD, ALBERT FREDERICK. *Factors in American History.* New York: The Macmillan Company, 1925.

SCHLESINGER, ARTHUR MEIER. *New Viewpoints in American History.* New York: The Macmillan Company, 1922.

——, AND FOX, DIXON RYAN, EDS. *The Cavalcade of America.* Springfield, Mass.: Milton Bradley Company, 1937-1938.

——, AND FOX, DIXON RYAN, EDS. *A History of American Life.* New York: The Macmillan Company, 1927-1936 (12 volumes).

TURNER, FREDERICK JACKSON. *The Frontier in American History.* New York: Henry Holt & Company, 1921.

——. *The Significance of Sections in American History.* New York: Henry Holt & Company, 1932.

WILLIAMS, BENJAMIN HARRISON. *American Diplomacy; Policies and Practice.* New York: McGraw-Hill Book Company, 1936.

WILSON, WOODROW. *A History of the American People.* New York: Harper & Brothers, 1918.

WOODWARD, W. E. *A New American History.* New York: Farrar & Rinehart, Inc., 1936.

BOOK I

ADAMS, JAMES TRUSLOW. *Provincial Society, 1690-1763* New York: The Macmillan Company, 1927.

ANDREWS, CHARLES M. *The Fathers of New England.* New Haven: Yale University Press, 1919.

BEER, GEORGE LOUIS. *British Colonial Policy.* New York. The Macmillan Company, 1922.

————. *The Old Colonial System.* New York: The Macmillan Company, 1912 (2 volumes).

BOLTON, HERBERT E. *The Spanish Borderlands.* New Haven: Yale University Press, 1921.

BRIGHAM, ALBERT PERRY. *Geographic Influences in American History.* Boston: Ginn & Company, 1903.

CHEYNEY, EDWARD POTTS. *European Background of American History, 1300-1600.* New York: Harper & Brothers, 1904.

DOW, GEORGE FRANCIS. *Slave Ships and Slaving.* Salem, Mass.: Marine Research Society, 1927.

EGGLESTON, EDWARD. *The Transit of Civilization from England to America, in the Seventeenth Century.* New York: D. Appleton & Company, 1901.

FAŸ, BERNARD. *L'Esprit Révolutionnaire en France et aux Etats-Unis à la fin du dix-huitième siècle.* Paris: Champion, 1925.

FISHER, SYDNEY G. *The Quaker Colonies.* New Haven: Yale University Press, 1919.

FISKE, JOHN. *The Discovery of America.* Boston: Houghton Mifflin Company, 1892 (2 volumes).

GODDARD, PLINY EARLE. *Indians of the Southwest.* New York: American Museum of Natural History, 1931.

GOODWIN, MAUD WILDER. *Dutch and English on the Hudson.* New Haven: Yale University Press, 1919.

GREENE, EVARTS BOUTELL. *The Provincial Governor in the English Colonies of North America.* Cambridge, Mass.: Harvard University Press, 1898.

HUNTINGTON, ELLSWORTH. *The Red Man's Continent: a Chronicle of Aboriginal America.* New Haven: Yale University Press, 1921.

JOHNSTON, MARY. *Pioneers of the Old South.* New Haven: Yale University Press, 1918.

MUNRO, WILLIAM BENNETT. *Crusaders of New France.* New Haven: Yale University Press, 1918.

PARKMAN, FRANCIS. *Prescott's Works.* Boston: Little, Brown & Company, 1902 (16 volumes).

PRESCOTT, WILLIAM HICKLING. *Conquest of Mexico.* New York: E. P. Dutton & Company, 1909 (2 volumes).

————. *History of the Conquest of Peru.* New York: E. P. Dutton & Company, 1909.

RICHMAN, IRVING BERDINE. *The Spanish Conquerors*. New Haven: Yale University Press, 1919.

SEMPLE, ELLEN CHURCHILL. *American History and Its Geographic Conditions*. Boston: Houghton Mifflin Company, 1903.

SKINNER, CONSTANCE LINDSAY. *Pioneers of the Old Southwest*. New Haven: Yale University Press, 1919.

WERTENBAKER, THOMAS JEFFERSON. *The First Americans, 1607-1690*. New York: The Macmillan Company, 1927.

————. *The Old South (The Founding of American Civilization)*. New York: Charles Scribner's Sons, 1942.

WISSLER, CLARK. *The American Indian: an Introduction to the Anthropology of the New World*. New York: Oxford University Press, 1922.

————. *North American Indians of the Plains*. New York: American Museum of Natural History, 1920.

WOOD, WILLIAM. *Elizabethan Sea Dogs*. New Haven: Yale University Press, 1919.

WRONG, GEORGE M. *The Conquest of New France*. New Haven: Yale University Press, 1918.

BOOK II

BECKER, CARL. *The Eve of the Revolution*. New Haven: Yale University Press, 1918.

BURKE, EDMUND. *Speeches and Letters on American Affairs*. London: J. M. Dent & Sons, Ltd., 1908.

FAŸ, BERNARD. *Benjamin Franklin*. Paris: Calmann-Lévy, 1929.

FISKE, JOHN. *The American Revolution*. Boston: Houghton Mifflin Company, 1893 (2 volumes).

HOSMER, JAMES KENDALL. *Samuel Adams*. Boston: Houghton Mifflin Company, 1885.

JANET, *père,* ed. *Correspondence inédite et secrète du Docteur B. Franklin, depuis l'année 1753 jus qu'en 1790*. Paris: 1817.

JUSSERAND, JEAN JULES. *With Americans of Past and Present Days*. New York: Charles Scribner's Sons, 1916.

PERKINS, JAMES BRECK. *France in the American Revolution*. Boston: Houghton Mifflin Company, 1911.

TOWER, CHARLEMANGE. *The Marquis de La Fayette and the American Revolution*. Philadelphia: J. B. Lippincott Company, 1895.

TREVELYAN, GEORGE OTTO. *The American Revolution*. New York: Longmans, Green & Company, 1905-1912 (4 volumes).

TYLER, MOSES COIT. *The Literary History of the American Revolution*. New York: G. P. Putnam's Sons, 1897 (2 volumes).

VAN DOREN, CARL. *Benjamin Franklin*. Garden City, N. Y.: Garden City Publishing Company, 1941.

VAN TYNE, CLAUDE HALSTEAD. *The American Revolution. 1776-1783.* New York: Harper & Brothers, 1905.

———. *The Loyalists in the American Revolution.* New York: The Macmillan Company, 1902.

WOODWARD, WILLIAM E. *Lafayette.* New York: Farrar & Rinehart, 1938.

WROTH, GEORGE M. *Washington and His Comrades in Arms.* New Haven: Yale University Press, 1921.

BOOK III

ADAMS, HENRY. *The Life of Albert Gallatin.* London: J. B. Lippincott Company, 1879.

ADAMS, JAMES TRUSLOW. *The Adams Family.* Boston: Little, Brown & Company, 1930.

———. *The Living Jefferson.* New York: Charles Scribner's Sons, 1936.

ADAMS, JOHN QUINCY. *The Diary of John Quincy Adams.* ed. by Allan Nevins. New York: Longmans, Green & Company, 1928.

BASSETT, JOHN SPENCER. *The Life of Andrew Jackson.* New York: The Macmillan Company, 1925.

BEVERIDGE, ALBERT JEREMIAH. *The Life of John Marshall.* Boston: Houghton Mifflin Company, 1929 (4 volumes).

BOWERS, CLAUDE GERNADE. *Jefferson and Hamilton; the Struggle for Democracy in America.* Boston: Houghton Mifflin Company, 1925.

BRANT, IRVING. *James Madison.* Indianapolis: The Bobbs-Merrill Company, 1941.

CHINARD, GILBERT. *George Washington as the French Knew Him.* Princeton, N. J.: Princeton University Press, 1940.

———. *Honest John Adams.* Boston: Little, Brown & Company, 1933.

———. *Thomas Jefferson, the Apostle of Americanism.* Boston: Little, Brown & Company, 1939.

CORWIN, EDWARD S. *John Marshall and the Constitution.* New Haven: Yale University Press, 1919.

FARRAND, MAX. *The Fathers of the Constitution.* New Haven: Yale University Press, 1921.

———. *The Framing of the Constitution of the United States.* New Haven: Yale University Press, 1913.

FAŸ, BERNARD. *George Washington, gentilhomme.* Paris: Bernard Grasset, 1932.

FISKE, JOHN. *The Critical Period of American History, 1783-1789.* Boston: Houghton Mifflin Company, 1889.

FORD, HENRY JONES. *Washington and His Colleagues.* New Haven: Yale University Press, 1918.

FORD, PAUL LEICESTER. *The True George Washington.* Philadelphia: J. B. Lippincott Company, 1896.

GAY, SYDNEY HOWARD. *James Madison*. Boston: Houghton Mifflin Company, 1909.

HAMILTON, J. G. DE ROULHAC, Ed. *The Best Letters of Jefferson*. Boston: Houghton Mifflin Company, 1926.

HART, ALBERT BUSHNELL. *George Washington*. Chicago: American Library Association, 1927.

———. *The Monroe Doctrine, an Interpretation*. Boston: Little, Brown & Company, 1917.

HUNT, GAILLARD. *Life of James Madison*. New York: Doubleday, Page & Company, 1902.

JAMES, MARQUIS. *Andrew Jackson, the Border Captain*. Indianapolis: The Bobbs-Merrill Company, 1933.

JOHNSON, ALLEN. *Jefferson and His Colleagues*. New Haven: Yale University Press, 1921.

LODGE, HENRY CABOT. *Alexander Hamilton*. Boston: Houghton Mifflin Company, 1898.

MEIGS, WILLIAM MONTGOMERY. *The Life of John Caldwell Calhoun*. New York: G. E. Stechert & Company, 1925.

OLIVER, FREDERICK SCOTT. *Alexander Hamilton, an Essay on American Union*. New York: G. P. Putnam's Sons, 1921.

RANDOLPH, SARAH N. *The Domestic Life of Thomas Jefferson*. Cambridge, Mass.: University Press, 1939.

SCHURZ, CARL. *Henry Clay*. Boston: Houghton Mifflin Company, 1887.

TOCQUEVILLE, ALEXIS DE. *La Démocratie en Amérique*. Paris: Pagnerre, 1848 (4 volumes).

TURNER, FREDERICK JACKSON. *Rise of the New West*. New York: Harper & Brothers, 1906.

WANDELL, SAMUEL HENRY, AND MINNIGERODE, MEADE. *Aaron Burr*. New York: G. P. Putnam's Sons, 1925.

BOOK IV

ADAMS, JAMES TRUSLOW. *The March of Democracy*. New York: Charles Scribner's Sons, 1932-1933 (2 volumes).

BENSON, GODFREY RATHBONE (Lord Charnwood). *Abraham Lincoln*. New York: Henry Holt & Company, 1917.

BOWERS, CLAUDE GERNADE. *The Party Battles of the Jackson Period*. Boston: Houghton Mifflin Company, 1922.

———. *The Tragic Era. The Revolution after Lincoln*. Boston: Houghton Mifflin Company, 1929.

BRADFORD, GAMALIEL. *Confederate Portraits. 1875-1900*. Boston: Houghton Mifflin Company, 1922.

———. *Union Portraits*. Boston: Houghton Mifflin Company, 1916.

CALKINS, EARNEST ELMO. *They Broke the Prairie*. New York: Charles Scribner's Sons, 1937.

CARNEGIE, DALE. *Lincoln the Unknown.* New York: D. Appleton-Century Company, 1932.

COOLIDGE, LOUIS ARTHUR. *Ulysses S. Grant.* Boston: Houghton Mifflin Company, 1922.

DAVIS, VARINA HOWELL. *Jefferson Davis, Ex-President of the Confederate States of America. A Memoir, by His Wife.* New York: The Bedford Company, 1890.

DODD, WILLIAM E. *The Cotton Kingdom.* New Haven: Yale University Press, 1919.

————. *Statesmen of the Old South: Thomas Jefferson. John C. Calhoun and Jefferson Davis.* New York: The Macmillan Company, 1911.

FLEMING, WALTER LYNWOOD. *The Sequel of Appomattox.* New Haven: Yale University Press, 1919.

FREEMAN, DOUGLAS SOUTHALL. *Lee's Lieutenants. A Study in Command.* New York: Charles Scribner's Sons, 1943 (2 volumes).

GRANT, ULYSSES SIMPSON. *Personal Memoirs.* New York: The Century Company, 1909.

HART, ALBERT BUSHNELL. *Slavery and Abolition, 1831-1841.* New York: Harper & Brothers, 1906.

HENDRICK, BURTON J. *Statesmen of the Lost Cause; Jefferson Davis and His Cabinet.* Boston: Little, Brown & Company, 1939.

HUNT, GAILLARD. *John C. Calhoun.* Philadelphia: George W. Jacobs & Company, 1907.

JOHNSON, ALLEN. *Stephen A. Douglas, a Study in American Politics.* New York: The Macmillan Company, 1908.

LEECH, MARGARET. *Reveille in Washington.* New York: Harper & Brothers, 1941.

LODGE, HENRY CABOT. *Daniel Webster.* Boston: Houghton Mifflin Company, 1917.

MACY, JESSE. *The Anti-Slavery Crusade.* New Haven: Yale University Press, 1919.

NEVINS, ALLAN, ED. *Polk, the Diary of a President.* New York: Longmans, Green & Company, 1929.

OGG, FREDERICK AUSTIN. *The Reign of Andrew Jackson.* New Haven: Yale University Press, 1919.

PARKMAN, FRANCIS. *The Oregon Trail.* (Volume XVI of Parkman's *Works.*) Boston: Little, Brown & Company, 1902.

PHILLIPS, ULRICH BONNELL. *American Negro Slavery.* New York: D. Appleton & Company, 1918.

SANDBURG, CARL. *Abraham Lincoln. The Prairie Years.* New York: Harcourt, Brace & Company, 1926.

————. *Abraham Lincoln. The War Years.* New York: Harcourt, Brace & Company, 1939.

SANDBURG, CARL. *Storm over the Land. A Profile of the Civil War.* New York: Harcourt, Brace & Company, 1942.

SHEPARD, EDWARD MORSE. *Martin Van Buren.* Boston: Houghton Mifflin Company, 1917.

SHERMAN, WILLIAM TECUMSEH. *Memoirs.* New York: D. Appleton & Company, 1875.

SKINNER, CONSTANCE LINDSAY. *Adventurers of Oregon.* New Haven: Yale University Press, 1920.

STEPHENSON, NATHANIEL W. *Abraham Lincoln and the Union.* New Haven: Yale University Press, 1918.

————. *The Day of the Confederacy.* New Haven: Yale University Press, 1919.

————. *Texas and the Mexican War.* New Haven: Yale University Press, 1921.

THAYER, WILLIAM ROSCOE. *The Life and Letters of John Hay.* Boston: Houghton Mifflin Company, 1915.

WOOD, WILLIAM. *Captains of the Civil War.* New Haven: Yale University Press, 1918.

WOODBURN, JAMES ALBERT. *The Life of Thaddeus Stevens.* Indianapolis: The Bobbs-Merrill Company, 1913.

BOOK V

ADAMS, HENRY. *The Education of Henry Adams.* Washington: Privately printed, 1907.

ANDREWS, E. BENJAMIN. *The United States in Our Own Times.* New York: Charles Scribner's Sons, 1903.

BEER, THOMAS. *Hanna.* New York: Alfred A. Knopf, 1929.

BOWERS, CLAUDE GERNADE. *The Tragic Era. The Revolution after Lincoln.* Boston: Houghton Mifflin Company, 1929.

CASH, W. J. *The Mind of the South.* New York: Alfred A. Knopf, 1941.

DABNEY, VIRGINIUS. *Below the Potomac, a Book about the New South.* New York: D. Appleton-Century Company, 1942.

DU BOIS, WILLIAM EDWARD BURGHARDT. *Black Reconstruction.* New York: Harcourt, Brace & Company, 1935.

DUNNING, WILLIAM ARCHIBALD. *Reconstruction, Political and Economic.* New York: Harper & Brothers, 1907.

FAULKNER, HAROLD UNDERWOOD, KEPNER, TYLER, AND BARTLETT, HALL. *The American Way of Life,* New York: Harper & Brothers, 1941.

FISH, CARL RUSSELL. *The Civil Service and the Patronage.* Cambridge, Mass.: Harvard University Press, 1905.

FORD, HENRY JONES. *The Cleveland Era.* New Haven: Yale University Press, 1919.

GARLAND, HAMLIN. "Ulysses S. Grant in the Mexican War," *McClure's Magazine,* New York, 1897.

GOMPERS, SAMUEL. *Seventy Years of Life and Labor, an Autobiography.* New York: E. P. Dutton & Company, 1925.

HAWORTH, PAUL LELAND. *The Hayes, Tilden Election.* Indianapolis: The Bobbs-Merrill Company, 1927.

HENDRICK, BURTON J. *The Age of Big Business.* New Haven: Yale University Press, 1921.

HULBERT, ARCHER B. *The Paths of Inland Commerce.* New Haven: Yale University Press, 1920.

MILTON, GEORGE FORT. *The Age of Hate. Andrew Johnson and the Radicals.* New York: Coward-McCann, 1930.

MOODY, JOHN. *The Railroad Builders.* New Haven: Yale University Press, 1920.

MUZZEY, DAVID SAVILLE. *James G. Blaine, a Political Idol of Other Days.* New York: Dodd, Mead & Company, 1934.

MYERS, GUSTAVUS. *America Strikes Back, a Record of Contrasts.* New York: Ives, Washburn, 1935.

————. *The Ending of Hereditary American Fortunes.* New York: Julian Messner, 1939.

NEVINS, ALLAN. *Grover Cleveland, a Study in Courage.* New York: Dodd, Mead & Company, 1933.

————. *The Emergence of Modern America.* New York: The Macmillan Company, 1927.

————. *Hamilton Fish, the Inner History of the Grant Administration.* New York: Dodd, Mead & Company, 1936.

OBERHOLTZER, ELLIS PAXSON. *Jay Cooke, Financier of the Civil War.* Philadelphia: George W. Jacobs & Company, 1907 (2 volumes).

OSGOOD, ERNEST STAPLES. *The Day of the Cattleman.* Minneapolis: University of Minnesota Press, 1929.

ROBINSON, HENRY MORTON. *Fantastic Interim.* New York: Harcourt, Brace & Company, 1943.

SCHLESINGER, ARTHUR MEIER. *The Rise of the City, 1878-1898.* New York: The Macmillan Company, 1933.

SMITH, ARTHUR D. HOWDEN. *Mr. House of Texas.* New York: Funk & Wagnalls Company, 1940.

STANWOOD, EDWARD. *James Gillespie Blaine.* Boston: Houghton Mifflin Company, 1917.

STEFFENS, LINCOLN. *The Autobiography of Lincoln Steffens.* New York: Harcourt, Brace & Company, 1931.

THOMAS, HOLLAND. *The Age of Invention.* New Haven: Yale University Press, 1921.

VANCE, RUPERT BAYLESS. *Human Geography of the South.* Chapel Hill, N. C.: University of North Carolina Press, 1932.

WEBB, WALTER PRESCOTT. *The Great Plains.* Boston: Ginn & Company, 1931.

WERNER, MORRIS ROBERT. *Bryan.* New York: Harcourt, Brace & Company, 1929.

WHITE, WILLIAM ALLEN. *Masks in a Pageant.* New York: The Macmillan Company, 1928.

WINKLER, JOHN K. *Morgan the Magnificent: the Life of J. Pierpont Morgan [1837-1913].* New York: The Vanguard Press, 1930.

WINSTON, ROBERT W. *Andrew Johnson, Plebeian and Patriot.* New York: Henry Holt & Company, 1928.

BOOK VI

BAKER, RAY STANNARD. *Woodrow Wilson, Life and Letters.* New York: Doubleday, Doran & Company, 1927-1939 (8 volumes).

BEER, THOMAS. *The Mauve Decade. American Life at the End of the Nineteenth Century.* New York: Alfred A. Knopf, 1926.

BENSON, GODFREY RATHBONE (Lord Charnwood). *Theodore Roosevelt.* Boston: Little, Brown & Company, 1923.

BUCK, SOLON J. *The Agrarian Crusade.* New Haven: Yale University Press, 1919.

CHAMBERLAIN, JOHN R. *Farewell to Reform.* New York: Liveright Publishing Corporation, 1932.

DUFFY, HERBERT SMITH. *William Howard Taft.* New York: Minton, Balch & Company, 1930.

DUMOND, DWIGHT LOWELL. *Roosevelt to Roosevelt. The United States in the Twentieth Century.* New York: Henry Holt & Company, 1937.

EMERSON, GUY. *The New Frontier.* New York: Henry Holt & Company, 1920.

FISH, CARL RUSSELL. *The Path of Empire.* New Haven: Yale University Press, 1919.

HAYES, CARLTON JOSEPH. *A Brief History of the Great War.* New York: The Macmillan Company, 1920.

HOWLAND, HAROLD. *Theodore Roosevelt and His Times.* New Haven: Yale University Press, 1919.

KERNEY, JAMES. *The Political Education of Woodrow Wilson.* New York: The Century Company, 1926.

LYND, ROBERT STAUGHTON AND HELEN MERRELL. *Middletown, a Study in Contemporary American Culture.* New York: Harcourt, Brace & Company, 1929.

MERRIAM, CHARLES EDWARD. *American Political Ideas; Studies in the Development of American Political Thought, 1865-1917.* New York: The Macmillan Company, 1920.

MERZ, CHARLES. *The Dry Decade.* New York: Doubleday, Doran & Company, 1931.

———. *The Great American Band Wagon.* New York: The John Day Company, 1928.

MOODY, JOHN. *The Masters of Capital.* New Haven: Yale University Press, 1919.

ORTH, SAMUEL P. *The Armies of Labor.* New Haven: Yale University Press, 1920.

———. *The Boss and the Machine.* New Haven: Yale University Press, 1919.

———. *Our Foreigners.* New Haven. Yale University Press, 1920.

PRINGLE, HENRY FOWLES. *Theodore Roosevelt, a Biography.* New York: Harcourt, Brace & Company, 1931.

REGIER, CORNELIUS C. *The Era of the Muckrakers.* Chapel Hill, N. C.: University of North Carolina Press, 1932.

ROBINSON, HENRY MORTON. *Fantastic Interim.* New York: Harcourt, Brace & Company, 1943.

SELDES, GILBERT VIVIAN. *The Years of the Locust. America, 1929-1932.* Boston: Little, Brown & Company, 1933.

SEYMOUR, CHARLES. *Woodrow Wilson and the World War, a Chronicle of Our Own Times.* New Haven: Yale University Press, 1921.

SLOSSON, EDWIN EMERY. *The American Spirit in Education.* New Haven: Yale University Press, 1921.

SLOSSON, PRESTON WILLIAM. *The Great Crusade and After (1914-1928).* New York: The Macmillan Company, 1930.

SULLIVAN, MARK. *Our Times. The United States, 1900-1925.* New York: Charles Scribner's Sons, 1926-1927.

THOMPSON, HOLLAND. *The New South.* New Haven: Yale University Press, 1919.

TUMULTY, JOSEPH PATRICK. *Woodrow Wilson as I Know Him.* Garden City, N. Y.: Garden City Publishing Company, 1925.

TWAIN, MARK. *Mark Twain in Eruption,* ed. by Bernard De Voto. New York: Harper & Brothers, 1940.

WHITE, LEONARD DUPEE, WOODY, CARROL HILL, AND WOOFTER, THOMAS JACKSON. *Recent Social Trends in the United States.* New York: McGraw-Hill Book Company, 1933-1934.

WHITE, WILLIAM ALLEN. *A Puritan in Babylon. The Story of Calvin Coolidge.* New York: The Macmillan Company, 1938.

———. *Woodrow Wilson, the Man, His Times and His Task.* Boston: Houghton Mifflin Company, 1924.

WILSON, EDITH BOLLING GALT (Mrs. Woodrow Wilson). *My Memoir.* Indianapolis: The Bobbs-Merrill Company, 1939.

INDEX